ENGLISH COMEDIES

ENGLISH COMEDIES

Edited, with an Introduction,
by JOHN GASSNER

E. M. HALE AND COMPANY

Eau Claire, Wisconsin

PRINTED IN THE UNITED STATES OF AMERICA
AMERICAN BOOK—STRATFORD PRESS, INC., NEW YORK

For MY FATHER
whose sense of humor belongs
to this vintage.

CONTENTS

INTRODUCTION

ENGLISH COMEDY IN THE CLASSIC AGE*

By John Gassner

The simplest matters can cause the greatest whirl of complication when we elect to ponder them. Take the case of comedy. It would seem that so simple a statement as Max Eastman's that the first law of humor is that "things can be funny only when we are in fun" would cover the case sufficiently. But even Eastman has written three hundred and fifty pages on the sense of humor, and has succeeded only in raising the ghosts of more questions than he has laid. The esthetics of comedy has filled many books, some so formidable that it is certain the authors were temperamentally unqualified to write on the subject. Even if we limit inquiry to English comedy, the morasses lie all around us. It is simply impossible to generalize on anything as varied as life itself. English comedy has run the entire gamut from horseplay to laughter of the mind, and the two have, as often as not, overlapped.

The classic period covered by the plays in this volume is fortunately more distinctive than any other. The purest English distillations of the comic spirit make their appearance in the years between the restoration of the monarchy in 1660 and the production of Sheridan's *School for Scandal* in 1777. That is, we can allow the claim, provided we concede that there were decades of drought even within this century, and that some of the worst comedies and most deleterious influences upon the art appeared then.

If the world were well ordered, excellence would never have to be explained. The world is not well ordered. Moreover, past and present are not co-existent for most of us, and especially in the case of humor the gap between two eras can be very wide. When John Palmer wrote that "laughter is the real frontier between races and kinds of people," he was not guilty of much exaggeration. The best comedies of the Restoration period and the eighteenth century differ from those to which we are habituated in one cardinal respect: their humor is *disengaged*. We are accustomed to admixtures of comedy and sentiment: to social satires, rooted in moral indignation or disapprobation; and to plays in which the laughter is gross rather than subtle. In the masterpieces of English classicism, we encounter a view of comedy largely or wholly free from contamination by either sentimentality or the moral faculty. Its world is small, for it consists of the social set. The characters who whirl about in it are always dressed in the height of fashion, as if for a continuous Easter parade, and they exhibit virtually no life beyond the puppetry of their social comportment. The one exception afforded by *The Beggar's Opera* and its sequel *Polly* proves to be no exception at all; John Gay's underworld characters do not differ in essence from Wycherley's and Congreve's dandies.

If, however, you take exception to this mode of characterization, if you protest that these peruked figures are egregiously unreal, they will smile at you with a disconcerting air of superiority. If you could follow the imputations of their periodic sentences, paraphrase them in the less impeccable speech of our times, you would know why they smile. "At most," you would hear them say, "we wear our cap and bells at a more rakish angle, the cap is made of better cloth, the bells are of silver not earned in the sweat of our brow. But no matter how low you descend in the social scale, or how far you forage in time and space, you will find humanity wearing the same unmistakable adornments. You will find the same unwarranted pretensions, the same egolatry and selfishness, and the same illogic and lack of balance. The difference at best is that our foibles and follies are more openly exhibited because we are less inhibited, and because our creators, the pestilential authors, were men of our kidney. Expecting no more from us than we could deliver, they enjoyed the spectacle we provided with untroubled eyes. Is it art you want to discuss? *Their* artistry was more complete because more single-minded, and more single-minded because less adulterated with anger or pity. We did not take the world more seriously than it should be taken, and neither did our authors. In any case, let us alone and don't try to touch our hearts with the tears of things; we cannot even cope with our follies! And if you press your social or private anguish closer, we will have to tell you that we have no heart at all. It won't be entirely true, but you will believe us, for we, who had the benefit of breeding, are past masters in the art of concealment."

One could have quite a conversation with this breed. And no wonder, since their creators were masterly conversationalists in an age of salons and coffee houses where the English tongue was filed to a fine cutting edge. It is some such conversation that George Meredith, whose ear was singularly attuned to it, tried to reduce to a number of critical distinctions in his famous essay on Comedy. "If you detect the ridicule," he wrote, "and your kindliness is chilled by it, you are slipping into the grasp of satire. . . . if you laugh all around him (around the ridiculous person), tumble him, roll him about, deal him a smack, and drop a tear on him. . . . it is the spirit of Humor that is moving you." Comedy is more objective or disengaged than either moral fervor or humanitarian sympathy will allow. It does not hover on the altitudes where the thunder is grown, nor does it snuggle in the valleys where humanity teems with activities and experiences that obliterate aloofness; it clings close to the temperate foothills of reason. The comic spirit, writes Meredith, is "the perceptive, the governing spirit, awakening and giving aim to those powers of laughter—" that is, to satire and humor. But it differs from satire "in not sharply driving into the quivering sensibilities," and from humor "in not comforting them and tucking them up." Its laughter is "impersonal and of unrivaled politeness, nearer a smile, often no more than a smile."

Comedy, so defined, is the peculiar possession of an epoch, more particularly of a class, and most particularly of specially slanted personalities. The class is what Veblen aptly termed "the leisure class"—the conglomeration of gallants or society folk augmented by a small intelligentsia that wrote for a living, when it had to, but greatly preferred patronage. The rare individuals who possessed this gift of comedy were the so-called wits, not all of whom committed their talent to paper. Those who wrote have a secure place in the history of English letters; Dryden, Pope, Swift, Addison, Steele, Fielding, Samuel Johnson and others contributed verses, essays, and novels that we would not willingly relinquish from our literary heritage. A few of them wrote comedies for the stage—Wycherley, Congreve, Gay, and Sheridan, who are represented in this collection; and there were a number of others, including Goldsmith, John Dryden, George Etherege, Mrs. Aphra Behn (the first woman to write for the English stage), Sir John Vanbrugh (the architect of Blenheim castle) Fielding, the novelist, and George Farquhar.

Their type of comedy—aptly termed, for the most part, "comedy of manners"—was the product, and the luxury, of an age that supported a settled upper-class devoted to the amenities. The world seemed very stable to its members. No new frontiers seemed necessary, no great adventures lay before them, no great changes seemed imperative. The Elizabethan world of promises and fluctuations of fortune, of wonder and of challenge, was past. That world had produced a comedy of romance, as in *As You Like It, A Midsummer Night's Dream* and *Twelfth Night;* and when social strife and insecurity darkened the horizon, it brought forth Shakespeare's so-called dark comedies (*All's Well That Ends Well, Measure for Measure*) and Ben Jonson's angry

satires. There was a portent in these works: There came revolution—
the Puritan revolution, the beheading of Charles I, and the flight of the
nobility to France. When Charles II returned, he took care to walk a
political tight-rope by interfering with government as little as possible,
by confining his prerogatives to the bedchamber and the world of
fashion. There was method in the merriment of the "Merry Monarch."
The aristocracy followed suit and led its own life as something apart,
adhering to the maxim of *carpe diem* with fine living and frivolity,
partly as a safe way of thumbing noses at an entrenched bourgeoisie,
partly because their vigor had been sapped. They became gallants and
courtiers, and, by a process of sublimation, wits instead of explorers
and buccaneers and military conquerors. The larger world of politics
and economics also settled down. England favored gradualism rather
than violent upheavals, evolution rather than revolution, and inched
along the road of constitutional monarchy. And the England of the
middle-class settled down to a business as usual policy whose rewards
filled horns of plenty. "Whatever is, is right," Alexander Pope's maxim,
expressed the prevailing attitude, the smugness of which probably
helped to drive Jonathan Swift mad, since he could not share his "savage
indignation" with anyone. To this we may add another maxim, tacitly
held by the leisure class, that "Whatever is, is funny." Indolence of a
kind no doubt contributed to this state of mind.

The period's masters of comedy were supremely intelligent, but their
moral laziness—call it indifference, if you will—kept them from seeing
much that wasn't in the least funny, such as the hangings for petty
crimes, the baiting of the hapless insane that passed for entertainment,
and the delight in unmitigated malice that made Pope's enemies twit
him because he was of dwarfish stature. "Humor," Ludovici writes in
The Secret of Laughter, "is the lazier principle to adopt in approaching
all questions." The questions, moreover, barely existed for them, and a
certain degree of petty malice, a little sadism, was actually a component
of their laughter. In a catastrophic age like our own we are likely to
feel very critical of these carefree writers. They took for granted that
they were possessors of civilization, and could be easily refuted. They
were strong believers in cultivation, in the manner of Lord Chesterfield's
letters to his son; they neglected to realize that the value of culture lies
in its effect on character. They made tolerable with laughter that which
the moralist or the social critic would find intolerable. We can reflect
that the social graces could blossom only by fortuitous benefit of freedom from want. We can note that the actual field of observation was
often as narrow as the Mall or Mayfair, that their microcosm could be
engraved on a guinea.

Nevertheless, their merits are considerable. Their concentrated light promotes crystal clarity. There is something undeniably civilized in their urbane detachment; their cerebral approach is bracing, and provides a tonic to frayed nerves. Their wit, a creation of unintimidated intellect, enables us to triumph momentarily over the confusions and intimidations of reality. It is always pleasurable, if not always useful, to make an excursion with someone who doesn't try to inform us. Above all, these writers were a merry lot. They knew what many of their colleagues, past and present, have overlooked—that the primary function of comedy is to entertain.

To varying degrees, the writers in this collection answer to this description. William Wycherley (1641–1715) had an unhappy marriage, fell upon evil days, had a long sojourn in debtors' prisons, and wrote one bitter play *The Plain Dealer*, based on Molière's *The Misanthrope*. But he was a dashing blade when he returned to England with the other royalists in 1660, enjoyed the exalted friendship of Charles II's mistress, the Duchess of Cleveland, was presented to the King, and had success with his first play, *Love in a Wood*, in 1671. His third play, *The Country Wife*, produced four years later, reveals him at the peak of his talent for sophisticated comedy. It is perhaps the most amusing treatment of jealousy in the English language, and Mistress Margery Pinchwife is an ingenue who has not been frequently surpassed.

William Congreve, the genial "Phoebus Apollo of the Mall," was wholly a son of the Restoration period. He was born in 1670 and surrendered himself completely to the spirit of the age. Excellently educated, the protégé of the reigning arbiter of letters, John Dryden, he had his first play, *The Old Bachelor*, polished by Dryden and performed by the leading stage couple of his time, Betterton and Mrs. Bracegirdle. His two masterpieces *Love for Love* (1695) and *The Way of the World* (1700) are generally considered the supreme achievements of the comic spirit in England. At any rate, they are the best examples of comedy of manners in the language. They may be caviar to the general, but they are the very best caviar.

Comedy began to decline from its zenith after these two productions. A withering blast from a polemical clergyman, Jeremy Collier, silenced its purveyors, and public taste, now largely dictated by the sedate burghers, favored sentimental plays. This change in the moral climate is a chapter in social history, as well as in the English theatre. But, fortunately, the comic spirit rallied for a few more pirouettes on the boards in the eighteenth century. It found an able and willing master of ceremonies in John Gay (1685–1732), an indolent fellow but an irrepressible wit, whose ballad-operas *The Beggar's Opera* (1728) and

its sequel *Polly* are imperishable. Congreve, who died in 1729 after a life
of pleasant patronage, sinecures, and friendships without writing another play after *The Way of the World*, lived to witness the return of
the unruly muse he had briefly served. Gay's comedies were political
satires aimed at England's first prime minister, Robert Walpole, but
their blithe insouciance and amorality are undated. Their prime subject
is the comedy of villainy. *The Beggar's Opera* fits any period. It was
adapted for the German stage shortly before the advent of Hitler and
his gang.

Henry Fielding, who is better known for the notable novels with
which he stemmed the tide of sentimentalism, also took a stand against
false art in the drama. *Tom Thumb the Great* (1730), one of several
comedies by Fielding, is a burlesque on fulsome heroic drama to which
the public had been partial. It is one of three literary satires (Bucking-
ham's *The Rehearsal* and Sheridan's *The Critic* were the other two) the
like of which was not to be seen in the English theatre until Gilbert and
Sullivan created Bunthorne. Then came the last capers with Oliver
Goldsmith's *She Stoops to Conquer* (1773) and Robert Brinsley Sheridan's two masterpieces *The Rivals* (1775) and *The School for Scandal*
(1777), none of them free from traces of concession to sentiment, but
sufficiently lively and perceptive to deserve their hold upon the English-
speaking world.

After these productions comes the deluge of lachrymose comedies,
romantic claptrap, and knockdown farce which lasts until the closing
decades of the nineteenth century. Wit is banished for a century or
more as either indecent or unfeeling. Sophistication becomes improper
in the Victorian period, and the public would no doubt have answered
any impertinent admirer of the older comedies with the dear Queen's
own words on Gilbert and Sullivan: "We are not amused." The renas-
cence of English comedy comes late, with Oscar Wilde, Gilbert and
Sullivan, and Bernard Shaw. On the non-musical stage, moreover,
comedy becomes subject to a major transformation, in keeping with
the climate of an age of rapidly intensified social awareness. Wilde's
one successful effort to return strictly to the Restoration, *The Importance of Being Earnest*, is not in the main stream of further develop-
ment. And yet we can go too far in denying the continuance of the
Restoration and eighteenth century spirit since 1890. The wit and
the comedy of manners are abundant in the work of Shaw, Maugham,
Coward, and the less celebrated practitioners of our day. The comic
spirit, in the twentieth century, no longer finds, and no longer creates,
so artificial a world. But it still makes use of dispassionate observation,
and a certain degree of artificiality in background and behavior. It also

still derives entertainment from man's divergences from common sense. Only the implications of such divergence are different today—larger and charged with the travail of a world in transition. At least this has been apparent in Shaw and Behrman, though still too infrequently in the work of other contemporaries.

WILLIAM MAKEPEACE THACKERAY
ON RESTORATION COMEDY

(from *The English Humourists*)

William Congreve's Pindaric Odes are still to be found in Johnson's *Poets*, that now unfrequented poets' corner, in which so many forgotten bigwigs have a niche; but though he was also voted to be one of the greatest tragic poets of any day, it was Congreve's wit and humour which first recommended him to courtly fortune. And it is recorded that his first play, the *Old Bachelor*, brought our author to the notice of that great patron of English muses, Charles Montague, Lord Halifax —who, being desirous to place so eminent a wit in a state of ease and tranquillity, instantly made him one of the Commissioners for licensing hackney-coaches, bestowed on him soon after a place in the Pipe Office, and likewise a post in the Custom House of the value of £600.

A commissionership of hackney-coaches—a post in the Custom House —a place in the Pipe Office, and all for writing a comedy! Doesn't it sound like a fable, that place in the Pipe Office? "Ah, l'heureux temps que celui de ces fables!" Men of letters there still be: but I doubt whether any Pipe Offices are left. The public has smoked them long ago.

Words, like men, pass current for a while with the public, and, being known everywhere abroad, at length take their places in society; so even the most secluded and refined ladies here present will have heard the phrase from their sons or brothers at school, and will permit me to call William Congreve, Esquire, the most eminent literary "swell" of his age. In my copy of Johnson's *Lives* Congreve's wig is the tallest, and put on with the jauntiest air of all the laurelled worthies. "I am the great Mr. Congreve," he seems to say, looking out from his voluminous curls. People called him the great Mr. Congreve. From the beginning of his career until the end everybody admired him. Having got his education in Ireland, at the same school and college with Swift, he came to live in the Middle Temple, London, where he luckily bestowed no attention to the law; but splendidly frequented the coffee-houses and theatres, and appeared in the side-box, the tavern, the Piazza, and the Mall, brilliant, beautiful, and victorious from the first. Everybody acknowledged the young chieftain. The great Mr. Dryden declared that he was equal to Shakspeare, and bequeathed to him his own undisputed poetical crown, and writes of him: "Mr. Congreve has done me the favour to review the *Æneis* and compare my version with the original. I shall never be ashamed to own that this excellent young man has showed me many faults which I have endeavoured to correct."

The "excellent young man" was but three or four and twenty when the great Dryden thus spoke of him: the greatest literary chief in England, the veteran field-marshal of letters, himself the marked man of all Europe, and the centre of a school of wits who daily gathered round his chair and tobacco-pipe at Will's. Pope dedicated his *Iliad* to him; Swift, Addison, Steele, all acknowledge Congreve's rank, and lavish compliments upon him. Voltaire went to wait upon him as on one of the Representatives of Literature; and the man who scarce praises any other living person—who flung abuse at Pope, and Swift, and Steele, and Addison—the Grub Street Timon, old John Dennis, was hat in hand to Mr. Congreve; and said that when he retired from the stage, Comedy went with him.

Nor was he less victorious elsewhere. He was admired in the drawing-rooms as well as the coffee-houses; as much beloved in the side-box as on the stage. He loved, and conquered, and jilted the beautiful Bracegirdle, the heroine of all his plays, the favourite of all the town of her day; and the Duchess of Marlborough, Marlborough's daughter, had such an admiration of him, that when he died she had an ivory figure made to imitate him, and a large wax doll with gouty feet to be dressed just as the great Congreve's gouty feet were dressed in his great lifetime. He saved some money by his Pipe office, and his Custom House office, and his Hackney-Coach office, and nobly left it, not to Bracegirdle, who wanted it, but to the Duchess of Marlborough, who didn't.

How can I introduce to you that merry and shameless Comic Muse who won him such a reputation? Nell Gwynn's servant fought the other footman for having called his mistress a bad name; and in like manner, and with pretty little epithets, Jeremy Collier attacked that godless reckless Jezebel, the English Comedy of his time, and called her what Nell Gwynn's man's fellow-servants called Nell Gwynn's man's mistress. The servants of the theatre, Dryden, Congreve, and others, defended themselves with the same success, and for the same cause which set Nell's lacquey fighting. She was a disreputable, daring, laughing, painted French baggage, that Comic Muse. She came over from the Continent with Charles (who chose many more of his female friends there) at the Restoration—a wild dishevelled Laïs, with eyes bright with wit and wine—a saucy Court-favourite that sat at the King's knees, and laughed in his face, and when she showed her bold cheeks at her

chariot-window, had some of the noblest and most famous people of
the land bowing round her wheel. She was kind and popular enough,
that daring Comedy, that audacious poor Nell: she was gay and generous, kind, frank as such people can afford to be! and the men who
lived with her and laughed with her, took her pay and drank her wine,
turned out when the Puritans hooted her, to fight and defend her. But
the jade was indefensible, and it is pretty certain her servants knew it.

There is life and death going on in everything: truth and lies always
at battle. Pleasure is always warring against self-restraint. Doubt is
always crying Psha! and sneering. A man in life, a humourist, in writing
about life, sways over to one principle or the other, and laughs with the
reverence for right and the love of truth in his heart, or laughs at these
from the other side. Didn't I tell you that dancing was a serious business
to Harlequin? I have read two or three of Congreve's plays over before
speaking of him; and my feelings were rather like those, which I dare
say most of us here have had, at Pompeii, looking at Sallust's house and
the relics of an orgy; a dried wine-jar or two, a charred supper-table,
the breast of a dancing-girl pressed against the ashes, the laughing skull
of a jester: a perfect stillness round about, as the cicerone twangs his
moral, and the blue sky shines calmly over the ruin. The Congreve
Muse is dead, and her song choked in Time's ashes. We gaze at the
skeleton, and wonder at the life which once revelled in its mad veins.
We take the skull up, and muse over the frolic and daring, the wit,
scorn, passion, hope, desire, with which that empty bowl once fer-
mented. We think of the glances that allured, the tears that melted, of
the bright eyes that shone in those vacant sockets; and of lips whispering
love, and cheeks dimpling with smiles, that once covered yon ghastly
yellow framework. They used to call those teeth pearls once. See,
there's the cup she drank from, the gold-chain she wore on her neck,
the vase which held the rouge for her cheeks, her looking-glass, and the
harp she used to dance to. Instead of a feast we find a gravestone, and
in place of a mistress, a few bones!

Reading in these plays now, is like shutting your ears and looking at
people dancing. What does it mean? the measures, the grimaces, the
bowing, shuffling and retreating, the *cavalier seul* advancing upon those
ladies—those ladies and men twirling round at the end in a mad galop,
after which everybody bows and the quaint rite is celebrated. Without
the music we can't understand that comic dance of the last century—
its strange gravity and gaiety, its decorum or its indecorum. It has a
jargon of its own quite unlike life; a sort of moral of its own quite unlike life too. I'm afraid it's a Heathen mystery, symbolising a Pagan
doctrine; protesting—as the Pompeians very likely were, assembled at

their theatre and laughing at their games; as Sallust and his friends, and their mistresses protested, crowned with flowers, with cups in their hands—against the new, hard, ascetic, pleasure-hating doctrine whose gaunt disciples, lately passed over from the Asian shores of the Mediterranean, were for breaking the fair images of Venus and flinging the altars of Bacchus down.

I fancy poor Congreve's theatre is a temple of Pagan delights, and mysteries not permitted except among heathens. I fear the theatre carries down that ancient tradition and worship, as masons have carried their secret signs and rites from temple to temple. When the libertine hero carries off the beauty in the play, and the dotard is laughed to scorn for having the young wife: in the ballad, when the poet bids his mistress to gather roses while she may, and warns her that old Time is still a-flying: in the ballet, when honest Corydon courts Phillis under the treillage of the pasteboard cottage, and leers at her over the head of grandpapa in red stockings, who is opportunely asleep; and when seduced by the invitations of the rosy youth she comes forward to the footlights, and they perform on each other's tiptoes that *pas* which you all know, and which is only interrupted by old grandpapa awaking from his doze at the pasteboard châlet (whither he returns to take another nap in case the young people get an encore): when Harlequin, splendid in youth, strength, and agility, arrayed in gold and a thousand colours, springs over the heads of countless perils, leaps down the throat of bewildered giants, and, dauntless and splendid, dances danger down: when Mr. Punch, that godless old rebel, breaks every law and laughs at it with odious triumph, outwits his lawyer, bullies the beadle, knocks his wife about the head, and hangs the hangman,—don't you see in the comedy, in the song, in the dance, in the ragged little Punch's puppet-show—the Pagan protest? Doesn't it seem as if Life puts in its plea and sings its comment? Look how the lovers walk and hold each other's hands and whisper! Sings the chorus—"There is nothing like love, there is nothing like youth, there is nothing like beauty of your springtime. Look! how old age tries to meddle with merry sport! Beat him with his own crutch, the wrinkled old dotard! There is nothing like youth, there is nothing like beauty, there is nothing like strength. Strength and valour win beauty and youth. Be brave and conquer. Be young and happy. Enjoy, enjoy, enjoy! Would you know the *Segreto per esser felice?* Here it is, in a smiling mistress and a cup of Falernian." As the boy tosses the cup and sings his song—hark! what is that chaunt coming nearer and nearer? What is that dirge which *will* disturb us? The lights of the festival burn dim—the cheeks turn pale—the voice quavers—and the cup drops on the floor. Who's there? Death and Fate are at the gate, and they *will* come in.

Congreve's comic feast flares with lights, and round the table, emptying their flaming bowls of drink, and exchanging the wildest jests and ribaldry, sit men and women, waited on by rascally valets and attendants as dissolute as their mistresses—perhaps the very worst company in the world. There doesn't seem to be a pretence of morals. At the head of the table sits Mirabel or Belmour (dressed in the French fashion and waited on by English imitators of Scapin and Frontin). Their calling is to be irresistible, and to conquer everywhere. Like the heroes of the chivalry story, whose long-winded loves and combats they were sending out of fashion, they are always splendid and triumphant—overcome all dangers, vanquish all enemies, and win the beauty at the end. Fathers, husbands, usurers, are the foes these champions contend with. They are merciless in old age, invariably, and an old man plays the part in the dramas which the wicked enchanter or the great blundering giant performs in the chivalry tales, who threatens and grumbles and resists—a huge stupid obstacle always overcome by the night. It is an old man with a money-box: Sir Belmour, his son or nephew, spends his money and laughs at him. It is an old man with a young wife whom he locks up: Sir Mirabel robs him of his wife, trips up his gouty old heels, and leaves the old hunks. The old fool, what business has he to hoard his money, or to lock up blushing eighteen? Money is for youth, love is for youth, away with the old people. When Millamant is sixty, having of course divorced the first Lady Millamant, and married his friend Doricourt's granddaughter out of the nursery—it will be his turn; and young Belmour will make a fool of him. All this pretty morality you have in the comedies of William Congreve, Esquire. They are full of wit. Such manners as he observes, he observes with great humour; but ah! it's a weary feast, that banquet of wit where no love is. It palls very soon; sad indigestions follow it, and lonely blank headaches in the morning. . . .

THE COUNTRY WIFE

by William Wycherley

DRAMATIS PERSONÆ

Mr. HORNER.
Mr. HARCOURT.
Mr. DORILANT.
Mr. PINCHWIFE.
Mr. SPARKISH.
Sir JASPER FIDGET.
A Boy.
A Quack.
Waiters, Servants, and Attendants.

Mrs. MARGERY PINCHWIFE.
ALITHEA, Sister of Pinchwife.
Lady FIDGET.
Mrs. DAINTY FIDGET, Sister of Sir Jasper.
Mrs. SQUEAMISH.
Old Lady SQUEAMISH.
LUCY, Alithea's Maid.

SCENE—LONDON.

PROLOGUE

POETS, like cudgelled bullies, never do
At first or second blow submit to you;
But will provoke you still, and ne'er have done,
Till you are weary first with laying on.
The late so baffled scribbler of this day,
Though he stands trembling, bids me boldly say,
What we before most plays are used to do,
For poets out of fear first draw on you;
In a fierce prologue the still pit defy,
And, ere you speak, like Castril give the lie.
But though our Bayes's battles oft I've fought,
And with bruised knuckles their dear conquests bought;
Nay, never yet feared odds upon the stage,
In prologue dare not hector with the age;
But would take quarter from your saving hands,
Though Bayes within all yielding countermands,
Says, you confederate wits no quarter give,
Therefore his play shan't ask your leave to live.
Well, let the vain rash fop, by huffing so,
Think to obtain the better terms of you;
But we, the actors, humbly will submit,
Now, and at any time, to a full pit;
Nay, often we anticipate your rage,
And murder poets for you on our stage:
We set no guards upon our tiring-room,
But when with flying colours there you come,
We patiently, you see, give up to you
Our poets, virgins, nay, our matrons too.

THE COUNTRY WIFE

ACT I

SCENE I.—HORNER's *Lodging*

Enter HORNER, *and* QUACK *following him at a distance.*

Horn. [*aside*]. A quack is as fit for a pimp, as a midwife for a bawd; they are still but in their way, both helpers of nature.—[*Aloud.*] Well, my dear doctor, hast thou done what I desired?

Quack. I have undone you for ever with the women, and reported you throughout the whole town as bad as an eunuch, with as much trouble as if I had made you one in earnest.

Horn. But have you told all the midwives you know, the orange wenches at the playhouses, the city husbands, and old fumbling keepers of this end of the town? for they'll be the readiest to report it.

Quack. I have told all the chambermaids, waiting-women, tire-women, and old women of my acquaintance; nay, and whispered it as a secret to 'em, and to the whisperers of Whitehall; so that you need not doubt 'twill spread, and you will be as odious to the handsome young women as——

Horn. As the small-pox. Well——

Quack. And to the married women of this end of the town, as——

Horn. As the great one; nay, as their own husbands.

Quack. And to the city dames, as aniseed Robin, of filthy and contemptible memory; and they will frighten their children with your name, especially their females.

Horn. And cry, Horner's coming to carry you away. I am only afraid 'twill not be believed. You told 'em it was by an English-French disaster, and an English-French chirurgeon, who has given me at once not only a cure, but an antidote for the future against that damned malady, and that worse distemper, love, and all other women's evils?

Quack. Your late journey into France has made it the more credible, and your being here a fortnight before you appeared in public, looks as if you apprehended the shame, which I wonder you do not. Well, I have been hired by young gallants to belie 'em t'other way; but you are the first would be thought a man unfit for women.

Horn. Dear Mr. Doctor, let vain rogues be contented only to be thought abler men than they are, generally 'tis all the pleasure they have; but mine lies another way.

Quack. You take, methinks, a very preposterous way to it, and as ridiculous as if we operators in physic should put forth bills to disparage our medicaments, with hopes to gain customers.

Horn. Doctor, there are quacks in love as well as physic, who get but the fewer and worse patients for their boasting; a good name is seldom got by giving it one's self; and women, no more than honour, are compassed by bragging. Come, come, Doctor, the wisest lawyer never discovers the merits of his cause till the trial; the wealthiest man conceals his riches, and the cunning gamester his play. Shy husbands and keepers, like old rooks, are not to be cheated but by a new unpractised trick: false friendship will pass now no more than false dice upon 'em; no, not in the city.

Enter Boy.

Boy. There are two ladies and a gentleman coming up.   [*Exit.*

Horn. A pox! some unbelieving sisters of my former acquaintance, who, I am afraid, expect their sense should be satisfied of the falsity of the report. No—this formal fool and women!

Enter Sir JASPER FIDGET, Lady FIDGET, *and* Mrs. DAINTY FIDGET.

Quack. His wife and sister.

Sir Jasp. My coach breaking just now before your door, sir, I look upon as an occasional reprimand to me, sir, for not kissing your hands, sir, since your coming out of France, sir; and so my disaster, sir, has been my good fortune, sir; and this is my wife and sister, sir.

Horn. What then, sir?

Sir Jasp. My lady, and sister, sir.—Wife, this is Master Horner.

Lady Fid. Master Horner, husband!

Sir Jasp. My lady, my Lady Fidget, sir.

Horn. So, sir.

Sir Jasp. Won't you be acquainted with her, sir?—[*Aside.*] So, the report is true, I find, by his coldness or aversion to the sex; but I'll play the wag with him.—[*Aloud.*] Pray salute my wife, my lady, sir.

Horn. I will kiss no man's wife, sir, for him, sir; I have taken my eternal leave, sir, of the sex already, sir.

Sir Jasp. [*aside*]. Ha! ha! ha! I'll plague him yet.—[*Aloud.*] Not know my wife, sir?

Horn. I do know your wife, sir; she's a woman, sir, and consequently a monster, sir, a greater monster than a husband, sir.

Sir Jasp. A husband! how, sir?

Horn. So, sir; but I make no more cuckolds, sir.   [*Makes horns.*

Sir Jasp. Ha! ha! ha! Mercury! Mercury!

Lady Fid. Pray, Sir Jasper, let us be gone from this rude fellow.

Mrs. Dain. Who, by his breeding, would think he had ever been in France?

Lady Fid. Foh! he's but too much a French fellow, such as hate women of quality and virtue for their love to their husbands. Sir Jasper, a woman is hated by 'em as much for loving her husband as for loving their money. But pray let's be gone.

Horn. You do well, madam; for I have nothing that you came for. I have brought over not so much as a bawdy picture, no new postures, nor the second part of the *Ecole des Filles;* nor——

Quack. Hold, for shame, sir! what d'ye mean? you'll ruin yourself for ever with the sex—— [*Apart to* HORNER.

Sir Jasp. Ha! ha! ha! he hates women perfectly, I find.

Mrs. Dain. What pity 'tis he should!

Lady Fid. Ay, he's a base fellow for't. But affectation makes not a woman more odious to them than virtue.

Horn. Because your virtue is your greatest affectation, madam.

Lady Fid. How, you saucy fellow! would you wrong my honour?

Horn. If I could.

Lady Fid. How d'ye mean, sir?

Sir Jasp. Ha! ha! ha! no, he can't wrong your ladyship's honour, upon my honour. He, poor man—hark you in your ear—a mere eunuch. [*Whispers.*

Lady Fid. O filthy French beast! foh! foh! why do we stay? let's be gone: I can't endure the sight of him.

Sir Jasp. Stay but till the chairs come; they'll be here presently.

Lady Fid. No.

Sir Jasp. Nor can I stay longer. 'Tis, let me see, a quarter and half quarter of a minute past eleven. The council will be sat; I must away. Business must be preferred always before love and ceremony with the wise, Mr. Horner.

Horn. And the impotent, Sir Jasper.

Sir Jasp. Ay, ay, the impotent, Master Horner; hah! hah! hah!

Lady Fid. What, leave us with a filthy man alone in his lodgings?

Sir Jasp. He's an innocent man now, you know. Pray stay, I'll hasten the chairs to you.—Mr. Horner, your servant; I should be glad to see you at my house. Pray come and dine with me, and play at cards with my wife after dinner; you are fit for women at that game yet, ha! ha!—[*Aside.*] 'Tis as much a husband's prudence to provide innocent diversion for a wife as to hinder her unlawful pleasures; and he had better employ her than let her employ herself.—[*Aloud.*] Farewell.

Horn. Your servant, Sir Jasper. [*Exit* Sir JASPER.

Lady Fid. I will not stay with him, foh!——

Horn. Nay, madam, I beseech you stay, if it be but to see I can be as civil to ladies yet as they would desire.

Lady Fid. No, no, foh! you cannot be civil to ladies.

Mrs. Dain. You as civil as ladies would desire?

Lady Fid. No, no, no, foh! foh! foh!

[*Exeunt* Lady FIDGET *and* Mrs. DAINTY FIDGET.

Quack. Now, I think, I, or you yourself, rather, have done your business with the women.

Horn. Thou art an ass. Don't you see already, upon the report, and my carriage, this grave man of business leaves his wife in my lodgings, invites me to his house and wife, who before would not be acquainted with me out of jealousy?

Quack. Nay, by this means you may be the more acquainted with the husbands, but the less with the wives.

Horn. Let me alone; if I can but abuse the husbands, I'll soon disabuse the wives. Stay—I'll reckon you up the advantages I am like to have by my stratagem. First, I shall be rid of all my old acquaintances, the most insatiable sort of duns, that invade our lodgings in a morning; and next to the pleasure of making a new mistress is that of being rid of an old one, and of all old debts. Love, when it comes to be so, is paid the most unwillingly.

Quack. Well, you may be so rid of your old acquaintances; but how will you get any new ones?

Horn. Doctor, thou wilt never make a good chemist, thou art so incredulous and impatient. Ask but all the young fellows of the town if they do not lose more time, like huntsmen, in starting the game, than in running it down. One knows not where to find 'em; who will or will not. Women of quality are so civil, you can hardly distinguish love from good breeding, and a man is often mistaken: but now I can be sure she that shows an aversion to me loves the sport, as those women that are gone, whom I warrant to be right. And then the next thing is, your women of honour, as you call 'em, are only chary of their reputations, not their persons; and 'tis scandal they would avoid, not men. Now may I have, by the reputation of an eunuch, the privileges of one, and be seen in a lady's chamber in a morning as early as her husband; kiss virgins before their parents or lovers; and may be, in short, the *passe-partout* of the town. Now, doctor.

Quack. Nay, now you shall be the doctor; and your process is so new that we do not know but it may succeed.

Horn. Not so new neither; *probatum est,* doctor.

Quack. Well, I wish you luck, and many patients, whilst I go to mine.

[*Exit.*

Enter HARCOURT *and* DORILANT.

Har. Come, your appearance at the play yesterday has, I hope, hardened you for the future against the women's contempt, and the men's raillery; and now you'll abroad as you were wont.

Horn. Did I not bear it bravely?

Dor. With a most theatrical impudence, nay, more than the orange-wenches show there, or a drunken vizard-mask, or a great-bellied actress; nay, or the most impudent of creatures, an ill poet; or what is yet more impudent, a second-hand critic.

Horn. But what say the ladies? have they no pity?

Har. What ladies? The vizard-masks, you know, never pity a man when all's gone, though in their service.

Dor. And for the women in the boxes, you'd never pity them when 'twas in your power.

Har. They say 'tis pity but all that deal with common women should be served so.

Dor. Nay, I dare swear they won't admit you to play at cards with them, go to plays with 'em, or do the little duties which other shadows of men are wont to do for 'em.

Horn. What do you call shadows of men?

Dor. Half-men.

Horn. What, boys?

Dor. Ay, your old boys, old *beaux garçons*, who, like superannuated stallions, are suffered to run, feed, and whinny with the mares as long as they live, though they can do nothing else.

Horn. Well, a pox on love and wenching! Women serve but to keep a man from better company. Though I can't enjoy them, I shall you the more. Good fellowship and friendship are lasting, rational, and manly pleasures.

Har. For all that, give me some of those pleasures you call effeminate too; they help to relish one another.

Horn. They disturb one another.

Har. No, mistresses are like books. If you pore upon them too much, they doze you, and make you unfit for company; but if used discreetly, you are the fitter for conversation by 'em.

Dor. A mistress should be like a little country retreat near the town; not to dwell in constantly, but only for a night and away, to taste the town the better when a man returns.

Horn. I tell you, 'tis as hard to be a good fellow, a good friend, and a lover of women, as 'tis to be a good fellow, a good friend, and a lover of money. You cannot follow both, then choose your side. Wine gives you liberty, love takes it away.

Dor. Gad, he's in the right on't.

Horn. Wine gives you joy; love, grief and tortures, besides surgeons. Wine makes us witty; love, only sots. Wine makes us sleep; love breaks it.

Dor. By the world he has reason, Harcourt.

Horn. Wine makes——

Dor. Ay, wine makes us—makes us princes; love makes us beggars, poor rogues, egad—and wine——

Horn. So, there's one converted.—No, no, love and wine, oil and vinegar.

Har. I grant it; love will still be uppermost.

Horn. Come, for my part, I will have only those glorious manly pleasures of being very drunk and very slovenly.

Enter Boy.

Boy. Mr. Sparkish is below, sir.   [*Exit.*

Har. What, my dear friend! a rogue that is fond of me only, I think, for abusing him.

Dor. No, he can no more think the men laugh at him than that women jilt him; his opinion of himself is so good.

Horn. Well, there's another pleasure by drinking I thought not of,—I shall lose his acquaintance, because he cannot drink: and you know 'tis a very hard thing to be rid of him; for he's one of those nauseous offerers at wit, who, like the worst fiddlers, run themselves into all companies.

Har. One that, by being in the company of men of sense, would pass for one.

Horn. And may so to the short-sighted world; as a false jewel amongst true ones is not discerned at a distance. His company is as troublesome to us as a cuckold's when you have a mind to his wife's.

Har. No, the rogue will not let us enjoy one another, but ravishes our conversation; though he signifies no more to't than Sir Martin Mar-all's gaping, and awkward thrumming upon the lute, does to his man's voice and music.

Dor. And to pass for a wit in town shows himself a fool every night to us, that are guilty of the plot.

Horn. Such wits as he are, to a company of reasonable men, like rooks to the gamesters; who only fill a room at the table. but are so far from contributing to the play, that they only serve to spoil the fancy of those that do.

Dor. Nay, they are used like rooks too, snubbed, checked, and abused; yet the rogues will hang on.

Horn. A pox on 'em, and all that force nature, and would be still what she forbids 'em! Affectation is her greatest monster.

Har. Most men are the contraries to that they would seem. Your bully, you see, is a coward with a long sword; the little humbly-fawning physician, with his ebony cane, is he that destroys men.

Dor. The usurer, a poor rogue, possessed of mouldy bonds and mortgages; and we they call spendthrifts, are only wealthy, who lay out his money upon daily new purchases of pleasure.

Horn. Ay, your arrantest cheat is your trustee or executor; your jealous man, the greatest cuckold; your churchman the greatest atheist; and your noisy pert rogue of a wit, the greatest fop, dullest ass, and worst company, as you shall see; for here he comes.

Enter SPARKISH.

Spark. How is't, sparks? how is't? Well, faith, Harry, I must rally thee a little, ha! ha! ha! upon the report in town of thee, ha! ha! ha! I can't hold i'faith; shall I speak?

Horn. Yes; but you'll be so bitter then.

Spark. Honest Dick and Frank here shall answer for me; I will not be extreme bitter, by the universe.

Har. We will be bound in a ten thousand pound bond, he shall not be bitter at all.

Dor. Nor sharp, nor sweet.

Horn. What, not downright insipid?

Spark. Nay then, since you are so brisk, and provoke me, take what follows. You must know, I was discoursing and rallying with some ladies yesterday, and they happened to talk of the fine new signs in town——

Horn. Very fine ladies, I believe.

Spark. Said I, I know where the best new sign is.—Where? says one of the ladies.—In Covent Garden, I replied.—Said another, In what street?—In

Russel Street, answered I.—Lord, says another, I'm sure there was never a fine new sign there yesterday.—Yes, but there was, said I again; and it came out of France, and has been there a fortnight.

Dor. A pox! I can hear no more, prithee.

Horn. No, hear him out; let him tune his crowd a while.

Har. The worst music, the greatest preparation.

Spark. Nay, faith, I'll make you laugh.—It cannot be, says a third lady.— Yes, yes, quoth I again.—Says a fourth lady——

Horn. Look to't, we'll have no more ladies.

Spark. No—then mark, mark, now. Said I to the fourth, Did you never see Mr. Horner? he lodges in Russel Street, and he's a sign of a man, you know, since he came out of France; ha! ha! ha!

Horn. But the devil take me if thine be the sign of a jest.

Spark. With that they all fell a-laughing, till they bepissed themselves. What, but it does not move you, methinks? Well, I see one had as good go to law without a witness, as break a jest without a laughter on one's side.— Come, come, sparks, but where do we dine? I have left at Whitehall an earl, to dine with you.

Dor. Why, I thought thou hadst loved a man with a title, better than a suit with a French trimming to't.

Har. Go to him again.

Spark. No, sir, a wit to me is the greatest title in the world.

Horn. But go dine with your earl, sir; he may be exceptious. We are your friends, and will not take it ill to be left, I do assure you.

Har. Nay, faith, he shall go to him.

Spark. Nay, pray, gentlemen.

Dor. We'll thrust you out, if you won't; what, disappoint anybody for us?

Spark. Nay, dear gentlemen, hear me.

Horn. No, no, sir, by no means; pray go, sir.

Spark. Why, dear rogues——

Dor. No, no.   [*They all thrust him out of the room.*

All. Ha! ha! ha!

Re-enter SPARKISH.

Spark. But, sparks, pray hear me. What, d'ye think I'll eat then with gay shallow fops and silent coxcombs? I think wit as necessary at dinner as a glass of good wine; and that's the reason I never have any stomach when I eat alone.—Come, but where do we dine?

Horn. Even where you will.

Spark. At Chateline's?

Dor. Yes, if you will.

Spark. Or at the Cock?

Dor. Yes, if you please.

Spark. Or at the Dog and Partridge?

Horn. Ay, if you have a mind to't; for we shall dine at neither.

Spark. Pshaw! with your fooling we shall lose the new play; and I would no more miss seeing a new play the first day, than I would miss sitting in the wit's row. Therefore I'll go fetch my mistress, and away.   [*Exit.*

Enter PINCHWIFE.

Horn. Who have we here? Pinchwife?

Pinch. Gentlemen, your humble servant.

Horn. Well, Jack, by thy long absence from the town, the grumness of thy countenance, and the slovenliness of thy habit, I should give thee joy, should I not, of marriage?

Pinch. [*aside*]. Death! does he know I'm married too? I thought to have concealed it from him at least.—[*Aloud.*] My long stay in the country will excuse my dress; and I have a suit of law that brings me up to town, that puts me out of humour. Besides, I must give Sparkish to-morrow five thousand pounds to lie with my sister.

Horn. Nay, you country gentlemen, rather than not purchase, will buy anything; and he is a cracked title, if we may quibble. Well, but am I to give thee joy? I heard thou wert married.

Pinch. What then?

Horn. Why, the next thing that is to be heard, is, thou'rt a cuckold.

Pinch. Insupportable name!   [*Aside.*

Horn. But I did not expect marriage from such a whoremaster as you; one that knew the town so much, and women so well.

Pinch. Why, I have married no London wife.

Horn. Pshaw! that's all one. That grave circumspection in marrying a country wife, is like refusing a deceitful pampered Smithfield jade, to go and be cheated by a friend in the country.

Pinch. [*aside*]. A pox on him and his simile!—[*Aloud.*] At least we are a little surer of the breed there, know what her keeping has been, whether foiled or unsound.

Horn. Come, come, I have known a clap gotten in Wales; and there are cousins, justices' clerks, and chaplains in the country, I won't say coachmen. But she's handsome and young?

Pinch. [*aside*]. I'll answer as I should do.—[*Aloud.*] No, no; she has no beauty but her youth, no attraction but her modesty: wholesome, homely, and huswifely; that's all.

Dor. He talks as like a grazier as he looks.

Pinch. She's too awkward, ill-favoured, and silly to bring to town.

Har. Then methinks you should bring her to be taught breeding.

Pinch. To be taught! no, sir, I thank you. Good wives and private soldiers should be ignorant—I'll keep her from your instructions, I warrant you.

Har. The rogue is as jealous as if his wife were not ignorant.   [*Aside.*

Horn. Why, if she be ill-favoured, there will be less danger here for you than by leaving her in the country. We have such variety of dainties that we are seldom hungry.

Dor. But they have always coarse, constant, swingeing stomachs in the country.

Har. Foul feeders indeed!

Dor. And your hospitality is great there.

Har. Open house; every man's welcome.

Pinch. So, so, gentlemen.

Horn. But prithee, why shouldst thou marry her? If she be ugly, ill-bred, and silly, she must be rich then.

Pinch. As rich as if she brought me twenty thousand pound out of this town; for she'll be as sure not to spend her moderate portion, as a London baggage would be to spend hers, let it be what it would: so 'tis all one. Then, because she's ugly, she's the likelier to be my own; and being ill-bred, she'll hate conversation; and since silly and innocent, will not know the difference betwixt a man of one-and-twenty and one of forty.

Horn. Nine—to my knowledge. But if she be silly, she'll expect as much from a man of forty-nine, as from him of one-and-twenty. But methinks wit is more necessary than beauty; and I think no young woman ugly that has it, and no handsome woman agreeable without it.

Pinch. 'Tis my maxim, he's a fool that marries; but he's a greater that does not marry a fool. What is wit in a wife good for, but to make a man a cuckold?

Horn. Yes, to keep it from his knowledge.

Pinch. A fool cannot contrive to make her husband a cuckold.

Horn. No; but she'll club with a man that can: and what is worse, if she cannot make her husband a cuckold, she'll make him jealous, and pass for one: and then 'tis all one.

Pinch. Well, well, I'll take care for one. My wife shall make me no cuckold, though she had your help, Mr. Horner. I understand the town, sir.

Dor. His help!   [*Aside.*

Har. He's come newly to town, it seems, and has not heard how things are with him.   [*Aside.*

Horn. But tell me, has marriage cured thee of whoring, which it seldom does?

Har. 'Tis more than age can do.

Horn. No, the word is, I'll marry and live honest: but a marriage vow is like a penitent gamester's oath, and entering into bonds and penalties to stint himself to such a particular small sum at play for the future, which makes him but the more eager; and not being able to hold out, loses his money again, and his forfeit to boot.

Dor. Ay, ay, a gamester will be a gamester whilst his money lasts, and a whoremaster whilst his vigour.

Har. Nay, I have known 'em, when they are broke, and can lose no more, keep a fumbling with the box in their hands to fool with only, and hinder other gamesters.

Dor. That had wherewithal to make lusty stakes.

Pinch. Well, gentlemen, you may laugh at me; but you shall never lie with my wife: I know the town.

Horn. But prithee, was not the way you were in better? is not keeping better than marriage?

Pinch. A pox on't! the jades would jilt me, I could never keep a whore to myself.

Horn. So, then you only married to keep a whore to yourself. Well, but let me tell you, women, as you say, are like soldiers, made constant and loyal by good pay, rather than by oaths and covenants. Therefore I'd advise my friends to keep rather than marry, since too I find, by your example, it does not serve one's turn; for I saw you yesterday in the eighteenpenny place with a pretty country-wench.

Pinch. How the devil! did he see my wife then? I sat there that she might not be seen. But she shall never go to a play again. *[Aside.*

Horn. What! dost thou blush, at nine-and-forty, for having been seen with a wench?

Dor. No, faith, I warrant 'twas his wife, which he seated there out of sight; for he's a cunning rogue, and understands the town.

Har. He blushes. Then 'twas his wife; for men are now more ashamed to be seen with them in public than with a wench.

Pinch. Hell and damnation! I'm undone, since Horner has seen her, and they know 'twas she. *[Aside.*

Horn. But prithee, was it thy wife? She was exceeding pretty: I was in love with her at that distance.

Pinch. You are like never to be nearer to her. Your servant, gentlemen.
[Offers to go.

Horn. Nay, prithee stay.

Pinch. I cannot; I will not.

Horn. Come, you shall dine with us.

Pinch. I have dined already.

Horn. Come, I know thou hast not: I'll treat thee, dear rogue; thou sha't spend none of thy Hampshire money to-day.

Pinch. Treat me! So, he uses me already like his cuckold. *[Aside.*

Horn. Nay, you shall not go.

Pinch. I must; I have business at home. *[Exit.*

Har. To beat his wife. He's as jealous of her as a Cheapside husband of a Covent Garden wife.

Horn. Why, 'tis as hard to find an old whoremaster without jealousy and the gout, as a young one without fear, or the pox:—

As gout in age from pox in youth proceeds,
So wenching past, then jealousy succeeds;
The worst disease that love and wenching breeds.

[Exeunt.

ACT II

SCENE I.—*A Room in* PINCHWIFE'S *House*

MRS. MARGERY PINCHWIFE *and* ALITHEA. PINCHWIFE *peeping behind at the door.*

Mrs. Pinch. Pray, sister, where are the best fields and woods to walk in, in London?

Alith. [*aside*]. A pretty question!—[*Aloud.*] Why, sister, Mulberry Garden and St. James's Park; and, for close walks, the New Exchange.

Mrs. Pinch. Pray, sister, tell me why my husband looks so grum here in town, and keeps me up so close, and will not let me go a-walking, nor let me wear my best gown yesterday.

Alith. O, he's jealous, sister.

Mrs. Pinch. Jealous! what's that?

Alith. He's afraid you should love another man.

Mrs. Pinch. How should he be afraid of my loving another man, when he will not let me see any but himself?

Alith. Did he not carry you yesterday to a play?

Mrs. Pinch. Ay; but we sat amongst ugly people. He would not let me come near the gentry, who sat under us, so that I could not see 'em. He told me, none but naughty women sat there, whom they toused and moused. But I would have ventured, for all that.

Alith. But how did you like the play?

Mrs. Pinch. Indeed I was weary of the play; but I liked hugeously the actors. They are the goodliest, properest men, sister!

Alith. O, but you must not like the actors, sister.

Mrs. Pinch. Ay, how should I help it, sister? Pray, sister, when my husband comes in, will you ask leave for me to go a-walking?

Alith. A-walking! ha! ha! Lord, a country-gentlewoman's pleasure is the drudgery of a footpost; and she requires as much airing as her husband's horses.—[*Aside.*] But here comes your husband: I'll ask, though I'm sure he'll not grant it.

Mrs. Pinch. He says he won't let me go abroad for fear of catching the pox.

Alith. Fy! the small pox you should say.

Enter PINCHWIFE.

Mrs. Pinch. O my dear, dear bud, welcome home! Why dost thou look so fropish? who has nangered thee?

Pinch. You're a fool.   [Mrs. PINCHWIFE *goes aside, and cries.*

Alith. Faith, so she is, for crying for no fault, poor tender creature!

Pinch. What, you would have her as impudent as yourself, as arrant a jilflirt, a gadder, a magpie; and to say all, a mere notorious town-woman?

Alith. Brother, you are my only censurer; and the honour of your family will sooner suffer in your wife there than in me, though I take the innocent liberty of the town.

Pinch. Hark you, mistress, do not talk so before my wife.—The innocent liberty of the town!

Alith. Why, pray, who boasts of any intrigue with me? what lampoon has made my name notorious? what ill women frequent my lodgings? I keep no company with any women of scandalous reputations.

Pinch. No, you keep the men of scandalous reputations company.

Alith. Where? would you not have me civil? answer 'em in a box at the plays, in the drawing-room at Whitehall, in St. James's Park, Mulberry Garden, or——

Pinch. Hold, hold! Do not teach my wife where the men are to be found: I believe she's the worse for your town-documents already. I bid you keep her in ignorance, as I do.

Mrs. Pinch. Indeed, be not angry with her, bud, she will tell me nothing of the town, though I ask her a thousand times a day.

Pinch. Then you are very inquisitive to know, I find?

Mrs. Pinch. Not I indeed, dear; I hate London. Our place-house in the country is worth a thousand of't: would I were there again!

Pinch. So you shall, I warrant. But were you not talking of plays and players when I came in?—[*To* ALITHEA.] You are her encourager in such discourses.

Mrs. Pinch. No, indeed, dear; she chid me just now for liking the player-men.

Pinch. [*aside*]. Nay, if she be so innocent as to own to me her liking them, there is no hurt in't.—[*Aloud.*] Come, my poor rogue, but thou likest none better than me?

Mrs. Pinch. Yes, indeed, but I do. The playermen are finer folks.

Pinch. But you love none better than me?

Mrs. Pinch. You are my own dear bud, and I know you. I hate a stranger.

Pinch. Ay, my dear, you must love me only; and not be like the naughty town-women, who only hate their husbands, and love every man else; love plays, visits, fine coaches, fine clothes, fiddles, balls, treats, and so lead a wicked town-life.

Mrs. Pinch. Nay, if to enjoy all these things be a town-life, London is not so bad a place, dear.

Pinch. How! if you love me, you must hate London.

Alith. The fool has forbid me discovering to her the pleasures of the town, and he is now setting her agog upon them himself. [*Aside*

Mrs. Pinch. But, husband, do the town-women love the playermen too?

Pinch. Yes, I warrant you.

Mrs. Pinch. Ay, I warrant you.

Pinch. Why, you do not, I hope?

Mrs. Pinch. No, no, bud. But why have we no playermen in the country?

Pinch. Ha!—Mrs. Minx, ask me no more to go to a play.

Mrs. Pinch. Nay, why, love? I did not care for going: but when you forbid me, you make me, as 'twere, desire it.

Alith. So 'twill be in other things, I warrant.   [*Aside.*

Mrs. Pinch. Pray let me go to a play, dear.

Pinch. Hold your peace, I wo' not.

Mrs. Pinch. Why, love?

Pinch. Why, I'll tell you.

Alith. Nay, if he tell her, she'll give him more cause to forbid her that place.   [*Aside.*

Mrs. Pinch. Pray why, dear?

Pinch. First, you like the actors; and the gallants may like you.

Mrs. Pinch. What, a homely country girl! No, bud, nobody will like me.

Pinch. I tell you yes, they may.

Mrs. Pinch. No, no, you jest—I won't believe you: I will go.

Pinch. I tell you then, that one of the lewdest fellows in town, who saw you there, told me he was in love with you.

Mrs. Pinch. Indeed! who, who, pray who was't?

Pinch. I've gone too far, and slipped before I was aware; how overjoyed she is!   [*Aside.*

Mrs. Pinch. Was it any Hampshire gallant, any of our neighbours? I promise you, I am beholden to him.

Pinch. I promise you, you lie; for he would but ruin you, as he has done hundreds. He has no other love for women but that; such as he look upon women, like basilisks, but to destroy 'em.

Mrs. Pinch. Ay, but if he loves me, why should he ruin me? answer me to that. Methinks he should not, I would do him no harm.

Alith. Ha! ha! ha!

Pinch. 'Tis very well; but I'll keep him from doing you any harm, or me either. But here comes company; get you in, get you in.

Mrs. Pinch. But, pray, husband, is he a pretty gentleman that loves me?

Pinch. In, baggage, in.   [*Thrusts her in, and shuts the door.*

Enter SPARKISH *and* HARCOURT.

What, all the lewd libertines of the town brought to my lodging by this easy coxcomb! 'sdeath, I'll not suffer it.

Spark. Here, Harcourt, do you approve my choice?—[*To* ALITHEA.] Dear little rogue, I told you I'd bring you acquainted with all my friends, the wits and——   [HARCOURT *salutes her.*

Pinch. Ay, they shall know her, as well as you yourself will, I warrant you.

Spark. This is one of those, my pretty rogue, that are to dance at your wedding to-morrow; and him you must bid welcome ever, to what you and I have.

Pinch. Monstrous!   [*Aside.*

Spark. Harcourt, how dost thou like her, faith? Nay, dear, do not look down; I should hate to have a wife of mine out of countenance at anything.

Pinch. Wonderful!   [*Aside.*

Spark. Tell me, I say, Harcourt, how dost thou like her? Thou hast stared upon her enough, to resolve me.

Har. So infinitely well, that I could wish I had a mistress too, that might differ from her in nothing but her love and engagement to you.

Alith. Sir, Master Sparkish has often told me that his acquaintance were all wits and raillieurs, and now I find it.

Spark. No, by the universe, madam, he does not rally now; you may believe him. I do assure you, he is the honestest, worthiest, true-hearted gentleman —a man of such perfect honour, he would say nothing to a lady he does not mean.

Pinch. Praising another man to his mistress!   [*Aside.*

Har. Sir, you are so beyond expectation obliging, that——

Spark. Nay, egad, I am sure you do admire her extremely; I see't in your eyes.—He does admire you, madam.—By the world, don't you?

Har. Yes, above the world, or the most glorious part of it, her whole sex: and till now I never thought I should have envied you, or any man about to marry, but you have the best excuse for marriage I ever knew.

Alith. Nay, now, sir, I'm satisfied you are of the society of the wits and raillieurs, since you cannot spare your friend, even when he is but too civil to you; but the surest sign is, since you are an enemy to marriage,—for that I hear you hate as much as business or bad wine.

Har. Truly, madam, I was never an enemy to marriage till now, because marriage was never an enemy to me before.

Alith. But why, sir, is marriage an enemy to you now? because it robs you of your friend here? for you look upon a friend married, as one gone into a monastery, that is, dead to the world.

Har. 'Tis indeed, because you marry him; I see, madam, you can guess my meaning. I do confess heartily and openly, I wish it were in my power to break the match; by Heavens I would.

Spark. Poor Frank!

Alith. Would you be so unkind to me?

Har. No, no, 'tis not because I would be unkind to you.

Spark. Poor Frank! no gad, 'tis only his kindness to me.

Pinch. Great kindness to you indeed! Insensible fop, let a man make love to his wife to his face!   [*Aside.*

Spark. Come, dear Frank, for all my wife there, that shall be, thou shalt enjoy me sometimes, dear rogue. By my honour, we men of wit condole for our deceased brother in marriage, as much as for one dead in earnest: I think that was prettily said of me, ha, Harcourt?—But come, Frank, be not melancholy for me.

Har. No, I assure you, I am not melancholy for you.

Spark. Prithee, Frank, dost think my wife that shall be, there, a fine person?

Har. I could gaze upon her till I became as blind as you are.

Spark. How as I am? how?

Har. Because you are a lover, and true lovers are blind, stock blind.

Spark. True, true; but by the world she has wit too, as well as beauty: go, go with her into a corner, and try if she has wit; talk to her anything, she's bashful before me.

Har. Indeed if a woman wants wit in a corner, she has it nowhere.

Alith. Sir, you dispose of me a little before your time——

[*Aside to* SPARKISH.

Spark. Nay, nay, madam, let me have an earnest of your obedience, or—go, go, madam——   [HARCOURT *courts* ALITHEA *aside.*

Pinch. How, sir! if you are not concerned for the honour of a wife, I am for that of a sister; he shall not debauch her. Be a pander to your own wife! bring men to her! let 'em make love before your face! thrust 'em into a corner together, then leave 'em in private! is this your town wit and conduct?

Spark. Ha! ha! ha! a silly wise rogue would make one laugh more than a stark fool, ha! ha! I shall burst. Nay, you shall not disturb 'em; I'll vex thee, by the world.

[*Struggles with* PINCHWIFE *to keep him from* HARCOURT *and* ALITHEA.

Alith. The writings are drawn, sir, settlements made; 'tis too late, sir, and past all revocation.

Har. Then so is my death.

Alith. I would not be unjust to him.

Har. Then why to me so?

Alith. I have no obligation to you.

Har. My love.

Alith. I had his before.

Har. You never had it; he wants, you see, jealousy, the only infallible sign of it.

Alith. Love proceeds from esteem; he cannot distrust my virtue: besides, he loves me, or he would not marry me.

Har. Marrying you is no more sign of his love than bribing your woman, that he may marry you, is a sign of his generosity. Marriage is rather a sign of interest than love; and he that marries a fortune covets a mistress, not loves her. But if you take marriage for a sign of love, take it from me immediately.

Alith. No, now you have put a scruple in my head; but in short, sir, to end our dispute, I must marry him, my reputation would suffer in the world else.

Har. No; if you do marry him, with your pardon, madam, your reputation suffers in the world, and you would be thought in necessity for a cloak.

Alith. Nay, now you are rude, sir.—Mr. Sparkish, pray come hither, your friend here is very troublesome, and very loving.

Har. Hold! hold!——   [*Aside to* ALITHEA.

Pinch. D'ye hear that?

Spark. Why, d'ye think I'll seem to be jealous, like a country bumpkin?

Pinch. No, rather be a cuckold, like a credulous cit.

Har. Madam, you would not have been so little generous as to have told him.

Alith. Yes, since you could be so little generous as to wrong him.

Har. Wrong him! no man can do't, he's beneath an injury: a bubble, a coward, a senseless idiot, a wretch so contemptible to all the world but you, that——

Alith. Hold, do not rail at him, for since he is like to be my husband, I am resolved to like him: nay, I think I am obliged to tell him you are not his friend.—Master Sparkish, Master Sparkish!

Spark. What, what?—[*To* Harcourt.] Now, dear rogue, has not she wit?

Har. Not so much as I thought, and hoped she had. [*Speaks surlily.*

Alith. Mr. Sparkish, do you bring people to rail at you?

Har. Madam——

Spark. How! no; but if he does rail at me, 'tis but in jest, I warrant: what we wits do for one another, and never take any notice of it.

Alith. He spoke so scurrilously of you, I had no patience to hear him; besides, he has been making love to me.

Har. True, damned tell-tale woman! [*Aside.*

Spark. Pshaw! to show his parts—we wits rail and make love often, but to show our parts: as we have no affections, so we have no malice, we——

Alith. He said you were a wretch below an injury——

Spark. Pshaw!

Har. Damned, senseless, impudent, virtuous jade! Well, since she won't let me have her, she'll do as good, she'll make me hate her. [*Aside.*

Alith. A common bubble——

Spark. Pshaw!

Alith. A coward——

Spark. Pshaw, pshaw!

Alith. A senseless, drivelling idiot——

Spark. How! did he disparage my parts? Nay, then, my honour's concerned, I can't put up that, sir, by the world—brother, help me to kill him—[*Aside*] I may draw now, since we have the odds of him:—'tis a good occasion, too, before my mistress—— [*Offers to draw.*

Alith. Hold, hold!

Spark. What, what?

Alith. [*aside*]. I must not let 'em kill the gentleman neither, for his kindness to me: I am so far from hating him, that I wish my gallant had his person and understanding. Nay, if my honour——

Spark. I'll be thy death.

Alith. Hold, hold! Indeed, to tell the truth, the gentleman said after all, that what he spoke was but out of friendship to you.

Spark. How! say, I am, I am a fool, that is, no wit, out of friendship to me?

Alith. Yes, to try whether I was concerned enough for you; and made love to me only to be satisfied of my virtue, for your sake.

Har. Kind, however. [*Aside.*

Spark. Nay, if it were so, my dear rogue, I ask thee pardon; but why would not you tell me so, faith?

Har. Because I did not think on't, faith.

Spark. Come, Horner does not come; Harcourt, let's be gone to the new play.—Come, madam.

Alith. I will not go, if you intend to leave me alone in the box, and run into the pit, as you use to do.

Spark. Pshaw! I'll leave Harcourt with you in the box to entertain you, and that's as good; if I sat in the box, I should be thought no judge but of trimmings.—Come away, Harcourt, lead her down.

[Exeunt SPARKISH, HARCOURT, and ALITHEA.

Pinch. Well, go thy ways, for the flower of the true town fops, such as spend their estates before they come to 'em, and are cuckolds before they're married. But let me go look to my own freehold.—How!

Enter Lady FIDGET, Mrs. DAINTY FIDGET, and Mrs. SQUEAMISH.

Lady Fid. Your servant, sir: where is your lady? We are come to wait upon her to the new play.

Pinch. New play!

Lady Fid. And my husband will wait upon you presently.

Pinch. [*aside*]. Damn your civility.—[*Aloud.*] Madam, by no means; I will not see Sir Jasper here, till I have waited upon him at home; nor shall my wife see you till she has waited upon your ladyship at your lodgings.

Lady Fid. Now we are here, sir?

Pinch. No, Madam.

Mrs. Dain. Pray, let us see her.

Mrs. Squeam. We will not stir till we see her.

Pinch. [*aside*]. A pox on you all!—[*Goes to the door, and returns.*] She has locked the door, and is gone abroad.

Lady Fid. No, you have locked the door, and she's within.

Mrs. Dain. They told us below she was here.

Pinch. [*aside*]. Will nothing do?—[*Aloud.*] Well, it must out then. To tell you the truth, ladies, which I was afraid to let you know before, lest it might endanger your lives, my wife has just now the small-pox come out upon her; do not be frightened; but pray be gone, ladies; you shall not stay here in danger of your lives; pray get you gone, ladies.

Lady Fid. No, no, we have all had 'em.

Mrs. Squeam. Alack, alack!

Mrs. Dain. Come, come, we must see how it goes with her; I understand the disease.

Lady Fid. Come!

Pinch. [*aside*]. Well, there is no being too hard for women at their own weapon, lying, therefore I'll quit the field.   [*Exit.*

Mrs. Squeam. Here's an example of jealousy!

Lady Fid. Indeed, as the world goes, I wonder there are no more jealous, since wives are so neglected.

Mrs. Dain. Pshaw! as the world goes, to what end should they be jealous?

Lady Fid. Foh! 'tis a nasty world.

Mrs. Squeam. That men of parts, great acquaintance, and quality, should take up with and spend themselves and fortunes in keeping little playhouse creatures, foh!

Lady Fid. Nay, that women of understanding, great acquaintance, and good quality, should fall a-keeping too of little creatures, foh!

Mrs. Squeam. Why, 'tis the men of quality's fault; they never visit women of honour and reputation as they used to do; and have not so much as common civility for ladies of our rank, but use us with the same indifference and ill-breeding as if we were all married to 'em.

Lady Fid. She says true; 'tis an arrant shame women of quality should be so slighted; methinks birth—birth should go for something; I have known men admired, courted, and followed for their titles only.

Mrs. Squeam. Ay, one would think men of honour should not love, no more than marry, out of their own rank.

Mrs. Dain. Fy, fy, upon 'em! they are come to think cross breeding for themselves best, as well as for their dogs and horses.

Lady Fid. They are dogs and horses for't.

Mrs. Squeam. One would think, if not for love, for vanity a little.

Mrs. Dain. Nay, they do satisfy their vanity upon us sometimes; and are kind to us in their report, tell all the world they lie with us.

Lady Fid. Damned rascals, that we should be only wronged by 'em! To report a man has had a person, when he has not had a person, is the greatest wrong in the whole world that can be done to a person.

Mrs. Squeam. Well, 'tis an arrant shame noble persons should be so wronged and neglected.

Lady Fid. But still 'tis an arranter shame for a noble person to neglect her own honour, and defame her own noble person with little inconsiderable fellows, foh!

Mrs. Dain. I suppose the crime against our honour is the same with a man of quality as with another.

Lady Fid. How! no sure, the man of quality is likest one's husband, and therefore the fault should be the less.

Mrs. Dain. But then the pleasure should be the less.

Lady Fid. Fy, fy, fy, for shame, sister! whither shall we ramble? Be continent in your discourse, or I shall hate you.

Mrs. Dain. Besides, an intrigue is so much the more notorious for the man's quality.

Mrs. Squeam. 'Tis true that nobody takes notice of a private man, and therefore with him 'tis more secret; and the crime's the less when 'tis not known.

Lady Fid. You say true; i'faith, I think you are in the right on't: 'tis not an injury to a husband, till it be an injury to our honours; so that a woman of honour loses no honour with a private person; and to say truth——

Mrs. Dain. So, the little fellow is grown a private person——with her——
                                    [*Apart to* Mrs. SQUEAMISH.
Lady Fid. But still my dear, dear honour——

Enter Sir JASPER FIDGET, HORNER, *and* DORILANT.

Sir Jasp. Ay, my dear, dear of honour, thou hast still so much honour in thy mouth——

Horn. That she has none elsewhere.   [*Aside.*

Lady Fid. Oh, what d'ye mean to bring in these upon us?

Mrs. Dain. Foh! these are as bad as wits.

Mrs. Squeam. Foh!

Lady Fid. Let us leave the room.

Sir Jasp. Stay, stay; faith, to tell you the naked truth——

Lady Fid. Fy, Sir Jasper! do not use that word naked.

Sir Jasp. Well, well, in short I have business at Whitehall, and cannot go to the play with you, therefore would have you go——

Lady Fid. With those two to a play?

Sir Jasp. No, not with t'other, but with Mr. Horner; there can be no more scandal to go with him than with Mr. Tattle, or Master Limberham.

Lady Fid. With that nasty fellow! no—no.

Sir Jasp. Nay, prithee, dear, hear me.   [*Whispers to* Lady FIDGET.

Horn. Ladies——
          [HORNER *and* DORILANT *draw near* Mrs. SQUEAMISH *and* Mrs. DAINTY
              FIDGET.

Mrs. Dain. Stand off.

Mrs. Squeam. Do not approach us.

Mrs. Dain. You herd with the wits, you are obscenity all over.

Mrs. Squeam. And I would as soon look upon a picture of Adam and Eve, without fig-leaves, as any of you, if I could help it; therefore keep off, and do not make us sick.

Dor. What a devil are these?

Horn. Why, these are pretenders to honour, as critics to wit, only by censuring others; and as every raw, peevish, out-of-humoured, affected, dull, tea-drinking, arithmetical fop, sets up for a wit by railing at men of sense, so these for honour, by railing at the court, and ladies of as great honour as quality.

Sir Jasp. Come, Mr. Horner, I must desire you to go with these ladies to the play, sir.

Horn. I, sir?

Sir Jasp. Ay, ay, come, sir.

Horn. I must beg your pardon, sir, and theirs; I will not be seen in women's company in public again for the world.

Sir Jasp. Ha, ha, strange aversion!

Mrs. Squeam. No, he's for women's company in private.

Sir Jasp. He—poor man—he—ha! ha! ha!

Mrs. Dain. 'Tis a greater shame amongst lewd fellows to be seen in virtuous women's company, than for the women to be seen with them.

Horn. Indeed, madam, the time was I only hated virtuous women, but now I hate the other too; I beg your pardon, ladies.

Lady Fid. You are very obliging, sir, because we would not be troubled with you.

Sir Jasp. In sober sadness, he shall go.

Dor. Nay, if he wo' not, I am ready to wait upon the ladies, and I think I am the fitter man.

Sir Jasp. You, sir! no, I thank you for that. Master Horner is a privileged man amongst the virtuous ladies, 'twill be a great while before you are so; he! he! he! he's my wife's gallant; he! he! he! No, pray withdraw, sir, for as I take it, the virtuous ladies have no business with you.

Dor. And I am sure he can have none with them. 'Tis strange a man can't come amongst virtuous women now, but upon the same terms as men are admitted into the Great Turk's seraglio. But heavens keep me from being an ombre player with 'em!—But where is Pinchwife?   [*Exit.*

Sir Jasp. Come, come, man; what, avoid the sweet society of womankind? that sweet, soft, gentle, tame, noble creature, woman, made for man's companion——

Horn. So is that soft, gentle, tame, and more noble creature a spaniel, and has all their tricks; can fawn, lie down, suffer beating, and fawn the more; barks at your friends when they come to see you, makes your bed hard, gives you fleas, and the mange sometimes. And all the difference is, the spaniel's the more faithful animal, and fawns but upon one master.

Sir Jasp. He! he! he!

Mrs. Squeam. O the rude beast!

Mrs. Dain. Insolent brute!

Lady Fid. Brute! stinking, mortified, rotten French wether, to dare——

Sir Jasp. Hold, an't please your ladyship.—For shame, Master Horner! your mother was a woman.—[*Aside.*] Now shall I never reconcile 'em.—[*Aside to* Lady Fidget.] Hark you, madam, take my advice in your anger. You know you often want one to make up your drolling pack of ombre players, and you may cheat him easily; for he's an ill gamester, and consequently loves play. Besides, you know you have but two old civil gentlemen (with stinking breaths too) to wait upon you abroad; take in the third into your service. The other are but crazy; and a lady should have a supernumerary gentleman-usher as a supernumerary coach-horse, lest sometimes you should be forced to stay at home.

Lady Fid. But are you sure he loves play, and has money?

Sir Jasp. He loves play as much as you, and has money as much as I.

Lady Fid. Then I am contented to make him pay for his scurrility. Money makes up in a measure all other wants in men.—Those whom we cannot make hold for gallants, we make fine.   [*Aside.*

Sir Jasp. [*aside*]. So, so; now to mollify, wheedle him.—[*Aside to*

HORNER.] Master Horner, will you never keep civil company? methinks 'tis time now, since you are only fit for them. Come, come, man, you must e'en fall to visiting our wives, eating at our tables, drinking tea with our virtuous relations after dinner, dealing cards to 'em, reading plays and gazettes to 'em, picking fleas out of their smocks for 'em, collecting receipts, new songs, women, pages, and footmen for 'em.

Horn. I hope they'll afford me better employment, sir.

Sir Jasp. He! he! he! 'tis fit you know your work before you come into your place. And since you are unprovided of a lady to flatter, and a good house to eat at, pray frequent mine, and call my wife mistress, and she shall call you gallant, according to the custom.

Horn. Who, I?

Sir Jasp. Faith, thou sha't for my sake; come, for my sake only.

Horn. For your sake——

Sir Jasp. Come, come, here's a gamester for you; let him be a little familiar sometimes; nay, what if a little rude? Gamesters may be rude with ladies, you know.

Lady Fid. Yes; losing gamesters have a privilege with women.

Horn. I always thought the contrary, that the winning gamester had most privilege with women; for when you have lost your money to a man, you'll lose anything you have, all you have, they say, and he may use you as he pleases.

Sir Jasp. He! he! he! well, win or lose, you shall have your liberty with her.

Lady Fid. As he behaves himself; and for your sake I'll give him admittance and freedom.

Horn. All sorts of freedom, madam?

Sir Jasp. Ay, ay, ay, all sorts of freedom thou canst take. And so go to her, begin thy new employment; wheedle her, jest with her, and be better acquainted one with another.

Horn. [*aside*]. I think I know her already; therefore may venture with her my secret for hers. [HORNER *and* Lady FIDGET *whisper.*

Sir Jasp. Sister cuz, I have provided an innocent playfellow for you there.

Mrs. Dain. Who, he?

Mrs. Squeam. There's a playfellow, indeed!

Sir Jasp. Yes sure.—What, he is good enough to play at cards, blindman's-buff, or the fool with, sometimes!

Mrs. Squeam. Foh! we'll have no such playfellows.

Mrs. Dain. No, sir; you shan't choose playfellows for us, we thank you.

Sir Jasp. Nay, pray hear me. [*Whispering to them.*

Lady Fid. But, poor gentleman, could you be so generous, so truly a man of honour, as for the sakes of us women of honour, to cause yourself to be reported no man? No man! and to suffer yourself the greatest shame that could fall upon a man, that none might fall upon us women by your conversation? but, indeed, sir, as perfectly, perfectly the same man as before your going into France, sir? as perfectly, perfectly, sir?

Horn. As perfectly, perfectly, madam. Nay, I scorn you should take my word; I desire to be tried only, madam.

Lady Fid. Well, that's spoken again like a man of honour: all men of honour desire to come to the test. But, indeed, generally you men report such things of yourselves, one does not know how or whom to believe; and it is come to that pass, we dare not take your words no more than your tailor's, without some staid servant of yours be bound with you. But I have so strong a faith in your honour, dear, dear, noble sir, that I'd forfeit mine for yours, at any time, dear sir.

Horn. No, madam, you should not need to forfeit it for me; I have given you security already to save you harmless, my late reputation being so well known in the world, madam.

Lady Fid. But if upon any future falling-out, or upon a suspicion of my taking the trust out of your hands, to employ some other, you yourself should betray your trust, dear sir? I mean, if you'll give me leave to speak obscenely, you might tell, dear sir.

Horn. If I did, nobody would believe me. The reputation of impotency is as hardly recovered again in the world as that of cowardice, dear madam.

Lady Fid. Nay, then, as one may say, you may do your worst, dear, **dear** sir.

Sir Jasp. Come, is your ladyship reconciled to him yet? have you agreed on matters? for I must be gone to Whitehall.

Lady Fid. Why, indeed, Sir Jasper, Master Horner is a thousand, thousand times a better man than I thought him. Cousin Squeamish, sister Dainty, I can name him now. Truly, not long ago, you know, I thought his very name obscenity; and I would as soon have lain with him as have named him.

Sir Jasp. Very likely, poor madam.

Mrs. Dain. I believe it.

Mrs. Squeam. No doubt on't.

Sir Jasp. Well, well—that your ladyship is as virtuous as any she, I know, and him all the town knows—he! he! he! therefore now you like him, get you gone to your business together, go, go to your business, I say, pleasure, whilst I go to my pleasure, business.

Lady Fid. Come, then, dear gallant.

Horn. Come away, my dearest mistress.

Sir Jasp. So, so; why, 'tis as I'd have it.   [*Exit.*

Horn. And as I'd have it.

Lady Fid. Who for his business from his wife will run,
              Takes the best care to have her business done.   [*Exeunt.*

ACT III

SCENE I.—*A Room in* PINCHWIFE'S *House*

Enter ALITHEA *and* MRS. PINCHWIFE.

Alith. Sister, what ails you? you are grown melancholy.

Mrs. Pinch. Would it not make any one melancholy to see you go every day fluttering about abroad, whilst I must stay at home like a poor lonely sullen bird in a cage?

Alith. Ay, sister; but you came young, and just from the nest to your cage: so that I thought you liked it, and could be as cheerful in't as others that took their flight themselves early, and are hopping abroad in the open air.

Mrs. Pinch. Nay, I confess I was quiet enough till my husband told me what pure lives the London ladies live abroad, with their dancing, meetings, and junketings, and dressed every day in their best gowns; and I warrant you, play at nine-pins every day of the week, so they do.

Enter PINCHWIFE.

Pinch. Come, what's here to do? you are putting the town-pleasures in her head, and setting her a-longing.

Alith. Yes, after nine-pins. You suffer none to give her those longings you mean but yourself.

Pinch. I tell her of the vanities of the town like a confessor.

Alith. A confessor! just such a confessor as he that, by forbidding a silly ostler to grease the horse's teeth, taught him to do't.

Pinch. Come, Mrs. Flippant, good precepts are lost when bad examples are still before us: the liberty you take abroad makes her hanker after it, and out of humour at home. Poor wretch! she desired not to come to London; I would bring her.

Alith. Very well.

Pinch. She has been this week in town, and never desired till this afternoon to go abroad.

Alith. Was she not at a play yesterday?

Pinch. Yes; but she ne'er asked me; I was myself the cause of her going.

Alith. Then if she ask you again, you are the cause of her asking, and not my example.

Pinch. Well, to-morrow night I shall be rid of you; and the next day, before 'tis light, she and I'll be rid of the town, and my dreadful apprehensions.—Come, be not melancholy; for thou sha't go into the country after to-morrow, dearest.

Alith. Great comfort!

Mrs. Pinch. Pish! what d'ye tell me of the country for?

Pinch. How's this! what, pish at the country?

Mrs. Pinch. Let me alone; I am not well.

Pinch. O, if that be all—what ails my dearest?

Mrs. Pinch. Truly, I don't know: but I have not been well since you told me there was a gallant at the play in love with me.

Pinch. Ha!——

Alith. That's by my example too!

Pinch. Nay, if you are not well, but are so concerned, because a lewd fellow chanced to lie, and say he liked you, you'll make me sick too.

Mrs. Pinch. Of what sickness?

Pinch. O, of that which is worse than the plague, jealousy.

Mrs. Pinch. Pish, you jeer! I'm sure there's no such disease in our receipt-book at home.

Pinch. No, thou never met'st with it, poor innocent.—Well, if thou cuckold me, 'twill be my own fault—for cuckolds and bastards are generally makers of their own fortune.   [*Aside.*

Mrs. Pinch. Well, but pray, bud, let's go to a play to-night.

Pinch. 'Tis just done, she comes from it. But why are you so eager to see a play?

Mrs. Pinch. Faith, dear, not that I care one pin for their talk there; but I like to look upon the playermen, and would see, if I could, the gallant you say loves me: that's all, dear bud.

Pinch. Is that all, dear bud?

Alith. This proceeds from my example!

Mrs. Pinch. But if the play be done, let's go abroad, however, dear bud.

Pinch. Come, have a little patience and thou shalt go into the country on Friday.

Mrs. Pinch. Therefore I would see first some sights to tell my neighbours of. Nay, I will go abroad, that's once.

Alith. I'm the cause of this desire too!

Pinch. But now I think on't, who, who was the cause of Horner's coming to my lodgings to-day? That was you.

Alith. No, you, because you would not let him see your handsome wife out of your lodging.

Mrs. Pinch. Why, O Lord! did the gentleman come hither to see me indeed?

Pinch. No, no.—You are not the cause of that damned question too, Mistress Alithea?—[*Aside.*] Well, she's in the right of it. He is in love with my wife—and comes after her—'tis so—but I'll nip his love in the bud; lest he should follow us into the country, and break his chariot-wheel near our house, on purpose for an excuse to come to't. But I think I know the town.

Mrs. Pinch. Come, pray, bud, let's go abroad before 'tis late; for I will go, that's flat and plain.

Pinch. [*aside*]. So! the obstinacy already of the town-wife; and I must, whilst she's here, humour her like one.—[*Aloud.*] Sister, how shall we do, that she may not be seen or known?

Alith. Let her put on her mask.

Pinch. Pshaw! a mask makes people but the more inquistive, and is as ridiculous a disguise as a stage-beard: her shape, stature, habit will be known. And if we should meet with Horner, he would be sure to take acquaintance with us, must wish her joy, kiss her, talk to her, leer upon her, and the devil and all. No, I'll not use her to a mask, 'tis dangerous; for masks have made more cuckolds than the best faces that ever were known.

Alith. How will you do then?

Mrs. Pinch. Nay, shall we go? The Exchange will be shut, and I have a mind to see that.

Pinch. So—I have it—I'll dress her up in the suit we are to carry down to her brother, little Sir James; nay, I understand the town-tricks. Come, let's go dress her. A mask! no—a woman masked, like a covered dish, gives a man curiosity and appetite; when, it may be, uncovered, 'twould turn his stomach: no, no.

Alith. Indeed your comparison is something a greasy one: but I had a gentle gallant used to say, A beauty masked, like the sun in eclipse, gathers together more gazers than if it shined out.   [*Exeunt.*

SCENE II.—*The New Exchange*

Enter HORNER, HARCOURT, *and* DORILANT.

Dor. Engaged to women, and not sup with us!

Horn. Ay, a pox on 'em all!

Har. You were much a more reasonable man in the morning, and had as noble resolutions against 'em as a widower of a week's liberty.

Dor. Did I ever think to see you keep company with women in vain?

Horn. In vain: no—'tis since I can't love 'em, to be revenged on 'em.

Har. Now your sting is gone, you looked in the box amongst all those women like a drone in the hive; all upon you, shoved and ill-used by 'em all, and thrust from one side to t'other.

Dor. Yet he must be buzzing amongst 'em still, like other beetle-headed liquorish drones. Avoid 'em, and hate 'em, as they hate you.

Horn. Because I do hate 'em, and would hate 'em yet more, I'll frequent 'em. You may see by marriage, nothing makes a man hate a woman more than her constant conversation. In short, I converse with 'em, as you do with rich fools, to laugh at 'em and use 'em ill.

Dor. But I would no more sup with women, unless I could lie with 'em, than sup with a rich coxcomb, unless I could cheat him.

Horn. Yes, I have known thee sup with a fool for his drinking; if he could set out your hand that way only, you were satisfied, and if he were a wine-swallowing mouth, 'twas enough.

Har. Yes, a man drinks often with a fool, as he tosses with a marker, only to keep his hand in use. But do the ladies drink?

Horn. Yes, sir; and I shall have the pleasure at least of laying 'em flat with a bottle, and bring as much scandal that way upon 'em as formerly t'other.

Har. Perhaps you may prove as weak a brother among 'em that way as t'other.

Dor. Foh! drinking with women is as unnatural as scolding with 'em. But 'tis a pleasure of decayed fornicators, and the basest way of quenching love.

Har. Nay, 'tis drowning love, instead of quenching it. But leave us for civil women too!

Dor. Ay, when he can't be the better for 'em. We hardly pardon a man that leaves his friend for a wench, and that's a pretty lawful call.

Horn. Faith, I would not leave you for 'em, if they would not drink.

Dor. Who would disappoint his company at Lewis's for a gossiping?

Har. Foh! Wine and women, good apart, together are as nauseous as sack and sugar. But hark you, sir, before you go, a little of your advice; an old maimed general, when unfit for action, is fittest for counsel. I have other designs upon women than eating and drinking with them; I am in love with Sparkish's mistress, whom he is to marry to-morrow: now how shall I get her?

Enter SPARKISH, *looking about.*

Horn. Why, here comes one will help you to her.

Har. He! he, I tell you, is my rival, and will hinder my love.

Horn. No; a foolish rival and a jealous husband assist their rival's designs; for they are sure to make their women hate them, which is the first step to their love for another man.

Har. But I cannot come near his mistress but in his company.

Horn. Still the better for you; for fools are most easily cheated when they themselves are accessories: and he is to be bubbled of his mistress as of his money, the common mistress, by keeping him company.

Spark. Who is that that is to be bubbled? Faith, let me snack; I han't met with a bubble since Christmas. 'Gad, I think bubbles are like their brother woodcocks, go out with the cold weather.

Har. A pox! he did not hear all, I hope.   [*Apart to* HORNER.

Spark. Come, you bubbling rogues you, where do we sup?—Oh, Harcourt, my mistress tells me you have been making fierce love to her all the play long: ha! ha!—But I——

Har. I make love to her!

Spark. Nay, I forgive thee, for I think I know thee, and I know her; but I am sure I know myself.

Har. Did she tell you so? I see all women are like these of the Exchange; who, to enhance the prize of their commodities, report to their fond customers offers which were never made 'em.

Horn. Ay, women are apt to tell before the intrigue, as men after it, and so show themselves the vainer sex. But hast thou a mistress, Sparkish? 'Tis as hard for me to believe it, as that thou ever hadst a bubble, as you bragged just now.

Spark. O, your servant, sir: are you at your raillery, sir? But we are some of us beforehand with you to-day at the play. The wits were something bold with you, sir; did you not hear us laugh?

Horn. Yes; but I thought you had gone to plays, to laugh at the poet's wit, not at your own.

Spark. Your servant, sir: no, I thank you. 'Gad, I go to a play as to a country treat; I carry my own wine to one, and my own wit to t'other, or else I'm sure I should not be merry at either. And the reason why we are so often louder than the players, is, because we think we speak more wit, and so become the poet's rivals in his audience: for to tell you the truth, we hate the silly rogues; nay, so much, that we find fault even with their bawdy upon the stage, whilst we talk nothing else in the pit as loud.

Horn. But why shouldst thou hate the silly poets? Thou hast too much wit to be one; and they, like whores, are only hated by each other: and thou dost scorn writing, I'm sure.

Spark. Yes; I'd have you to know I scorn writing: but women, women, that make men do all foolish things, make 'em write songs too. Everybody does it. 'Tis even as common with lovers, as playing with fans; and you can no more help rhyming to your Phillis, than drinking to your Phillis.

Har. Nay, poetry in love is no more to be avoided than jealousy.

Dor. But the poets damned your songs, did they?

Spark. Damn the poets! they have turned 'em into burlesque, as they call it. That burlesque is a hocus-pocus trick they have got, which, by the virtue of *Hictius doctius topsy turvy*, they make a wise and witty man in the world, a fool upon the stage you know not how: and 'tis therefore I hate 'em too, for I know not but it may be my own case; for they'll put a man into a play for looking asquint. Their predecessors were contented to make serving-men only their stage-fools: but these rogues must have gentlemen, with a pox to 'em, nay, knights; and, indeed, you shall hardly see a fool upon the stage but he's a knight. And to tell you the truth, they have kept me these six years from being a knight in earnest, for fear of being knighted in a play, and dubbed a fool.

Dor. Blame 'em not, they must follow their copy, the age.

Har. But why shouldst thou be afraid of being in a play, who expose yourself every day in the play-houses, and at public places?

Horn. 'Tis but being on the stage, instead of standing on a bench in the pit.

Dor. Don't you give money to painters to draw you like? and are you afraid of your pictures at length in a playhouse, where all your mistresses may see you?

Spark. A pox! painters don't draw the small-pox or pimples in one's face. Come, damn all your silly authors whatever, all books and booksellers, by the world; and all readers, courteous or uncourteous!

Har. But who comes here, Sparkish?

Enter PINCHWIFE *and* Mrs. PINCHWIFE *in man's clothes,*
ALITHEA *and* LUCY.

Spark. Oh, hide me! There's my mistress too.

[SPARKISH *hides himself behind* HARCOURT.

Har. She sees you.

Spark. But I will not see her. 'Tis time to go to Whitehall, and I must not fail the drawing-room.

Har. Pray, first carry me, and reconcile me to her.

Spark. Another time. Faith, the king will have supped.

Har. Not with the worse stomach for thy absence. Thou art one of those fools that think their attendance at the king's meals as necessary as his physicians, when you are more troublesome to him than his doctors or his dogs.

Spark. Pshaw! I know my interest, sir. Prithee hide me.

Horn. Your servant, Pinchwife.—What, he knows us not!

Pinch. Come along.   [*To his* Wife *aside.*

Mrs. Pinch. Pray, have you any ballads? give me sixpenny worth.

Bookseller. We have no ballads.

Mrs. Pinch. Then give me "Covent Garden Drollery," and a play or two— Oh, here's "Tarugo's Wiles," and "The Slighted Maiden"; I'll have them.

Pinch. No; plays are not for your reading. Come along; will you discover yourself?   [*Apart to her.*

Horn. Who is that pretty youth with him, Sparkish?

Spark. I believe his wife's brother, because he's something like her: but I never saw her but once.

Horn. Extremely handsome; I have seen a face like it too. Let us follow 'em.

[*Exeunt* PINCHWIFE, Mrs. PINCHWIFE, ALITHEA, *and* LUCY;
HORNER *and* DORILANT *following them.*

Har. Come, Sparkish, your mistress saw you, and will be angry you go not to her. Besides, I would fain be reconciled to her, which none but you can do, dear friend.

Spark. Well, that's a better reason, dear friend. I would not go near her now for hers or my own sake; but I can deny you nothing: for though I have known thee a great while, never go, if I do not love thee as well as a new acquaintance.

Har. I am obliged to you indeed, dear friend. I would be well with her, only to be well with thee still; for these ties to wives usually dissolve all ties to friends. I would be contented she should enjoy you a-nights, but I would have you to myself a-days as I have had, dear friend.

Spark. And thou shalt enjoy me a-days, dear, dear friend, never stir: and I'll be divorced from her, sooner than from thee. Come along.

Har. [*aside*]. So, we are hard put to't, when we make our rival our procurer; but neither she nor her brother would let me come near her now. When all's done, a rival is the best cloak to steal to a mistress under, without suspicion; and when we have once got to her as we desire, we throw him off like other cloaks.   [*Exit* SPARKISH, HARCOURT *following him.*

Re-enter PINCHWIFE *and* Mrs. PINCHWIFE.

Pinch. [*to* ALITHEA]. Sister, if you will not go, we must leave you.— [*Aside.*] The fool her gallant and she will muster up all the young saunterers of this place, and they will leave their dear sempstresses to follow us. What a swarm of cuckolds and cuckold-makers are here!—Come, let's be gone, Mistress Margery.

Mrs. Pinch. Don't you believe that; I han't half my bellyfull of sights yet.

Pinch. Then walk this way.

Mrs. Pinch. Lord, what a power of brave signs are here! stay—the Bull's-Head, the Ram's-Head, and the Stag's-Head, dear——

Pinch. Nay, if every husband's proper sign here were visible, they would be all alike.

Mrs. Pinch. What d'ye mean by that, bud?

Pinch. 'Tis no matter—no matter, bud.

Mrs. Pinch. Pray tell me: nay, I will know.

Pinch. They would be all Bulls, Stags, and Rams-heads.

[*Exeunt* PINCHWIFE *and* Mrs. PINCHWIFE.

Re-enter SPARKISH, HARCOURT, ALITHEA, *and* LUCY,
at the other side.

Spark. Come, dear madam, for my sake you shall be reconciled to him.

Alith. For your sake I hate him.

Har. That's something too cruel, madam, to hate me for his sake.

Spark. Ay indeed, madam, too, too cruel to me, to hate my friend for my sake.

Alith. I hate him because he is your enemy; and you ought to hate him too, for making love to me, if you love me.

Spark. That's a good one! I hate a man for loving you! If he did love you, 'tis but what he can't help; and 'tis your fault, not his, if he admires you. I hate a man for being of my opinion! I'll n'er do't, by the world.

Alith. Is it for your honour, or mine, to suffer a man to make love to me, who am to marry you to-morrow?

Spark. Is it for your honour, or mine, to have me jealous? That he makes love to you, is a sign you are handsome; and that I am not jealous, is a sign you are virtuous. That I think is for your honour.

Alith. But 'tis your honour too I am concerned for.

Har. But why, dearest madam, will you be more concerned for his honour than he is himself? Let his honour alone, for my sake and his. He! he has no honour——

Spark. How's that?

Har. But what my dear friend can guard himself.

Spark. O ho—that's right again.

Har. Your care of his honour argues his neglect of it, which is no honour to my dear friend here. Therefore once more, let his honour go which way it will, dear madam.

Spark. Ay, ay; were it for my honour to marry a woman whose virtue I suspected, and could not trust her in a friend's hands?

Alith. Are you not afraid to lose me?

Har. He afraid to lose you, madam! No, no—you may see how the most estimable and most glorious creature in the world is valued by him. Will you not see it?

Spark. Right, honest Frank, I have that noble value for her that I cannot be jealous of her.

Alith. You mistake him. He means, you care not for me, nor who has me.

Spark. Lord, madam, I see you are jealous! Will you wrest a poor man's meaning from his words?

Alith. You astonish me, sir, with your want of jealousy.

Spark. And you make me giddy, madam, with your jealousy and fears, and virtue and honour. 'Gad, I see virtue makes a woman as troublesome as a little reading or learning.

Alith. Monstrous!

Lucy. Well, to see what easy husbands these women of quality can meet with! a poor chambermaid can never have such ladylike luck. Besides, he's thrown away upon her. She'll make no use of her fortune, her blessing, none to a gentleman, for a pure cuckold; for it requires good breeding to be a cuckold. [*Aside.*

Alith. I tell you then plainly, he pursues me to marry me.

Spark. Pshaw!

Har. Come, madam, you see you strive in vain to make him jealous of me. My dear friend is the kindest creature in the world to me.

Spark. Poor fellow!

Har. But his kindness only is not enough for me, without your favour, your good opinion, dear madam: 'tis that must perfect my happiness. Good gentleman, he believes all I say: would you would do so! Jealous of me! I would not wrong him nor you for the world.

Spark. Look you there. Hear him, hear him, and do not walk away so.
[ALITHEA *walks carelessly to and fro.*

Har. I love you, madam, so——

Spark. How's that? Nay, now you begin to go too far indeed.

Har. So much, I confess, I say, I love you, that I would not have you miserable, and cast yourself away upon so unworthy and inconsiderable a thing as what you see here.
[*Clapping his hand on his breast, points at* SPARKISH.

Spark. No, faith, I believe thou wouldst not: now his meaning is plain; but I knew before thou wouldst not wrong me, nor her.

Har. No, no, Heaven forbid the glory of her sex should fall so low, as into the embraces of such a contemptible wretch, the least of mankind—my friend here—I injure him! [*Embracing* SPARKISH.

Alith. Very well.

Spark. No, no, dear friend, I knew it.—Madam, you see he will rather wrong himself than me, in giving himself such names.

Alith. Do not you understand him yet?

Spark. Yes: how modestly he speaks of himself, poor fellow!

Alith. Methinks he speaks impudently of yourself, since—before yourself too; insomuch that I can no longer suffer his scurrilous abusiveness to you, no more than his love to me.   [*Offers to go.*

Spark. Nay, nay, madam, pray stay—his love to you! Lord, madam, has he not spoke yet plain enough?

Alith. Yes, indeed, I should think so.

Spark. Well then, by the world, a man can't speak civilly to a woman now, but presently she says, he makes love to her. Nay, madam, you shall stay, with your pardon, since you have not yet understood him, till he has made an eclaircissement of his love to you, that is, what kind of love it is. Answer to thy catechism, friend; do you love my mistress here?

Har. Yes, I wish she would not doubt it.

Spark. But how do you love her?

Har. With all my soul.

Alith. I thank him, methinks he speaks plain enough now.

Spark. [*to* ALITHEA]. You are out still.—But with what kind of love, Harcourt?

Har. With the best and the truest love in the world.

Spark. Look you there then, that is with no matrimonial love, I'm sure.

Alith. How's that? do you say matrimonial love is not best?

Spark. 'Gad, I went too far ere I was aware. But speak for thyself, Harcourt, you said you would not wrong me nor her.

Har. No, no, madam, e'en take him for Heaven's sake.

Spark. Look you there, madam.

Har. Who should in all justice be yours, he that loves you most.

[*Claps his hand on his breast.*

Alith. Look you there, Mr. Sparkish, who's that?

Spark. Who should it be?—Go on, Harcourt.

Har. Who loves you more than women titles, or fortune fools.

[*Points at* SPARKISH.

Spark. Look you there, he means me still, for he points at me.

Alith. Ridiculous!

Har. Who can only match your faith and constancy in love.

Spark. Ay.

Har. Who knows, if it be possible, how to value so much beauty and virtue.

Spark. Ay.

Har. Whose love can no more be equalled in the world, than that heavenly form of yours.

Spark. No.

Har. Who could no more suffer a rival, than your absence, and yet could no more suspect your virtue, than his own constancy in his love to you.

Spark. No.

Har. Who, in fine, loves you better than his eyes, that first made him love you.

Spark. Ay—Nay, madam, faith, you shan't go till——

Alith. Have a care, lest you make me stay too long.

Spark. But till he has saluted you; that I may be assured you are friends, after his honest advice and declaration. Come, pray, madam, be friends with him.

Re-enter PINCHWIFE *and* Mrs. PINCHWIFE.

Alith. You must pardon me, sir, that I am not yet so obedient to you.

Pinch. What, invite your wife to kiss men? Monstrous! are you not ashamed? I will never forgive you.

Spark. Are you not ashamed, that I should have more confidence in the chastity of your family than you have? You must not teach me, I am a man of honour, sir, though I am frank and free; I am frank, sir——

Pinch. Very frank, sir, to share your wife with your friends.

Spark. He is an humble, menial friend, such as reconciles the differences of the marriage bed; you know man and wife do not always agree; I design him for that use, therefore would have him well with my wife.

Pinch. A menial friend!—you will get a great many menial friends, by showing your wife as you do.

Spark. What then? It may be I have a pleasure in't, as I have to show fine cloths at a play-house, the first day, and count money before poor rogues.

Pinch. He that shows his wife or money, will be in danger of having them borrowed sometimes.

Spark. I love to be envied, and would not marry a wife that I alone could love; loving alone is as dull as eating alone. Is it not a frank age? and I am a frank person; and to tell you the truth, it may be, I love to have rivals in a wife, they make her seem to a man still but as a kept mistress; and so good night, for I must to Whitehall.—Madam, I hope you are now reconciled to my friend; and so I wish you a good night, madam, and sleep if you can: for to-morrow you know I must visit you early with a canonical gentleman. Good night, dear Harcourt. [*Exit.*

Har. Madam, I hope you will not refuse my visit to-morrow, if it should be earlier with a canonical gentleman than Mr. Sparkish's.

Pinch. This gentlewoman is yet under my care, therefore you must yet forbear your freedom with her, sir.

[*Coming between* ALITHEA *and* HARCOURT.

Har. Must, sir?

Pinch. Yes, sir, she is my sister.

Har. 'Tis well she is, sir—for I must be her servant, sir.—Madam——

Pinch. Come away, sister, we had been gone, if it had not been for you, and so avoided these lewd rake-hells, who seem to haunt us.

Re-enter HORNER *and* DORILANT.

Horn. How now, Pinchwife!

Pinch. Your servant.

Horn. What! I see a little time in the country makes a man turn wild and unsociable, and only fit to converse with his horses, dogs, and his herds.

Pinch. I have business, sir, and must mind it; your business is pleasure, therefore you and I must go different ways.

Horn. Well, you may go on, but this pretty young gentleman——

[*Takes hold of* Mrs. PINCHWIFE.

Har. The lady——

Dor. And the maid——

Horn. Shall stay with us; for I suppose their business is the same with ours, pleasure.

Pinch. 'Sdeath, he knows her, she carries it so sillily! yet if he does not, I should be more silly to discover it first.   [*Aside.*

Alith. Pray, let us go, sir.

Pinch. Come, come——

Horn. [*to* Mrs. PINCHWIFE]. Had you not rather stay with us?—Prithee, Pinchwife, who is this pretty young gentleman?

Pinch. One to whom I'm a guardian.—[*Aside.*] I wish I could keep her out of your hands.

Horn. Who is he? I never saw anything so pretty in all my life.

Pinch. Pshaw! do not look upon him so much, he's a poor bashful youth, you'll put him out of countenance.—Come away, brother.

[*Offers to take her away.*

Horn. O, your brother!

Pinch. Yes, my wife's brother.—Come, come, she'll stay supper for us.

Horn. I thought so, for he is very like her I saw you at the play with, whom I told you I was in love with.

Mrs. Pinch. [*aside*]. O jeminy! is that he that was in love with me? I am glad on't, I vow, for he's a curious fine gentleman, and I love him already, too.—[*To* PINCHWIFE.] Is this he, bud?

Pinch. Come away, come away.   [*To his* Wife.

Horn. Why, what haste are you in? why won't you let me talk with him?

Pinch. Because you'll debauch him; he's yet young and innocent, and I would not have him debauched for anything in the world.—[*Aside.*] How she gazes on him! the devil!

Horn. Harcourt, Dorilant, look you here, this is the likeness of that dowdy he told us of, his wife; did you ever see a lovelier creature? The rogue has reason to be jealous of his wife, since she is like him, for she would make all that see her in love with her.

Har. And, as I remember now, she is as like him here as can be.

Dor. She is indeed very pretty, if she be like him.

Horn. Very pretty? a very pretty commendation!—she is a glorious creature, beautiful beyond all things I ever beheld.

Pinch. So, so.

Har. More beautiful than a poet's first mistress of imagination.

Horn. Or another man's last mistress of flesh and blood.

Mrs. Pinch. Nay, now you jeer, sir; pray don't jeer me.

Pinch. Come, come.—[*Aside.*] By Heavens, she'll discover herself!

Horn. I speak of your sister, sir.

Pinch. Ay, but saying she was handsome, if like him, made him blush.—[*Aside.*] I am upon a rack!

Horn. Methinks he is so handsome he should not be a man.

Pinch. [*aside*]. O, there 'tis out! he has discovered her! I am not able to suffer any longer.—[*To his* Wife.] Come, come away, I say.

Horn. Nay, by your leave, sir, he shall not go yet.—[*Aside to them.*] Harcourt, Dorilant, let us torment this jealous rogue a little.

Har. Dor. How?

Horn. I'll show you.

Pinch. Come, pray let him go, I cannot stay fooling any longer; I tell you his sister stays supper for us.

Horn. Does she? Come then, we'll all go to sup with he and thee.

Pinch. No, now I think on't, having stayed so long for us, I warrant she's gone to bed.—[*Aside.*] I wish she and I were well out of their hands.—[*To his* Wife.] Come, I must rise early to-morrow, come.

Horn. Well then, if she be gone to bed, I wish her and you a good night. But pray, young gentleman, present my humble service to her.

Mrs. Pinch. Thank you heartily, sir.

Pinch. [*aside*]. 'Sdeath, she will discover herself yet in spite of me.—[*Aloud.*] He is something more civil to you, for your kindness to his sister, than I am, it seems.

Horn. Tell her, dear sweet little gentleman, for all your brother there, that you have revived the love I had for her at first sight in the play-house.

Mrs. Pinch. But did you love her indeed, and indeed?

Pinch. [*aside*]. So, so.—[*Aloud.*] Away, I say.

Horn. Nay, stay.—Yes, indeed, and indeed, pray do you tell her so, and give her this kiss from me.   [*Kisses her.*

Pinch. [*aside*]. O Heavens! what do I suffer? Now 'tis too plain he knows her, and yet——

Horn. And this, and this——   [*Kisses her again.*

Mrs. Pinch. What do you kiss me for? I am no woman.

Pinch. [*aside*]. So, there, 'tis out.—[*Aloud.*] Come, I cannot, nor will stay any longer.

Horn. Nay, they shall send your lady a kiss too. Here, Harcourt, Dorilant, will you not?   [*They kiss her.*

Pinch. [*aside*]. How! do I suffer this? Was I not accusing another just now for this rascally patience, in permitting his wife to be kissed before his face? Ten thousand ulcers gnaw away their lips.—[*Aloud.*] Come, come.

Horn. Good night, dear little gentleman; madam, good night; farewell,

Pinchwife.—[*Apart to* HARCOURT *and* DORILANT.] Did not I tell you I would raise his jealous gall?   [*Exeunt* HORNER, HARCOURT, *and* DORILANT.

Pinch. So, they are gone at last; stay, let me see first if the coach be at this door.   [*Exit.*

Re-enter HORNER, HARCOURT, *and* DORILANT.

Horn. What, not gone yet? Will you be sure to do as I desired you, sweet sir?

Mrs. Pinch. Sweet sir, but what will you give me then?

Horn. Anything. Come away into the next walk.

          [*Exit, haling away* Mrs. PINCHWIFE.

Alith. Hold! hold! what d'ye do?

Lucy. Stay, stay, hold——

Har. Hold, madam, hold, let him present him—he'll come presently; nay, I will never let you go till you answer my question.

Lucy. For God's sake, sir, I must follow 'em.

          [ALITHEA *and* LUCY, *struggling with* HARCOURT *and* DORILANT.

Dor. No, I have something to present you with too, you shan't follow them.

Re-enter PINCHWIFE.

Pinch. Where?—how—what's become of?—gone!—whither?

Lucy. He's only gone with the gentleman, who will give him something, an't please your worship.

Pinch. Something!—give him something, with a pox!—where are they?

Alith. In the next walk only, brother.

Pinch. Only, only! where, where?

          [*Exit and returns presently, then goes out again.*

Har. What's the matter with him? why so much concerned? But, dearest madam——

Alith. Pray let me go, sir; I have said and suffered enough already.

Har. Then you will not look upon, nor pity, my sufferings?

Alith. To look upon 'em, when I cannot help 'em, were cruelty, not pity; therefore, I will never see you more.

Har. Let me then, madam, have my privilege of a banished lover, complaining or railing, and giving you but a farewell reason why, if you cannot condescend to marry me, you should not take that wretch, my rival.

Alith. He only, not you, since my honour is engaged so far to him, can give me a reason why I should not marry him; but if he be true, and what I think him to me, I must be so to him. Your servant, sir.

Har. Have women only constancy when 'tis a vice, and are, like Fortune, only true to fools?

Dor. Thou sha't not stir, thou robust creature; you see I can deal with you, therefore you should stay the rather, and be kind.

          [*To* LUCY, *who struggles to get from him.*

Re-enter PINCHWIFE.

Pinch. Gone, gone, not to be found! quite gone! ten thousand plagues go with 'em! Which way went they?

Alith. But into t'other walk, brother.

Lucy. Their business will be done presently sure, an't please your worship; it can't be long in doing, I'm sure on't.

Alith. Are they not there?

Pinch. No, you know where they are, you infamous wretch, eternal shame of your family, which you do not dishonour enough yourself you think, but you must help her to do it too, thou legion of bawds!

Alith. Good brother——

Pinch. Damned, damned sister!

Alith. Look you here, she's coming.

Re-enter Mrs. PINCHWIFE *running, with her hat full of oranges and dried fruit under her arm,* HORNER *following.*

Mrs. Pinch. O dear bud, look you here what I have got, see!

Pinch. And what I have got here too, which you can't see.

[*Aside, rubbing his forehead.*

Mrs. Pinch. The fine gentleman has given me better things yet.

Pinch. Has he so?—[*Aside.*] Out of breath and coloured!—I must hold yet.

Horn. I have only given your little brother an orange, sir.

Pinch. [*to* HORNER]. Thank you, sir.—[*Aside.*] You have only squeezed my orange, I suppose, and given it me again; yet I must have a city patience. —[*To his* Wife.] Come, come away.

Mrs. Pinch. Stay, till I have put up my fine things, bud.

Enter Sir JASPER FIDGET.

Sir Jasp. O, Master Horner, come, come, the ladies stay for you; your mistress, my wife, wonders you make not more haste to her.

Horn. I have stayed this half hour for you here, and 'tis your fault I am not now with your wife.

Sir Jasp. But, pray, don't let her know so much; the truth on't is, I was advancing a certain project to his majesty about—I'll tell you.

Horn. No, let's go, and hear it at your house. Good night, sweet little gentleman; one kiss more, you'll remember me now, I hope.   [*Kisses her.*

Dor. What, Sir Jasper, will you separate friends? He promised to sup with us, and if you take him to your house, you'll be in danger of our company too.

Sir Jasp. Alas! gentlemen, my house is not fit for you; there are none but civil women there, which are not for your turn. He, you know, can bear with the society of civil women now, ha! ha! ha! besides, he's one of my family—he's—he! he! he!

Dor. What is he?

Sir Jasp. Faith, my eunuch, since you'll have it; he! he! he!

[*Exeunt* Sir Jasper Fidget *and* Horner.

Dor. I rather wish thou wert his or my cuckold. Harcourt, what a good cuckold is lost there for want of a man to make him one? Thee and I cannot have Horner's privilege, who can make use of it.

Har. Ay, to poor Horner 'tis like coming to an estate at threescore, when a man can't be the better for't.

Pinch. Come.

Mrs. Pinch. Presently, bud.

Dor. Come, let us go too.—[*To* Alithea.] Madam, your servant.—[*To* Lucy.] Good night, strapper.

Har. Madam, though you will not let me have a good day or night, I wish you one; but dare not name the other half of my wish.

Alith. Good night, sir, for ever.

Mrs. Pinch. I don't know where to put this here, dear bud, you shall eat it; nay, you shall have part of the fine gentleman's good things, or treat, as you call it, when we come home.

Pinch. Indeed, I deserve it, since I furnished the best part of it.

[*Strikes away the orange.*

The gallant treats presents, and gives the ball;
But 'tis the absent cuckold pays for all.   [*Exeunt.*

ACT IV

SCENE I.—Pinchwife's *House in the morning*

Enter Alithea *dressed in new clothes, and* Lucy.

Lucy. Well—madam, now have I dressed you, and set you out with so many ornaments, and spent upon you ounces of essence and pulvillio; and all this for no other purpose but as people adorn and perfume a corpse for a stinking second-hand grave: such, or as bad, I think Master Sparkish's bed.

Alith. Hold your peace.

Lucy. Nay, madam, I will ask you the reason why you would banish poor Master Harcourt for ever from your sight; how could you be so hard-hearted?

Alith. 'Twas because I was not hard-hearted.

Lucy. No, no; 'twas stark love and kindness, I warrant.

Alith. It was so; I would see him no more because I love him.

Lucy. Hey day, a very pretty reason!

Alith. You do not understand me.

Lucy. I wish you may yourself.

Alith. I was engaged to marry, you see, another man, whom my justice will not suffer me to deceive or injure.

Lucy. Can there be a greater cheat or wrong done to a man than to give him your person without your heart? I should make a conscience of it.

Alith. I'll retrieve it for him after I am married a while.

Lucy. The woman that marries to love better, will be as much mistaken as the wencher that marries to live better. No, madam, marrying to increase love is like gaming to become rich; alas! you only lose what little stock you had before.

Alith. I find by your rhetoric you have been bribed to betray me.

Lucy. Only by his merit, that has bribed your heart, you see, against your word and rigid honour. But what a devil is this honour! 'tis sure a disease in the head, like the megrim or falling-sickness, that always hurries people away to do themselves mischief. Men lose their lives by it; women, what's dearer to 'em, their love, the life of life.

Alith. Come, pray talk you no more of honour, nor Master Harcourt; I wish the other would come to secure my fidelity to him and his right in me.

Lucy. You will marry him then?

Alith. Certainly, I have given him already my word, and will my hand too, to make it good, when he comes.

Lucy. Well, I wish I may never stick pin more, if he be not an arrant natural, to t'other fine gentleman.

Alith. I own he wants the wit of Harcourt, which I will dispense with al for another want he has, which is want of jealousy, which men of wit seldom want.

Lucy. Lord, madam, what should you do with a fool to your husband? You intend to be honest, don't you? then that husbandly virtue, credulity, is thrown away upon you.

Alith. He only that could suspect my virtue should have cause to do it; 'tis Sparkish's confidence in my truth that obliges me to be so faithful to him.

Lucy. You are not sure his opinion may last.

Alith. I am satisfied, 'tis impossible for him to be jealous after the proofs I have had of him. Jealousy in a husband—Heaven defend me from it! it begets a thousand plagues to a poor woman, the loss of her honour, her quiet, and her——

Lucy. And her pleasure.

Alith. What d'ye mean, impertinent?

Lucy. Liberty is a great pleasure, madam.

Alith. I say, loss of her honour, her quiet, nay, her life sometimes; and what's as bad almost, the loss of this town; that is, she is sent into the country, which is the last ill-usage of a husband to a wife, I think.

Lucy [*aside*]. O, does the wind lie there?—[*Aloud.*] Then of necessity, madam, you think a man must carry his wife into the country, if he be wise. The country is as terrible, I find, to our young English ladies, as a monastery to those abroad; and on my virginity, I think they would rather marry a London jailer, than a high sheriff of a county, since neither can stir from his employment. Formerly women of wit married fools for a great estate. a fine seat, or the like; but now 'tis for a pretty seat only in Lincoln's Inn Fields, St. James's Fields, or the Pall Mall.

Enter Sparkish, *and* Harcourt, *dressed like a* Parson.

Spark. Madam, your humble servant, a happy day to you, and to us all.
Har. Amen.
Alith. Who have we here?
Spark. My chaplain, faith—O madam, poor Harcourt remembers his humble service to you; and, in obedience to your last commands, refrains coming into your sight.
Alith. Is not that he?
Spark. No, fy, no; but to show that he ne'er intended to hinder our match, has sent his brother here to join our hands. When I get me a wife, I must get her a chaplain, according to the custom; that is his brother, and my chaplain.
Alith. His brother!
Lucy. And your chaplain, to preach in your pulpit then——   [*Aside.*
Alith. His brother!
Spark. Nay, I knew you would not believe it.—I told you, sir, she would take you for your brother Frank.
Alith. Believe it!
Lucy. His brother! ha! ha! he! he has a trick left still, it seems.   [*Aside.*
Spark. Come, my dearest, pray let us go to church before the canonical hour is past.
Alith. For shame, you are abused still.
Spark. By the world, 'tis strange now you are so incredulous.
Alith. 'Tis strange you are so credulous.
Spark. Dearest of my life, hear me. I tell you this is Ned Harcourt of Cambridge, by the world; you see he has a sneaking college look. 'Tis true he's something like his brother Frank; and they differ from each other no more than in their age, for they were twins.
Lucy. Ha! ha! ha!
Alith. Your servant, sir; I cannot be so deceived, though you are. But come, let's hear, how do you know what you affirm so confidently?
Spark. Why I'll tell you all. Frank Harcourt coming to me this morning to wish me joy, and present his service to you, I asked him if he could help me to a parson. Whereupon he told me, he had a brother in town who was in orders; and he went straight away, and sent him, you see there, to me.
Alith. Yes, Frank goes and puts on a black coat, then tells you he is Ned; that's all you have for't.
Spark. Pshaw! pshaw! I tell you, by the same token, the midwife put her garter about Frank's neck, to know 'em asunder, they were so like.
Alith. Frank tells you this too?
Spark. Ay, and Ned there too: nay, they are both in a story.
Alith. So, so; very foolish.

Spark. Lord, if you won't believe one, you had best try him by your chambermaid there; for chambermaids must needs know chaplains from other men, they are so used to 'em.

Lucy. Let's see: nay, I'll be sworn he has the canonical smirk, and the filthy clammy palm of a chaplain.

Alith. Well, most reverend doctor, pray let us make an end of this fooling.

Har. With all my soul, divine heavenly creature, when you please.

Alith. He speaks like a chaplain indeed.

Spark. Why, was there not soul, divine, heavenly, in what he said?

Alith. Once more, most impertinent black coat, cease your persecution, and let us have a conclusion of this ridiculous love.

Har. I had forgot, I must suit my style to my coat, or I wear it in vain.
　　　　　　　　　　　　　　　　　　　　　　　　　　　　　　　　[Aside.

Alith. I have no more patience left; let us make once an end of this troublesome love, I say.

Har. So be it, seraphic lady, when your honour shall think it meet and convenient so to do.

Spark. 'Gad, I'm sure none but a chaplain could speak so, I think.

Alith. Let me tell you, sir, this dull trick will not serve your turn; though you delay our marriage, you shall not hinder it.

Har. Far be it from me, munificent patroness, to delay your marriage; I desire nothing more than to marry you presently, which I might do, if you yourself would; for my noble, good-natured, and thrice generous patron here would not hinder it.

Spark. No, poor man, not I, faith.

Har. And now, madam, let me tell you plainly nobody else shall marry you; by Heavens! I'll die first, for I'm sure I should die after it.

Lucy. How his love has made him forget his function, as I have seen it in real parsons!

Alith. That was spoken like a chaplain too? now you understand him, I hope.

Spark. Poor man, he takes it heinously to be refused; I can't blame him, 'tis putting an indignity upon him, not to be suffered; but you'll pardon me, madam, it shan't be; he shall marry us; come away, pray, madam.

Lucy. Ha! ha! he! more ado! 'tis late.

Alith. Invincible stupidity! I tell you, he would marry me as your rival, not as your chaplain.

Spark. Come, come, madam.　　　　　　　　　　　　　*[Pulling her away.*

Lucy. I pray, madam, do not refuse this reverend divine the honour and satisfaction of marrying you; for I dare say, he has set his heart upon't, good doctor.

Alith. What can you hope or design by this?

Har. I could answer her, a reprieve for a day only, often revokes a hasty doom. At worst, if she will not take mercy on me, and let me marry her, I have at least the lover's second pleasure, hindering my rival's enjoyment, though but for a time.　　　　　　　　　　　　　　　　　　　*[Aside.*

Spark. Come, madam, 'tis e'en twelve o'clock, and my mother charged me never to be married out of the canonical hours. Come, come; Lord, here's such a deal of modesty, I warrant, the first day.

Lucy. Yes, an't please your worship, married women show all their modesty the first day, because married men show all their love the first day.

[*Exeunt*.

SCENE II.—*A Bedchamber in* PINCHWIFE'S *House*

PINCHWIFE *and* MRS. PINCHWIFE *discovered*.

Pinch. Come, tell me, I say.

Mrs. Pinch. Lord! han't I told it a hundred times over?

Pinch. [*aside*]. I would try, if in the repetition of the ungrateful tale, I could find her altering it in the least circumstance; for if her story be false, she is so too.—[*Aloud*.] Come, how was't, baggage?

Mrs. Pinch. Lord, what pleasure you take to hear it sure!

Pinch. No, you take more in telling it I find; but speak, how was't?

Mrs. Pinch. He carried me up into the house next to the Exchange.

Pinch. So, and you two were only in the room!

Mrs. Pinch. Yes, for he sent away a youth that was there, for some dried fruit, and China oranges.

Pinch. Did he so? Damn him for it—and for——

Mrs. Pinch. But presently came up the gentlewoman of the house.

Pinch. O, 'twas well she did; but what did he do whilst the fruit came?

Mrs. Pinch. He kissed me a hundred times, and told me he fancied he kissed my fine sister, meaning me, you know, whom he said he loved with all his soul, and bid me be sure to tell her so, and to desire her to be at her window, by eleven of the clock this morning, and he would walk under it at that time.

Pinch. And he was as good as his word, very punctual; a pox reward him for't.   [*Aside*.

Mrs. Pinch. Well, and he said if you were not within, he would come up to her, meaning me, you know, bud, still.

Pinch. [*aside*]. So—he knew her certainly; but for this confession, I am obliged to her simplicity.—[*Aloud*.] But what, you stood very still when he kissed you?

Mrs. Pinch. Yes, I warrant you; would you have had me discovered myself?

Pinch. But you told me he did some beastliness to you, as you call it; what was't?

Mrs. Pinch. Why, he put——

Pinch. What?

Mrs. Pinch. Why, he put the tip of his tongue between my lips, and so mousled me—and I said, I'd bite it.

Pinch. An eternal canker seize it, for a dog!

Mrs. Pinch. Nay, you need not be so angry with him neither, for to say truth, he has the sweetest breath I ever knew.

Pinch. The devil! you were satisfied with it then, and would do it again?

Mrs. Pinch. Not unless he should force me.

Pinch. Force you, changeling! I tell you, no woman can be forced.

Mrs. Pinch. Yes, but she may sure, by such a one as he, for he's a proper, goodly, strong man; 'tis hard, let me tell you, to resist him.

Pinch. [*aside*]. So, 'tis plain she loves him, yet she has not love enough to make her conceal it from me; but the sight of him will increase her aversion for me and love for him; and that love instruct her how to deceive me and satisfy him, all idiot as she is. Love! 'twas he gave women first their craft, their art of deluding. Out of Nature's hands they came plain, open, silly, and fit for slaves, as she and Heaven intended 'em; but damned Love— well—I must strangle that little monster whilst I can deal with him.— [*Aloud.*] Go fetch pen, ink, and paper out of the next room.

Mrs. Pinch. Yes, bud.   [*Exit.*

Pinch. Why should women have more invention in love than men? It can only be, because they have more desires, more soliciting passions, more lust, and more of the devil.

Re-enter Mrs. PINCHWIFE.

Come, minx, sit down and write.

Mrs. Pinch. Ay, dear bud, but I can't do't very well.

Pinch. I wish you could not at all.

Mrs. Pinch. But what should I write for?

Pinch. I'll have you write a letter to your lover.

Mrs. Pinch. O Lord, to the fine gentleman a letter!

Pinch. Yes, to the fine gentleman.

Mrs. Pinch. Lord, you do but jeer: sure you jest.

Pinch. I am not so merry: come, write as I bid you.

Mrs. Pinch. What, do you think I am a fool?

Pinch. [*aside*]. She's afraid I would not dictate any love to him, therefore she's unwilling.—[*Aloud.*] But you had best begin.

Mrs. Pinch. Indeed, and indeed, but I won't, so I won't.

Pinch. Why?

Mrs. Pinch. Because he's in town; you may send for him if you will.

Pinch. Very well, you would have him brought to you; is it come to this? I say, take the pen and write, or you'll provoke me.

Mrs. Pinch. Lord, what d'ye make a fool of me for? Don't I know that letters are never writ but from the country to London, and from London into the country? Now he's in town, and I am in town too; therefore I can't write to him, you know.

Pinch. [*aside*]. So, I am glad it is no worse; she is innocent enough yet.— [*Aloud.*] Yes, you may, when your husband bids you, write letters to people that are in town.

Mrs. Pinch. O, may I so? then I'm satisfied.

Pinch. Come, begin:—"Sir"—— [*Dictates.*

Mrs. Pinch. Shan't I say, "Dear Sir?"—You know one says always something more than bare "Sir."

Pinch. Write as I bid you, or I will write whore with this penknife in your face.

Mrs. Pinch. Nay, good bud—"Sir"—— [*Writes.*

Pinch. "Though I suffered last night your nauseous, loathed kisses and embraces"—Write!

Mrs. Pinch. Nay, why should I say so? You know I told you he had a sweet breath.

Pinch. Write!

Mrs. Pinch. Let me but put out "loathed."

Pinch. Write, I say!

Mrs. Pinch. Well then. [*Writes.*

Pinch. Let's see, what have you writ?—[*Takes the paper and reads.*] "Though I suffered last night your kisses and embraces"—Thou impudent creature! where is "nauseous" and "loathed"?

Mrs. Pinch. I can't abide to write such filthy words.

Pinch. Once more write as I'd have you, and question it not, or I will spoil thy writing with this. I will stab out those eyes that cause my mischief.

[*Holds up the penknife.*

Mrs. Pinch. O Lord! I will.

Pinch. So—so—let's see now.—[*Reads.*] "Though I suffered last night your nauseous, loathed kisses and embraces"—go on—"yet I would not have you presume that you shall ever repeat them"—so—— [*She writes.*

Mrs. Pinch. I have writ it.

Pinch. On, then—"I then concealed myself from your knowledge, to avoid your insolencies."—— [*She writes.*

Mrs. Pinch. So——

Pinch. "The same reason, now I am out of your hands"—— [*She writes.*

Mrs. Pinch. So——

Pinch. "Makes me own to you my unfortunate, though innocent frolic, of being in man's clothes"—— [*She writes.*

Mrs. Pinch. So——

Pinch. "That you may for evermore cease to pursue her, who hates and detests you"—— [*She writes on.*

Mrs. Pinch. So—heigh! [*Sighs.*

Pinch. What, do you sigh?—"detests you—as much as she loves her husband and her honour."

Mrs. Pinch. I vow, husband, he'll ne'er believe I should write such a letter.

Pinch. What, he'd expect a kinder from you? Come, now your name only.

Mrs. Pinch. What, shan't I say "Your most faithful humble servant till death?"

Pinch. No, tormenting fiend!—[*Aside.*] Her style, I find, would be very soft.—[*Aloud.*] Come, wrap it up now, whilst I go fetch wax and a candle; and write on the backside, "For Mr. Horner." [*Exit.*

Mrs. Pinch. "For Mr. Horner."—So, I am glad he has told me his name. Dear Mr. Horner! but why should I send thee such a letter that will vex thee, and make thee angry with me?—Well, I will not send it.—Ay, but then my husband will kill me—for I see plainly he won't let me love Mr. Horner—but what care I for my husband?—I won't, so I won't, send poor Mr. Horner such a letter—But then my husband—but oh, what if I writ at bottom my husband made me write it?—Ay, but then my husband would see't—Can one have no shift? ah, a London woman would have had a hundred presently. Stay—what if I should write a letter, and wrap it up like this, and write upon't too? Ay, but then my husband would see't—I don't know what to do.—But yet evads I'll try, so I will—for I will not send this letter to poor Mr. Horner, come what will on't.

"Dear, sweet Mr. Horner"—[*Writes and repeats what she writes.*]—so—"my husband would have me send you a base, rude, unmannerly letter; but I won't"—so—"and would have me forbid you loving me; but I won't"—so—"and would have me say to you, I hate you, poor Mr. Horner; but I won't tell a lie for him"—there—"for I'm sure if you and I were in the country at cards together"—so—"I could not help treading on your toe under the table"—so—"or rubbing knees with you, and staring in your face, till you saw me"—very well—"and then looking down, and blushing for an hour together"—so—"but I must make haste before my husband comes: and now he has taught me to write letters, you shall have longer ones from me, who am, dear, dear, poor, dear Mr. Horner, your most humble friend, and servant to command till death,—Margery Pinchwife."

Stay, I must give him a hint at bottom—so—now wrap it up just like t'other—so—now write "For Mr. Horner"—But oh now, what shall I do with it? for here comes my husband.

Re-enter PINCHWIFE.

Pinch. [*aside*]. I have been detained by a sparkish coxcomb, who pretended a visit to me; but I fear 'twas to my wife—[*Aloud.*] What, have you done?

Mrs. Pinch. Ay, ay, bud, just now.

Pinch. Let's see't: what d'ye tremble for? what, you would not have it go?

Mrs. Pinch. Here—[*aside.*] No, I must not give him that: so I had been served if I had given him this.   [*He opens and reads the first letter.*

Pinch. Come, where's the wax and seal?

Mrs. Pinch. [*aside*]. Lord, what shall I do now? Nay, then I have it—[*aloud.*] Pray let me see't. Lord, you think me so arrant a fool, I cannot seal a letter; I will do't, so I will.

[*Snatches the letter from him, changes it for the other, seals it, and delivers it to him.*

Pinch. Nay, I believe you will learn that, and other things too, which I would not have you.

Mrs. Pinch. So, han't I done it curiously?—[*Aside.*] I think I have; there's my letter going to Mr. Horner, since he'll needs have me send letters to folks.

Pinch. 'Tis very well; but I warrant, you would not have it go now?

Mrs. Pinch. Yes, indeed, but I would, bud, now.

Pinch. Well, you are a good girl then. Come, let me lock you up in your chamber, till I come back; and be sure you come not within three strides of the window when I am gone, for I have a spy in the street.—[*Exit Mrs.* PINCHWIFE, PINCHWIFE *locks the door.*] At least, 'tis fit she thinks so. If we do not cheat women, they'll cheat us, and fraud may be justly used with secret enemies, of which a wife is the most dangerous; and he that has a handsome one to keep, and a frontier town, must provide against treachery, rather than open force. Now I have secured all within, I'll deal with the foe without, with false intelligence.   [*Holds up the letter. Exit.*

SCENE III.—HORNER's *Lodging*

Enter HORNER *and* Quack.

Quack. Well, sir, how fadges the new design? have you not the luck of all your brother projectors, to deceive only yourself at last?

Horn. No, good domine doctor, I deceive you, it seems, and others too; for the grave matrons, and old, rigid husbands think me as unfit for love, as they are; but their wives, sisters, and daughters know, some of 'em, better things already.

Quack. Already!

Horn. Already, I say. Last night I was drunk with half-a-dozen of your civil persons, as you call 'em, and people of honour, and so was made free of their society and dressing-rooms for ever hereafter; and am already come to the privileges of sleeping upon their pallets, warming smocks, tying shoes and garters, and the like, doctor, already, already, doctor.

Quack. You have made good use of your time, sir.

Horn. I tell thee, I am now no more interruption to 'em, when they sing, or talk bawdy, than a little squab French page who speaks no English.

Quack. But do civil persons and women of honour drink, and sing bawdy songs?

Horn. O, amongst friends, amongst friends. For your bigots in honour are just like those in religion; they fear the eye of the world more than the eye of Heaven; and think there is no virtue, but railing at vice, and no sin, but giving scandal. They rail at a poor, little, kept player, and keep themselves some young, modest pulpit comedian to be privy to their sins in their closets, not to tell 'em of them in their chapels.

Quack. Nay, the truth on't is, priests, amongst the women now, have quite got the better of us lay-confessors, physicians.

Horn. And they are rather their patients; but——

Enter Lady FIDGET, *looking about her.*

Now we talk of women of honour, here comes one. Step behind the screen there, and but observe, if I have not particular privileges with the women of reputation already, doctor, already.   [*Quack retires.*

Lady Fid. Well, Horner, am not I a woman of honour? you see, I'm as good as my word.

Horn. And you shall see, madam, I'll not be behind-hand with you in honour; and I'll be as good as my word too, if you please but to withdraw into the next room.

Lady Fid. But first, my dear sir, you must promise to have a care of my dear honour.

Horn. If you talk a word more of your honour, you'll make me incapable to wrong it. To talk of honour in the mysteries of love, is like talking of Heaven or the Deity, in an operation of witchcraft, just when you are employing the devil: it makes the charm impotent.

Lady Fid. Nay, fy! let us not be smutty. But you talk of mysteries and bewitching to me; I don't understand you.

Horn. I tell you, madam, the word money in a mistress's mouth, at such a nick of time, is not a more disheartening sound to a younger brother, than that of honour to an eager lover like myself.

Lady Fid. But you can't blame a lady of my reputation to be chary.

Horn. Chary! I have been chary of it already, by the report I have caused of myself.

Lady Fid. Ay, but if you should ever let other women know that dear secret, it would come out. Nay, you must have a great care of your conduct; for my acquaintance are so censorious (oh, 'tis a wicked, censorious world, Mr. Horner!), I say, are so censorious, and detracting, that perhaps they'll talk to the prejudice of my honour, though you should not let them know the dear secret.

Horn. Nay, madam, rather than they shall prejudice your honour, I'll prejudice theirs; and, to serve you, I'll lie with 'em all, make the secret their own, and then they'll keep it. I am a Machiavel in love, madam.

Lady Fid. O, no, sir, not that way.

Horn. Nay, the devil take me, if censorious women are to be silenced any other way.

Lady Fid. A secret is better kept, I hope, by a single person than a multitude; therefore pray do not trust anybody else with it, dear, dear Mr. Horner. [*Embracing him.*

Enter Sir JASPER FIDGET.

Sir Jasp. How now!

Lady Fid. [*aside*]. O my husband!—prevented—and what's almost as bad, found with my arms about another man—that will appear too much—what shall I say?—[*Aloud.*] Sir Jasper, come hither: I am trying if Mr. Horner were ticklish, and he's as ticklish as can be. I love to torment the confounded toad; let you and I tickle him.

Sir Jasp. No, your ladyship will tickle him better without me, I suppose. But is this your buying china? I thought you had been at the china-house.

Horn. [*aside*]. China-house! that's my cue, I must take it.—[*Aloud.*] A pox! can't you keep your impertinent wives at home? Some men are troubled with the husbands, but I with the wives; but I'd have you to know, since I cannot be your journeyman by night, I will not be your drudge by day, to squire your wife about, and be your man of straw, or scarecrow only to pies and jays, that would be nibbling at your forbidden fruit; I shall be shortly the hackney gentleman-usher of the town.

Sir Jasp. [*aside*]. He! he! he! poor fellow, he's in the right on't, faith. To squire women about for other folks is as ungrateful an employment, as to tell money for other folks.—[*Aloud.*] He! he! he! be'n't angry, Horner.

Lady Fid. No, 'tis I have more reason to be angry, who am left by you, to go abroad indecently alone; or, what is more indecent, to pin myself upon such ill-bred people of your acquaintance as this is.

Sir Jasp. Nay, prithee, what has he done?

Lady Fid. Nay, he has done nothing.

Sir Jasp. But what d'ye take ill, if he has done nothing?

Lady Fid. Ha! ha! ha! faith, I can't but laugh however; why, d'ye think the unmannerly toad would come down to me to the coach? I was fain to come up to fetch him, or go without him, which I was resolved not to do; for he knows china very well, and has himself very good, but will not let me see it, lest I should beg some; but I will find it out, and have what I came for yet.

Horn. [*apart to* Lady FIDGET, *as he follows her to the door*]. Lock the door, madam.—[*Exit* Lady FIDGET, *and locks the door.*]—[*Aloud.*] So, she has got into my chamber and locked me out. Oh the impertinency of womankind! Well, Sir Jasper, plain-dealing is a jewel; if ever you suffer your wife to trouble me again here, she shall carry you home a pair of horns; by my lord mayor she shall; though I cannot furnish you myself, you are sure, yet I'll find a way.

Sir Jasp. Ha! ha! he!—[*Aside.*] At my first coming in, and finding her arms about him, tickling him it seems, I was half jealous, but now I see my folly.—[*Aloud.*] He! he! he! poor Horner.

Horn. Nay, though you laugh now, 'twill be my turn ere long. Oh women, more impertinent, more cunning, and more mischievous than their monkeys, and to me almost as ugly!—Now is she throwing my things about and rifling all I have; but I'll get in to her the back way, and so rifle her for it.

Sir Jasp. Ha! ha! ha! poor angry Horner.

Horn. Stay here a little, I'll ferret her out to you presently, I warrant.

[*Exit at the other door.*

[Sir JASPER *talks through the door to his* Wife, *she answers from within.*

Sir Jasp. Wife! my Lady Fidget! wife! he is coming in to you the back way.

Lady Fid. Let him come, and welcome, which way he will.

Sir Jasp. He'll catch you, and use you roughly, and be too strong for you.

Lady Fid. Don't you trouble yourself, let him if he can.

Quack. [*aside*]. This indeed I could not have believed from him, nor any but my own eyes.

Enter Mrs. Squeamish.

Mrs. Squeam. Where's this woman-hater, this toad, this ugly, greasy, dirty sloven?

Sir Jasp. [*aside*]. So, the women all will have him ugly: methinks he is a comely person, but his wants make his form contemptible to 'em; and 'tis e'en as my wife said yesterday, talking of him, that a proper handsome eunuch was as ridiculous a thing as a gigantic coward.

Mrs. Squeam. Sir Jasper, your servant: where is the odious beast?

Sir Jasp. He's within in his chamber, with my wife; she's playing the wag with him.

Mrs. Squeam. Is she so? and he's a clownish beast, he'll give her no quarter, he'll play the wag with her again, let me tell you: come, let's go help her.— What, the door's locked?

Sir Jasp. Ay, my wife locked it.

Mrs. Squeam. Did she so? let's break it open then.

Sir Jasp. No, no, he'll do her no hurt.

Mrs. Squeam. [*aside*]. But is there no other way to get in to 'em? whither goes this? I will disturb 'em. [*Exit at another door.*

Enter Old Lady Squeamish.

Lady Squeam. Where is this harlotry, this impudent baggage, this rambling tomrigg? O Sir Jasper, I'm glad to see you here; did you not see my vile grandchild come in hither just now?

Sir Jasp. Yes.

Lady Squeam. Ay, but where is she then? where is she? Lord, Sir Jasper, I have e'en rattled myself to pieces in pursuit of her: but can you tell what she makes here? they say below, no woman lodges here.

Sir Jasp. No.

Lady Squeam. No! what does she here then? say, if it be not a woman's lodging, what makes she here? But are you sure no woman lodges here?

Sir Jasp. No, nor no man neither, this is Mr. Horner's lodging.

Lady Squeam. Is it so, are you sure?

Sir Jasp. Yes, yes.

Lady Squeam. So; then there's no hurt in't, I hope. But where is he?

Sir Jasp. He's in the next room with my wife.

Lady Squeam. Nay, if you trust him with your wife, I may with my Biddy. They say, he's a merry harmless man now, e'en as harmless a man as ever came out of Italy with a good voice, and as pretty, harmless company for a lady, as a snake without his teeth.

Sir Jasp. Ay, ay, poor man.

Re-enter Mrs. Squeamish.

Mrs. Squeam. I can't find 'em.—Oh, are you here, grandmother? I followed, you must know, my Lady Fidget hither; 'tis the prettiest lodging, and I have been staring on the prettiest pictures——

Re-enter Lady FIDGET *with a piece of china in her hand, and* HORNER *following.*

Lady Fid. And I have been toiling and moiling for the prettiest piece of china, my dear.

Horn. Nay, she has been too hard for me, do what I could.

Mrs. Squeam. Oh, lord, I'll have some china too. Good Mr. Horner, don't think to give other people china, and me none; come in with me too.

Horn. Upon my honour, I have none left now.

Mrs. Squeam. Nay, nay, I have known you deny your china before now, but you shan't put me off so. Come.

Horn. This lady had the last there.

Lady Fid. Yes indeed, madam, to my certain knowledge, he has no more left.

Mrs. Squeam. O, but it may be he may have some you could not find.

Lady Fid. What, d'ye think if he had had any left, I would not have had it too? for we women of quality never think we have china enough.

Horn. Do not take it ill, I cannot make china for you all, but I will have a roll-waggon for you too, another time.

Mrs. Squeam. Thank you, dear toad.

Lady Fid. What do you mean by that promise?   [*Aside to* HORNER.

Horn. Alas, she has an innocent, literal understanding.

                                      [*Aside to* Lady FIDGET.

Lady Squeam. Poor Mr. Horner! he has enough to do to please you all, I see.

Horn. Ay, madam, you see how they use me.

Lady Squeam. Poor gentleman, I pity you.

Horn. I thank you, madam: I could never find pity, but from such reverend ladies as you are; the young ones will never spare a man.

Mrs. Squeam. Come, come, beast, and go dine with us; for we shall want a man at ombre after dinner.

Horn. That's all their use of me, madam, you see.

Mrs. Squeam. Come, sloven, I'll lead you, to be sure of you.

                                     [*Pulls him by the cravat.*

Lady Squeam. Alas, poor man, how she tugs him! Kiss, kiss her; that's the way to make such nice women quiet.

Horn. No, madam, that remedy is worse than the torment; they know I dare suffer anything rather than do it.

Lady Squeam. Prithee kiss her, and I'll give you her picture in little, that you admired so last night; prithee do.

Horn. Well, nothing but that could bribe me: I love a woman only in effigy, and good painting as much as I hate them.—I'll do't, for I could adore the devil well painted.   [*Kisses* Mrs. SQUEAMISH.

Mrs. Squeam. Foh, you filthy toad! nay, now I've done jesting.

Lady Squeam. Ha! ha! ha! I told you so.

Mrs. Squeam. Foh! a kiss of his——

Sir Jasp. Has no more hurt in't than one of my spaniel's.

Mrs. Squeam. Nor no more good neither.

Quack. I will now believe anything he tells me.   [*Aside.*

Enter PINCHWIFE.

Lady Fid. O lord, here's a man! Sir Jasper, my mask, my mask! I would not be seen here for the world.

Sir Jasp. What, not when I am with you?

Lady Fid. No, no, my honour—let's be gone.

Mrs. Squeam. Oh grandmother, let's be gone; make haste, make haste, I know not how he may censure us.

Lady Fid. Be found in the lodging of anything like a man!—Away.

[*Exeunt* Sir JASPER FIDGET, Lady FIDGET, Old Lady SQUEAMISH, *and* Mrs. SQUEAMISH.

Quack. What's here? another cuckold? he looks like one, and none else sure have any business with him.   [*Aside.*

Horn. Well, what brings my dear friend hither?

Pinch. Your impertinency.

Horn. My impertinency!—why, you gentlemen that have got handsome wives, think you have a privilege of saying anything to your friends, and are as brutish as if you were our creditors.

Pinch. No, sir, I'll ne'er trust you any way.

Horn. But why not, dear Jack? why diffide in me thou know'st so well?

Pinch. Because I do know you so well.

Horn. Han't I been always thy friend, honest Jack, always ready to serve thee, in love or battle, before thou wert married, and am so still?

Pinch. I believe so, you would be my second now, indeed.

Horn. Well then, dear Jack, why so unkind, so grum, so strange to me? Come, prithee kiss me, dear rogue: gad, I was always, I say, and am still as much thy servant as——

Pinch. As I am yours, sir. What, you would send a kiss to my wife, is that it?

Horn. So, there 'tis—a man can't show his friendship to a married man, but presently he talks of his wife to you. Prithee, let thy wife alone, and let thee and I be all one, as we were wont. What, thou art as shy of my kindness as a Lombard Street alderman of a courtier's civility at Locket's!

Pinch. But you are over-kind to me, as kind as if I were your cuckold already; yet I must confess you ought to be kind and civil to me, since I am so kind, so civil to you, as to bring you this: look you there, sir.

[*Delivers him a letter.*

Horn. What is't?

Pinch. Only a love-letter, sir.

Horn. From whom?—how! this is from your wife—hum—and hum——

[*Reads.*

Pinch. Even from my wife, sir: am I not wondrous kind and civil to you now too?—[*Aside.*] But you'll not think her so.

Horn. Ha! is this a trick of his or hers?   [*Aside.*

Pinch. The gentleman's surprised I find.—What, you expected a kinder letter?

Horn. No faith, not I, how could I?

Pinch. Yes, yes, I'm sure you did. A man so well made as you are, must needs be disappointed, if the women declare not their passion at first sight or opportunity.

Horn. [*aside*]. But what should this mean? Stay, the postscript.—[*Reads aside.*] "Be sure you love me, whatsoever my husband says to the contrary, and let him not see this, lest he should come home and pinch me, or kill my squirrel."—It seems he knows not what the letter contains.

Pinch. Come, ne'er wonder at it so much.

Horn. Faith, I can't help it.

Pinch. Now, I think I have deserved your infinite friendship and kindness, and have showed myself sufficiently an obliging kind friend and husband; am I not so, to bring a letter from my wife to her gallant?

Horn. Ay, the devil take me, art thou, the most obliging, kind friend and husband in the world, ha! ha!

Pinch. Well, you may be merry, sir; but in short I must tell you, sir, my honour will suffer no jesting.

Horn. What dost thou mean?

Pinch. Does the letter want a comment? Then, know, sir, though I have been so civil a husband, as to bring you a letter from my wife, to let you kiss and court her to my face, I will not be a cuckold, sir, I will not.

Horn. Thou art mad with jealousy. I never saw thy wife in my life but at the play yesterday, and I know not if it were she or no. I court her, kiss her!

Pinch. I will not be a cuckold, I say; there will be danger in making me a cuckold.

Horn. Why, wert thou not well cured of thy last clap?

Pinch. I wear a sword.

Horn. It should be taken from thee, lest thou shouldst do thyself a mischief with it; thou art mad, man.

Pinch. As mad as I am, and as merry as you are, I must have more reason from you ere we part. I say again, though you kissed and courted last night my wife in man's clothes, as she confesses in her letter——

Horn. Ha!   [*Aside.*

Pinch. Both she and I say, you must not design it again, for you have mistaken your woman, as you have done your man.

Horn. [*aside*]. O—I understand something now—[*Aloud.*] Was that thy wife! Why wouldst thou not tell me 'twas she? Faith, my freedom with her was your fault, not mine.

Pinch. Faith, so 'twas.   [*Aside.*

Horn. Fy! I'd never do't to a woman before her husband's face, sure.

Pinch. But I had rather you should do't to my wife before my face, than behind my back; and that you shall never do.

Horn. No—you will hinder me.

Pinch. If I would not hinder you, you see by her letter she would.

Horn. Well, I must e'en acquiesce then, and be contented with what she writes.

Pinch. I'll assure you 'twas voluntarily writ; I had no hand in't you may believe me.

Horn. I do believe thee, faith.

Pinch. And believe her too, for she's an innocent creature, has no dissembling in her: and so fare you well, sir.

Horn. Pray, however, present my humble service to her, and tell her, I will obey her letter to a tittle, and fulfil her desires, be what they will, or with what difficulty soever I do't; and you shall be no more jealous of me, I warrant her, and you.

Pinch. Well then, fare you well; and play with any man's honour but mine, kiss any man's wife but mine, and welcome.   [*Exit.*

Horn. Ha! ha! ha! doctor.

Quack. It seems, he has not heard the report of you, or does not believe it.

Horn. Ha! ha!—now, doctor, what think you?

Quack. Pray let's see the letter—hum—"for—dear—love you——"

[*Reads the letter.*

Horn. I wonder how she could contrive it! What say'st thou to't? 'tis an original.

Quack. So are your cuckolds too originals: for they are like no other common cuckolds, and I will henceforth believe it not impossible for you to cuckold the Grand Signior amidst his guards of eunuchs, that I say.

Horn. And I say for the letter, 'tis the first love-letter that ever was without flames, darts, fates, destinies, lying and dissembling in't.

Enter Sparkish *pulling in* Pinchwife.

Spark. Come back, you are a pretty brother-in-law, neither go to church nor to dinner with your sister bride!

Pinch. My sister denies her marriage, and you see is gone away from you dissatisfied.

Spark. Pshaw! upon a foolish scruple, that our parson was not in lawful orders, and did not say all the common-prayer; but 'tis her modesty only I believe. But let all women be never so modest the first day, they'll be sure to come to themselves by night, and I shall have enough of her then. In the meantime, Harry Horner, you must dine with me: I keep my wedding at my aunt's in the Piazza.

Horn. Thy wedding! what stale maid has lived to despair of a husband, or what young one of a gallant?

Spark. O, your servant, sir—this gentleman's sister then,—no stale maid.

Horn. I'm sorry for't.

Pinch. How comes he so concerned for her?   [*Aside*

Spark. You sorry for't? why, do you know any ill by her?

Horn. No, I know none but by thee; 'tis for her sake, not yours, and another man's sake that might have hoped, I thought.

Spark. Another man! another man! what is his name?

Horn. Nay, since 'tis past, he shall be nameless.—[*Aside.*] Poor Harcourt! I am sorry thou hast missed her.

Pinch. He seems to be much troubled at the match.   [*Aside.*

Spark. Prithee, tell me—Nay, you shan't go, brother.

Pinch. I must of necessity, but I'll come to you to dinner.   [*Exit.*

Spark. But, Harry, what, have I a rival in my wife already? But with all my heart, for he may be of use to me hereafter; for though my hunger is now my sauce, and I can fall on heartily without, the time will come when a rival will be as good sauce for a married man to a wife, as an orange to veal.

Horn. O thou damned rogue! thou hast set my teeth on edge with thy orange.

Spark. Then let's to dinner—there I was with you again. Come.

Horn. But who dines with thee?

Spark. My friends and relations, my brother Pinchwife, you see, of your acquaintance.

Horn. And his wife?

Spark. No, 'gad, he'll ne'er let her come amongst us good fellows; your stingy country coxcomb keeps his wife from his friends, as he does his little firkin of ale, for his own drinking, and a gentleman can't get a smack on't; but his servants, when his back is turned, broach it at their pleasures, and dust it away, ha! ha! ha!—'Gad, I am witty, I think, considering I was married to-day, by the world; but come——

Horn. No, I will not dine with you, unless you can fetch her too.

Spark. Pshaw! what pleasure canst thou have with women now, Harry?

Horn. My eyes are not gone; I love a good prospect yet, and will not dine with you unless she does too; go fetch her, therefore, but do not tell her husband 'tis for my sake.

Spark. Well, I'll go try what I can do; in the meantime, come away to my aunt's lodging, 'tis in the way to Pinchwife's.

Horn. The poor woman has called for aid, and stretched forth her hand, doctor; I cannot but help her over the pale out of the briars.   [*Exeunt.*

SCENE IV.—*A Room in* PINCHWIFE'S *House*

Mrs. PINCHWIFE *alone, leaning on her elbow.—A table, pen, ink, and paper.*

Mrs. Pinch. Well, 'tis e'en so, I have got the London disease they call love; I am sick of my husband, and for my gallant. I have heard this distemper called a fever, but methinks 'tis like an ague; for when I think of my husband, I tremble, and am in a cold sweat, and have inclinations to vomit; but when I think of my gallant, dear Mr. Horner, my hot fit comes, and I am all in a fever indeed; and, as in other fevers, my own chamber is tedious to me, and I would fain be removed to his, and then methinks I should be well. Ah, poor Mr. Horner! Well, I cannot, will not stay here; therefore I'll make an end of my letter to him, which shall be a finer letter than my last, because I have studied it like anything. Oh sick, sick!　　*[Takes the pen and writes.*

Enter PINCHWIFE, *who seeing her writing, steals softly behind her and looking over her shoulder, snatches the paper from her.*

Pinch. What, writing more letters?

Mrs. Pinch. O Lord, bud, why d'ye fright me so?

[She offers to run out; he stops her, and reads.

Pinch. How's this? nay, you shall not stir, madam:—"Dear, dear, dear Mr. Horner"—very well—I have taught you to write letters to good purpose —but let us see't. "First, I am to beg your pardon for my boldness in writing to you, which I'd have you to know I would not have done, had not you said first you loved me so extremely, which if you do, you will never suffer me to lie in the arms of another man whom I loathe, nauseate, and detest."— Now you can write these filthy words. But what follows?—"Therefore, I hope you will speedily find some way to free me from this unfortunate match, which was never, I assure you, of my choice, but I'm afraid 'tis already too far gone; however, if you love me, as I do you, you will try what you can do; but you must help me away before to-morrow, or else, alas! I shall be for ever out of your reach, for I can defer no longer our—our——" what is to follow "our"?—speak, what—our journey into the country I suppose—Oh woman, damned woman! and Love, damned Love, their old tempter! for this is one of his miracles; in a moment he can make those blind that could see, and those see that were blind, those dumb that could speak, and those prattle who were dumb before; nay, what is more than all, make these dough-baked, senseless, indocile animals, women, too hard for us their politic lords and rulers, in a moment. But make an end of your letter, and then I'll make an end of you thus, and all my plagues together.

[Draws his sword.

Mrs. Pinch. O Lord, O Lord, you are such a passionate man, bud!

Enter SPARKISH.

Spark. How now, what's here to do?

Pinch. This fool here now!

Spark. What! drawn upon your wife? You should never do that, but at night in the dark, when you can't hurt her. This is my sister-in-law, is it not? ay, faith, e'en our country Margery [*pulls aside her handkerchief*]; one may know her. Come, she and you must go dine with me; dinner's ready, come. But where's my wife? is she not come home yet? where is she?

Pinch. Making you a cuckold; 'tis that they all do, as soon as they can.

Spark. What, the wedding-day? no, a wife that designs to make a cully of her husband will be sure to let him win the first stake of love, by the world. But come, they stay dinner for us: come, I'll lead down our Margery.

Pinch. No—sir, go, we'll follow you.

Spark. I will not wag without you.

Pinch. This coxcomb is a sensible torment to me amidst the greatest in the world.   [*Aside.*

Spark. Come, come, Madam Margery.

Pinch. No; I'll lead her my way: what, would you treat your friends with mine, for want of your own wife?—[*Leads her to the other door, and locks her in and returns.*] I am contented my rage should take breath—— [*Aside.*

Spark. I told Horner this.

Pinch. Come now.

Spark. Lord, how shy you are of your wife! but let me tell you, brother, we men of wit have amongst us a saying, that cuckolding, like the small-pox, comes with a fear; and you may keep your wife as much as you will out of danger of infection, but if her constitution incline her to't, she'll have it sooner or later, by the world, say they.

Pinch. [*aside*]. What a thing is a cuckold, that every fool can make him ridiculous!—[*Aloud.*] Well, sir—but let me advise you, now you are come to be concerned, because you suspect the danger, not to neglect the means to prevent it, especially when the greatest share of the malady will light upon your own head, for

Hows'e'er the kind wife's belly comes to swell,
The husband breeds for her, and first is ill.   [*Exeunt.*

ACT V

SCENE I.—Pinchwife's *House*

Enter Pinchwife *and* Mrs. Pinchwife. *A table and candle.*

Pinch. Come, take the pen and make an end of the letter, just as you intended; if you are false in a tittle, I shall soon perceive it, and punish you as you deserve.—[*Lays his hand on his sword.*] Write what was to follow—let's see—"You must make haste, and help me away before to-morrow, or else I shall be for ever out of your reach, for I can defer no longer our"—What follows "our"?

Mrs. Pinch. Must all out, then, bud?—Look you there, then.
                                                                      [Mrs. Pinchwife *takes the pen and writes.*

Pinch. Let's see—"For I can defer no longer our—wedding—Your slighted Alithea."—What's the meaning of this? my sister's name to't? speak, unriddle.

Mrs. Pinch. Yes, indeed, bud.

Pinch. But why her name to't? speak—speak, I say.

Mrs. Pinch. Ay, but you'll tell her then again. If you would not tell her again——

Pinch. I will not:—I am stunned, my head turns round.—Speak.

Mrs. Pinch. Won't you tell her, indeed, and indeed?

Pinch. No; speak, I say.

Mrs. Pinch. She'll be angry with me; but I had rather she should be angry with me than you, bud; and, to tell you the truth, 'twas she made me write the letter, and taught me what I should write.

Pinch. [*aside*]. Ha! I thought the style was somewhat better than her own. —[*Aloud.*] Could she come to you to teach you, since I had locked you up alone?

Mrs. Pinch. O, through the key-hole, bud.

Pinch. But why should she make you write a letter for her to him, since she can write herself?

Mrs. Pinch. Why, she said because—for I was unwilling to do it——

Pinch. Because what—because?

Mrs. Pinch. Because, lest Mr. Horner should be cruel, and refuse her; or be vain afterwards, and show the letter, she might disown it, the hand not being hers.

Pinch. [*aside*]. How's this? Ha!—then I think I shall come to myself again. —This changeling could not invent this lie: but if she could, why should she? she might think I should soon discover it.—Stay—now I think on't too, Horner said he was sorry she had married Sparkish; and her disowning her marriage to me makes me think she has evaded it for Horner's sake: yet why should she take this course? But men in love are fools; women may well be so—[*aloud.*] But hark you, madam, your sister went out in the morning, and I have not seen her within since.

Mrs. Pinch. Alack-a-day, she has been crying all day above, it seems, in a corner.

Pinch. Where is she? let me speak with her.

Mrs. Pinch. [*aside*]. O Lord, then she'll discover all!—[*Aloud.*] Pray hold, bud; what, d'ye mean to discover me? she'll know I have told you then. Pray, bud, let me talk with her first.

Pinch. I must speak with her, to know whether Horner ever made her any promise, and whether she be married to Sparkish or no.

Mrs. Pinch. Pray, dear bud, don't, till I have spoken with her, and told her that I have told you all; for she'll kill me else.

Pinch. Go then, and bid her come out to me.

Mrs. Pinch. Yes, yes, bud.

Pinch. Let me see—— [*Pausing.*

Mrs. Pinch. [*aside*]. I'll go, but she is not within to come to him: I have just got time to know of Lucy her maid, who first set me on work, what lie I shall tell next; for I am e'en at my wit's end. [*Exit.*

Pinch. Well, I resolve it, Horner shall have her: I'd rather give him my sister than lend him my wife; and such an alliance will prevent his pretensions to my wife, sure. I'll make him of kin to her, and then he won't care for her.

Re-enter Mrs. PINCHWIFE.

Mrs. Pinch. O Lord, bud! I told you what anger you would make me with my sister.

Pinch. Won't she come hither?

Mrs. Pinch. No, no. Lack-a-day, she's ashamed to look you in the face: and she says, if you go in to her, she'll run away downstairs, and shamefully go herself to Mr. Horner, who has promised her marriage, she says; and she will have no other, so she won't.

Pinch. Did he so?—promise her marriage!—then she shall have no other. Go tell her so; and if she will come and discourse with me a little concerning the means, I will about it immediately. Go.—[*Exit* Mrs. PINCHWIFE.] His estate is equal to Sparkish's, and his extraction is much better than his, as his parts are; but my chief reason is, I'd rather be akin to him by the name of brother-in-law than that of cuckold.

Re-enter Mrs. PINCHWIFE.

Well, what says she now?

Mrs. Pinch. Why, she says, she would only have you lead her to Horner's lodging; with whom she first will discourse the matter before she talks with you, which yet she cannot do; for alack, poor creature, she says she can't so much as look you in the face, therefore she'll come to you in a mask. And you must excuse her, if she make you no answer to any question of yours, till you have brought her to Mr. Horner; and if you will not chide her, nor question her, she'll come out to you immediately.

Pinch. Let her come: I will not speak a word to her, nor require a word from her.

Mrs. Pinch. Oh, I forgot: besides, she says she cannot look you in the face, though through a mask; therefore would desire you to put out the candle.

Pinch. I agree to all. Let her make haste.—There, 'tis out.—[*Puts out the candle. Exit* Mrs. PINCHWIFE.] My case is something better: I'd rather fight with Horner for not lying with my sister, than for lying with my wife; and of the two, I had rather find my sister too forward than my wife. I expected no other from her free education, as she calls it, and her passion for the town. Well, wife and sister are names which make us expect love and duty, pleasure and comfort; but we find 'em plagues and torments, and are equally, though differently, troublesome to their keeper; for we have as much ado to get people to lie with our sisters as to keep 'em from lying with our wives.

Re-enter Mrs. PINCHWIFE *masked, and in hoods and scarfs, and a night-gown and petticoat of* ALITHEA'S.

What, are you come, sister? let us go then.—But first, let me lock up my wife. Mrs. Margery, where are you?

Mrs. Pinch. Here, bud.

Pinch. Come hither, that I may lock you up: get you in.—[*Locks the door.*] Come, sister, where are you now?

[Mrs. PINCHWIFE *gives him her hand; but when he lets her go, she steals softly on to the other side of him, and is led away by him for his* Sister, ALITHEA.

SCENE II.—Horner's *Lodging*

Horner *and* Quack.

Quack. What, all alone? not so much as one of your cuckolds here, nor one of their wives! They use to take their turns with you, as if they were to watch you.

Horn. Yes, it often happens that a cuckold is but his wife's spy, and is more upon family duty when he is with her gallant abroad, hindering his pleasure, than when he is at home with her playing the gallant. But the hardest duty a married woman imposes upon a lover is keeping her husband company always.

Quack. And his fondness wearies you almost as soon as hers.

Horn. A pox! keeping a cuckold company, after you have had his wife, is as tiresome as the company of a country squire to a witty fellow of the town, when he has got all his money.

Quack. And as at first a man makes a friend of the husband to get the wife, so at last you are fain to fall out with the wife to be rid of the husband.

Horn. Ay, most cuckold-makers are true courtiers; when once a poor man has cracked his credit for 'em, they can't abide to come near him.

Quack. But at first, to draw him in, are so sweet, so kind, so dear! just as you are to Pinchwife. But what becomes of that intrigue with his wife?

Horn. A pox! he's as surly as an alderman that has been bit; and since he's so coy, his wife's kindness is in vain, for she's a silly innocent.

Quack. Did she not send you a letter by him?

Horn. Yes; but that's a riddle I have not yet solved. Allow the poor creature to be willing, she is silly too, and he keeps her up so close——

Quack. Yes, so close, that he makes her but the more willing, and adds but revenge to her love; which two, when met, seldom fail of satisfying each other one way or other.

Horn. What! here's the man we are talking of, I think.

Enter Pinchwife, *leading in his* Wife *masked, muffled, and in her* Sister's *gown.*

Pshaw!

Quack. Bringing his wife to you is the next thing to bringing a love-letter from her.

Horn. What means this?

Pinch. The last time, you know, sir, I brought you a love-letter; now, you see, a mistress; I think you'll say I am a civil man to you.

Horn. Ay, the devil take me, will I say thou art the civilest man I ever met with; and I have known some. I fancy I understand thee now better than I did the letter. But, hark thee, in thy ear——

Pinch. What?

Horn. Nothing but the usual question, man: is she sound, on thy word?

Pinch. What, you take her for a wench, and me for a pimp?

Horn. Pshaw! wench and pimp, paw words; I know thou art an honest fellow, and hast a great acquaintance among the ladies, and perhaps hast made love for me, rather than let me make love to thy wife.

Pinch. Come, sir, in short, I am for no fooling.

Horn. Nor I neither: therefore prithee, let's see her face presently. Make her show, man: art thou sure I don't know her?

Pinch. I am sure you do know her.

Horn. A pox! why dost thou bring her to me then?

Pinch. Because she's a relation of mine——

Horn. Is she, faith, man? then thou art still more civil and obliging, dear rogue.

Pinch. Who desired me to bring her to you.

Horn. Then she is obliging, dear rogue.

Pinch. You'll make her welcome for my sake, I hope.

Horn. I hope she is handsome enough to make herself welcome. Prithee let her unmask.

Pinch. Do you speak to her; she would never be ruled by me.

Horn. Madam—— [Mrs. PINCHWIFE *whispers to* HORNER.] She says she must speak with me in private. Withdraw, prithee.

Pinch. [*aside*]. She's unwilling, it seems, I should know all her indecent conduct in this business.—[*Aloud.*] Well then, I'll leave you together, and hope when I am gone, you'll agree; if not, you and I shan't agree, sir.

Horn. What means the fool? if she and I agree 'tis no matter what you and I do.

[*Whispers to* Mrs. PINCHWIFE, *who makes signs with her hand for him to be gone.*

Pinch. In the meantime I'll fetch a parson, and find out Sparkish, and disabuse him. You would have me fetch a parson, would you not? Well then—now I think I am rid of her, and shall have no more trouble with her—our sisters and daughters, like usurers' money, are safest when put out; but our wives, like their writings, never safe, but in our closets under lock and key.   [*Exit.*

Enter Boy.

Boy. Sir Jasper Fidget, sir, is coming up.   [*Exit.*

Horn. Here's the trouble of a cuckold now we are talking of. A pox on him! has he not enough to do to hinder his wife's sport, but he must other women's too?—Step in here, madam.   [*Exit* Mrs. PINCHWIFE.

Enter Sir JASPER FIDGET.

Sir Jasp. My best and dearest friend.

Horn. [*aside to* Quack]. The old style, doctor.—[*Aloud.*] Well, be short, for I am busy. What would your impertinent wife have now?

Sir Jasp. Well guessed, i'faith; for I do come from her.

Horn. To invite me to supper! Tell her, I can't come: go.

Sir Jasp. Nay, now you are out, faith; for my lady, and the whole knot of the virtuous gang, as they call themselves, are resolved upon a frolic of coming to you to-night in masquerade, and are all dressed already.

Horn. I shan't be at home.

Sir Jasp. [*aside*]. Lord, how churlish he is to women!—[*Aloud.*] Nay, prithee don't disappoint 'em; they'll think 'tis my fault: prithee don't. I'll send in the banquet and the fiddles. But make no noise on't; for the poor virtuous rogues would not have it known, for the world, that they go a-masquerading; and they would come to no man's ball but yours.

Horn. Well, well—get you gone; and tell 'em, if they come, 'will be at the peril of their honour and yours.

Sir Jasp. He! he! he!—we'll trust you for that: farewell.   [*Exit.*

Horn. Doctor, anon you too shall be my guest,
But now I'm going to a private feast.   [*Exeunt.*

SCENE III.—*The Piazza of Covent Garden*

Enter SPARKISH *with a letter in his hand,* PINCHWIFE *following.*

Spark. But who would have thought a woman could have been false to me? By the world, I could not have thought it.

Pinch. You were for giving and taking liberty: she has taken it only, sir, now you find in that letter. You are a frank person, and so is she, you see there.

Spark. Nay, if this be her hand—for I never saw it.

Pinch. 'Tis no matter whether that be her hand or no; I am sure this hand, at her desire, led her to Mr. Horner, with whom I left her just now, to go fetch a parson to 'em at their desire too, to deprive you of her for ever; for it seems yours was but a mock marriage.

Spark. Indeed, she would needs have it that 'twas Harcourt himself, in a parson's habit, that married us; but I'm sure he told me 'twas his brother Ned.

Pinch. O, there 'tis out; and you were deceived, not she: for you are such a frank person. But I must be gone.—You'll find her at Mr. Horner's. Go, and believe your eyes.   [*Exit.*

Spark. Nay, I'll to her, and call her as many crocodiles, sirens, harpies, and other heathenish names, as a poet would do a mistress who had refused to hear his suit, nay more, his verses on her.—But stay, is not that she following a torch at t'other end of the Piazza? and from Horner's certainly—'tis so.

Enter ALITHEA *following a torch, and* LUCY *behind.*

You are well met, madam, though you don't think so. What, you have made a short visit to Mr. Horner? but I suppose you'll return to him presently, by that time the parson can be with him.

Alith. Mr. Horner and the parson, sir!

Spark. Come, madam, no more dissembling, no more jilting; for I am no more a frank person.

Alith. How's this?

Lucy. So, 'twill work, I see. [*Aside.*

Spark. Could you find out no easy country fool to abuse? none but me, a gentleman of wit and pleasure about the town? But it was your pride to be too hard for a man of parts, unworthy false woman! false as a friend that lends a man money to lose; false as dice, who undo those that trust all they have to 'em.

Lucy. He has been a great bubble, by his similes, as they say. [*Aside.*

Alith. You have been too merry, sir, at your wedding-dinner, sure.

Spark. What, d'ye mock me too?

Alith. Or you have been deluded.

Spark. By you.

Alith. Let me understand you.

Spark. Have you the confidence (I should call it something else, since you know your guilt) to stand my just reproaches? you did not write an impudent letter to Mr. Horner? who I find now has clubbed with you in deluding me with his aversion for women, that I might not, forsooth, suspect him for my rival.

Lucy. D'ye think the gentleman can be jealous now, madam? [*Aside.*

Alith. I write a letter to Mr. Horner!

Spark. Nay, madam, do not deny it. Your brother showed it me just now; and told me likewise, he left you at Horner's lodging to fetch a parson to marry you to him: and I wish you joy, madam, joy, joy; and to him too, much joy; and to myself more joy, for not marrying you.

Alith. [*aside*]. So, I find my brother would break off the match; and I can consent to't, since I see this gentleman can be made jealous.—[*Aloud.*] O Lucy, by his rude usage and jealousy, he makes me almost afraid I am married to him. Art thou sure 'twas Harcourt himself, and no parson, that married us?

Spark. No, madam, I thank you. I suppose, that was a contrivance too of Mr. Horner's and yours, to make Harcourt play the parson; but I would as little as you have him one now, no, not for the world. For, shall I tell you another truth? I never had any passion for you till now, for now I hate you. 'Tis true, I might have married your portion, as other men of parts of the town do sometimes: and so, your servant. And to show my unconcernedness, I'll come to your wedding, and resign you with as much joy, as I would a stale wench to a new cully; nay, with as much joy as I would after the first night, if I had been married to you. There's for you; and so your servant, servant. [*Exit.*

Alith. How was I deceived in a man!

Lucy. You'll believe then a fool may be made jealous now? for that easiness in him that suffers him to be led by a wife, will likewise permit him to be persuaded against her by others.

Alith. But marry Mr. Horner! my brother does not intend it, sure: if I thought he did, I would take thy advice, and Mr. Harcourt for my husband. And now I wish, that if there be any over-wise woman of the town, who, like me, would marry a fool for fortune, liberty, or title, first, that her husband may love play, and be a cully to all the town but her, and suffer none but Fortune to be mistress of his purse; then, if for liberty, that he may send her into the country, under the conduct of some huswifely mother-in-law; and if for title, may the world give 'em none but that of cuckold.

Lucy. And for her greater curse, madam, may he not deserve it.

Alith. Away, impertinent! Is not this my old Lady Lanterlu's?

Lucy. Yes, madam.—[*Aside.*] And here I hope we shall find Mr. Harcourt.   [*Exeunt.*

SCENE IV.—Horner's *Lodging. A table, banquet, and bottles*

Enter Horner, Lady Fidget, Mrs. Dainty Fidget, *and* Mrs. Squeamish.

Horn. A pox! they are come too soon—before I have sent back my new mistress. All that I have now to do is to lock her in, that they may not see her.   [*Aside.*

Lady Fid. That we may be sure of our welcome, we have brought our entertainment with us, and are resolved to treat thee, dear toad.

Mrs. Dain. And that we may be merry to purpose, have left Sir Jasper and my old Lady Squeamish quarrelling at home at backgammon.

Mrs. Squeam. Therefore let us make use of our time, lest they should chance to interrupt us.

Lady Fid. Let us sit then.

Horn. First, that you may be private, let me lock this door and that, and I'll wait upon you presently.

Lady Fid. No, sir, shut 'em only, and your lips for ever; for we must trust you as much as our women.

Horn. You know all vanity's killed in me; I have no occasion for talking.

Lady Fid. Now, ladies, supposing we had drank each of us two bottles, let us speak the truth of our hearts.

Mrs. Dain. and Mrs. Squeam. Agreed.

Lady Fid. By this brimmer, for truth is nowhere else to be found—[*aside to Horner*] not in thy heart, false man!

Horn. You have found me a true man, I'm sure.   [*Aside to* Lady Fidget.

Lady Fid. [*aside to* Horner]. Not every way.—But let us sit and be merry.   [*Sings.*

> Why should our damned tyrants oblige us to live
> On the pittance of pleasure which they only give?
>   We must not rejoice
>   With wine and with noise:
> In vain we must wake in a dull bed alone,
> Whilst to our warm rival the bottle they're gone.
>   Then lay aside charms,
>   And take up these arms.

'Tis wine only gives 'em their courage and wit;
Because we live sober, to men we submit.
If for beauties you'd pass,
Take a lick of the glass,
'Twill mend your complexions, and when they are gone,
The best red we have is the red of the grape:
Then, sisters, lay't on,
And damn a good shape.

Mrs. Dain. Dear brimmer! Well, in token of our openness and plain-dealing, let us throw our masks over our heads.

Horn. So, 'twill come to the glasses anon.   [*Aside.*

Mrs. Squeam. Lovely brimmer! let me enjoy him first.

Lady Fid. No, I never part with a gallant till I've tried him. Dear brimmer! that makest our husbands short-sighted.

Mrs. Dain. And our bashful gallants bold.

Mrs. Squeam. And, for want of a gallant, the butler lovely in our eyes.—Drink, eunuch.

Lady Fid. Drink, thou representative of a husband.—Damn a husband!

Mrs. Dain. And, as it were a husband, an old keeper.

Mrs. Squeam. And an old grandmother.

Horn. And an English bawd, and a French surgeon.

Lady Fid. Ay, we have all reason to curse 'em.

Horn. For my sake, ladies?

Lady Fid. No, for our own; for the first spoils all young gallants' industry.

Mrs. Dain. And the other's art makes 'em bold only with common women.

Mrs. Squeam. And rather run the hazard of the vile distemper amongst them, than of a denial amongst us.

Mrs. Dain. The filthy toads choose mistresses now as they do stuffs, for having been fancied and worn by others.

Mrs. Squeam. For being common and cheap.

Lady Fid. Whilst women of quality, like the richest stuffs, lie untumbled, and unasked for.

Horn. Ay, neat, and cheap, and new, often they think best.

Mrs. Dain. No, sir, the beasts will be known by a mistress longer than by a suit.

Mrs. Squeam. And 'tis not for cheapness neither.

Lady Fid. No; for the vain fops will take up druggets and embroider 'em. But I wonder at the depraved appetites of witty men; they use to be out of the common road, and hate imitation. Pray tell me, beast, when you were a man, why you rather chose to club with a multitude in a common house for an entertainment, than to be the only guest at a good table.

Horn. Why, faith, ceremony and expectation are unsufferable to those that are sharp bent. People always eat with the best stomach at an ordinary, where every man is snatching for the best bit.

Lady Fid. Though he get a cut over the fingers.—But I have heard, that people eat most heartily of another man's meat, that is, what they do not pay for.

Horn. When they are sure of their welcome and freedom; for ceremony in love and eating is as ridiculous as in fighting: falling on briskly is all should be done on those occasions.

Lady Fid. Well then, let me tell you, sir, there is nowhere more freedom than in our houses; and we take freedom from a young person as a sign of good breeding; and a person may be as free as he pleases with us, as frolic, as gamesome, as wild as he will.

Horn. Han't I heard you all declaim against wild men?

Lady Fid. Yes; but for all that, we think wildness in a man as desirable a quality as in a duck or rabbit: a tame man! foh!

Horn. I know not, but your reputations frightened me as much as your faces invited me.

Lady Fid. Our reputation! Lord, why should you not think that we women make use of our reputation, as you men of yours, only to deceive the world with less suspicion? Our virtue is like the statesman's religion, the quaker's word, the gamester's oath, and the great man's honour; but to cheat those that trust us.

Mrs. Squeam. And that demureness, coyness, and modesty, that you see in our faces in the boxes at plays, is as much a sign of a kind woman, as a vizard-mask in the pit.

Mrs. Dain. For, I assure you, women are least masked when they have the velvet vizard on.

Lady Fid. You would have found us modest women in our denials only.

Mrs. Squeam. Our bashfulness is only the reflection of the men's.

Mrs. Dain. We blush when they are shamefaced.

Horn. I beg your pardon, ladies, I was deceived in you devilishly. But why that mighty pretence to honour?

Lady Fid. We have told you; but sometimes 'twas for the same reason you men pretend business often, to avoid ill company, to enjoy the better and more privately those you love.

Horn. But why would you ne'er give a friend a wink then?

Lady Fid. Faith, your reputation frightened us, as much as ours did you, you were so notoriously lewd.

Horn. And you so seemingly honest.

Lady Fid. Was that all that deterred you?

Horn. And so expensive—you allow freedom, you say.

Lady Fid. Ay, ay.

Horn. That I was afraid of losing my little money, as well as my little time, both which my other pleasures required.

Lady Fid. Money! foh! you talk like a little fellow now: do such as we expect money?

Horn. I beg your pardon, madam, I must confess, I have heard that great ladies, like great merchants, set but the higher prices upon what they have. because they are not in necessity of taking the first offer.

Mrs. Dain. Such as we make sale of our hearts?

Mrs. Squeam. We bribed for our love? foh!

Horn. With your pardon, ladies, I know, like great men in offices, you seem to exact flattery and attendance only from your followers; but you have receivers about you, and such fees to pay, a man is afraid to pass your grants. Besides, we must let you win at cards, or we lose your hearts; and if you make an assignation, 'tis at a goldsmith's, jeweller's, or china-house; where for your honour you deposit to him, he must pawn his to the punctual cit, and so paying for what you take up, pays for what he takes up.

Mrs. Dain. Would you not have us assured of our gallants' love?

Mrs. Squeam. For love is better known by liberality than by jealousy.

Lady Fid. For one may be dissembled, the other not.—[*Aside.*] But my jealousy can be no longer dissembled, and they are telling ripe.—[*Aloud.*]— Come, here's to our gallants in waiting, whom we must name, and I'll begin. This is my false rogue. [*Claps him on the back.*

Mrs. Squeam. How!

Horn. So, all will out now. [*Aside.*

Mrs. Squeam. Did you not tell me, 'twas for my sake only you reported yourself no man? [*Aside to* HORNER.

Mrs. Dain. Oh, wretch! did you not swear to me, 'twas for my love and honour you passed for that thing you do? [*Aside to* HORNER.

Horn. So, so.

Lady Fid. Come, speak, ladies: this is my false villain.

Mrs. Squeam. And mine too.

Mrs. Dain. And mine.

Horn. Well then, you are all three my false rogues too, and there's an end on't.

Lady Fid. Well then, there's no remedy; sister sharers, let us not fall out, but have a care of our honour. Though we get no presents, no jewels of him, we are savers of our honour, the jewel of most value and use, which shines yet to the world unsuspected, though it be counterfeit.

Horn. Nay, and is e'en as good as if it were true, provided the world think so; for honour, like beauty now, only depends on the opinion of others.

Lady Fid. Well, Harry Common, I hope you can be true to three. Swear; but 'tis to no purpose to require your oath, for you are as often forsworn as you swear to new women.

Horn. Come, faith, madam, let us e'en pardon one another; for all the difference I find betwixt we men and you women, we forswear ourselves at the beginning of an amour, you as long as it lasts.

Enter Sir JASPER FIDGET, *and* Old Lady SQUEAMISH.

Sir Jasp. Oh, my Lady Fidget, was this your cunning, to come to Mr. Horner without me? but you have been nowhere else, I hope.

Lady Fid. No, Sir Jasper.

Lady Squeam. And you came straight hither, Biddy?

Mrs. Squeam. Yes, indeed, lady grandmother.

Sir Jasp. 'Tis well, 'tis well; I knew when once they were thoroughly acquainted with poor Horner, they'd ne'er be from him: you may let her masquerade it with my wife and Horner, and I warrant her reputation safe.

Enter Boy.

Boy. O, sir, here's the gentleman come, whom you bid me not suffer to come up, without giving you notice, with a lady too, and other gentlemen.

Horn. Do you all go in there, whilst I send 'em away; and, boy, do you desire 'em to stay below till I come, which shall be immediately.

[*Exeunt* Sir JASPER FIDGET, Lady FIDGET, Lady SQUEAMISH, Mrs. SQUEAMISH, *and* Mrs. DAINTY FIDGET.

Boy. Yes, sir. [*Exit.*

[*Exit* HORNER *at the other door, and returns with* Mrs. PINCHWIFE.

Horn. You would not take my advice, to be gone home before your husband came back, he'll now discover all; yet pray, my dearest, be persuaded to go home, and leave the rest to my management; I'll let you down the back way.

Mrs. Pinch. I don't know the way home, so I don't.

Horn. My man shall wait upon you.

Mrs. Pinch. No, don't you believe that I'll go at all; what, are you weary of me already?

Horn. No, my life, 'tis that I may love you long, 'tis to secure my love, and your reputation with your husband; he'll never receive you again else.

Mrs. Pinch. What care I? d'ye think to frighten me with that? I don't intend to go to him again; you shall be my husband now.

Horn. I cannot be your husband, dearest, since you are married to him.

Mrs. Pinch. O, would you make me believe that? Don't I see every day at London here, women leave their first husbands, and go and live with other men as their wives? pish, pshaw! you'd make me angry, but that I love you so mainly.

Horn. So, they are coming up—In again, in, I hear 'em.—[*Exit* Mrs. PINCHWIFE.] Well, a silly mistress is like a weak place, soon got, soon lost, a man has scarce time for plunder; she betrays her husband first to her gallant, and then her gallant to her husband.

Enter PINCHWIFE, ALITHEA, HARCOURT, SPARKISH, LUCY, *and a* Parson.

Pinch. Come, madam, 'tis not the sudden change of your dress, the confidence of your asseverations, and your false witness there, shall persuade me I did not bring you hither just now; here's my witness, who cannot deny it, since you must be confronted.—Mr. Horner, did not I bring this lady to you just now?

Horn. Now must I wrong one woman for another's sake,—but that's no new thing with me, for in these cases I am still on the criminal's side against the innocent. [*Aside.*

Alith. Pray speak, sir.

Horn. It must be so. I must be impudent, and try my luck; impudence uses to be too hard for truth. [*Aside.*

Pinch. What, you are studying an evasion or excuse for her! Speak, sir.

Horn. No, faith, I am something backward only to speak in women's affairs or disputes.

Pinch. She bids you speak.

Alith. Ah, pray, sir, do, pray satisfy him.

Horn. Then truly, you did bring that lady to me just now.

Pinch. O ho!

Alith. How, sir?

Har. How, Horner?

Alith. What mean you, sir? I always took you for a man of honour.

Horn. Ay, so much a man of honour, that I must save my mistress, I thank you, come what will on't. [*Aside.*

Spark. So, if I had had her, she'd have made me believe the moon had been made of a Christmas pie.

Lucy. Now could I speak, if I durst, and solve the riddle, who am the author of it. [*Aside.*

Alith. O unfortunate woman! A combination against my honour! which most concerns me now, because you share in my disgrace, sir, and it is your censure, which I must now suffer, that troubles me, not theirs.

Har. Madam, then have no trouble, you shall now see 'tis possible for me to love too, without being jealous; I will not only believe your innocence myself, but make all the world believe it.—[*Aside to* HORNER.] Horner, I must now be concerned for this lady's honour.

Horn. And I must be concerned for a lady's honour too.

Har. This lady has her honour, and I will protect it.

Horn. My lady has not her honour, but has given it me to keep, and I will preserve it.

Har. I understand you not.

Horn. I would not have you.

Mrs. Pinch. What's the matter with 'em all? [*Peeping in behind.*

Pinch. Come, come, Mr. Horner, no more disputing; here's the parson, I brought him not in vain.

Har. No, sir, I'll employ him, if this lady please.

Pinch. How! what d'ye mean?

Spark. Ay, what does he mean?

Horn. Why, I have resigned your sister to him, he has my consent.

Pinch. But he has not mine, sir; a woman's injured honour, no more than a man's, can be repaired or satisfied by any but him that first wronged it; and you shall marry her presently, or—— [*Lays his hand on his sword.*

Re-enter Mrs. PINCHWIFE.

Mrs. Pinch. O Lord, they'll kill poor Mr. Horner! besides, he shan't marry her whilst I stand by, and look on; I'll not lose my second husband so.

Pinch. **What do I see?**

Alith. My sister in my clothes!

Spark. Ha!

Mrs. Pinch. Nay, pray now don't quarrel about finding work for the par-son, he shall marry me to Mr. Horner; or now, I believe, you have enough of me.   [*To* PINCHWIFE.

Horn. Damned, damned loving changeling!   [*Aside.*

Mrs. Pinch. Pray, sister, pardon me for telling so many lies of you.

Horn. I suppose the riddle is plain now.

Lucy. No, that must be my work.—Good sir, hear me.

     [*Kneels to* PINCHWIFE, *who stands doggedly with his hat over his eyes.*

Pinch. I will never hear woman again, but make 'em all silent thus——

                                   [*Offers to draw upon his* Wife.

Horn. No, that must not be.

Pinch. You then shall go first, 'tis all one to me.

          [*Offers to draw on* HORNER, *but is stopped by* HARCOURT.

Har. Hold!

Re-enter Sir JASPER FIDGET, Lady FIDGET, Lady SQUEAMISH, Mrs. DAINTY FIDGET, *and* Mrs. SQUEAMISH.

Sir Jasp. What's the matter? what's the matter? pray, what's the matter, sir? I beseech you communicate, sir.

Pinch. Why, my wife has communicated, sir, as your wife may have done too, sir, if she knows him, sir.

Sir Jasp. Pshaw, with him! ha! ha! he!

Pinch. D'ye mock me, sir? a cuckold is a kind of a wild beast; have a care, sir.

Sir Jasp. No, sure, you mock me, sir. He cuckold you! it can't be, ha! ha! he! why, I'll tell you, sir——   [*Offers to whisper.*

Pinch. I tell you again, he has whored my wife, and yours too, if he knows her, and all the women he comes near; 'tis not his dissembling, his hypocrisy, can wheedle me.

Sir Jasp. How! does he dissemble? is he a hypocrite? Nay, then—how—wife—sister, is he a hypocrite?

Lady Squeam. A hypocrite! a dissembler! Speak, young harlotry, speak, how?

Sir Jasp. Nay, then—O my head too!—O thou libidinous lady!

Lady Squeam. O thou harloting harlotry! hast thou done't then?

Sir Jasp. Speak, good Horner, art thou a dissembler, a rogue? hast thou——

Horn. So!

Lucy. I'll fetch you off, and her too, if she will but hold her tongue.

                                   [*Apart to* HORNER.

Horn. Canst thou? I'll give thee——   [*Apart to* LUCY.

Lucy [*to* PINCHWIFE]. Pray have but patience to hear me, sir, who am the unfortunate cause of all this confusion. Your wife is innocent, I only culpable; for I put her upon telling you all these lies concerning my mistress, in order to the breaking off the match between Mr. Sparkish and her, to make way for Mr. Harcourt.

Spark. Did you so, eternal rotten tooth? Then, it seems, my mistress was not false to me, I was only deceived by you. Brother, that should have been, now man of conduct, who is a frank person now, to bring your wife to her lover, ha?

Lucy. I assure you, sir, she came not to Mr. Horner out of love, for she loves him no more——

Mrs. Pinch. Hold, I told lies for you, but you shall tell none for me, for I do love Mr. Horner with all my soul, and nobody shall say me nay; pray, don't you go to make poor Mr. Horner believe to the contrary; 'tis spitefully done of you, I'm sure.

Horn. Peace, dear idiot.   [*Aside to* Mrs. PINCHWIFE.

Mrs. Pinch. Nay, I will not peace.

Pinch. Not till I make you.

Enter DORILANT *and* Quack.

Dor. Horner, your servant; I am the doctor's guest, he must excuse our intrusion.

Quack. But what's the matter, gentlemen? for Heaven's sake, what's the matter?

Horn. Oh, 'tis well you are come. 'Tis a censorious world we live in; you may have brought me a reprieve, or else I had died for a crime I never committed, and these innocent ladies had suffered with me; therefore, pray satisfy these worthy, honourable, jealous gentlemen—that——   [*Whispers.*

Quack. O, I understand you, is that all?—Sir Jasper, by Heavens, and upon the word of a physician, sir——   [*Whispers to* Sir JASPER.

Sir Jasp. Nay, I do believe you truly.—Pardon me, my virtuous lady, and dear of honour.

Lady Squeam. What, then all's right again?

Sir Jasp. Ay, ay, and now let us satisfy him too.

                    [*They whisper with* PINCHWIFE.

Pinch. An eunuch! Pray, no fooling with me.

Quack. I'll bring half the chirurgeons in town to swear it.

Pinch. They!—they'll swear a man that bled to death through his wounds, died of an apoplexy.

Quack. Pray, hear me, sir—why, all the town has heard the report of him.

Pinch. But does all the town believe it?

Quack. Pray, inquire a little, and first of all these.

Pinch. I'm sure when I left the town, he was the lewdest fellow in't.

Quack. I tell you, sir, he has been in France since; pray, ask but these ladies and gentlemen, your friend Mr. Dorilant. Gentlemen and ladies, han't you all heard the late sad report of poor Mr. Horner?

All the Ladies. Ay, ay, ay.

Dor. Why, thou jealous fool, dost thou doubt it? he's an arrant French capon.

Mrs. Pinch. 'Tis false, sir, you shall not disparage poor Mr. Horner, for to my certain knowledge——

Lucy. O, hold!

Mrs. Squeam. Stop her mouth!   [*Aside to* LUCY

Lady Fid. Upon my honour, sir, 'tis as true——   [*To* PINCHWIFE

Mrs. Dain. D'ye think we would have been seen in his company?

Mrs. Squeam. Trust our unspotted reputations with him?

Lady Fid. This you get, and we too, by trusting your secret to a fool.

[*Aside to* HORNER

Horn. Peace, madam.—[*Aside to* Quack.] Well, doctor, is not this a good design, that carries a man on unsuspected, and brings him off safe?

Pinch. Well, if this were true—but my wife——   [*Aside.*

[DORILANT *whispers with* Mrs. PINCHWIFE.

Alith. Come, brother, your wife is yet innocent, you see; but have a care of too strong an imagination, lest, like an over-concerned timorous gamester, by fancying an unlucky cast, it should come. Women and fortune are truest still to those that trust 'em.

Lucy. And any wild thing grows but the more fierce and hungry for being kept up, and more dangerous to the keeper.

Alith. There's doctrine for all husbands, Mr. Harcourt.

Har. I edify, madam, so much, that I am impatient till I am one.

Dor. And I edify so much by example, I will never be one.

Spark. And because I will not disparage my parts, I'll ne'er be one.

Horn. And I, alas! can't be one.

Pinch. But I must be one—against my will to a country wife, with a country murrain to me!

Mrs. Pinch. And I must be a country wife still too, I find; for I can't, like a city one, be rid of my musty husband, and do what I list.   [*Aside.*

Horn. Now, sir, I must pronounce your wife innocent, though I blush whilst I do it; and I am the only man by her now exposed to shame, which I will straight drown in wine, as you shall your suspicion; and the ladies' troubles we'll divert with a ballad.—Doctor, where are your maskers?

Lucy. Indeed, she's innocent, sir, I am her witness; and her end of coming out was but to see her sister's wedding; and what she has said to your face of her love to Mr. Horner, was but the usual innocent revenge on a husband's jealousy;—was it not, madam, speak?

Mrs. Pinch. [*aside to* LUCY *and* HORNER]. Since you'll have me tell more lies—[*Aloud.*] Yes, indeed, bud.

Pinch. For my own sake fain I would all believe;
    Cuckolds, like lovers, should themselves deceive.
    But——   [*Sighs.*
    His honour is least safe (too late I find)
    Who trusts it with a foolish wife or friend.

A Dance of Cuckolds.

Horn. Vain fops but court and dress, and keep a pother,
  To pass for women's men with one another;
  But he who aims by women to be prized,
  First by the men, you see, must be despised.   [*Exeunt.*

EPILOGUE

SPOKEN BY MRS. KNEP

Now you the vigorous, who daily here
O'er vizard-mask in public dominere,
And what you'd do to her, if in place where;
Nay, have the confidence to cry, "Come out!"
Yet when she says, "Lead on!" you are not stout;
But to your well-dressed brother straight turn round,
And cry, "Pox on her, Ned, she can't be sound!"
Then slink away, a fresh one to engage,
With so much seeming heat and loving rage,
You'd frighten listening actress on the stage;
Till she at last has seen you huffing come,
And talk of keeping in the tiring-room,
Yet cannot be provoked to lead her home.
Next, you Falstaffs of fifty, who beset
Your buckram maidenheads, which your friends get;
And whilst to them you of achievements boast,
They share the booty, and laugh at your cost.
In fine, you essenced boys, both old and young,
Who would be thought so eager, brisk, and strong,
Yet do the ladies, not their husbands wrong;
Whose purses for your manhood make excuse,
And keep your Flanders mares for show not use;
Encouraged by our woman's man to-day,
A Horner's part may vainly think to play;
And may intrigues so bashfully disown,
That they may doubted be by few or none;
May kiss the cards at picquet, ombre, loo,
And so be taught to kiss the lady too;
But, gallants, have a care, faith, what you do.
The world, which to no man his due will give,
You by experience know you can deceive,
And men may still believe you vigorous,
But then we women—there's no cozening us.

THE WAY OF THE WORLD

A COMEDY

by William Congreve

Audire eft Operæ pretium, procedere recte
Qui mæchis non vultis —— Hor. Sat. 2. l. 1.
—— *Metuat doti deprenfa.* —— Ibid.

Mr. CONGREVE,

Occasion'd by his

COMEDY

CALL'D

The WAY of the WORLD.

When Pleasure's falling to the low Delight,
In the vain Joys of the uncertain Sight,
No sense of Wit when rude Spectators know,
But in distorted Gesture, Farce and Show;
How could, Great Author, your Aspiring Mind
Dare to Write only to the Few Refin'd!
Yet tho' that nice Ambition you pursue,
'Tis not in Congreve's *Power to please but few.*
Implicitly devoted to his Fame,
Well-dress'd Barbarians know his awful Name;
Tho' senseless they're of Mirth, but when they laugh,
As they feel Wine, but when, 'till drunk, they quaff.

    On you, from Fate, a lavish Portion fell
In ev'ry way of Writing to excell.
Your Muse Applause to Arabella *brings,*
In Notes as sweet as Arabella *Sings.*
When e'er you draw an undissembled Woe,
With sweet Distress your Rural Numbers flow
Pastora's the Complaint of ev'ry Swain,
Pastora still the Eccho of the Plain!
Or if your Muse describe, with warming Force,
The wounded Frenchman *falling from his Horse;*
And her own William *glorious in the Strife,*
Bestowing on the prostrate Foe his Life:
You the great Act as gen'rously rehearse,
And all the English *Fury's in your Verse.*
By your selected Scenes, and handsome Choice,
Ennobled Comedy exalts her Voice;
You check unjust Esteem and fond Desire,
And teach to Scorn, what else we should Admire;

The just Impression taught by you we bear,
The Player acts the World, the World the Player,
Whom still that World unjustly disesteems,
Tho' he, alone, professes what he seems:
But when your Muse assumes her Tragick Part,
She conquers and she reigns in ev'ry Heart;
To mourn with her Men cheat their private Woe,
And gen'rous Pity's all the Grief they know;
The Widow, who impatient of Delay,
From the Town-joys must mask it to the Play,
Joyns with your Mourning-Bride's resistless Moan,
And weeps at Loss she slighted, when her own;
You give us Torment, and you give us Ease,
And vary our Afflictions as you please;
Is not a Heart so kind as yours in Pain,
To load your Friends with Cares you only feign;
Your Friends in Grief, compos'd your self, to leave?
But 'tis the only way you'll e'er deceive.
Then still, great Sir, your moving Pow'r employ,
To lull our Sorrow, and correct our Joy.

                                        R. STEELE

To the Right Honourable

RALPH,

Earl of *MOUNTAGUE,* &c.

My LORD,
Whether the World will arraign me of Vanity, or not, that I have presum'd to Dedicate this Comedy to Your Lordship, I am yet in Doubt: Tho'
it may be it is some degree of Vanity even to doubt of it. One who has at
any time had the Honour of Your Lordship's Conversation, cannot be suppos'd to think very meanly of that which he wou'd prefer to Your Perusal:
Yet it were to incur the Imputation of too much Sufficiency, to pretend to
such a Merit as might abide the Test of Your Lordship's Censure.

Whatever Value may be wanting to this Play while yet it is mine, will be
sufficiently made up to it, when it is once become Your Lordship's; and it
is my Security, that I cannot have overrated it more by my Dedication, than
Your Lordship will dignifie it by Your Patronage.

That it succeeded on the Stage, was almost beyond my Expectation; for
but little of it was prepar'd for that general Taste which seems now to be
predominant in the Pallats of our Audience.

Those Characters which are meant to be ridicul'd in most of our Comedies,
are of Fools so gross, that in my humble Opinion, they shou'd rather disturb
than divert the well-natur'd and reflecting Part of an Audience; they are
rather Objects of Charity than Contempt; and instead of moving our Mirth,
they ought very often to excite our Compassion.

This Reflection mov'd me to design some Characters, which shou'd appear
ridiculous not so much thro' a natural Folly (which is incorrigible, and therefore not proper for the Stage) as thro' an affected Wit; a Wit, which at
the same time that it is affected, is also false. As there is some Difficulty in
the Formation of a Character of this Nature, so there is some Hazard which
attends the Progress of its Success, upon the Stage: For many come to a
Play, so over-charg'd with Criticism, that they very often let fly their Censure, when thro' their Rashness they have mistaken their Aim. This I had
Occasion lately to observe: For this Play had been acted two or three Days,
before some of these hasty Judges cou'd find the leisure to distinguish betwixt the Character of a *Witwoud* and a *Truewit.*

I must beg Your Lordship's Pardon for this Digression from the true
Course of this Epistle; but that it may not seem altogether impertinent, I
beg, that I may plead the Occasion of it, in part of that Excuse of which I
stand in need, for recommending this Comedy to Your Protection. It is
only by the Countenance of Your Lordship, and the *Few* so qualify'd, that

such who write with Care and Pains can hope to be distinguish'd: For th
Prostituted Name of *Poet* promiscuously levels all that bear it.

Terence, the most correct Writer in the World, had a *Scipio* and a *Leliu*
if not to assist him, at least to support him in his Reputation: And notwith
standing his extraordinary Merit, it may be, their Countenance was not mor
than necessary.

The purity of his Stile, the Delicacy of his Turns, and the Justness of h
Characters, were all of them Beauties, which the greater Part of his Audienc
were incapable of Tasting: Some of the coursest Strokes of *Plautus*, s
severely censur'd by *Horace*, were more likely to affect the Multitude; sucl
who come with expectation to laugh at the last Act of a Play, and are bette
entertain'd with two or three unseasonable Jests, than with the artful Solu
tion of the *Fable*.

As *Terence* excell'd in his Performances, so had he great Advantages t
encourage his Undertakings; for he built most on the Foundations o
Menander: His Plots were generally modell'd, and his Characters read
drawn to his Hand. He copied *Menander*; and *Menander* had no less Ligh
in the Formation of his Characters, from the Observations of *Theophrastu*
of whom he was a Disciple; and *Theophrastus* it is known was not only th
Disciple, but the immediate Successor of *Aristotle*, the first and greates
Judge of Poetry. These were great Models to design by; and the furthe
Advantage which *Terence* possess'd, towards giving his Plays the due Orna
ments of Purity of Stile, and Justness of Manners, was not less Considerable
from the Freedom of Conversation, which was permitted him with *Leliu*
and *Scipio*, two of the greatest and most polite Men of his Age. And indeed
the Privilege of such a Conversation, is the only certain Means of attainin
to the Perfection of Dialogue.

If it has happen'd in any Part of this Comedy, that I have gain'd a Turi
of Stile, or Expression more Correct, or at least more Corrigible than ii
those which I have formerly written, I must, with equal Pride and Gratitude
ascribe it to the Honour of Your Lordship's admitting me into Your Con
versation, and that of a Society where every body else was so well worthy o
You, in Your Retirement last Summer from the Town: For it was immedi
ately after, that this Comedy was written. If I have fail'd in my Performance
it is only to be regretted, where there were so many, not inferior either to
Scipio or a *Lelius*, that there shou'd be one wanting, equal in Capacity to
Terence.

If I am not mistaken, Poetry is almost the only Art, which has not yet laie
Claim to your Lordship's Patronage. Architecture, and Painting, to the grea
Honour of our Country, have flourish'd under Your Influence and Protec
tion. In the meantime, Poetry, the eldest Sister of all Arts, and Parent o
most, seems to have design'd her Birth-right, by having neglected to pay hei
Duty to Your Lordship; and by permitting others of a later Extraction, te
prepossess that Place in Your Esteem, to which none can pretend a bettei
Title. Poetry, in its Nature, is sacred to the Good and Great; the Relatior
between them is reciprocal, and they are ever propitious to it. It is the

Privilege of Poetry to address to them, and it is their Prerogative alone to give it Protection.

This receiv'd Maxim is a general Apology for all Writers who Consecrate their Labours to great Men: But I could wish, at this time, that this Address were exempted from the common Pretence of all Dedications; and that as I can distinguish Your Lordship even among the most Deserving, so this Offering might become remarkable by some particular Instance of Respect, which should assure Your Lordship, that I am, with all due sense of Your extream Worthiness and Humanity,

My LORD,
Your Lordship's most Obedient
and most Oblig'd Humble Servant,
Will. Congreve.

PROLOGUE

Spoken by Mr. *Betterton*.

Of those few Fools, who with ill Stars are curst,
Sure, scribbling Fools, call'd Poets, fare the worst:
For they're a sort of Fools which Fortune *makes,*
And after she has made 'em Fools, forsakes.
With Nature's *Oafs 'tis quite a diff'rent Case,*
For Fortune *favours all her Idiot-Race:*
In her own Nest the Cuckow-Eggs *we find,*
O'er which she broods to hatch the Changling-Kind.
No Portion for her own she has to spare,
So much she doats on her adopted Care.

   Poets are Bubbles, by the Town drawn in,
Suffer'd at first some trifling Stakes to win:
But what unequal Hazards do they run!
Each time they write they venture all they've won:
The Squire that's butter'd still, is sure to be undone.
This Author, heretofore, has found your Favour,
But pleads no Merit from his past Behaviour;
To build on that might prove a vain Presumption,
Shou'd Grants to Poets made, admit Resumption:
And in Parnassus *he must lose his Seat,*
If that be found a forfeited Estate.

   He owns, with Toil, he wrought the following Scenes,
But if they're naught ne'er spare him for his Pains:
Damn him the more; have no Commiseration
For Dulness on mature Deliberation.
He swears he'll not resent one hiss'd-off Scene
Nor, like those peevish Wits, his Play maintain,
Who, to assert their Sense, your Taste arraign.
Some Plot we think he has, and some new Thought;
Some Humour too, no Farce; but that's a Fault.
Satire, he thinks, you ought not to expect;
For so Reform'd a Town, who dares Correct?
To Please, this Time, has been his sole Pretence,
He'll not instruct, lest it shou'd give Offence.
Shou'd he by chance a Knave or Fool expose,
That hurts none here, sure here are none of those.
In short, our Play shall (with your leave to shew it)
Give you one Instance of a Passive Poet.
Who to your Judgments yields all Resignation;
So Save or Damn, after your own Discretion.

DRAMATIS PERSONÆ.

MEN.

ainall, In Love with Mrs. *Marwood*.

Mirabell, In Love with Mrs. *Millamant*.

Witwoud, ⎫
tulant, ⎭ Followers of Mrs. *Millamant*.

r Wilfull Witwoud, Half Brother to *Witwoud*, and Nephew to Lady
Wishfort.

aitwell, Servant to *Mirabell*.

WOMEN.

dy Wishfort, Enemy to *Mirabell*, for having falsely pretended Love to
her.

rs. Millamant, A fine Lady, Neice to Lady *Wishfort*, and loves *Mirabell*.

rs. Marwood, Friend to Mr. *Fainall*, and likes *Mirabell*.

rs. Fainall, Daughter to Lady *Wishfort*, and Wife to *Fainall*, formerly
Friend to *Mirabell*.

ible, Woman to Lady *Wishfort*.

incing, Woman to Mrs. *Millamant*.

Dancers, Footmen, *and* Attendants.

SCENE—LONDON.

The Time equal to that of the Presentation.

THE WAY OF THE WORLD

ACT I.

SCENE I.—*A Chocolate-House.*

MIRABELL *and* FAINALL [*Rising from Cards.*] BETTY *waiting.*

Mira. You are a fortunate Man, Mr. *Fainall.*

Fain. Have we done?

Mira. What you please. I'll play on to entertain you.

Fain. No, I'll give you your Revenge another time, when you are not so indifferent; you are thinking of something else now, and play too negligently; the Coldness of a losing Gamester lessens the Pleasure of the Winner. I'd no more play with a Man that slighted his ill Fortune, than I'd make Love to a Woman who undervalu'd the Loss of her Reputation.

Mira. You have a Taste extreamly delicate, and are for refining on your Pleasures.

Fain. Prithee, why so reserv'd? Something has put you out of Humour.

Mira. Not at all: I happen to be grave to Day; and you are gay; that's all.

Fain. Confess, *Millamant* and you quarrell'd last Night, after I left you; my fair Cousin has some Humours that wou'd tempt the Patience of a Stoick. What, some Coxcomb came in, and was well receiv'd by her, while you were by.

Mira. Witwoud and *Petulant;* and what was worse, her Aunt, your Wife's Mother, my evil Genius; or to sum up all in her own Name, my old Lady *Wishfort* came in.——

Fain. O there it is then——She has a lasting Passion for you, and with Reason.——What, then my Wife was there?

Mira. Yes, and Mrs. *Marwood* and three or four more, whom I never saw before; seeing me, they all put on their grave Faces, whisper'd one another; then complain'd aloud of the Vapours, and after fell into a profound Silence.

Fain. They had a mind to be rid of you.

Mira. For which good Reason I resolv'd not to stir. At last the good old Lady broke thro' her painful Taciturnity, with an Invective against long Visits. I would not have understood her, but *Millamant* joining in the Argument, I rose and with a constrain'd Smile told her, I thought nothing was so easie as to know when a Visit began to be troublesome; she reden'd and I withdrew, without expecting her reply.

Fain. You were to blame to resent what she spoke only in Compliance with her Aunt.

Mira. She is more Mistress of her self, than to be under the necessity of such a Resignation.

Fain. What? tho' half her Fortune depends upon her Marrying with my Lady's Approbation?

Mira. I was then in such a Humour, that I shou'd have been better pleas'd if she had been less discreet.

Fain. Now I remember, I wonder not they were weary of you; last Night was one of their Cabal-Nights; they have 'em three times a Week, and meet by turns, at one another's Apartments, where they come together like the Coroner's Inquest, to sit upon the murder'd Reputations of the Week. You and I are excluded; and it was once propos'd that all the Male Sex shou'd be excepted; but some body mov'd that to avoid Scandal there might be one Man of the Community; upon which *Witwoud* and *Petulant* were enroll'd Members.

Mira. And who may have been the Foundress of this Sect? My Lady *Wishfort*, I warrant, who publishes her Detestation of Mankind; and full of the Vigour of Fifty five, declares for a Friend and *Ratafia;* and let Posterity shift for it self, she'll breed no more.

Fain. The Discovery of your sham Addresses to her, to conceal your Love to her Neice, has provok'd this Separation: Had you dissembl'd better, Things might have continu'd in the State of Nature.

Mira. I did as much as Man cou'd, with any reasonable Conscience; I proceeded to the very last Act of Flattery with her, and was guilty of a Song in her Commendation. Nay, I got a Friend to put her into a Lampoon, and compliment her with the Imputation of an Affair with a young Fellow, which I carry'd so far, that I told her the malicious Town took notice that she was grown fat of a sudden; and when she lay in of a Dropsie, persuaded her she was reported to be in Labour. The Devil's in't, if an old Woman is to be flatter'd further, unless a Man shou'd endeavour downright personally to debauch her; and that my Vertue forbad me. But for the Discovery of this Amour, I am indebted to your Friend, or your Wife's Friend, Mrs. *Marwood.*

Fain. What shou'd provoke her to be your Enemy, unless she has made you Advances, which you have slighted? Women do not easily forgive Omissions of that Nature.

Mira. She was always civil to me, 'till of late; I confess I am not one of those Coxcombs who are apt to interpret a Woman's good Manners to her Prejudice; and think that she who does not refuse 'em ev'ry thing, can refuse 'em nothing.

Fain. You are a gallant Man, *Mirabell;* and tho' you may have Cruelty enough, not to satisfie a Lady's longing; you have too much Generosity, not to be tender of her Honour. Yet you speak with an Indifference which seems to be affected; and confesses you are conscious of a Negligence.

Mira. You pursue the Argument with a Distrust that seems to be unaffected, and confesses you are conscious of a Concern for which the Lady is more indebted to you, than is your Wife.

Fain. Fie, fie Friend, if you grow censorious I must leave you;——I'll look upon the Gamesters in the next Room.

Mira. Who are they?

Fain. Petulant and *Witwoud*—Bring me some Chocolate.

Mira. Betty, what says your Clock?

Bet. Turn'd of the last Canonical Hour, Sir.

Mira. How pertinently the Jade answers me! Ha? almost one a Clock! [*Looking on his Watch.*] O, y'are come—

SCENE II.

MIRABELL *and* FOOTMAN.

Mira. Well; is the grand Affair over? You have been something tedious.

Serv. Sir, there's such Coupling at *Pancras*, that they stand behind one another, as 'twere in a Country Dance. Ours was the last Couple to lead up; and no Hopes appearing of Dispatch, besides, the Parson growing hoarse, we were afraid his Lungs wou'd have fail'd before it came to our Turn; so we drove round to *Duke's-Place;* and there they were rivetted in a trice.

Mira. So, so, you are sure they are married.

Serv. Married and Bedded, Sir: I am Witness.

Mira. Have you the Certificate?

Serv. Here it is, Sir.

Mira. Has the Tailor brought *Waitwell's* Cloaths home, and the new Liveries?

Serv. Yes, Sir.

Mira. That's well. Do you go home again, d'ye hear, and adjourn the Consummation 'till farther Order; bid *Waitwell* shake his Ears, and Dame *Partlet* rustle up her Feathers, and meet me at One a Clock by *Rosamond's* Pond; that I may see her before she returns to her Lady: And as you tender your Ears be secret.

SCENE III.

MIRABELL, FAINALL, BETTY.

Fain. Joy of your Success, *Mirabell;* you look pleas'd.

Mira. Ay; I have been engag'd in a Matter of some sort of Mirth, which is not yet ripe for Discovery. I am glad this is not a Cabal-Night. I wonder, *Fainall*, that you who are married, and of consequence should be discreet, will suffer your Wife to be of such a Party.

Fain. Faith, I am not jealous. Besides, most who are engag'd are Women and Relations; and for the Men, they are of a Kind too contemptible to give Scandal.

Mira. I am of another Opinion. The greater the Coxcomb, always the more the Scandal: For a Woman who is not a Fool, can have but one Reason for associating with a Man who is one.

Fain. Are you jealous as often as you see *Witwoud* entertain'd by *Millamant?*

Mira. Of her Understanding I am, if not of her Person.

Fain. You do her wrong; for to give her her Due, she has Wit.

Mira. She has Beauty enough to make any Man think so; and Complaisance enough not to contradict him who shall tell her so.

Fain. For a passionate Lover, methinks you are a Man somewhat too discerning in the Failings of your Mistress.

Mira. And for a discerning Man, somewhat too passionate a Lover; for I like her with all her Faults; nay, like her for her Faults. Her Follies are so natural, or so artful, that they become her; and those Affectations which in another Woman wou'd be odious, serve but to make her more agreeable. I'll tell thee, *Fainall*, she once us'd me with that Insolence, that in Revenge I took her to pieces; sifted her, and separated her Failings; I study'd 'em, and got 'em by Rote. The Catalogue was so large, that I was not without Hopes, one Day or other to hate her heartily: To which end I so us'd my self to think of 'em, that at length, contrary to my Design and Expectation, they gave me ev'ry Hour less and less Disturbance; 'till in a few Days it became habitual to me, to remember 'em without being displeas'd. They are now grown as familiar to me as my own Frailties; and in all probability in a little time longer I shall like 'em as well.

Fain. Marry her, marry her; be half as well acquainted with her Charms, as you are with her Defects, and my Life on't, you are your own Man again.

Mira. Say you so?

Fain. Ay, ay, I have Experience: I have a Wife, and so forth.

SCENE IV.

[*To them*] MESSENGER.

Mess. Is one Squire *Witwoud* here?

Bet. Yes; What's your Business?

Mess. I have a Letter for him, from his Brother Sir *Wilfull*, which I am charg'd to deliver into his own Hands.

Bet. He's in the next Room, Friend—That way.

SCENE V.

MIRABELL, FAINALL, BETTY.

Mira. What, is the chief of that noble Family in Town, Sir *Wilfull Witwoud?*

Fain. He is expected to Day. Do you know him?

Mira. I have seen him, he promises to be an extraordinary Person; I think you have the Honour to be related to him.

Fain. Yes; he is half Brother to this *Witwoud* by a former Wife, who was Sister to my Lady *Wishfort*, my Wife's Mother. If you marry *Millamant*, you must call Cousins too.

Mira. I had rather be his Relation than his Acquaintance.

Fain. He comes to Town in order to Equip himself for Travel.

Mira. For Travel! Why the Man that I mean is above Forty.

Fain. No matter for that; 'tis for the Honour of *England*, that all *Europe* should know that we have Blockheads of all Ages.

Mira. I wonder there is not an Act of Parliament to save the Credit of the Nation, and prohibit the Exportation of Fools.

Fain. By no means, 'tis better as 'tis; 'tis better to Trade with a little Loss, than to be quite eaten up, with being overstock'd.

Mira. Pray, are the Follies of this Knight-Errant, and those of the Squire his Brother, any thing related?

Fain. Not at all; *Witwoud* grows by the Knight, like a Medlar grafted on a Crab. One will melt in your Mouth, and t'other set your Teeth on edge; one is all Pulp, and the other all Core.

Mira. So one will be Rotten before he be Ripe, and the other will be Rotten without ever being Ripe at all.

Fain. Sir *Wilfull* is an odd Mixture of Bashfulness and Obstinacy.——But when he's drunk, he's as loving as the Monster in the Tempest; and much after the same manner. To give t'other his due; he has something of good Nature, and does not always want Wit.

Mira. Not always; but as often as his Memory fails him, and his common Place of Comparisons. He is a Fool with a good Memory, and some few Scraps of other Folks Wit. He is one whose Conversation can never be approv'd, yet it is now and then to be endur'd. He has indeed one good Quality, he is not Exceptious; for he so passionately affects the Reputation of understanding Raillery, that he will construe an Affront into a Jest; and call downright Rudeness and ill Language, Satire and Fire.

Fain. If you have a mind to finish his Picture, you have an Opportunity to do it at full length. Behold the Original.

SCENE VI.

[*To them*] WITWOUD.

Wit. Afford me your Compassion, my Dears; pity me, *Fainall*, *Mirabell*, pity me.

Mira. I do from my Soul.

Fain. Why, what's the Matter?

Wit. No Letters for me, *Betty*?

Bet. Did not a Messenger bring you one but now, Sir?

Wit. Ay, but no other?

Bet. No, Sir.

Wit. That's hard, that's very hard;—A Messenger, a Mule, a Beast of Burden, he has brought me a Letter from the Fool my Brother, as heavy as a Panegyrick in a Funeral Sermon, or a Copy of Commendatory Verses from one Poet to another. And what's worse, 'tis as sure a Forerunner of the Author, as an Epistle Dedicatory.

Mira. A Fool, and your Brother, *Witwoud!*

Wit. Ay, ay, my half Brother. My half Brother he is, no nearer upon Honour.

Mira. Then 'tis possible he may be but half a Fool.

Wit. Good, good, *Mirabell*, *le Drole!* Good, good, hang him, don't let's talk of him;——*Fainall*, how does your Lady? Gad. I say any thing in the World to get this Fellow out of my Head. I beg Pardon that I shou'd ask a Man of Pleasure, and the Town, a Question at once so Foreign and Domestick. But I Talk like an old Maid at a Marriage, I don't know what I say: But she's the best Woman in the World.

Fain. 'Tis well you don't know what you say, or else your Commendation wou'd go near to make me either Vain or Jealous.

Wit. No Man in Town lives well with a Wife but *Fainall.* Your Judgment, *Mirabell?*

Mira. You had better step and ask his Wife; if you wou'd be credibly inform'd.

Wit. Mirabell.

Mira. Ay.

Wit. My Dear, I ask Ten Thousand Pardons;——Gad I have forgot what I was going to say to you.

Mira. I thank you heartily, heartily.

Wit. No, but prithee excuse me,——my Memory is such a Memory.

Mira. Have a care of such Apologies, *Witwoud;*——for I never knew a Fool but he affected to complain, either of the Spleen or his Memory.

Fain. What have you done with *Petulant?*

Wit. He's reckoning his Mony,——my Mony it was——I have no Luck to Day.

Fain. You may allow him to win of you at Play;——for you are sure to be too hard for him at Repartee: Since you monopolize the Wit that is between you, the Fortune must be his of Course.

Mira. I don't find that *Petulant* confesses the Superiority of Wit to be your Talent, *Witwoud.*

Wit. Come, come, you are malicious now, and wou'd breed Debates—— *Petulant's* my Friend, and a very honest Fellow, and a very pretty Fellow, and has a smattering——Faith and Troth a pretty deal of an odd sort of a small Wit: Nay, I'll do him Justice. I'm his Friend, I won't wrong him.—— And if he had any Judgment in the World,——he wou'd not be altogether contemptible. Come, come, don't detract from the Merits of my Friend.

Fain. You don't take your Friend to be over-nicely bred.

Wit. No, no, hang him, the Rogue has no Manners at all, that I must own

—No more Breeding than a Bum-bailey, that I grant you,——'Tis pity; the Fellow has Fire and Life.

Mira. What, Courage?

Wit. Hum, faith I don't know as to that,——I can't say as to that.——Yes, faith, in a Controversie he'll contradict any Body.

Mira. Tho' 'twere a Man whom he fear'd, or a Woman whom he lov'd.

Wit. Well, well, he does not always think before he speaks;——We have all our Failings; you are too hard upon him, you are faith. Let me excuse him, ——I can defend most of his Faults, except one or two; one he has, that's the Truth on't, if he were my Brother, I cou'd not acquit him——That indeed I cou'd wish were otherwise.

Mira. Ay marry, what's that, *Witwoud?*

Wit. O pardon me——Expose the Infirmities of my Friend.——No, my Dear, excuse me there.

Fain. What I warrant he's unsincere, or 'tis some such Trifle.

Wit. No, no, what if he be? 'Tis no matter for that, his Wit will excuse that: A Wit shou'd no more be sincere, than a Woman constant; one argues a Decay of Parts, as t'other of Beauty.

Mira. May be you think him too positive?

Wit. No, no, his being positive is an Incentive to Argument, and keeps up Conversation.

Fain. Too illiterate.

Wit. That! that's his Happiness——His want of Learning gives him the more Opportunities to shew his natural Parts.

Mira. He wants Words.

Wit. Ay; but I like him for that now; for his want of Words gives me the Pleasure very often to explain his Meaning.

Fain. He's Impudent.

Wit. No, that's not it.

Mira. Vain.

Wit. No.

Mira. What, he speaks unseasonable Truths sometimes, because he has not Wit enough to invent an Evasion.

Wit. Truths! Ha, ha, ha! No, no, since you will have it,——I mean, he never speaks Truth at all,—That's all. He will lie like a Chambermaid, or a Woman of Quality's Porter. Now that is a Fault.

SCENE VII.

[*To them*] Coachman.

Coach. Is Master *Petulant* here, Mistress?

Bet. Yes.

Coach. Three Gentlewomen in a Coach would speak with him.

Fain. O brave *Petulant*, Three!

Bet. I'll tell him.

Coach. You must bring Two Dishes of Chocolate and a Glass of Cinnamon-water.

SCENE VIII.

MIRABELL, FAINALL, WITWOUD.

Wit. That should be for Two fasting Strumpets, and a Bawd troubled with Wind. Now you may know what the Three are.

Mira. You are free with your Friend's Acquaintance.

Wit. Ay, ay, Friendship without Freedom is as dull as Love without Enjoyment, or Wine without Toasting; but to tell you a Secret, these are Trulls whom he allows Coach-hire, and something more by the Week, to call on him once a Day at publick Places.

Mira. How!

Wit. You shall see he won't go to 'em because there's no more Company here to take notice of him——Why this is nothing to what he us'd to do;—— Before he found out this way, I have known him call for himself——

Fain. Call for himself? What dost thou mean?

Wit. Mean, why he wou'd slip you out of this Chocolate-house, just when you had been talking to him——As soon as your Back was turn'd——Whip he was gone;——Then trip to his Lodging, clap on a Hood and Scarf, and a Mask, slap into a Hackney-Coach, and drive hither to the Door again in a trice; where he wou'd send in for himself, that I mean, call for himself, wait for himself, nay and what's more, not finding himself, sometimes leave a Letter for himself.

Mira. I confess this is something extraordinary——I believe he waits for himself now, he is so long a coming; O I ask his Pardon.

SCENE IX.

PETULANT, MIRABELL, FAINALL, WITWOUD, BETTY.

Bet. Sir, the Coach stays.

Pet. Well, well; I come——'Sbud a Man had as good be a profess'd Midwife, as a profess'd Whoremaster, at this rate; to be knock'd up and rais'd at all Hours, and in all Places. Pox on 'em, I won't come——D'ye hear, tell 'em I won't come.——Let 'em snivel and cry their Hearts out.

Fain. You are very cruel, *Petulant.*

Pet. All's one, let it pass——I have a Humour to be cruel.

Mira. I hope they are not Persons of Condition that you use at this rate.

Pet. Condition, Condition's a dry'd Fig, if I am not in Humour——By this Hand, if they were your—a—a—your What-dee-call-'ems themselves, they must wait or rub off, if I want Appetite.

Mira. What-dee-call-'ems! What are they, *Witwoud?*

Wit. Empresses, my Dear—By your What-dee-call-'ems he means Sultana Queens.

Pet. Ay, *Roxolana's.*

Mira. Cry you Mercy.

Fain. Witwoud says they are——

Pet. What does he say th'are?

Wit. I; fine Ladies I say.

Pet. Pass on, *Witwoud*——Harkee, by this Light his Relations——Two Co-heiresses his Cousins, and an old Aunt, who loves Catterwauling better than a Conventicle.

Wit. Ha, ha, ha; I had a Mind to see how the Rogue wou'd come off—— Ha, ha, ha; Gad I can't be angry with him; if he had said they were my Mother and my Sisters.

Mira. No!

Wit. No; the Rogue's Wit and Readiness of Invention charm me, dear *Petulant.*

Bet. They are gone, Sir, in great Anger.

Pet. Enough, let 'em trundle. Anger helps Complexion, saves Paint.

Fain. This Continence is all dissembled; this is in order to have something to brag of the next time he makes Court to *Millamant*, and swear he has abandoned the whole Sex for her Sake.

Mira. Have you not left off your impudent Pretensions there yet? I shall cut your Throat, sometime or other, *Petulant*, about that Business.

Pet. Ay, ay, let that pass—There are other Throats to be cut.——

Mira. Meaning mine, Sir?

Pet. Not I——I mean no Body——I know nothing.——But there are Uncles and Nephews in the World——And they may be Rivals——What then? All's one for that——

Mira. How! Harkee *Petulant*, come hither——Explain, or I shall call your Interpreter.

Pet. Explain; I know nothing—Why you have an Uncle, have you not, lately come to Town, and lodges by my Lady *Wishfort's?*

Mira. True.

Pet. Why that's enough——You and he are not Friends; and if he shou'd marry and have a Child, you may be disinherited, ha?

Mira. Where hast thou stumbled upon all this Truth?

Pet. All's one for that; why then say I know something.

Mira. Come, thou art an honest Fellow *Petulant*, and shalt make Love to my Mistress, thou sha't, Faith. What hast thou heard of my Uncle?

Pet. I, nothing I. If Throats are to be cut, let Swords clash; snug's the Word, I shrug and am silent.

Mira. O Raillery, Raillery. Come, I know thou art in the Women's Secrets —What you're a Cabalist, I know you staid at *Millamant's* last Night, after I went. Was there any Mention made of my Uncle, or me? Tell me; if thou hadst but good Nature equal to thy Wit *Petulant, Tony Witwoud*, who is now thy Competitor in Fame, would shew as dim by thee as a dead Whiting's Eye by a Pearl of Orient; he wou'd no more be seen by thee, than *Mercury* is by the Sun: Come, I'm sure thou wo't tell me.

Pet. If I do, will you grant me common Sense then, for the future?

Mira. Faith I'll do what I can for thee, and I'll pray that Heav'n may grant it thee in the mean time.

Pet. Well, harkee.

Fain. *Petulant* and you both will find *Mirabell* as warm a Rival as a Lover.

Wit. Pshaw, pshaw, that she laughs at *Petulant* is plain. And for my part ——But that it is almost a Fashion to admire her, I should——Harkee——To tell you a Secret, but let it go no further—Between Friends, I shall never break my Heart for her.

Fain. How!

Wit. She's handsome; but she's a sort of an uncertain Woman.

Fain. I thought you had dy'd for her.

Wit. Umh——No——

Fain. She has Wit.

Wit. 'Tis what she will hardly allow any body else—Now, Demme, I shou'd hate that, if she were as handsome as *Cleopatra. Mirabell* is not so sure of her as he thinks for.

Fain. Why do you think so?

Wit. We staid pretty late there last Night; and heard something of an Uncle to *Mirabell,* who is lately come to Town——and is between him and the best part of his Estate; *Mirabell* and he are at some Distance, as my Lady *Wishfort* has been told; and you know she hates *Mirabell,* worse than a Quaker hates a Parrot, or than a Fishmonger hates a hard Frost. Whether this Uncle has seen Mrs. *Millamant* or not, I cannot say; but there were Items of such a Treaty being in Embrio; and if it shou'd come to Life, poor *Mirabell* wou'd be in some sort unfortunately fobb'd i'faith.

Fain. 'Tis impossible *Millamant* shou'd harken to it.

Wit. Faith, my Dear, I can't tell; she's a Woman and a kind of a Humorist.

Mira. And this is the Sum of what you cou'd collect last Night.

Pet. The Quintessence. May be *Witwoud* knows more, he stay'd longer—— Besides they never mind him; they say any thing before him.

Mira. I thought you had been the greatest Favourite.

Pet. Ay *tete a tete;* But not in publick, because I make Remarks.

Mira. You do?

Pet. Ay, ay, pox I'm malicious, Man. Now he's soft, you know, they are not in awe of him——The Fellow's well bred, he's what you call a——What-d'ye-call-'em. A fine Gentleman, but he's silly withal.

Mira. I thank you, I know as much as my Curiosity requires. *Fainall,* are you for the *Mall?*

Fain. Ay, I'll take a Turn before Dinner.

Wit. Ay, we'll all walk in the Park, the Ladies talk'd of being there.

Mira. I thought you were oblig'd to watch for your Brother Sir *Wilfull's* Arrival.

Wit. No, no, he's come to his Aunt's, my Lady *Wishfort;* pox on him, I shall be troubled with him too; what shall I do with the Fool?

Pet. Beg him for his Estate; that I may beg you afterwards; and so have but one Trouble with you both.

Wit. O rare *Petulant;* thou art as quick as Fire in a frosty Morning; thou shalt to the *Mall* with us; and we'll be very severe.

Pet. Enough, I'm in a Humour to be severe.

Mira. Are you? Pray then walk by your selves,——Let not us be accessory to your putting the Ladies out of Countenance, with your senseless Ribaldry; which you roar out aloud as often as they pass by you; and when you have made a handsome Woman blush, then you think you have been severe.

Pet. What, what? Then let 'em either shew their Innocence by not understanding what they hear, or else shew their Discretion by not hearing what they wou'd not be thought to understand.

Mira. But hast not thou then Sense enough to know that thou ought'st to be most asham'd thy self, when thou hast put another out of Countenance.

Pet. Not I, by this Hand——I always take Blushing either for a Sign of Guilt, or ill Breeding.

Mira. I confess you ought to think so. You are in the right, that you may plead the Error of your Judgment in defence of your Practice.

Where Modesty's ill Manners, 'tis but fit
That Impudence and Malice pass for Wit.

End of the First Act.

ACT II.
SCENE I.—*St. James's Park.*

Mrs. FAINALL *and Mrs.* MARWOOD.

Mrs. Fainall. Ay, ay, dear *Marwood*, if we will be happy, we must find the Means in our selves, and among our selves. Men are ever in Extreams; either doating or averse. While they are Lovers, if they have Fire and Sense, their Jealousies are insupportable: And when they cease to Love, (we ought to think at least) they loath; they look upon us with Horror and Distaste; they meet us like the Ghosts of what we were, and as from such, fly from us.

Mrs. Mar. True, 'tis an unhappy Circumstance of Life, that Love shou'd ever die before us; and that the Man so often shou'd out-live the Lover. But say what you will, 'tis better to be left, than never to have been lov'd. To pass our Youth in dull Indifference, to refuse the Sweets of Life because they once must leave us, is as preposterous, as to wish to have been born Old, because we one Day must be Old. For my part, my Youth may wear and waste, but it shall never rust in my Possession.

Mrs. Fain. Then it seems you dissemble an Aversion to Mankind, only in compliance to my Mother's Humour.

Mrs. Mar. Certainly. To be free; I have no Taste of those insipid dry Discourses, with which our Sex of force must entertain themselves, apart from Men. We may affect Endearments to each other, profess eternal Friendships, and seem to dote like Lovers; but 'tis not in our Natures long to persevere. Love will resume his Empire in our Breasts, and every Heart, or soon or late, receive and readmit him as its lawful Tyrant.

Mrs. Fain. Bless me, how have I been deceiv'd! Why you profess a Libertine.

Mrs. Mar. You see my Friendship by my Freedom. Come, be as sincere, acknowledge that your Sentiments agree with mine.

Mrs. Fain. Never.

Mrs. Mar. You hate Mankind?

Mrs. Fain. Heartily, Inveterately.

Mrs. Mar. Your Husband?

Mrs. Fain. Most transcendently; ay, tho' I say it, meritoriously.

Mrs. Mar. Give me your Hand upon it.

Mrs. Fain. There.

Mrs. Mar. I join with you; what I have said has been to try you.

Mrs. Fain. Is it possible? Dost thou hate those Vipers Men?

Mrs. Mar. I have done hating 'em, and am now come to despise 'em; the next thing I have to do, is eternally to forget 'em.

Mrs. Fain. There spoke the Spirit of an Amazon, a *Penthesilea.*

Mrs. Mar. And yet I am thinking sometimes to carry my Aversion further.

Mrs. Fain. How?

Mrs. Mar. Faith by marrying; if I cou'd but find one that lov'd me very well, and would be throughly sensible of ill Usage, I think I should do my self the Violence of undergoing the Ceremony.

Mrs. Fain. You wou'd not make him a Cuckold?

Mrs. Mar. No; but I'd make him believe I did, and that's as bad.

Mrs. Fain. Why had not you as good do it?

Mrs. Mar. O if he shou'd ever discover it, he wou'd then know the worst, and be out of his Pain; but I wou'd have him ever to continue upon the Rack of Fear and Jealousie.

Mrs. Fain. Ingenious Mischief! Wou'd thou wert married to *Mirabell.*

Mrs. Mar. Wou'd I were.

Mrs. Fain. You change Colour.

Mrs. Mar. Because I hate him.

Mrs. Fain. So do I; but I can hear him nam'd. But what Reason have you to hate him in particular?

Mrs. Mar. I never lov'd him; he is, and always was insufferably proud.

Mrs. Fain. By the Reason you give for your Aversion, one wou'd think it dissembled; for you have laid a Fault to his Charge, of which his Enemies must acquit him.

Mrs. Mar. O then it seems you are one of his favourable Enemies. Methinks you look a little pale, and now you flush again.

Mrs. Fain. Do I? I think I am a little sick o' the sudden.

Mrs. *Mar.* What ails you?

Mrs. *Fain:* My Husband. Don't you see him? He turn'd short upon me unawares, and has almost overcome me.

SCENE II.

[*To them*] FAINALL *and* MIRABELL.

Mrs. *Mar.* Ha, ha, ha; he comes opportunely for you.

Mrs. *Fain.* For you, for he has brought *Mirabell* with him.

Fain. My Dear.

Mrs. *Fain.* My Soul.

Fain. You don't look well to Day, Child.

Mrs. *Fain.* D'ye think so?

Mira. He is the only Man that does, Madam.

Mrs. *Fain.* The only Man that wou'd tell me so at least; and the only Man from whom I cou'd hear it without Mortification.

Fain. O my Dear I am satisfy'd of your Tenderness; I know you cannot resent any thing from me; especially what is an effect of my Concern.

Mrs. *Fain.* Mr. *Mirabell*, my Mother interrupted you in a pleasant Relation last Night: I wou'd fain hear it out.

Mira. The Persons concern'd in that Affair, have yet a tolerable Reputation.——I am afraid Mr. *Fainall* will be censorious.

Mrs. *Fain.* He has a Humour more prevailing than his Curiosity, and will willingly dispence with the hearing of one scandalous Story, to avoid giving an Occasion to make another by being seen to walk with his Wife. This way Mr. *Mirabell,* and I dare promise you will oblige us both.

SCENE III.

FAINALL, *Mrs.* MARWOOD.

Fain. Excellent Creature! Well, sure if I shou'd live to be rid of my Wife, I shou'd be a miserable Man.

Mrs. *Mar.* Ay!

Fain. For having only that one Hope, the accomplishment of it, of Consequence must put an end to all my Hopes; and what a Wretch is he who must survive his Hopes! Nothing remains when that Day comes, but to sit down and weep like *Alexander,* when he wanted other Worlds to conquer.

Mrs. *Mar.* Will you not follow 'em?

Fain. Faith, I think not.

Mrs. *Mar.* Pray let us; I have a Reason.

Fain. You are not Jealous?

Mrs. *Mar.* Of whom?

Fain. Of *Mirabell.*

Mrs. *Mar.* If I am, is it inconsistent with my Love to you that I am tender of your Honour?

Fain. You wou'd intimate then, as if there were a fellow-feeling between my Wife and him.

Mrs. *Mar.* I think she does not hate him to that degree she wou'd be thought.

Fain. But he, I fear, is too Insensible.

Mrs. *Mar.* It may be you are deceiv'd.

Fain. It may be so. I do not now begin to apprehend it.

Mrs. *Mar.* What?

Fain. That I have been deceiv'd, Madam, and you are false.

Mrs. *Mar.* That I am false! What mean you?

Fain. To let you know I see through all your little Arts——Come, you both love him; and both have equally dissembl'd your Aversion. Your mutual Jealousies of one another have made you clash 'till you have both struck Fire. I have seen the warm Confession red'ning on your Cheeks, and sparkling from your Eyes.

Mrs. *Mar.* You do me wrong.

Fain. I do not——'Twas for my ease to oversee and wilfully neglect the gross Advances made him by my Wife; that by permitting her to be engag'd, I might continue unsuspected in my Pleasures; and take you oftner to my Arms in full Security. But cou'd you think, because the nodding Husband wou'd not wake, that e'er the watchful Lover slept?

Mrs. *Mar.* And wherewithal can you reproach me?

Fain. With Infidelity, with loving another, with Love of *Mirabell.*

Mrs. *Mar.* 'Tis false. I challenge you to shew an Instance that can confirm your groundless Accusation. I hate him.

Fain. And wherefore do you hate him? He is insensible, and your Resentment follows his Neglect. An Instance! The Injuries you have done him are a Proof: Your interposing in his Love. What cause had you to make Discoveries of his pretended Passion? To undeceive the credulous Aunt, and be the officious Obstacle of his Match with *Millamant?*

Mrs. *Mar.* My Obligations to my Lady urg'd me: I had profess'd a Friendship to her; and cou'd not see her easie Nature so abus'd by that Dissembler.

Fain. What, was it Conscience then? Profess'd a Friendship! O the pious Friendships of the Female Sex!

Mrs. *Mar.* More tender, more sincere, and more enduring, than all the vain and empty Vows of Men, whether professing Love to us, or mutual Faith to one another.

Fain. Ha, ha, ha; you are my Wife's Friend too.

Mrs. *Mar.* Shame and Ingratitude! Do you reproach me? You, you upbraid me! Have I been false to her, thro' strict Fidelity to you, and sacrific'd my Friendship to keep my Love inviolate? And have you the Baseness to charge me with the Guilt, unmindful of the Merit! To you it shou'd be meritorious, that I have been vicious: And do you reflect that Guilt upon me, which shou'd lie buried in your Bosom?

Fain. You misinterpret my Reproof. I meant but to remind you of the slight Account you once cou'd make of strictest Ties, when set in Competition with your Love to me.

Mrs. Mar. 'Tis false, you urg'd it with deliberate Malice——'Twas spoke in scorn, and I never will forgive it.

Fain. Your Guilt, not your Resentment, begets your Rage. If yet you lov'd, you cou'd forgive a Jealousie: But you are stung to find you are discover'd.

Mrs. Mar. It shall be all discover'd. You too shall be discover'd; be sure you shall. I can but be expos'd——If I do it my self I shall prevent your Baseness.

Fain. Why, what will you do?

Mrs. Mar. Disclose it to your Wife; own what has past between us.

Fain. Frenzy!

Mrs. Mar. By all my Wrongs I'll do't——I'll publish to the World the Injuries you have done me, both in my Fame and Fortune: With both I trusted you, you Bankrupt in Honour, as indigent of Wealth.

Fain. Your Fame I have preserv'd. Your Fortune has been bestow'd as the Prodigality of your Love would have it, in Pleasures which we both have shar'd. Yet, had not you been false, I had e'er this repaid it——'Tis true—— had you permitted *Mirabell* with *Millamant* to have stoll'n their Marriage, my Lady had been incens'd beyond all Means of Reconcilement: *Millamant* had forfeited the Moiety of her Fortune; which then wou'd have descended to my Wife;——And wherefore did I marry, but to make lawful Prize of a rich Widow's Wealth, and squander it on Love and you?

Mrs. Mar. Deceit and frivolous Pretence.

Fain. Death, am I not married? What's Pretence? Am I not imprison'd, fetter'd? Have I not a Wife? Nay a Wife that was a Widow, a young Widow, a handsome Widow; and wou'd be again a Widow, but that I have a Heart of Proof, and something of a Constitution to bustle thro' the ways of Wedlock and this World. Will you yet be reconcil'd to Truth and me?

Mrs. Mar. Impossible. Truth and you are inconsistent——I hate you, and shall for ever.

Fain. For loving you?

Mrs. Mar. I loath the Name of Love after such Usage; and next to the Guilt with which you wou'd asperse me, I scorn you most. Farewel.

Fain. Nay, we must not part thus.

Mrs. Mar. Let me go.

Fain. Come, I'm sorry.

Mrs. Mar. I care not——Let me go——Break my Hands, do——I'd leave 'em to get loose.

Fain. I wou'd not hurt you for the World. Have I no other Hold to keep you here?

Mrs. Mar. Well, I have deserv'd it all.

Fain. You know I love you.

Mrs. *Mar.* Poor dissembling!——O that——Well, it is not yet——

Fain. What? What is it not? What is it not yet? It is not yet too late——

Mrs. *Mar.* No, it is not yet too late—I have that Comfort.

Fain. It is, to love another.

Mrs. *Mar.* But not to loath, detest, abhor Mankind, my self and the whole treacherous World.

Fain. Nay, this is Extravagance——Come, I ask your Pardon——No Tears—I was to blame, I cou'd not love you and be easie in my Doubts——Pray forbear——I believe you; I'm convinc'd I've done you wrong; and any way, ev'ry way will make amends;——I'll hate my Wife yet more, Damn her, I'll part with her, rob her of all she's worth, and we'll retire somewhere, any where, to another World, I'll marry thee——Be pacify'd——'Sdeath they come, hide your Face, your Tears——You have a Mask, wear it a moment. This way, this way, be persuaded.

SCENE IV.

Mirabell *and* Mrs. Fainall.

Mrs. *Fain.* They are here yet.

Mira. They are turning into the other Walk.

Mrs. *Fain.* While I only hated my Husband, I cou'd bear to see him; but since I have despis'd him, he's too offensive.

Mira. O you shou'd hate with Prudence.

Mrs. *Fain.* Yes, for I have lov'd with Indiscretion.

Mira. You shou'd have just so much Disgust for your Husband, as may be sufficient to make you relish your Lover.

Mrs. *Fain.* You have been the Cause that I have lov'd without Bounds, and wou'd you set Limits to that Aversion, of which you have been the Occasion? Why did you make me marry this Man?

Mira. Why do we daily commit disagreeable and dangerous Actions? To save that Idol Reputation. If the Familiarities of our Loves had produc'd that Consequence, of which you were apprehensive, where cou'd you have fix'd a Father's Name with Credit, but on a Husband? I knew *Fainall* to be a Man lavish of his Morals, an interested and professing Friend, a false and a designing Lover; yet one whose Wit and outward fair Behaviour, have gain'd a Reputation with the Town, enough to make that Woman stand excus'd, who has suffer'd her self to be won by his Addresses. A better Man ought not to have been sacrific'd to the Occasion; a worse had not answer'd to the Purpose. When you are weary of him, you know your Remedy.

Mrs. *Fain.* I ought to stand in some Degree of Credit with you, *Mirabell*.

Mira. In Justice to you, I have made you privy to my whole Design, and put it in your Pow'r to ruin or advance my Fortune.

Mrs. *Fain.* Whom have you instructed to represent your pretended Uncle?

Mira. Waitwell, my Servant.

Mrs. *Fain*. He is an humble Servant to *Foible* my Mother's Woman, and may win her to your Interest.

Mira. Care is taken for that——She is won and worn by this time. They were married this Morning.

Mrs. *Fain*. Who?

Mira. Waitwell and *Foible*. I wou'd not tempt my Servant to betray me by trusting him too far. If your Mother, in hopes to ruin me, shou'd consent to marry my pretended Uncle, he might, like *Mosca* in the *Fox*, stand upon Terms; so I made him sure before-hand.

Mrs. *Fain*. So, if my poor Mother is caught in a Contract, you will discover the Imposture betimes; and release her by producing a Certificate of her Gallant's former Marriage.

Mira. Yes, upon Condition that she consent to my Marriage with her Neice, and surrender the Moiety of her Fortune in her Possession.

Mrs. *Fain*. She talk'd last Night of endeavouring at a Match between *Millamant* and your Uncle.

Mira. That was by *Foible's* Direction, and my Instruction, that she might seem to carry it more privately.

Mrs. *Fain*. Well, I have an Opinion of your Success; for I believe my Lady will do any thing to get an Husband; and when she has this, which you have provided for her, I suppose she will submit to any thing to get rid of him.

Mira. Yes, I think the good Lady wou'd marry any thing that resembl'd a Man, though 'twere no more than what a Butler could pinch out of a Napkin.

Mrs. *Fain*. Female Frailty! We must all come to it, if we live to be Old, and feel the craving of a false Appetite when the true is decay'd.

Mira. An old Woman's Appetite is deprav'd like that of a Girl——'Tis the Green-Sickness of a second Childhood; and like the faint Offer of a latter Spring, serves but to usher in the Fall; and withers in an affected Bloom.

Mrs. *Fain*. Here's your Mistress.

SCENE V.

[*To them*] Mrs. MILLAMANT, WITWOUD, MINCING.

Mira. Here she comes i'faith full Sail, with her Fan spread and Streamers out, and a Shoal of Fools for Tenders——Ha, no, I cry her Mercy.

Mrs. *Fain*. I see but one poor empty Sculler; and he tows her Woman after him.

Mira. You seem to be unattended, Madam,——You us'd to have the *Beaumond* Throng after you; and a Flock of gay fine Perukes hovering round you.

Wit. Like Moths about a Candle——I had like to have lost my Comparison for want of Breath.

Milla. O I have deny'd my self Airs to Day. I have walk'd as fast through the Croud——

Wit. As a Favourite just disgrac'd; and with as few Followers.

Milla. Dear Mr. *Witwoud*, Truce with your Similitudes: For I am as Sick of 'em—

Wit. As a Physician of a good Air——I cannot help it, Madam, tho' 'tis against my self.

Milla. Yet again! *Mincing*, stand between me and his Wit.

Wit. Do, Mrs. *Mincing*, like a Skreen before a great Fire. I confess I do blaze to Day, I am too bright.

Mrs. Fain. But dear *Millamant*, why were you so long?

Milla. Long! Lord, have I not made violent haste? I have ask'd every living Thing I met for you; I have enquir'd after you, as after a new Fashion.

Wit. Madam, Truce with your Similitudes——No, you met her Husband, and did not ask him for her.

Mira. By your leave *Witwoud*, that were like enquiring after an old Fashion, to ask a Husband for his Wife.

Wit. Hum, a hit, a hit, a palpable hit, I confess it.

Mrs. Fain. You were dress'd before I came abroad.

Milla. Ay, that's true——O but then I had——*Mincing*, what had I? Why was I so long?

Minc. O Mem, your Laship staid to peruse a Pacquet of Letters.

Milla. O ay, Letters——I had Letters——I am persecuted with Letters——I hate Letters——No Body knows how to write Letters; and yet one has 'em, one does not know why——They serve one to pin up one's Hair.

Wit. Is that the way? Pray, Madam, do you pin up your Hair with all your Letters; I find I must keep Copies.

Milla. Only with those in Verse, Mr. *Witwoud*. I never pin up my Hair with Prose. I think I try'd once, *Mincing*.

Minc. O Mem, I shall never forget it.

Milla. Ay, poor *Mincing* tift and tift all the Morning.

Minc. 'Till I had the Cramp in my Fingers, I'll vow Mem. And all to no purpose. But when your Laship pins it up with Poetry, it sits so pleasant the next Day as any Thing, and is so pure and so crips.

Wit. Indeed, so crips?

Minc. You're such a Critick, Mr. *Witwoud*.

Milla. *Mirabell*, Did you take Exceptions last Night? O ay, and went away ——Now I think on't I'm angry——No, now I think on't I'm pleas'd——For I believe I gave you some Pain.

Mira. Does that please you?

Milla. Infinitely; I love to give Pain.

Mira. You wou'd affect a Cruelty which is not in your Nature; your true Vanity is in the Power of pleasing.

Milla. O I ask your Pardon for that—One's Cruelty is one's Power, and when one parts with one's Cruelty, one parts with one's Power; and when one has parted with that, I fancy one's old and ugly.

Mira. Ay, ay, suffer your Cruelty to ruin the Object of your Power, to destroy your Lover—And then how vain, how lost a Thing you'll be? Nay, 'tis true: You are no longer handsome when you've lost your Lover; your Beauty dies upon the Instant: For Beauty is the Lover's Gift; 'tis he bestows your Charms——Your Glass is all a Cheat. The Ugly and the Old, whom the Looking-glass mortifies, yet after Commendation can be flatter'd by it, and discover Beauties in it: For that reflects our Praises, rather than your Face.

Milla. O the Vanity of these Men! *Fainall,* d'ye hear him? If they did not commend us, we were not handsome! Now you must know they cou'd not commend one, if one was not handsome. Beauty the Lover's Gift——Lord, what is a Lover, that it can give? Why one makes Lovers as fast as one pleases, and they live as long as one pleases, and they die as soon as one pleases: And then if one pleases one makes more.

Wit. Very pretty. Why you make no more of making of Lovers, Madam, than of making so many Card-matches.

Milla. One no more owes one's Beauty to a Lover, than one's Wit to an Eccho: They can but reflect what we look and say; vain empty Things if we are silent or unseen, and want a Being.

Mira. Yet, to those two vain empty Things, you owe two of the greatest Pleasures of your Life.

Milla. How so?

Mira. To your Lover you owe the Pleasure of hearing your selves prais'd; and to an Eccho the Pleasure of hearing your selves talk.

Wit. But I know a Lady that loves Talking so incessantly, she won't give an Eccho fair play; she has that everlasting Rotation of Tongue, that an Eccho must wait 'till she dies, before it can catch her last Words.

Milla. O Fiction; *Fainall,* let us leave these Men.

Mira. Draw off *Witwoud.*   [*Aside to Mrs.* Fainall.

Mrs. Fain. Immediately; I have a Word or two for Mr. *Witwoud.*

SCENE VI.

MILLAMANT, MIRABELL, MINCING

Mira. I wou'd beg a little private Audience too——You had the Tyranny to deny me last Night; tho' you knew I came to impart a Secret to you that concern'd my Love.

Milla. You saw I was engag'd.

Mira. Unkind. You had the leisure to entertain a Herd of Fools; Things who visit you from their excessive Idleness; bestowing on your Easiness that Time, which is the Incumbrance of their Lives. How can you find Delight in such Society? It is impossible they shou'd admire you, they are not capable: Or if they were, it shou'd be to you as a Mortification; for sure to please a Fool is some degree of Folly.

Milla. I please my self——Besides, sometimes to converse with Fools is for my Health.

Mira. Your Health! Is there a worse Disease than the Conversation of Fools?

Milla. Yes, the Vapours; Fools are Physick for it, next to *Assa-fœtida.*

Mira. You are not in a Course of Fools?

Milla. Mirabell, if you persist in this offensive Freedom—you'll displease me——I think I must resolve after all, not to have you——We shan't agree.

Mira. Not in our Physick it may be.

Milla. And yet our Distemper in all likelihood will be the same; for we shall be sick of one another. I shan't endure to be reprimanded, nor instructed; 'tis so dull to act always by Advice, and so tedious to be told of one's Faults——I can't bear it. Well, I won't have you *Mirabell*——I'm resolv'd —I think——You may go—Ha, ha, ha. What wou'd you give, that you cou'd help loving me?

Mira. I wou'd give something that you did not know, I cou'd not help it.

Milla. Come, don't look grave then. Well, what do you say to me?

Mira. I say that a Man may as soon make a Friend by his Wit, or a Fortune by his Honesty, as win a Woman with Plain-dealing and Sincerity.

Milla. Sententious *Mirabell!* Prithee don't look with that violent and inflexible wise Face, like *Solomon* at the dividing of the Child in an old Tapestry Hanging.

Mira. You are merry, Madam, but I would persuade you for a Moment to be serious.

Milla. What, with that Face? No, if you keep your Countenance, 'tis impossible I shou'd hold mine. Well, after all, there is something very moving in a Lovesick Face. Ha, ha, ha——Well I won't laugh, don't be peevish—— Heigho! Now I'll be melancholy, as melancholy as a Watchlight. Well *Mirabell,* if ever you will win me woo me now——Nay, if you are so tedious, fare you well;——I see they are walking away.

Mira. Can you not find in the variety of your Disposition one Moment——

Milla. To hear you tell me *Foible's* Marry'd, and your Plot like to speed ——No.

Mira. But how you came to know it——

Milla. Without the help of the Devil, you can't imagine; unless she should tell me her self. Which of the two it may have been, I will leave you to consider; and when you have done thinking of that, think of me.

SCENE VII.

MIRABELL *alone.*

Mira. I have something more——Gone——Think of you! To think of a Whirlwind, tho' 'twere in a Whirlwind, were a Case of more steady Contemplation; a very Tranquility of Mind and Mansion. A Fellow that lives in a Windmill, has not a more whimsical Dwelling than the Heart of a Man that is lodg'd in a Woman. There is no Point of the Compass to which they cannot turn, and by which they are not turn'd; and by one as well as another; for Motion not Method is their Occupation. To know this, and yet continue to be in Love, is to be made wise from the Dictates of Reason, and yet persevere to play the Fool by the force of Instinct.——O here come my Pair of Turtles,——What, billing so sweetly! Is not *Valentine's* Day over with you yet?

SCENE VIII.

[*To him*] Waitwell, Foible.

Mira. Sirrah, *Waitwell,* why sure you think you were marry'd for your own Recreation, and not for my Conveniency.

Wait. Your Pardon, Sir. With Submission, we have indeed been solacing in lawful Delights; but still with an Eye to Business, Sir. I have instructed her as well as I could. If she can take your Directions as readily as my Instructions, Sir, your Affairs are in a prosperous way.

Mira. Give you Joy, Mrs. *Foible.*

Foib. O-las, Sir, I'm so asham'd——I'm afraid my Lady has been in a Thousand Inquietudes for me. But I protest, Sir, I made as much haste as I could.

Wait. That she did indeed, Sir. It was my Fault that she did not make more.

Mira. That I believe.

Foib. But I told my Lady as you instructed me, Sir. That I had a prospect of seeing Sir *Rowland* your Uncle; and that I wou'd put her Ladiship's Picture in my Pocket to shew him; which I'll be sure to say has made him so enamour'd of her Beauty, that he burns with Impatience to lye at her Ladiship's Feet and worship the Original.

Mira. Excellent *Foible!* Matrimony has made you eloquent in Love.

Wait. I think she has profited, Sir. I think so.

Foib. You have seen Madam *Millamant,* Sir?

Mira. Yes.

Foib. I told her, Sir, because I did not know that you might find an Opportunity; she had so much Company last Night.

Mira. Your Diligence will merit more—In the mean time— [*Gives Mony.*

Foib. O dear Sir, your humble Servant.

Wait. Spouse.

Mira. Stand off Sir, not a Penny——Go on and prosper, *Foible*——The Lease shall be made good and the Farm stock'd, if we succeed.

Foib. I don't question your Generosity, Sir: And you need not doubt of Success. If you have no more Commands, Sir, I'll be gone; I'm sure my Lady is at her Toilet, and can't dress 'till I come.——O dear, I'm sure that [*looking out*] was Mrs. *Marwood* that went by in a Mask; if she has seen

me with you I'm sure she'll tell my Lady. I'll make haste home and prevent
her. Your Servant Sir. B'w'y *Waitwell.*

SCENE IX.

MIRABELL, WAITWELL.

Wait. Sir *Rowland* if you please. The Jade's so pert upon her Preferment
she forgets her self.

Mira. Come Sir, will you endeavour to forget your self——and transform
into Sir *Rowland.*

Wait. Why Sir; it will be impossible I shou'd remember my self——
Marry'd, Knighted and attended all in one Day! 'Tis enough to make any
Man forget himself. The Difficulty will be how to recover my Acquaintance
and Familiarity with my former self; and fall from my Transformation to
a Reformation into *Waitwell.* Nay, I shan't be quite the same *Waitwell*
neither——for now I remember me, I'm marry'd, and can't be my own Man
again.

> *Ay there's my Grief; that's the sad Change of Life;*
> *To lose my Title, and yet keep my Wife.*

End of the Second Act.

ACT III.

SCENE I.—*A Room in Lady* Wishfort's *House.*

Lady WISHFORT *at her Toilet,* PEG *waiting.*

Lady. Merciful, no news of *Foible* yet?

Peg. No, Madam.

Lady. I have no more Patience—If I have not fretted my self 'till I am
pale again, there's no Veracity in me. Fetch me the Red——the Red, do you
hear, Sweet-heart? An errant Ash colour, as I'm a Person. Look you how
this Wench stirs! Why dost thou not fetch me a little Red? Didst thou not
hear me, Mopus?

Peg. The red *Ratafia* does your Ladiship mean, or the Cherry-Brandy?

Lady. Ratafia, Fool. No, Fool. Not the *Ratafia,* Fool——Grant me Patience!
I mean the *Spanish* Paper, Idiot, Complexion Darling. Paint, Paint, Paint,
dost thou understand that, Changeling, dangling thy Hands like Bobbins
before thee? Why dost thou not stir, Puppet? thou wooden Thing upon
Wires.

Peg. Lord, Madam, your Ladiship is so impatient——I cannot come at the
Paint, Madam, Mrs. *Foible* has lock'd it up, and carry'd the Key with her.

Lady. A Pox take you both—Fetch me the Cherry-Brandy then.

SCENE II.

Lady. I'm as pale and as faint, I look like Mrs. *Qualmsick* the Curate's Wife that's always breeding—Wench, come, come, Wench, what art thou doing, Sipping? Tasting? Save thee, dost thou not know the Bottle?

SCENE III.

Lady WISHFORT, PEG *with a Bottle and China Cup.*

Peg. Madam, I was looking for a Cup.

Lady. A Cup, save thee, and what a Cup hast thou brought! Dost thou take me for a *Fairy,* to drink out of an *Acorn?* Why didst thou not bring thy Thimble? Hast thou ne'er a Brass-Thimble clinking in thy Pocket with a bit of Nutmeg? I warrant thee. Come, fill, fill.——So——again. See who that is——[*One knocks.*] Set down the Bottle first. Here, here, under the Table ——What, wou'dst thou go with the Bottle in thy Hand like a Tapster. As I'm a Person, this Wench has liv'd in an Inn upon the Road, before she came to me, like *Maritornes* the *Asturian* in *Don Quixote.* No *Foible* yet?

Peg. No Madam, Mrs. *Marwood.*

Lady. O *Marwood,* let her come in. Come in good *Marwood.*

SCENE IV.

[*To them*] *Mrs.* MARWOOD.

Mrs. Mar. I'm surpriz'd to find your Ladiship in *dishabillé* at this time of Day.

Lady. Foible's a lost Thing; has been abroad since Morning, and never heard of since.

Mrs. Mar. I saw her but now, as I came mask'd through the Park, in Conference with *Mirabell.*

Lady. With *Mirabell!* You call my Blood into my Face, with mentioning that Traitor. She durst not have the Confidence. I sent her to negotiate an Affair, in which if I'm detected I'm undone. If that wheadling Villain has wrought upon *Foible* to detect me, I'm ruin'd. Oh my dear Friend, I'm a Wretch of Wretches if I'm detected.

Mrs. Mar. O Madam, you cannot suspect Mrs. *Foible's* Integrity.

Lady. O, he carries Poison in his Tongue that wou'd corrupt Integrity it self. If she has given him an Opportunity, she has as good as put her Integrity into his Hands. Ah dear *Marwood,* what's Integrity to an Opportunity?——Hark! I hear her——Dear Friend retire into my Closet, that I may examine her with more Freedom——You'll pardon me, dear Friend, I can make bold with you——There are Books over the Chimney——*Quarles* and *Pryn*, and the *Short View of the Stage*, with *Bunyan's* Works to entertain you.——Go, you Thing, and send her in.   [*To* Peg.

SCENE V.

Lady WISHFORT, FOIBLE.

Lady. O *Foible*, where hast thou been? what hast thou been doing?

Foib. Madam, I have seen the Party.

Lady. But what hast thou done?

Foib. Nay, 'tis your Ladiship has done, and are to do; I have only promis'd. But a Man so enamour'd——so transported! Well, if worshipping of Pictures be a Sin——Poor Sir *Rowland*, I say.

Lady. The Miniature has been counted like——But hast thou not betray'd me, *Foible?* Hast thou not detected me to that faithless *Mirabell?*——What hadst thou to do with him in the Park? Answer me, has he got nothing out of thee?

Foib. So, the Devil has been beforehand with me, what shall I say?—— Alas, Madam, cou'd I help it, if I met that confident Thing? Was I in Fault? If you had heard how he us'd me, and all upon your Ladiship's Account, I'm sure you wou'd not suspect my Fidelity. Nay, if that had been the worst I cou'd have born: But he had a Fling at your Ladiship too; and then I cou'd not hold: But i'faith I gave him his own.

Lady. Me? What did the filthy Fellow say?

Foib. O Madam; 'tis a Shame to say what he said——With his Taunts and his Fleers, tossing up his Nose. Humh (says he) what you are a hatching some Plot (says he) you are so early abroad, or Catering (says he) ferreting for some disbanded Officer, I warrant——Half Pay is but thin Subsistance (says he)——Well, what Pension does your Lady propose? Let me see (says he) what she must come down pretty deep now, she's superannuated (says he) and——

Lady. Ods my Life, I'll have him, I'll have him murder'd. I'll have him poison'd. Where does he eat? I'll marry a Drawer to have him poison'd in his Wine. I'll send for *Robin* and *Lockets*–Immediately.

Foib. Poison him? Poisoning's too good for him. Starve him, Madam, starve him; marry Sir *Rowland*, and get him disinherited. O you wou'd bless your self, to hear what he said.

Lady. A Villain, superannuated!

Foib. Humh (says he) I hear you are laying Designs against me too (says he) and Mrs. *Millamant* is to marry my Uncle (he does not suspect a Word of your Ladiship;) but (says he) I'll fit you for that, I warrant you (says he) I'll hamper you for that (says he) you and your old Frippery too (says he) I'll handle you–

Lady. Audacious Villain! handle me, wou'd he durst——Frippery? old Frippery! Was there ever such a foul-mouth'd Fellow? I'll be marry'd to Morrow, I'll be contracted to Night.

Foib. The sooner the better, Madam.

Lady. Will Sir *Rowland* be here, say'st thou? when, *Foible?*

Foib. Incontinently, Madam. No new Sheriff's Wife expects the Return of her Husband after Knighthood, with that Impatience in which Sir *Rowland* burns for the dear Hour of kissing your Ladiship's Hand after Dinner.

Lady. Frippery! superannuated Frippery! I'll Frippery the Villain; I'll reduce him to Frippery and Rags: A Tatterdemallion——I hope to see him hung with Tatters, like a *Long-Lane* Penthouse, or a Gibbet-Thief. A slander-mouth'd Railer: I warrant the Spendthrift Prodigal's in Debt as much as the Million Lottery, or the whole Court upon a Birth-Day. I'll spoil his Credit with his Tailor. Yes, he shall have my Neice with her Fortune, he shall.

Foib. He! I hope to see him lodge in *Ludgate* first, and angle into *Black-Fryars* for Brass Farthings, with an old Mitten.

Lady. Ay dear *Foible;* thank thee for that, dear *Foible.* He has put me out of all Patience. I shall never recompose my Features, to receive Sir *Rowland* with any Oeconomy of Face. This Wretch has fretted me that I am absolutely decay'd. Look *Foible.*

Foib. Your Ladiship has frown'd a little too rashly, indeed Madam. There are some Cracks discernable in the white Vernish.

Lady. Let me see the Glass—Cracks, say'st thou? Why I am arrantly flea'd —I look like an old peel'd Wall. Thou must repair me, *Foible,* before Sir *Rowland* comes; or I shall never keep up to my Picture.

Foib. I warrant you, Madam; a little Art once made your Picture like you; and now a little of the same Art must make you like your Picture. Your Picture must sit for you, Madam.

Lady. But art thou sure Sir *Rowland* will not fail to come? Or will a not fail when he does come? Will he be Importunate, *Foible,* and push? For if he shou'd not be importunate–I shall never break Decorums——I shall die with Confusion, if I am forc'd to advance——Oh no, I can never advance——I shall swoon if he should expect Advances. No, I hope Sir *Rowland* is better bred, than to put a Lady to the Necessity of breaking her forms. I won't be too coy neither.——I won't give him Despair——But a little Disdain is not amiss; a little Scorn is alluring.

Foib. A little Scorn becomes your Ladiship.

Lady. Yes, but Tenderness becomes me best——A sort of Dyingness—— You see that Picture has a sort of a——Ha *Foible?* A Swimmingness in the Eyes——Yes, I'll look so——My Neice affects it; but she wants Features. Is Sir *Rowland* handsome? Let my Toilet be remov'd—I'll dress above. I'll receive Sir *Rowland* here. Is he handsome? Don't answer me. I won't know: I'll be surpriz'd. I'll be taken by Surprize.

Foib. By Storm, Madam. Sir *Rowland's* a brisk Man.

Lady. Is he! O then he'll importune, if he's a brisk Man. I shall save

Decorums if Sir *Rowland* importunes. I have a mortal Terror at the Apprehension of offending against Decorums. O I'm glad he's a brisk Man. Let my Things be remov'd, good *Foible*.

SCENE VI.

Mrs. Fainall, Foible.

Mrs. Fain. O *Foible*, I have been in a Fright, lest I shou'd come too late. That Devil, *Marwood*, saw you in the Park with *Mirabell*, and I'm afraid will discover it to my Lady.

Foib. Discover what, Madam?

Mrs. Fain. Nay, nay, put not on that strange Face. I am privy to the whole Design, and know *Waitwell*, to whom thou wert this Morning marry'd, is to personate *Mirabell's* Uncle, and as such, winning my Lady, to involve her in those Difficulties from which *Mirabell* only must release her, by his making his Conditions to have my Cousin and her Fortune left to her own Disposal.

Foib. O dear Madam, I beg your Pardon. It was not my Confidence in your Ladiship that was deficient; but I thought the former good Correspondence between your Ladiship and Mr. *Mirabell*, might have hinder'd his communicating this Secret.

Mrs. Fain. Dear *Foible*, forget that.

Foib. O dear Madam, Mr. *Mirabell* is such a sweet winning Gentleman ——But your Ladiship is the Pattern of Generosity.——Sweet Lady, to be so good! Mr. *Mirabell* cannot chuse but to be grateful. I find your Ladiship has his Heart still. Now, Madam, I can safely tell your Ladiship our Success, Mrs. *Marwood* had told my Lady; but I warrant I manag'd my self. I turn'd it all for the better. I told my Lady that Mr. *Mirabell* rail'd at her. I laid horrid Things to his Charge, I'll vow; and my Lady is so incens'd, that she'll be contracted to Sir *Rowland* to Night, she says;——I warrant I work'd her up, that he may have her for asking for, as they say of a *Welsh* Maidenhead.

Mrs. Fain. O rare *Foible*!

Foib. Madam, I beg your Ladiship to acquaint Mr. *Mirabell* of his Success. I would be seen as little as possible to speak to him——besides, I believe Madam *Marwood* watches me.——She has a Month's Mind; but I know Mr. *Mirabell* can't abide her.——[*Calls.*] *John*—remove my Lady's Toilet. Madam, your Servant. My Lady is so impatient, I fear she'll come for me, if I stay.

Mrs. Fain. I'll go with you up the back Stairs, lest I shou'd meet her.

SCENE VII.

Mrs. MARWOOD alone.

Mrs. Mar. Indeed, Mrs. Engine, is it thus with you? Are you become a go-between of this Importance? Yes, I shall watch you. Why this Wench is the *Pass-par-toute*, a very Master-Key to every Body's strong Box. My Friend *Fainall*, have you carry'd it so swimmingly? I thought there was something in it; but it seems it's over with you. Your Loathing is not from a want of Appetite then, but from a Surfeit. Else you could never be so cool to fall from a Principal to be an Assistant; to procure for him! A Pattern of Generosity, that I confess. Well, Mr. *Fainall*, you have met with your Match.——O Man, Man! Woman, Woman! The Devil's an Ass: If I were a Painter, I would draw him like an Idiot, a Driveler with a Bib and Bells. Man shou'd have his Head and Horns, and Woman the rest of him. Poor simple Fiend! Madam *Marwood* has a Month's Mind, but he can't abide her ——'Twere better for him you had not been his Confessor in that Affair; without you could have kept his Counsel closer. I shall not prove another Pattern of Generosity——he has not oblig'd me to that with those Excesses of himself; and now I'll have none of him. Here comes the good Lady, panting ripe; with a Heart full of Hope, and a Head full of Care, like any Chymist upon the Day of Projection.

SCENE VIII.

[*To her*] Lady WISHFORT.

Lady. O dear *Marwood*, what shall I say for this rude Forgetfulness—— But my dear Friend is all Goodness.

Mrs. Mar. No Apologies, dear Madam. I have been very well entertain'd.

Lady. As I'm a Person I am in a very Chaos to think I shou'd so forget my self——But I have such an Olio of Affairs really I know not what to do——[*Calls.*]——Foible——I expect my Nephew Sir *Wilfull* ev'ry Moment too:—Why *Foible*——He means to travel for Improvement.

Mrs. Mar. Methinks Sir *Wilfull* shou'd rather think of marrying than travelling at his Years. I hear he is turn'd of forty.

Lady. O he's in less Danger of being spoil'd by his Travels——I am against my Nephew's marrying too Young. It will be time enough when he comes back, and has acquir'd Discretion to chuse for himself.

Mrs. Mar. Methinks Mrs. *Millamant* and he wou'd make a very fit Match. He may travel afterwards. 'Tis a Thing very usual with young Gentlemen.

Lady. I promise you I have thought on't——And since 'tis your Judgment, I'll think on't again. I assure you I will; I value your Judgment extreamly. On my Word I'll propose it.

SCENE IX.

[*To them*] FOIBLE.

Lady. Come, come *Foible*—I had forgot my Nephew will be here before
Dinner——I must make haste.

Foib. Mr. *Witwoud* and Mr. *Petulant* are come to dine with your Ladiship.

Lady. O Dear, I can't appear 'till I am dress'd. Dear *Marwood* shall I be
free with you again, and beg you to entertain 'em. I'll make all imaginable
haste. Dear Friend excuse me.

SCENE X.

Mrs. MARWOOD, Mrs. MILLAMANT, MINCING.

Milla. Sure never any thing was so Unbred as that odious Man.—*Marwood*,
your Servant.

Mrs. *Mar*. You have a Colour, what's the matter?

Milla. That horrid Fellow *Petulant* has provok'd me into a Flame——I have
broke my Fan——*Mincing*, lend me yours;——Is not all the Powder out of
my Hair?

Mrs. *Mar*. No. What has he done?

Milla. Nay, he has done nothing; he has only talk'd——Nay, he has said
nothing neither; but he has contradicted ev'ry Thing that has been said.
For my part, I thought *Witwoud* and he wou'd have quarrell'd.

Minc. I vow Mem, I thought once they wou'd have fitt.

Milla. Well, 'tis a lamentable thing I swear, that one has not the Liberty
of chusing one's Acquaintance as one does one's Cloaths.

Mrs. *Mar*. If we had that Liberty, we shou'd be as weary of one Set of
Acquaintance, tho' never so good, as we are of one Suit, tho' never so fine.
A Fool and a *Doily* Stuff wou'd now and then find Days of Grace, and be
worn for Variety.

Milla. I could consent to wear 'em, if they would wear alike; but Fools
never wear out——They are such *Drap-de-berry* Things! Without one
cou'd give 'em to one's Chamber-Maid after a Day or two.

Mrs. *Mar*. 'Twere better so indeed. Or what think you of the Play-house?
A fine gay glossy Fool shou'd be given there, like a new masking Habit,
after the Masquerade is over, and we have done with the Disguise. For a
Fool's Visit is always a Disguise; and never admitted by a Woman of Wit,
but to blind her Affair with a Lover of Sense. If you wou'd but appear
bare-fac'd now, and own *Mirabell;* you might as easily put off *Petulant* and
Witwoud, as your Hood and Scarf. And indeed 'tis time, for the Town has

found it: The Secret is grown too big for the Pretence: 'Tis like Mrs. *Primly's* great Belly; she may lace it down before, but it burnishes on her Hips. Indeed, *Millamant*, you can no more conceal it, than my Lady *Strammel* can her Face, that goodly Face, which in Defiance of her Rhenish-wine Tea, will not be comprehended in a Mask.

Milla. I'll take my Death, *Marwood*, you are more Censorious than a decay'd Beauty, or a discarded Toast; *Mincing*, tell the Men they may come up. My Aunt is not dressing here; their Folly is less provoking than your Malice.

SCENE XI.

MILLAMANT, MARWOOD.

Milla. The Town has found it. What has it found? That *Mirabell* loves me is no more a Secret, than it is a Secret that you discover'd it to my Aunt, or than the Reason why you discover'd it is a Secret.

Mrs. *Mar.* You are nettl'd.

Milla. You're mistaken. Ridiculous!

Mrs. *Mar.* Indeed, my Dear, you'll tear another Fan, if you don't mitigate those violent Airs.

Milla. O silly! Ha, ha, ha. I cou'd laugh immoderately. Poor *Mirabell!* His Constancy to me has quite destroy'd his Complaisance for all the World beside. I swear, I never enjoin'd it him, to be so coy——If I had the Vanity to think he wou'd obey me; I wou'd command him to shew more Gallantry ——'Tis hardly well bred to be so particular on one Hand, and so insensible on the other. But I despair to prevail, and so let him follow his own Way. Ha, ha, ha. Pardon me, dear Creature, I must laugh, ha, ha, ha; tho' I grant you 'tis a little barbarous, ha, ha, ha.

Mrs. *Mar.* What pity 'tis, so much fine Raillery, and deliver'd with so significant Gesture, shou'd be so unhappily directed to miscarry.

Milla. Hæ? Dear Creature I ask your Pardon——I swear I did not mind you.

Mrs. *Mar.* Mr. *Mirabell* and you both may think it a Thing impossible, when I shall tell him by telling you——

Milla. O dear, what? for it is the same thing, if I hear it——Ha, ha, ha.

Mrs. *Mar.* That I detest him, hate him, Madam.

Milla. O Madam, why so do I——And yet the Creature loves me, ha, ha, ha. How can one forbear laughing to think of it—I am a Sybil if I am not amaz'd to think what he can see in me. I'll take my Death, I think you are handsomer—and within a Year or two as young.——If you cou'd but stay for me, I shou'd overtake you——But that cannot be——Well, that Thought makes me melancholick——Now I'll be sad.

Mrs. *Mar.* Your merry Note may be chang'd sooner than you think.

Milla. D'ye say so? Then I'm resolv'd I'll have a Song to keep up my Spirits.

SCENE XII.

[*To them*] MINCING.

Minc. The Gentlemen stay but to Comb, Madam; and will wait on you.

Milla. Desire Mrs. —— that is in the next Room to sing the Song I wou'd have learnt Yesterday. You shall hear it, Madam——Not that there's any great Matter in it——But 'tis agreeable to my Humour.

SONG.

Set by Mr. JOHN ECCLES.

I.

Love's but the Frailty of the Mind,
When 'tis not with Ambition join'd;
A sickly Flame, which if not fed expires;
And feeding, wastes in Self-consuming Fires.

II.

'Tis not to wound a wanton Boy
Or am'rous Youth, that gives the Joy;
But 'tis the Glory to have pierc'd a Swain,
For whom inferior Beauties sigh'd in vain.

III.

Then I alone the Conquest prize,
When I insult a Rival's Eyes:
If there's Delight in Love, 'tis when I see
That Heart which others bleed for, bleed for me.

SCENE XIII.

[*To them*] PETULANT, WITWOUD.

Milla. Is your Animosity compos'd, Gentlemen?

Wit. Raillery, Raillery, Madam, we have no Animosity——We hit off a little Wit now and then, but no Animosity——The falling out of Wits is like the falling out of Lovers——We agree in the main, like Treble and Base. Ha, *Petulant!*

Pet. Ay in the main—But when I have a Humour to contradict——

Wit. Ay, when he has a Humour to contradict, then I contradict too. What, I know my Cue. Then we contradict one another like two Battledores; For Contradictions beget one another like *Jews.*

Pet. If he says Black's Black—If I have a Humour to say 'tis Blue——Let that pass——All's one for that. If I have a Humour to prove it, it must be granted.

Wit. Not positively must—But it may—It may.

Pet. Yes, it positively must, upon Proof positive.

Wit. Ay, upon Proof positive it must; but upon Proof presumptive it only may. That's a Logical Distinction now, Madam.

Mrs. Mar. I perceive your Debates are of Importance, and very learnedly handled.

Pet. Importance is one Thing, and Learning's another; but a Debate's a Debate, that I assert.

Wit. *Petulant's* an Enemy to Learning; he relies altogether on his Parts.

Pet. No, I'm no Enemy to Learning; it hurts not me.

Mrs. Mar. That's a Sign indeed it's no Enemy to you.

Pet. No, no, it's no Enemy to any Body, but them that have it.

Milla. Well, an illiterate Man's my Aversion, I wonder at the Impudence of any illiterate Man, to offer to make Love.

Wit. That I confess I wonder at too.

Milla. Ah! to marry an Ignorant! that can hardly Read or Write.

Pet. Why should a Man be any further from being Marry'd tho' he can't read, than he is from being Hang'd. The Ordinary's paid for setting the *Psalm,* and the Parish-Priest for reading the Ceremony. And for the rest which is to follow in both Cases, a Man may do it without Book——So all's one for that.

Milla. D'ye hear the Creature? Lord, here's Company, I'll be gone.

SCENE XIV.

Sir WILFULL WITWOUD *in a riding Dress, Mrs.* MARWOOD, PETULANT, WITWOUD, FOOTMAN.

Wit. In the Name of *Bartlemew* and his Fair, what have we here?

Mrs. Mar. 'Tis your Brother, I fancy. Don't you know him?

Wit. Not I—Yes, I think it is he—I've almost forgot him; I have not seen him since the Revolution.

Foot. Sir, my Lady's dressing. Here's Company; if you please to walk in, in the mean time.

Sir Wil. Dressing! What, it's but Morning here I warrant with you in *London;* we shou'd count it towards Afternoon in our Parts, down in *Shropshire*—Why then belike my Aunt han't din'd yet——Ha, Friend?

Foot. Your Aunt, Sir?

Sir Wil. My Aunt, Sir, yes my Aunt, Sir, and your Lady, Sir; your Lady is my Aunt, Sir——Why, what do'st thou not know me, Friend? Why then send some Body hither that does. How long hast thou liv'd with thy Lady, Fellow, ha?

Foot. A Week, Sir; longer than any Body in the House, except my Lady's Woman.

Sir *Wil.* Why then belike thou do'st not know thy Lady, if thou see'st her, ha Friend?

Foot. Why truly Sir, I cannot safely swear to her Face in a Morning, before she is dress'd. 'Tis like I may give a shrewd guess at her by this time.

Sir *Wil.* Well, prithee try what thou canst do; if thou canst not guess, enquire her out, do'st hear, Fellow? And tell her, her Nephew, Sir *Wilfull Witwoud*, is in the House.

Foot. I shall, Sir.

Sir *Wil.* Hold ye, hear me, Friend; a Word with you in your Ear, prithee who are these Gallants?

Foot. Really, Sir, I can't tell; here come so many here, 'tis hard to know 'em all.

SCENE XV.

Sir WILFULL WITWOUD, PETULANT, WITWOUD, *Mrs.* MARWOOD.

Sir *Wil.* Oons this Fellow knows less than a Starling; I don't think a'knows his own Name.

Mrs. *Mar.* Mr. *Witwoud*, your Brother is not behind hand in Forget-fulness——I fancy he has forgot you too.

Wit. I hope so——The Devil take him that remembers first, I say.

Sir *Wil.* Save you Gentlemen and Lady.

Mrs. *Mar.* For shame, Mr. *Witwoud*; why don't you speak to him?—— And you, Sir.

Wit. Petulant speak.

Pet. And you, Sir.

Sir *Wil.* No Offence, I hope.

[*Salutes* Marwood.

Mrs. *Mar.* No sure, Sir.

Wit. This is a vile Dog, I see that already. No Offence! Ha, ha, ha, to him; to him, *Petulant*, smoke him.

Pet. It seems as if you had come a Journey, Sir; hem, hem.

[*Surveying him round.*

Sir *Wil.* Very likely, Sir, that it may seem so.

Pet. No Offence, I hope, Sir.

Wit. Smoke the Boots, the Boots; *Petulant*, the Boots; Ha, ha, ha.

Sir *Wil.* May be not, Sir; thereafter as 'tis meant, Sir.

Pet. Sir, I presume upon the Information of your Boots.

Sir *Wil.* Why, 'tis like you may, Sir: If you are not satisfy'd with the Information of my Boots, Sir, if you will step to the Stable, you may en-quire further of my Horse, Sir.

Pet. Your Horse, Sir! Your Horse is an Ass, Sir!

Sir *Wil.* Do you speak by way of Offence, Sir?

Mrs. Mar. The Gentleman's merry, that's all, Sir——'Slife, we shall have a Quarrel betwixt an Horse and an Ass, before they find one another out. You must not take any thing amiss from your Friends, Sir. You are among your Friends, here, tho' it may be you don't know it—If I am not mistaken, you are Sir *Wilfull Witwoud*.

Sir Wil. Right Lady; I am Sir *Wilfull Witwoud*, so I write my self; no Offence to any Body, I hope; and Nephew to the Lady *Wishfort* of this Mansion.

Mrs. Mar. Don't you know this Gentleman, Sir?

Sir Wil. Hum! What, sure 'tis not—Yea by'r Lady, but 'tis—'Sheart I know not whether 'tis or no——Yea but 'tis, by the *Wrekin*. Brother *Antony!* What *Tony*, i'faith! What do'st thou not know me? By'r Lady nor I thee, thou art so Becravated, and so Beperriwig'd—'Sheart why do'st not speak? Art thou o'erjoy'd?

Wit. Odso Brother, is it you? Your Servant, Brother.

Sir Wil. Your Servant! Why yours, Sir. Your Servant again——'Sheart, and your Friend and Servant to that——And a——(*puff*) and a Flap Dragon for your Service, Sir: And a Hare's Foot, and a Hare's Scut for your Service, Sir; an you be so cold and so courtly!

Wit. No Offence, I hope, Brother.

Sir Wil. 'Sheart, Sir, but there is, and much Offence.——A Pox, is this your Inns o' Court Breeding, not to know your Friends and your Relations, your Elders, and your Betters?

Wit. Why, Brother *Wilfull of Salop*, you may be as short as a *Shrewsbury* Cake, if you please. But I tell you 'tis not modish to know Relations in Town. You think you're in the Country, where great lubberly Brothers slabber and kiss one another when they meet, like a Call of Serjeants—— 'Tis not the Fashion here; 'tis not indeed, dear Brother.

Sir Wil. The Fashion's a Fool; and you're a Fop, dear Brother. 'Sheart, I've suspected this——By'r Lady I conjectur'd you were a Fop, since you began to change the Stile of your Letters, and write in a scrap of Paper gilt round the Edges, no bigger than a *Subpœna*. I might expect this when you left off Honour'd Brother; and hoping you are in good Health, and so forth——To begin with a Rat me, Knight, I'm so sick of a last Night's Debauch——Ods Heart, and then tell a familiar Tale of a Cock and a Bull, and a Whore and a Bottle, and so conclude——You cou'd write News before you were out of your Time, when you liv'd with honest *Pumple-Nose* the Attorney of *Furnival's* Inn——You cou'd intreat to be remember'd then to your Friends round the *Wrekin*. We could have Gazettes then, and *Dawks's* Letter, and the Weekly Bill, 'till of late Days.

Pet. 'Slife, *Witwoud*, were you ever an Attorney's Clerk? Of the Family of the *Furnivals*. Ha, ha, ha!

Wit. Ay, ay, but that was but for a while. Not long, not long; pshaw, I was not in my own Power then. An Orphan, and this Fellow was my Guardian; ay, ay, I was glad to consent to that Man to come to *London*. He had the Disposal of me then. If I had not agreed to that, I might have

been bound Prentice to a Felt-maker in *Shrewsbury;* this Fellow would
have bound me to a Maker of Felts.

Sir *Wil.* 'Sheart, and better than to be bound to a Maker of Fops; where,
I suppose, you have serv'd your Time; and now you may set up for your
self.

Mrs. *Mar.* You intend to Travel, Sir, as I'm inform'd.

Sir *Wil.* Belike I may, Madam. I may chance to sail upon the salt Seas,
if my Mind hold.

Pet. And the Wind serve.

Sir *Wil.* Serve or not serve, I shan't ask License of you, Sir; nor the
Weather-Cock your Companion. I direct my Discourse to the Lady, Sir;
'Tis like my Aunt may have told you, Madam——Yes, I have settl'd my
Concerns, I may say now, and am minded to see Foreign Parts. If an how
that the Peace holds, whereby that is Taxes abate.

Mrs. *Mar.* I thought you had designed for *France* at all Adventures.

Sir *Wil.* I can't tell that; 'tis like I may, and 'tis like I may not. I am somewhat dainty in making a Resolution,——because when I make it I keep it. I
don't stand shill I, shall I, then; if I say't, I'll do't: But I have Thoughts to
tarry a small matter in Town, to learn somewhat of your *Lingo* first, before
I cross the Seas. I'd gladly have a spice of your *French* as they say, whereby
to hold Discourse in Foreign Countries.

Mrs. *Mar.* Here's an Academy in Town for that use.

Sir *Wil.* There is? 'Tis like there may.

Mrs. *Mar.* No doubt you will return very much improv'd.

Wit. Yes, refin'd like a *Dutch* Skipper from a Whale-fishing.

SCENE XVI.

[*To them*] *Lady* WISHFORT *and* FAINALL.

Lady. Nephew, you are welcome.

Sir *Wil.* Aunt, your Servant.

Fain. Sir *Wilfull*, your most faithful Servant.

Sir *Wil.* Cousin *Fainall*, give me your Hand.

Lady. Cousin *Witwoud*, your Servant; Mr. *Petulant*, your Servant——
Nephew, you are welcome again. Will you drink any Thing after your
Journey, Nephew, before you eat? Dinner's almost ready.

Sir *Wil.* I'm very well I thank you, Aunt——However, I thank you for
your courteous Offer. 'Sheart I was afraid you wou'd have been in the
Fashion too, and have remember'd to have forgot your Relations. Here's
your Cousin *Tony*, belike, I mayn't call him Brother for fear of Offence.

Lady. O he's a Rallier, Nephew——My Cousin's a Wit: And your great
Wits always rally their best Friends to chuse. When you have been Abroad,
Nephew, you'll understand Raillery better.

[*Fain. and Mrs.* Marwood *talk apart.*

Sir *Wil.* Why then let him hold his Tongue in the mean Time; and rail when that Day comes.

SCENE XVII.

[*To them*] MINCING.

Minc. Mem, I come to acquaint your Laship that Dinner is impatient.

Sir *Wil.* Impatient? Why then belike it won't stay 'till I pull off my Boots. Sweet-heart, can you help me to a pair of Slippers?——My Man's with his Horses, I warrant.

Lady. Fie, fie, Nephew, you wou'd not pull off your Boots here——Go down into the Hall——Dinner shall stay for you——My Nephew's a little unbred, you'll pardon him, Madam,——Gentlemen will you walk? *Marwood?*

Mrs. *Mar.* I'll follow you, Madam,——Before Sir *Wilfull* is ready.

SCENE XVIII.

MARWOOD, FAINALL.

Fain. Why then *Foible's* a Bawd, an Errant, Rank, Matchmaking Bawd. And I it seems am a Husband, a Rank-Husband; and my Wife a very Errant, Rank-Wife,—all in the Way of the *World.* 'Sdeath to be a Cuckold by Anticipation, a Cuckold in Embrio? Sure I was born with budding Antlers like a young Satyr, or a Citizen's Child. 'Sdeath to be Out-witted, to be Out-jilted——Out-Matrimony'd,——If I had kept my Speed like a Stag, 'twere somewhat,——but to crawl after, with my Horns like a Snail, and be out-stripp'd by my Wife—'tis Scurvy Wedlock.

Mrs. *Mar.* Then shake it off, you have often wish'd for an Opportunity to part;——and now you have it. But first prevent their Plot,——the half of *Millamant's* Fortune is too considerable to be parted with, to a Foe, to *Mirabell.*

Fain. Dam him, that had been mine——had you not made that fond Discovery——That had been forfeited, had they been Married. My Wife had added Lustre to my Horns, by that Encrease of Fortune, I cou'd have worn 'em tipt with Gold, tho' my Forehead had been furnish'd like a Deputy-Lieutenant's-Hall.

Mrs. *Mar.* They may prove a Cap of Maintenance to you still, if you can away with your Wife. And she's no worse than when you had her—I dare swear she had given up her Game, before she was Marry'd.

Fain. Hum! That may be——

Mrs. *Mar.* You Married her to keep you; and if you can contrive to have her keep you better than you expected; why should you not keep her longer than you intended?

Fain. The Means, the Means.

Mrs. Mar. Discover to my Lady your Wife's Conduct; threaten to part with her——My Lady loves her, and will come to any Composition to save her Reputation. Take the Opportunity of breaking it, just upon the Discovery of this Imposture. My Lady will be enrag'd beyond Bounds, and sacrifice Neice, and Fortune, and all at that Conjuncture. And let me alone to keep her warm; if she shou'd flag in her part, I will not fail to prompt her.

Fain. Faith this has an Appearance.

Mrs. Mar. I'm sorry I hinted to my Lady to endeavour a Match between *Millamant* and Sir *Wilfull*, that may be an Obstacle.

Fain. O for that matter leave me to manage him; I'll disable him for that, he will drink like a *Dane:* after Dinner, I'll set his Hand in.

Mrs. Mar. Well, how do you stand affected towards your Lady?

Fain. Why faith I'm thinking of it.——Let me see——I am Marry'd already; so that's over—My Wife has plaid the Jade with me—Well, that's over too—I never lov'd her, or if I had, why that wou'd have been over too by this time—Jealous of her I cannot be, for I am certain; so there's an end of Jealousie. Weary of her, I am and shall be——No, there's no end of that; No, no, that were too much to·hope. Thus far concerning my Repose. Now for my Reputation,——As to my own, I Marry'd not for it; so that's out of the Question.——And as to my Part in my Wife's——Why she had parted with hers before; so bringing none to me, she can take none from me; 'tis against all rule of Play, that I should lose to one, who has not wherewithal to stake.

Mrs. Mar. Besides you forget, Marriage is honourable.

Fain. Hum! Faith and that's well thought on; Marriage is honourable, as you say; and if so, wherefore should Cuckoldom be a Discredit, being deriv'd from so honourable a Root?

Mrs. Mar. Nay I know not; if the Root be honourable, why not the Branches?

Fain. So, so, why this Point's clear.——Well, how do we proceed?

Mrs. Mar. I will contrive a Letter which shall be deliver'd to my Lady at the time when that Rascal who is to act Sir *Rowland* is with her. It shall come as from an unknown Hand——for the less I appear to know of the Truth, the better I can play the Incendiary. Besides, I wou'd not have *Foible* provok'd if I cou'd help it,——because you know she knows some Passages ——Nay I expect all will come out——But let the Mine be sprung first, and then I care not if I am discover'd.

Fain. If the worst come to the worst,——I'll turn my Wife to Grass——I have already a Deed of Settlement of the best part of her Estate; which I wheadl'd out of her; and that you shall partake at least.

Mrs. Mar. I hope you are convinc'd that I hate *Mirabell* now: You'll be no more Jealous?

Fain. Jealous, no,——by this Kiss——let Husbands be Jealous; but let the Lover still believe: Or if he doubt, let it be only to endear his Pleasure, and prepare the Joy that follows, when he proves his Mistress true. But let Husbands Doubts convert to endless Jealousie; or if they have Belief, let it corrupt to Superstition, and blind Credulity. I am single, and will herd no more with 'em. True, I wear the Badge, but I'll disown the Order. And since I take my Leave of 'em, I care not if I leave 'em a common Motto to their common Crest.

All Husbands must, or Pain, or Shame, endure;
The Wise too jealous are, Fools too secure.

End of the Third Act.

ACT IV.

SCENE I.—SCENE *Continues*.

Lady WISHFORT *and* FOIBLE.

Lady. Is Sir *Rowland* coming say'st thou, *Foible?* and are things in Order?

Foib. Yes, Madam. I have put Wax-Lights in the Sconces; and plac'd the Footmen in a Row in the Hall, in their best Liveries, with the Coachman and Postilion to fill up the Equipage.

Lady. Have you pullvill'd the Coachman and Postilion, that they may not stink of the Stable, when Sir *Rowland* comes by?

Foib. Yes, Madam.

Lady. And are the Dancers and the Musick ready, that he may be entertain'd in all Points with Correspondence to his Passion?

Foib. All is ready, Madam.

Lady. And——well——and how do I look, *Foible?*

Foib. Most killing well, Madam.

Lady. Well, and how shall I receive him? In what Figure shall I give his Heart the first Impression? There is a great deal in the first Impression. Shall I sit?——No, I won't sit——I'll walk——ay I'll walk from the Door upon his Entrance; and then turn full upon him——No, that will be too sudden. I'll lye——ay, I'll lye down—I'll receive him in my little Dressing-Room, there's a Couch—Yes, yes, I'll give the first Impression on a Couch——I won't lye neither, but loll and lean upon one Elbow; with one Foot a little dangling off, jogging in a thoughtful way—Yes—and then as soon as he appears, start, ay, start and be surpriz'd, and rise to meet him in a pretty Disorder—Yes—O, nothing is more alluring than a Levee from a Couch in some Confusion—It shews the Foot to advantage, and furnishes with Blushes, and recomposing Airs beyond Comparison. Hark! There's a Coach.

Foib. 'Tis he, Madam.

Lady. O dear, has my Nephew made his Addresses to *Millamant?* I order'd him.

Foib. Sir *Wilfull* is set in to Drinking, Madam, in the Parlour.

Lady. Ods my Life, I'll send him to her. Call her down, *Foible;* bring her hither. I'll send him as I go——When they are together, then come to me *Foible*, that I may not be too long alone with Sir *Rowland*.

SCENE II.

Mrs. Millamant, *Mrs.* Fainall, Foible.

Foib. Madam, I stay'd here, to tell your Ladiship that Mr. *Mirabell* has waited this half Hour for an Opportunity to talk with you. Tho' my Lady's Orders were to leave you and Sir *Wilfull* together. Shall I tell Mr. *Mirabell* that you are at leisure?

Milla. No——What wou'd the dear Man have? I am thoughtful, and wou'd amuse my self,——bid him come another time.

> *There never yet was Woman made,*
> *Nor shall, but to be curs'd.*
>
> [*Repeating and walking about.*

That's hard!

Mrs. Fain. You are very fond of Sir *John Suckling* to day, *Millamant,* and the Poets.

Milla. He? Ay, and filthy Verses——So I am.

Foib. Sir *Wilfull* is coming, Madam. Shall I send Mr. *Mirabell* away?

Milla. Ay, if you please, *Foible,* send him away,–Or send him hither,– just as you will, dear *Foible.*——I think I'll see him——Shall I? Ay, let the Wretch come.

> *Thyrsis, a Youth of the Inspir'd Train.*
>
> [*Repeating.*

Dear *Fainall,* entertain Sir *Wilfull*——Thou hast Philosophy to undergo a Fool, thou art marry'd and hast Patience——I would confer with my own Thoughts.

Mrs. Fain. I am oblig'd to you, that you would make me your Proxy in this Affair; but I have Business of my own.

SCENE III.

[*To them*] *Sir* Wilfull.

Mrs. Fain. O Sir *Wilfull;* you are come at the Critical Instant. There's your Mistress up to the Ears in Love and Contemplation, pursue your Point, now or never.

Sir Wil. Yes; my Aunt will have it so,——I would gladly have been en- courag'd with a Bottle or two, because ⎰ *This while* Milla. *walks about* I'm somewhat wary at first, before ⎱ *repeating to her self.* I am acquainted;–But I hope, after a time, I shall break my Mind——that is upon further Acquaintance——So for the present, Cousin, I'll take my leave——If so be you'll be so kind to make my Excuse, I'll return to my Company——

Mrs. Fain. O fie, Sir *Wilfull!* What, you must not be daunted.

Sir *Wil.* Daunted, no, that's not it, it is not so much for that——for if so be that I set on't, I'll do't. But only for the present, 'tis sufficient 'till further Acquaintance, that's all——your Servant.

Mrs. *Fain.* Nay, I'll swear you shall never lose so favourable an Opportunity, if I can help it. I'll leave you together, and lock the Door.

SCENE IV.

Sir WILFULL, MILLAMANT.

Sir *Wil.* Nay, nay Cousin,——I have forgot my Gloves,——What d'ye do? 'Sheart a'has lock'd the Door indeed, I think——Nay, Cousin *Fainall*, open the Door—Pshaw, what a Vixon Trick is this?——Nay, now a'has seen me too——Cousin, I made bold to pass thro' as it were——I think this Door's inchanted——

Milla. [*repeating.*]
  I prithee spare me, gentle Boy,
  Press me no more for that slight Toy.

Sir *Wil.* Anan? Cousin, your Servant.

Milla.—*That foolish Trifle of a Heart*——Sir *Wilfull!*

Sir *Wil.* Yes——your Servant. No Offence I hope, Cousin.

Milla. [*Repeating.*]
  I swear it will not do its Part,
Tho' thou dost thine, employ'st thy Power and Art.
Natural, easie *Suckling!*

Sir *Wil.* Anan? *Suckling?* No such Suckling neither, Cousin, nor Stripling: I thank Heav'n I'm no Minor.

Milla. Ah Rustick, ruder than *Gothick*.

Sir *Wil.* Well, well, I shall understand your *Lingo* one of these Days, Cousin, in the mean while I must answer in plain *English*.

Milla. Have you any Business with me, Sir *Wilfull?*

Sir *Wil.* Not at present, Cousin,——Yes, I made bold to see, to come and know if that how you were dispos'd to fetch a Walk this Evening, if so be that I might not be troublesome, I would have sought a Walk with you.

Milla. A Walk? What then?

Sir *Wil.* Nay nothing——Only for the Walk's sake, that's all——

Milla. I nauseate Walking; 'tis a Country Diversion, I loath the Country and every thing that relates to it.

Sir *Wil.* Indeed! Hah! Look ye, look ye, you do? Nay, 'tis like you may ——Here are choice of Pastimes here in Town, as Plays and the like, that must be confess'd indeed.——

Milla. Ah l'etourdie! I hate the Town too.

Sir *Wil.* Dear Heart, that's much——Hah! that you should hate 'em both! Hah! 'tis like you may; there are some can't relish the Town, and others can't away with the Country,——'tis like you may be one of those, Cousin.

Milla. Ha, ha, ha. Yes, 'tis like I may.——You have nothing further to say to me?

Sir *Wil.* Not at present, Cousin.—'Tis like when I have an Opportunity to be more private,—I may break my Mind in some measure—I conjecture you partly guess—However that's as time shall try,—But spare to speak and spare to speed, as they say.

Milla. If it is of no great Importance, Sir *Wilfull*, you will oblige me to leave me: I have just now a little Business.—

Sir *Wil.* Enough, enough, Cousin: Yes, yes, all a case—When you're dispos'd, when you're dispos'd. Now's as well as another time; and another time as well as now. All's one for that,—Yes, yes, if your Concerns call you, there's no haste; it will keep cold as they say—Cousin, your Servant.——I think this Door's lock'd.

Milla. You may go this way, Sir.

Sir *Wil.* Your Servant, then with your leave I'll return to my Company.

Milla. Ay, ay; ha, ha, ha.

Like Phœbus *sung the no less am'rous Boy.*

SCENE V.

Millamant, Mirabell.

Mira.—Like Daphne *she, as Lovely and as Coy.* Do you lock your self up from me, to make my Search more curious? Or is this pretty Artifice contriv'd, to signifie that here the Chace must end, and my Pursuit be crown'd, for you can fly no further?—

Milla. Vanity! No——I'll fly and be follow'd to the last Moment, tho' I am upon the very Verge of Matrimony, I expect you should sollicit me as much as if I were wavering at the Grate of a Monastery, with one Foot over the Threshold. I'll be sollicited to the very last, nay and afterwards.

Mira. What, after the last?

Milla. O, I should think I was poor and had nothing to bestow, if I were reduc'd to an inglorious Ease; and freed from the agreeable Fatigues of Sollicitation.

Mira. But do not you know, that when Favours are conferr'd upon instant and tedious Sollicitation, that they diminish in their Value, and that both the Giver loses the Grace, and the Receiver lessens his Pleasure?

Milla. It may be in Things of common Application; but never sure in Love. O, I hate a Lover, that can dare to think he draws a Moment's Air, independent on the Bounty of his Mistress. There is not so impudent a Thing in Nature, as the sawcy Look of an assured Man, confident of Success. The Pedantick Arrogance of a very Husband, has not so Pragmatical an Air. Ah! I'll never marry, unless I am first made sure of my Will and Pleasure.

Mira. Would you have 'em both before Marriage? Or will you be contented with the first now, and stay for the other 'till after Grace?

Milla. Ah don't be impertinent—My dear Liberty, shall I leave thee? My faithful Solitude, my darling Contemplation, must I bid you then Adieu? Ay-h adieu—My Morning Thoughts, agreeable Wakings, indolent Slumbers, all ye *douceurs*, ye *Someils du Matin*, adieu—I can't do't, 'tis more than impossible—Positively *Mirabell*, I'll lye a-bed in a Morning as long as I please.

Mira. Then I'll get up in a Morning as early as I please.

Milla. Ah! Idle Creature, get up when you will——And d'ye hear, I won't be call'd Names after I'm Marry'd; positively I won't be call'd Names.

Mira. Names!

Milla. Ay, as Wife, Spouse, my Dear, Joy, Jewel, Love, Sweet-heart, and the rest of that nauseous Cant, in which Men and their Wives are so fulsomly familiar,——I shall never bear that——Good *Mirabell* don't let us be familiar or fond, nor kiss before Folks, like my Lady *Fadler* and Sir *Francis:* Nor go to *Hide-Park* together the first *Sunday* in a new Chariot, to provoke Eyes and Whispers; And then never be seen there together again; as if we were proud of one another the first Week, and asham'd of one another ever after. Let us never Visit together, nor go to a Play together, but let us be very strange and well bred: Let us be as strange as if we had been marry'd a great while; and as well bred as if we were not marry'd at all.

Mira. Have you any more Conditions to offer? Hitherto your Demands are pretty reasonable.

Milla. Trifles,——As Liberty to pay and receive Visits to and from whom I please; to write and receive Letters, without Interrogatories or wry Faces on your part; to wear what I please; and chuse Conversation with regard only to my own Taste; to have no Obligation upon me to converse with Wits that I don't like, because they are your Acquaintance; or to be intimate with Fools, because they may be your Relations. Come to Dinner when I please, dine in my Dressing-Room when I'm out of Humour, without giving a Reason. To have my Closet inviolate; to be sole Empress of my Tea-Table, which you must never presume to approach without first asking leave. And lastly where-ever I am, you shall always knock at the Door before you come in. These Articles subscrib'd, if I continue to endure you a little longer, I may by degrees dwindle into a Wife.

Mira. Your Bill of Fare is something advanc'd in this latter Account. Well, have I Liberty to offer Conditions——That when you are dwindled into a Wife, I may not be beyond measure enlarg'd into a Husband.

Milla. You have free leave, propose your utmost, speak and spare not.

Mira. I thank you. *Inprimis* then, I covenant that your Acquaintance be general; that you admit no sworn Confident, or Intimate of your own Sex; no she Friend to skreen her Affairs under your Countenance, and tempt you to make Trial of a mutual Secresie. No Decoy-Duck to wheadle you a *fop* —*scrambling* to the Play in a Mask——Then bring you home in a pretended Fright, when you think you shall be found out—And rail at me for missing the Play, and disappointing the Frolick which you had to pick me up and prove my Constancy.

Milla. Detestable *Inprimis!* I go to the Play in a Mask!

Mira. *Item,* I Article, that you continue to like your own Face, as long as I shall: And while it passes currant with me, that you endeavour not to new Coin it. To which end, together with all Vizards for the Day, I prohibit all Masks for the Night, made of Oil'd-skins and I know not what——Hog's Bones, Hare's Gall, Pig Water, and the Marrow of a roasted Cat. In short, I forbid all Commerce with the Gentlewoman in *what-d'ye-call-it* Court. *Item,* I shut my Doors against all Bauds with Baskets, and penny-worths of *Muslin, China, Fans, Atlasses,* &c.——*Item,* when you shall be Breeding——

Milla. Ah! Name it not.

Mira. Which may be presum'd, with a Blessing on our Endeavours——

Milla. Odious Endeavours!

Mira. I denounce against all strait Lacing, squeezing for a Shape, 'till you mould my Boy's Head like a Sugar-loaf; and instead of a Man-Child, make me Father to a Crooked-billet. Lastly, to the Dominion of the *Tea-Table* I submit.——But with *proviso,* that you exceed not in your Province; but restrain your self to native and simple *Tea-Table* Drinks, as *Tea, Chocolate,* and *Coffee.* As likewise to Genuine and Authoriz'd *Tea-Table* Talk——Such as mending of Fashions, spoiling Reputations, railing at absent Friends, and so forth——But that on no Account you encroach upon the Mens Prerogative, and presume to drink Healths, or toast Fellows; for prevention of which, I banish all *Foreign Forces,* all Auxiliaries to the *Tea-Table,* as *Orange-Brandy,* all *Anniseed, Cinamon, Citron,* and *Barbado's-Waters,* together with *Ratafia* and the most noble Spirit of *Clary.*——But for *Couslip-Wine, Poppy-Water,* and all *Dormitives,* those I allow.——These *Proviso's* admitted, in other things I may prove a tractable and complying Husband.

Milla. O horrid *Proviso's!* filthy strong Waters! I toast Fellows, Odious Men! I hate your odious *Proviso's.*

Mira. Then we're agreed. Shall I kiss your Hand upon the Contract? and here comes one to be a Witness to the Sealing of the Deed.

SCENE VI.

[*To them*] Mrs. FAINALL.

Milla. Fainall, what shall I do? Shall I have him? I think I must have him.

Mrs. *Fain.* Ay, ay, take him, take him, what shou'd you do?

Milla. Well then—I'll take my Death I'm in a horrid Fright——*Fainall,* I shall never say it——Well——I think——I'll endure you.

Mrs. *Fain.* Fy, fy, have him, have him, and tell him so in plain Terms: For I am sure you have a Mind to him.

Milla. Are you? I think I have——and the horrid Man looks as if he thought so too——Well, you ridiculous thing you, I'll have you——I won't be kiss'd, nor I won't be thank'd——Here kiss my Hand tho'——So, hold your Tongue now, don't say a Word.

Mrs. *Fain. Mirabell,* there's a Necessity for your Obedience;——You have neither time to talk nor stay. My Mother is coming; and in my Conscience if she shou'd see you, wou'd fall into Fits, and may be not recover, time enough to return to Sir *Rowland;* who, as *Foible* tells me, is in a fair Way to succeed. Therefore spare your Extacies for another Occasion, and slip down the back Stairs, where *Foible* waits to consult you.

Milla. Ay, go, go. In the mean time I suppose you have said something to please me.

Mira. I am all Obedience.

SCENE VII.

MILLAMANT, *Mrs.* FAINALL.

Mrs. Fain. Yonder Sir *Wilfull's* drunk; and so noisie that my Mother has been forc'd to leave Sir *Rowland* to appease him; but he answers her only with Singing and Drinking——What they may have done by this time I know not; but *Petulant* and he were upon quarrelling as I came by.

Milla. Well, If *Mirabell* should not make a good Husband, I am a lost thing;——for I find I love him violently.

Mrs. Fain. So it seems; for you mind not what's said to you.——If you doubt him, you had best take up with Sir *Wilfull.*

Milla. How can you name that superannuated Lubber? foh!

SCENE VIII.

[*To them*] WITWOUD *from drinking.*

Mrs. Fain. So, is the Fray made up, that you have left 'em?

Wit. Left 'em? I could stay no longer——I have laugh'd like ten Christnings ——I am tipsie with laughing——If I had staid any longer I should have burst, ——I must have been let out and piec'd in the Sides like an unsiz'd Camlet—— Yes, yes, the Fray is compos'd; my Lady came in like a *Noli prosequi,* and stopt the Proceedings.

Milla. What was the Dispute?

Wit. That's the Jest; there was no Dispute. They could neither of 'em speak for Rage; and so fell a sputt'ring at one another like two roasting Apples.

SCENE IX.

[*To them*] PETULANT *Drunk.*

Wit. Now *Petulant?* all's over, all's well? Gad my Head begins to whim it about——Why dost thou not speak? thou art both as drunk and as mute as a Fish.

Pet. Look you, Mrs. *Millamant*——if you can love me, dear Nymph—say it—and that's the Conclusion—pass on, or pass off,——that's all.

Wit. Thou hast utter'd *Volumes, Folios,* in less than *Decimo Sexto,* my dear *Lacedemonian.* Sirrah, *Petulant,* thou art an Epitomizer of Words.

Pet. Witwoud——You are an Annihilator of Sense.

Wit. Thou art a Retailer of Phrases; and dost deal in Remnants of Remnants, like a Maker of Pincushions—thou art in truth (metaphorically speaking) a Speaker of Short-hand.

Pet. Thou art (without a Figure) just one half of an Ass, and *Baldwin* yonder, thy half Brother, is the rest—A *Gemini* of Asses split, would make just four of you.

Wit. Thou dost bite, my dear Mustard-seed; kiss me for that.

Pet. Stand off——I'll kiss no more Males,——I have kiss'd your *Twin* yonder in a humour of Reconciliation, 'till he (*hiccup*) rises upon my Stomach like a Radish.

Milla. Eh! filthy Creature—what was the Quarrel?

Pet. There was no Quarrel—there might have been a Quarrel.

Wit. If there had been Words enow between 'em to have express'd Provocation, they had gone together by the Ears like a pair of Castanets.

Pet. You were the Quarrel.

Milla. Me!

Pet. If I have a Humour to quarrel, I can make less Matters conclude Premises,—If you are not handsom, what then; If I have a Humour to prove it?—If I shall have my Reward, say so; if not, fight for your Face the next time your self—I'll go sleep.

Wit. Do, wrap thy self up like a *Woodlouse,* and dream Revenge—And hear me, if thou canst learn to write by to Morrow Morning, pen me a Challenge—I'll carry it for thee.

Pet. Carry your Mistress's *Monkey* a *Spider,*——go flea Dogs, and read Romances——I'll go to Bed to my Maid.

Mrs. Fain. He's horridly Drunk——how came you all in this Pickle?

Wit. A Plot, a Plot, to get rid of the Knight,——Your Husband's Advice; but he sneak'd off.

SCENE X.

Sir WILFULL *Drunk, Lady* WISHFORT, WITWOUD, MILLAMANT, *Mrs.* FAINALL.

Lady. Out upon't, out upon't, at Years of Discretion, and comport your self at this Rantipole rate.

Sir Wil. No Offence, Aunt.

Lady. Offence? As I'm a Person, I'm asham'd of you——Fogh! how you stink of Wine! D'ye think my Neice will ever endure such a *Borachio!* you're an absolute *Borachio.*

Sir *Wil. Borachio!*

Lady. At a time when you shou'd commence an Amour, and put your best Foot foremost——

Sir *Wil.* 'Sheart, an you grutch me your Liquor, make a Bill——Give me more Drink, and take my Purse.

Sings.   *Prithee fill me the Glass*
            'Till it laugh in my Face,
      With Ale that is Potent and Mellow;
            He that whines for a Lass
            Is an ignorant Ass,
      For a Bumper has not its Fellow.

But if you wou'd have me marry my Cousin,——say the Word, and I'll do't——*Wilfull* will do't, that's the Word——*Wilfull* will do't, that's my Crest——my Motto I have forgot.

Lady. My Nephew's a little overtaken, Cousin——but 'tis with drinking your Health——O' my Word you are oblig'd to him——

Sir *Wil. In Vino Veritas,* Aunt:——If I drunk your Health to Day, Cousin, ——I am a *Borachio.* But if you have a Mind to be marry'd, say the Word, and send for the Piper, *Wilfull* will do't. If not, dust it away, and let's have t'other Round——*Tony,* Ods-heart where's *Tony——Tony's* an honest Fellow, but he spits after a Bumper, and that's a Fault.

Sings.   *We'll drink and we'll never ha' done Boys,*
            Put the Glass then around with the Sun Boys,
      Let Apollo's Example invite us;
            For he's drunk ev'ry Night,
            And that makes him so bright,
      That he's able next Morning to light us.

The Sun's a good Pimple, an honest Soaker, he has a Cellar at your *Antipodes.* If I travel, Aunt, I touch at your *Antipodes*——your *Antipodes* are a good rascally sort of topsie turvy Fellows——If I had a Bumper I'd stand upon my Head and drink a Health to 'em——A Match or no Match, Cousin, with the hard Name——Aunt, *Wilfull* will do't. If she has her Maidenhead let her look to't; if she has not, let her keep her own Counsel in the mean time, and cry out at the Nine Months End.

Milla. Your Pardon, Madam, I can stay no longer——Sir *Wilfull* grows very powerful, Egh! how he smells; I shall be overcome if I stay. Come, Cousin.

SCENE XI.

Lady WISHFORT, *Sir* WILFULL WITWOUD, *Mr.* WITWOUD, FOIBLE.

Lady. Smells! he would poison a Tallow-Chandler and his Family. Beastly Creature, I know not what to do with him.——Travel quoth a; ay travel,

travel, get thee gone, get thee but far enough, to the *Saracens*, or the *Tartars*, or the *Turks*——for thou art not fit to live in a Christian Commonwealth, thou beastly Pagan.

Sir *Wil*. *Turks*, no; no *Turks*, Aunt: Your *Turks* are Infidels, and believe not in the Grape. Your *Mahometan*, your *Mussulman* is a dry Stinkard—— No Offence, Aunt. My Map says that your *Turk* is not so honest a Man as your Christian——I cannot find by the Map that your *Mufti* is Orthodox—— Whereby it is a plain Case, that Orthodox is a hard Word, Aunt, and (*hiccup*) Greek for Claret.

Sings.   *To Drink is a Christian Diversion.*
          Unknown to the Turk *or the* Persian:
              Let Mahometan *Fools*
              Live by Heathenish Rules,
          And be damn'd over Tea-Cups and Coffee.
              But let British *Lads sing,*
              Crown a Health to the King,
          And a Fig for your Sultan *and* Sophy.

Ah, *Tony!*   [Foible *whispers Lady* W.
   Lady. Sir *Rowland* impatient? Good lack! what shall I do with this beastly Tumbril?——Go lie down and sleep, you Sot——Or as I'm a Person, I'll have you bastinado'd with Broom-sticks. Call up the Wenches with Broom-sticks.
   Sir *Wil*. Ahay? Wenches, where are the Wenches?
   Lady. Dear Cousin *Witwoud* get him away, and you will bind me to you inviolably. I have an Affair of moment that invades me with some Precipitation——You will oblige me to all Futurity.
   Wit. Come, Knight——Pox on him, I don't know what to say to him—— Will you go to a Cock-match?
   Sir *Wil*. With a Wench, *Tony?* Is she a shake-bag, Sirrah? Let me bite your Cheek for that.
   Wit. Horrible! He has a Breath like a Bagpipe—Ay, ay, come will you march, my *Salopian?*
   Sir *Wil*. Lead on, little *Tony*——I'll follow thee my *Anthony*, my *Tantony*, Sirrah thou shalt be my *Tantony*, and I'll be thy *Pig*.

——*And a Fig for your* Sultan *and* Sophy.

   Lady. This will never do. It will never make a Match.——At least before he has been abroad.

SCENE XII.

Lady WISHFORT, WAITWELL *disguis'd as for Sir* ROWLAND.

   Lady. Dear Sir *Rowland*, I am confounded with Confusion at the Retrospection of my own Rudeness,——I have more Pardons to ask than the *Pope* distributes in the Year of *Jubile*. But I hope where there is likely to be so near an Alliance,——we may unbend the Severity of *Decorum*——and dispense with a little Ceremony.

Wait. My Impatience, Madam, is the Effect of my Transport;——and 'till I have the Possession of your adorable Person, I am tantaliz'd on the Rack; and do but hang, Madam, on the Tenter of Expectation.

Lady. You have Excess of Gallantry, Sir *Rowland;* and press things to a Conclusion, with a most prevailing Vehemence.——But a Day or two for Decency of Marriage.——

Wait. For Decency of Funeral, Madam. The Delay will break my Heart— or if that should fail, I shall be Poison'd. My Nephew will get an inkling of my Designs, and poison me,—and I would willingly starve him before I die ——I would gladly go out of the World with that Satisfaction.—That would be some Comfort to me, if I could but live so long as to be reveng'd on that unnatural Viper.

Lady. Is he so unnatural, say you? Truly I would contribute much both to the saving of your Life, and the accomplishment of your Revenge——Not that I respect my self; tho' he has been a perfidious Wretch to me.

Wait. Perfidious to you!

Lady. O Sir *Rowland*, the Hours that he has dy'd away at my Feet, the Tears that he has shed, the Oaths that he has sworn, the Palpitations that he has felt, the Trances and the Tremblings, the Ardors and the Ecstacies, the Kneelings, and the Risings, the Heart-heavings and the Hand-gripings, the Pangs and the Pathetick Regards of his protesting Eyes! Oh no Memory can Register.

Wait. What, my Rival! Is the Rebel my Rival? a'dies.

Lady. No, don't kill him at once, Sir *Rowland,* starve him gradually Inch by Inch.

Wait. I'll do't. In three Weeks he shall be bare-foot; in a Month out at Knees with begging an Alms,——he shall starve upward and upward, 'till he has nothing living but his Head, and then go out in a Stink like a Candle's End upon a Saveall.

Lady. Well, Sir *Rowland*, you have the way,——You are no Novice in the Labyrinth of Love——You have the Clue——But as I am a Person, Sir *Rowland*, you must not attribute my yielding to any sinister Appetite, or Indigestion of Widowhood; nor impute my Complacency to any Lethargy of Continence——I hope you do not think me prone to any Iteration of Nuptials.——

Wait. Far be it from me——

Lady. If you do, I protest I must recede——or think that I have made a Prostitution of Decorums, but in the Vehemence of Compassion, and to save the Life of a Person of so much Importance——

Wait. I esteem it so——

Lady. Or else you wrong my Condescension——

Wait. I do not, I do not——

Lady. Indeed you do.

Wait. I do not, fair Shrine of Virtue.

Lady. If you think the least Scruple of Carnality was an Ingredient——
Wait. Dear Madam, no. You are all *Camphire* and *Frankincense*, all *Chastity* and *Odour*.
Lady. Or that——

SCENE XIII.

[*To them*] FOIBLE.

Foib. Madam, the Dancers are ready, and there's one with a Letter, who must deliver it into your own Hands.
Lady. Sir *Rowland*, will you give me leave? Think favourably, judge candidly, and conclude you have found a Person who would suffer Racks in Honour's Cause, dear Sir *Rowland*, and will wait on you incessantly.

SCENE XIV.

WAITWELL, FOIBLE.

Wait. Fie, fie!—What a Slavery have I undergone; Spouse, hast thou any *Cordial*, I want *Spirits*.
Foib. What a washy Rogue art thou, to pant thus for a Quarter of an Hours Lying and Swearing to a fine Lady?
Wait. O, she is the Antidote to Desire. Spouse, thou wilt fare the worse for't——I shall have no Appetite to Iteration of Nuptials——this eight and forty Hours——By this Hand I'd rather be a Chairman in the Dog-days—— than act Sir *Rowland* 'till this time to Morrow.

SCENE XV.

[*To them*] LADY *with a Letter.*

Lady. Call in the Dancers;——Sir *Rowland*, we'll sit, if you please, and see the Entertainment.   [*Dance.*
Now with your Permission, Sir *Rowland*, I will peruse my Letter—I would open it in your Presence, because I would not make you uneasie. If it should make you uneasie I would burn it——speak if it does——but you may see, the Superscription is like a Woman's Hand.
Foib. By Heav'n! Mrs. *Marwood's*, I know it,——my Heart akes——get it from her——   [*To him.*
Wait. A Woman's Hand? No, Madam, that's no Woman's Hand, I see that already. That's some Body whose Throat must be cut.
Lady. Nay, Sir *Rowland*, since you give me a Proof of your Passion by

your Jealousie, I promise you I'll make a Return, by a frank Communication ——You shall see it—we'll open it together——look you here.

Reads.——*Madam, though unknown to you,* [Look you there, 'tis from no Body that I know.]——*I have that Honour for your Character, that I think my self oblig'd to let you know you are abus'd. He who pretends to be Sir* Rowland *is a Cheat and a Rascal——*

Oh Heav'ns! what's this?

Foib. Unfortunate, all's ruin'd.

Wait. How, how, let me see, let me see——reading, *A Rascal and disguis'd, and suborn'd for that Imposture,*—O Villany! O Villany!——*by the Contrivance of——*

Lady. I shall faint, I shall die, oh!

Foib. Say, 'tis your Nephew's Hand.—Quickly, his Plot, swear, swear it.—
                                                            [*To him.*

Wait. Here's a Villain! Madam, don't you perceive it, don't you see it?

Lady. Too well, too well. I have seen too much.

Wait. I told you at first I knew the Hand—A Woman's Hand? The Rascal writes a sort of a large Hand; your *Roman* Hand—I saw there was a Throat to be cut presently. If he were my Son, as he is my Nephew, I'd pistol him—

Foib. O Treachery! But are you sure, Sir *Rowland*, it is his Writing?

Wait. Sure? Am I here? do I live? do I love this Pearl of *India?* I have twenty Letters in my Pocket from him, in the same Character.

Lady. How!

Foib. O what Luck it is, Sir *Rowland*, that you were present at this Juncture! This was the Business that brought Mr. *Mirabell* disguis'd to Madam *Millamant* this Afternoon. I thought something was contriving, when he stole by me and would have hid his Face.

Lady. How, how!—I heard the Villain was in the House indeed; and now I remember, my Neice went away abruptly, when Sir *Wilfull* was to have made his Addresses.

Foib. Then, then Madam, Mr. *Mirabell* waited for her in her Chamber; but I would not tell your Ladiship to discompose you when you were to receive Sir *Rowland*.

Wait. Enough, his Date is short.

Foib. No, good Sir *Rowland*, don't incur the Law.

Wait. Law! I care not for Law. I can but die, and 'tis in a good Cause—My Lady shall be satisfy'd of my Truth and Innocence, tho' it cost me my Life.

Lady. No, dear Sir *Rowland*, don't fight, if you should be kill'd I must never shew my Face; or hang'd,—O consider my Reputation, Sir *Rowland*— No you shan't fight,—I'll go and examine my Neice; I'll make her confess. I conjure you Sir *Rowland* by all your Love not to fight.

Wait. I am charm'd Madam, I obey. But some Proof you must let me give you;—I'll go for a black Box, which contains the Writings of my whole Estate, and deliver that into your Hands.

Lady. Ay dear Sir *Rowland*, that will be some Comfort, bring the black Box.

Wait. And may I presume to bring a Contract to be sign'd this Night? May I hope so far?

Lady. Bring what you will; but come alive, pray come alive. O this is a happy Discovery.

Wait. Dead or alive I'll come—and married we will be in spight of Treachery; ay and get an Heir that shall defeat the last remaining Glimpse of Hope in my abandon'd Nephew. Come, my Buxom Widow:

E'er long you shall substantial Proof receive
That I'm an arrant Knight——
Foib. Or arrant Knave.

End of the Fourth Act.

ACT V.

SCENE I.—SCENE *Continues.*

Lady WISHFORT *and* FOIBLE.

Lady. Out of my House, out of my House, thou *Viper,* thou *Serpent,* that I have foster'd; thou bosom Traitress, that I rais'd from nothing——Begone, begone, begone, go, go,——That I took from washing of old Gause and weaving of dead Hair, with a bleak blue Nose, over a Chafing-dish of starv'd Embers, and Dining behind a Traverse Rag, in a shop no bigger than a Bird-Cage,——go, go, starve again, do, do.

Foib. Dear Madam, I'll beg Pardon on my Knees.

Lady. Away, out, out, go set up for your self again——do, drive a Trade, do, with your Three-penny-worth of small Ware, flaunting upon a Pack-thread, under a Brandy-sellers Bulk, or against a dead Wall by a Ballad-monger. Go, hang out an old *Frisoneer-gorget,* with a Yard of Yellow *Colberteen* again; do; an old gnaw'd Mask, two Rows of Pins and a Child's Fiddle; A Glass Necklace with the Beads broken, and a Quilted Night-cap with one Ear. Go, go, drive a Trade,——These were your Commodities, you treacherous Trull, this was the Merchandize you dealt in, when I took you into my House, plac'd you next my self, and made you Governante of my whole Family. You have forgot this, have you, now you have feather'd your Nest?

Foib. No, no, dear Madam. Do but hear me, have but a Moment's Patience——I'll confess all. Mr. *Mirabell* seduc'd me! I am not the first that he has wheadled with his dissembling Tongue; Your Ladiship's own Wisdom has been deluded by him, then how should I, a poor Ignorant, defend my self? O Madam, if you knew but what he promis'd me, and how he assur'd me your Ladiship should come to no Damage——Or else the Wealth of the *Indies* should not have brib'd me to conspire against so Good, so Sweet, so Kind a Lady as you have been to me.

Lady. No Damage? What to betray me, to marry me to a Cast-serving-

Man; to make me a Receptacle, an Hospital for a decay'd Pimp? No Damage? O thou frontless Impudence, more than a big-belly'd Actress.

Foib. Pray do but hear me Madam, he could not marry your Ladiship, Madam——No indeed his Marriage was to have been void in Law; for he was marry'd to me first, to secure your Ladiship. He could not have bedded your Ladiship; for if he had consummated with your Ladiship, he must have run the risque of the Law, and been put upon his Clergy——Yes indeed, I enquir'd of the Law in that case before I would meddle or make.

Lady. What, then I have been your Property, have I? I have been convenient to you, it seems,——while you were catering for *Mirabell;* I have been Broaker for you? What, have you made a passive Bawd of me?——this exceeds all Precedent; I am brought to fine Uses, to become a Botcher of second-hand Marriages between *Abigails* and *Andrews!* I'll couple you. Yes, I'll baste you together, you and your *Philander.* I'll *Duke's-Place* you, as I'm a Person. Your Turtle is in Custody already: You shall Coo in the same Cage, if there be Constable or Warrant in the Parish.

Foib. O that ever I was born, O that I was ever marry'd,——a Bride, ay I shall be a *Bridewell*[1]-Bride. Oh!

SCENE II.

Mrs. FAINALL, FOIBLE.

Mrs. Fain. Poor *Foible,* what's the matter?

Foib. O Madam, my Lady's gone for a Constable; I shall be had to a Justice, and put to *Bridewell* to beat Hemp; poor *Waitwell's* gone to Prison already.

Mrs. Fain. Have a good Heart, *Foible, Mirabell's* gone to give Security for him. This is all *Marwood's* and my Husband's doing.

Foib. Yes, yes, I know it, Madam; she was in my Lady's Closet, and overheard all that you said to me before Dinner. She sent the Letter to my Lady; and that missing Effect, Mr. *Fainall* laid this Plot to arrest *Waitwell,* when he pretended to go for the Papers; and in the mean time Mrs. *Marwood* declar'd all to my Lady.

Mrs. Fain. Was there no Mention made of me in the Letter?——My Mother does not suspect my being in the Confederacy? I fancy *Marwood* has not told her, tho' she has told my Husband.

Foib. Yes, Madam; but my Lady did not see that Part: We stifled the Letter before she read so far. Has that mischievous Devil told Mr. *Fainall* of your Ladiship then?

Mrs. Fain. Ay, all's out, my Affair with *Mirabell,* every thing discover'd. This is the last Day of our living together, that's my Comfort.

Foib. Indeed Madam, and so 'tis a Comfort if you knew all,——he has been even with your Ladiship; which I cou'd have told you long enough since, but

[1] Bridewell was a house of correction.

I love to keep Peace and Quietness by my good Will: I had rather bring Friends together, than set 'em at Distance. But Mrs. *Marwood* and he are nearer related than ever their Parents thought for.

Mrs. Fain. Say'st thou so, *Foible?* Canst thou prove this?

Foib. I can take my Oath of it, Madam, so can Mrs. *Mincing;* we have had many a fair Word from Madam *Marwood,* to conceal something that passed in our Chamber one Evening when you were at *Hide-Park;*——and we were thought to have gone a Walking: But we went up unawares,——tho' we were sworn to Secresie too; Madam *Marwood* took a Book and swore us upon it: But it was but a Book of Poems,——So long as it was not a Bible-Oath, we may break it with a safe Conscience.

Mrs. Fain. This Discovery is the most opportune Thing I cou'd wish. Now *Mincing?*

SCENE III.

[*To them*] MINCING.

Minc. My Lady wou'd speak with Mrs. *Foible, Mem.* Mr. *Mirabell* is with her; he has set your Spouse at liberty, Mrs. *Foible,* and wou'd have you hide your self in my Lady's Closet, 'till my old Lady's Anger is abated. O, my old Lady is in a perilous Passion, at something Mr. *Fainall* has said; he swears, and my old Lady cries. There's a fearful Hurricane I vow. He says *Mem,* how that he'll have my Lady's Fortune made over to him, or he'll be divorc'd.

Mrs. Fain. Does your Lady or *Mirabell* know that?

Minc. Yes *Mem,* they have sent me to see if Sir *Wilfull* be sober, and to bring him to them. My Lady is resolved to have him I think, rather than lose such a vast Sum as Six Thousand Pound. O, come Mrs. *Foible,* I hear my old Lady.

Mrs. Fain. Foible, you must tell *Mincing,* that she must prepare to vouch when I call her.

Foib. Yes, yes, Madam.

Minc. O yes *Mem,* I'll vouch any thing for your Ladiship's Service, be what it will.

SCENE IV.

Mrs. FAINALL, Lady WISHFORT, MARWOOD.

Lady. O my dear Friend, how can I enumerate the Benefits that I have receiv'd from your Goodness? To you I owe the timely Discovery of the false Vows of *Mirabell;* to you I owe the Detection of the Impostor Sir *Rowland.* And now you are become an Intercessor with my Son-in-Law, to save the Honour of my House, and compound for the Frailties of my Daughter. Well Friend, You are enough to reconcile me to the bad World, or else I would retire to Desarts and Solitudes; and feed harmless Sheep by Groves and purling Streams. Dear *Marwood*, let us leave the World, and retire by our selves and be Shepherdesses.

Mrs. Mar. Let us first dispatch the Affair in Hand, Madam. We shall have Leisure to think of Retirement afterwards. Here is one who is concerned in the Treaty.

Lady. O Daughter, Daughter, is it possible thou should'st be my Child, Bone of my Bone, and Flesh of my Flesh, and as I may say, another Me, and yet trangress the most minute Particle of severe Virtue? Is it possible you should lean aside to Iniquity, who have been cast in the direct Mold of Virtue? I have not only been a Mold but a Pattern for you, and a Model for you, after you were brought into the World.

Mrs. Fain. I don't understand your Ladiship.

Lady. Not understand? Why have you not been Naught? Have you not been Sophisticated? Not understand? Here I am ruin'd to compound for your *Caprices* and your *Cuckoldoms*. I must pawn my Plate and my Jewels, and ruin my Neice, and all little enough——

Mrs. Fain. I am wrong'd and abus'd, and so are you. 'Tis a false Accusation, as false as Hell, as false as your Friend there, ay or your Friend's Friend, my false Husband.

Mrs. Mar. My Friend, Mrs. *Fainall?* Your Husband my Friend, what do you mean?

Mrs. Fain. I know what I mean, Madam, and so do you; and so shall the World at a Time convenient.

Mrs. Mar. I am sorry to see you so passionate, Madam. More Temper would look more like Innocence. But I have done. I am sorry my Zeal to serve your Ladiship and Family should admit of Misconstruction, or make me liable to Affront. You will pardon me, Madam, if I meddle no more with an Affair, in which I am not personally concern'd.

Lady. O dear Friend, I am so asham'd that you should meet with such Returns;——You ought to ask Pardon on your Knees, ungrateful Creature; she deserves more from you, than all your Life can accomplish——O don't leave me destitute in this Perplexity;——No, stick to me, my good Genius.

Mrs. Fain. I tell you, Madam, you're abus'd—Stick to you? ay, like a Leach, to suck your best Blood——she'll drop off when she's full. Madam, you shan't pawn a Bodkin, nor part with a Brass Counter, in Composition for me. I defie 'em all. Let 'em prove their Aspersions: I know my own Innocence, and dare stand a Trial.

SCENE V.

Lady WISHFORT, MARWOOD.

Lady. Why, if she should be innocent, if she should be wrong'd after all, ha? I don't know what to think,——and I promise you, her Education has been unexceptionable——I may say it; for I chiefly made it my own Care to initiate her very Infancy in the Rudiments of Virtue, and to impress upon her tender Years a young Odium and Aversion to the very sight of Men,——ay Friend, she would have shriek'd if she had but seen a Man, 'till she was in her Teens. As I'm a Person 'tis true——She was never suffer'd to play with a Male-Child, tho' but in Coats; Nay her very Babies were of the *Feminine Gender*,——O, she never look'd a Man in the Face but her own Father, or the Chaplain, and him we made a shift to put upon her for a Woman, by the help of his long Garments, and his sleek Face; 'till she was going in her Fifteen.

Mrs. Mar. 'Twas much she should be deceiv'd so long.

Lady. I warrant you, or she would never have born to have been catechiz'd by him; and have heard his long Lectures against Singing and Dancing, and such Debaucheries; and going to filthy Plays; and prophane Musick-meetings, where the lewd Trebles squeek nothing but Bawdy, and the Bases roar Blasphemy. O, she would have swoon'd at the Sight or Name of an obscene Play-Book——and can I think after all this, that my Daughter can be Naught? What, a Whore? And thought it Excommunication to set her Foot within the Door of a Play-house. O dear Friend, I can't believe it, no, no; as she says, let him prove it, let him prove it.

Mrs. Mar. Prove it, Madam? What, and have your Name prostituted in a publick Court; yours and your Daughter's Reputation worry'd at the Bar by a Pack of bawling Lawyers? To be usher'd in with an *O Yes* of Scandal; and have your Case open'd by an old fumbler Leacher in a Quoif like a Man Midwife, to bring your Daughter's Infamy to Light; to be a Theme for legal Punsters, and Quiblers by the Statute; and become a Jest, against a Rule of Court, where there is no Precedent for a Jest in any Record; not even in *Dooms-day-Book:* To discompose the Gravity of the Bench, and provoke naughty Interrogatories in more naughty Law *Latin;* while the good Judge, tickl'd with the Proceeding, simpers under a Grey Beard, and figes off and on his Cushion as if he had swallow'd *Cantharides,* or sate upon *Cow-Itch.*

Lady. O, 'tis very hard!

Mrs. Mar. And then to have my young Revellers of the *Temple* take Notes, like Prentices at a Conventicle; and after talk it over again in Commons, or before Drawers in an Eating-House.

Lady. Worse and worse.

Mrs. Mar. Nay this is nothing; if it would end here 'twere well. But it must after this be consign'd by the Short-hand Writers to the publick Press; and from thence be transferr'd to the Hands nay into the Throats and Lungs of Hawkers, with Voices more licentious than the loud Flounderman's: And this you must hear 'till you are stunn'd; nay, you must hear nothing else for some Days.

Lady. O, 'tis insupportable. No, no, dear Friend, make it up, make it up; ay, ay, I'll Compound. I'll give up all, my self and my all, my Neice and her all——any thing, every thing for Composition.

Mrs. Mar. Nay, Madam. I advise nothing, I only lay before you, as a

Friend, the Inconveniences which perhaps you have overseen. Here comes Mr. *Fainall*, if he will be satisfy'd to huddle up all in Silence, I shall be glad. You must think I would rather Congratulate than Condole with you.

SCENE VI.

FAINALL, Lady WISHFORT, Mrs. MARWOOD.

Lady. Ay, ay, I do not doubt it, dear *Marwood:* No, no, I do not doubt it.

Fain. Well, Madam; I have suffer'd my self to be overcome by the Importunity of this Lady your Friend; and am content you shall enjoy your own proper Estate during Life; on Condition you oblige your self never to marry, under such Penalty as I think convenient.

Lady. Never to marry?

Fain. No more Sir *Rowlands*,——the next Imposture may not be so timely detected.

Mrs. Mar. That Condition, I dare answer, my Lady will consent to, without Difficulty; she has already but too much experienc'd the Perfidiousness of Men. Besides, Madam, when we retire to our Pastoral Solitude we shall bid adieu to all other Thoughts.

Lady. Ay, that's true; but in case of Necessity; as of Health, or some such Emergency——

Fain. O, if you are prescrib'd Marriage, you shall be consider'd; I will only reserve to my self the Power to chuse for you. If your Physick be wholsome, it matters not who is your Apothecary. Next, my Wife shall settle on me the Remainder of her Fortune, not made over already; and for her Maintenance depend entirely on my Discretion.

Lady. This is most inhumanly savage; exceeding the Barbarity of a *Muscovite* Husband.

Fain. I learn'd it from his *Czarish* Majesty's Retinue, in a Winter Evening's Conference over Brandy and Pepper, amongst other Secrets of Matrimony and Policy, as they are at present practis'd in the Northern Hemisphere. But this must be agreed unto, and that positively. Lastly, I will be endow'd, in right of my Wife, with that six thousand Pound, which is the Moiety of Mrs. *Millamant's* Fortune in your Possession; and which she has forfeited (as will appear by the last Will and Testament of your deceas'd Husband, Sir *Jonathan Wishfort*) by her Disobedience in Contracting her self against your Consent or Knowledge; and by refusing the offer'd Match with Sir *Wilfull Witwoud*, which you, like a careful Aunt, had provided for her.

Lady. My Nephew was *non Compos;* and could not make his Addresses.

Fain. I come to make Demands——I'll hear no Objections.

Lady. You will grant me Time to consider?

Fain. Yes, while the Instrument is drawing, to which you must set your Hand 'till more sufficient Deeds can be perfected: which I will take Care shall be done with all possible speed. In the mean while I will go for the said

Instrument, and 'till my Return you may ballance this Matter in your own Discretion.

SCENE VII.

Lady WISHFORT, Mrs. MARWOOD.

Lady. This Insolence is beyond all Precedent, all Parallel; must I be subject to this merciless Villain?

Mrs. Mar. 'Tis severe indeed, Madam, that you shou'd smart for your Daughter's Wantonness.

Lady. 'Twas against my Consent that she marry'd this Barbarian, but she wou'd have him, tho' her Year was not out.—Ah! her first Husband, my Son *Languish,* wou'd not have carry'd it thus. Well, that was my Choice, this is hers; she is match'd now with a Witness——I shall be mad, dear Friend, is there no Comfort for me? Must I live to be confiscated at this Rebel-rate? ——Here comes two more of my *Egyptian* Plagues too.

SCENE VIII.

[To them] MILLIMANT, Sir WILFULL.

Sir Wil. Aunt, your Servant.

Lady. Out *Caterpillar,* call not me Aunt; I know thee not.

Sir Wil. I confess I have been a little in Disguise, as they say,——'Sheart! and I'm sorry for't. What wou'd you have? I hope I committed no Offence, Aunt—and if I did I am willing to make Satisfaction; and what can a Man say fairer? If I have broke any thing I'll pay for't, an it cost a Pound. And so let that content for what's past, and make no more Words. For what's to come, to pleasure you I'm willing to marry my Cousin. So pray let's all be Friends, she and I are agreed upon the Matter before a Witness.

Lady. How's this, dear Neice? Have I any Comfort? Can this be true?

Milla. I am content to be a Sacrifice to your Repose, Madam; and to convince you that I had no Hand in the Plot, as you were misinform'd, I have laid my Commands on *Mirabell* to come in Person, and be a Witness that I give my Hand to this Flower of *Knighthood;* and for the Contract that pass'd between *Mirabell* and me, I have oblig'd him to make a Resignation of it in your Ladiship's Presence;——He is without, and waits your leave for Admittance.

Lady. Well, I'll swear I am something reviv'd at this Testimony of your Obedience; but I cannot admit that Traitor,——I fear I cannot fortifie my self to support his Appearance. He is as terrible to me as a *Gorgon;* if I see him I fear I shall turn to Stone, petrifie incessantly.

Milla. If you disoblige him he may resent your Refusal, and insist upon the Contract still. Then 'tis the last time he will be offensive to you.

Lady. Are you sure it will be the last time?——If I were sure of that—— shall I never see him again?

Milla. Sir *Wilfull*, you and he are to Travel together, are you not?

Sir Wil. 'Sheart the Gentleman's a Civil Gentleman, Aunt, let him come in; why we are sworn Brothers and Fellow-Travellers.——We are to be *Pylades* and *Orestes*, he and I——He is to be my Interpreter in Foreign Parts. He has been Overseas once already; and with *proviso* that I marry my Cousin, will cross 'em once again, only to bear me Company.—'Sheart, I'll call him in,——an I set on't once, he shall come in; and see who'll hinder him.

[*Goes to the Door and hems.*

Mrs. *Mar.* This is precious Fooling, if it wou'd pass; but I'll know the Bottom of it.

Lady. O dear *Marwood*, you are not going?

Mar. Not far, Madam; I'll return immediately.

SCENE IX.

Lady WISHFORT, MILLAMANT, *Sir* WILFULL, MIRABELL.

Sir Wil. Look up, Man, I'll stand by you, 'sbud and she do frown, she can't kill you;——Besides—harkee she dare not frown desperately, because her Face is none of her own; 'Sheart, and she shou'd her Forehead wou'd wrinkle like the Coat of a Cream-cheese; but mum for that, Fellow-Traveller.

Mira. If a deep Sense of the many Injuries I have offer'd to so good a Lady, with a sincere Remorse, and a hearty Contrition, can but obtain the least Glance of Compassion, I am too happy,——Ah Madam, there was a time ——But let it be forgotten——I confess I have deservedly forfeited the high Place I once held, of sighing at your Feet; nay kill me not, by turning from me in Disdain—I come not to plead for Favour;—Nay not for Pardon; I am a Suppliant only for Pity—I am going where I never shall behold you more——

Sir Wil. How, Fellow-Traveller!——You shall go by your self then.

Mira. Let me be pitied first; and afterwards forgotten——I ask no more.

Sir Wil. By'r Lady a very reasonable Request, and will cost you nothing, Aunt,—Come, come, forgive and forget Aunt, why you must an you are a Christian.

Mira. Consider Madam, in reality, you cou'd not receive much Prejudice; it was an innocent Device; tho' I confess it had a Face of Guiltiness,—it was at most an Artifice which Love contriv'd——And Errors which Love produces have ever been accounted *Venial*. At least think it is Punishment enough, that I have lost what in my Heart I hold most dear, that to your cruel Indignation, I have offer'd up this Beauty, and with her my Peace and Quiet; nay all my Hopes of future Comfort.

Sir Wil. An he does not move me, wou'd I may never be *O' the Quorum*, —An it were not as good a Deed as to drink, to give her to him again,——

I wou'd I might never take Shipping——Aunt, if you don't forgive quickly; I shall melt, I can tell you that. My Contract went no farther than a little Mouth-Glew, and that's hardly dry;——One doleful Sigh more from my Fellow-Traveller and 'tis dissolv'd.

Lady. Well Nephew, upon your Account——Ah, he has a false insinuating Tongue——Well Sir, I will stifle my just Resentment at my Nephew's Request.——I will endeavour what I can to forget,——but on *proviso* that you resign the Contract with my Neice immediately.

Mira. It is in Writing and with Papers of Concern; but I have sent my Servant for it, and will deliver it to you, with all Acknowledgments for your transcendent Goodness.

Lady. Oh, he has Witchcraft in his Eyes and Tongue;——When I did not see him I cou'd have brib'd a Villain to his Assassination; but his Appearance rakes the Embers which have so long lain smother'd in my Breast.——

[*Aside.*

SCENE X.

[*To them*] FAINALL, *Mrs.* MARWOOD.

Fain. Your Date of Deliberation, Madam, is expir'd. Here is the Instrument, are you prepar'd to sign?

Lady. If I were prepar'd, I am not impower'd. My Neice exerts a lawful Claim, having match'd her self by my Direction to Sir *Wilfull.*

Fain. That Sham is too gross to pass on me——tho' 'tis impos'd on you, Madam.

Milla. Sir, I have given my Consent.

Mira. And, Sir, I have resign'd my Pretensions.

Sir *Wil.* And, Sir, I assert my Right; and will maintain it in defiance of you, Sir, and of your Instrument. 'Sheart an you talk of an Instrument Sir, I have an old Fox by my Thigh shall hack your Instrument of *Ram Vellam* to Shreds, Sir. It shall not be sufficient for a *Mittimus* or a Tailor's Measure; therefore withdraw your Instrument Sir, or by'r Lady I shall draw mine.

Lady. Hold, Nephew, hold.

Milla. Good Sir *Wilfull* respite your Valour.

Fain. Indeed? Are you provided of your Guard, with your single Beefeater there? But I'm prepared for you; and insist upon my first Proposal. You shall submit your own Estate to my Management, and absolutely make over my Wife's to my sole use; as pursuant to the Purport and Tenor of this other Covenant.——I suppose, Madam, your Consent is not requisite in this Case; nor, Mr. *Mirabell*, your Resignation; nor, Sir *Wilfull*, your Right—— You may draw your Fox if you please Sir, and make a *Bear-Garden* flourish somewhere else: For here it will not avail. This, my Lady *Wishfort*, must be subscrib'd, or your Darling Daughter's turn'd a-drift, like a leaky Hulk to sink or swim, as she and the Current of this lewd Town can agree.

Lady. Is there no Means, no Remedy, to stop my Ruin? Ungrateful Wretch! dost thou not owe thy Being, thy Subsistance to my Daughter's Fortune?

Fain. I'll answer you when I have the rest of it in my Possession.

Mira. But that you wou'd not accept of a Remedy from my Hands——I own I have not deserv'd you shou'd owe any Obligation to me; or else perhaps I cou'd advise,——

Lady. O what? what? to save me and my Child from Ruin, from Want, I'll forgive all that's past; nay I'll consent to any Thing to come, to be deliver'd from this Tyranny.

Mira. Ay Madam; but that is too late, my Reward is intercepted. You have dispos'd of her, who only cou'd have made me a Compensation for all my Services;——But be it as it may, I am resolv'd I'll serve you, you shall not be wrong'd in this Savage manner.

Lady. How! Dear Mr. *Mirabell*, can you be so generous at last! But it is not possible. Harkee, I'll break my Nephew's Match, you shall have my Neice yet, and all her Fortune; if you can but save me from this imminent Danger.

Mira. Will you? I take you at your Word. I ask no more. I must have leave for two Criminals to appear.

Lady. Ay, ay, any body, any body.

Mira. Foible is one, and a Penitent.

SCENE XI.

[To them] Mrs. FAINALL, FOIBLE, MINCING.

Mrs. *Mar.* O My Shame! these corrupt things ⎰ *Mira. and Lady go to* are brought hither to expose me.   ⎱ *Mrs.* Fain. *and* Foib.

Fain. If it must all come out, why let 'em know it, 'tis but the *Way of the World*. That shall not urge me to relinquish or abate one Tittle of my Terms, no, I will insist the more.

Foib. Yes indeed Madam, I'll take my Bible-oath of it.

Minc. And so will I *Mem*.

Lady. O *Marwood, Marwood*, art thou false? my Friend deceive me? Hast thou been a wicked Accomplice with that profligate Man?

Mrs. *Mar.* Have you so much Ingratitude and Injustice, to give Credit against your Friend, to the Aspersions of Two such mercenary Truls?

Minc. Mercenary, *Mem*? I scorn your Words. 'Tis true we found you and Mr. *Fainall* in the blue Garret; by the same Token, you swore us to Secresie upon *Messalinas's* Poems. Mercenary? No, if we wou'd have been Mercenary, we shou'd have held our Tongues; you wou'd have brib'd us sufficiently.

Fain. Go, you are an insignificant Thing.——Well, what are you the better for this! Is this Mr. *Mirabell's* Expedient? I'll be put off no longer——You,

Thing, that was a Wife, shall smart for this. I will not leave thee wherewithal to hide thy Shame: Your Body shall be Naked as your Reputation.

Mrs. Fain. I despise you, and defie your Malice——You have aspers'd me wrongfully——I have prov'd your Falsehood——Go you and your treacherous ——I will not name it, but starve together——Perish.

Fain. Not while you are worth a Groat, indeed my Dear. Madam, I'll be fool'd no longer.

Lady. Ah Mr. *Mirabell*, this is small Comfort, the Detection of this Affair.

Mira. O in good time——Your leave for the other Offender and Penitent to appear, Madam.

SCENE XII.

[*To them*] WAITWELL *with a Box of Writings.*

Lady. O Sir *Rowland*——Well, Rascal.

Wait. What your Ladiship pleases.——I have brought the Black-Box at last, Madam.

Mira. Give it me. Madam, you remember your Promise.

Lady. Ay, dear Sir.

Mira. Where are the Gentlemen?

Wait. At hand Sir, rubbing their Eyes,——just risen from Sleep.

Fain. S'death what's this to me? I'll not wait your private Concerns.

SCENE XIII.

[*To them*] PETULANT, WITWOUD.

Pet. How now? what's the matter? who's Hand's out?

Wit. Hey day! what are you all got together, like Players at the End of the last Act?

Mira. You may remember, Gentlemen, I once requested your Hands as Witnesses to a certain Parchment.

Wit. Ay I do, my Hand I remember—*Petulant* set his Mark.

Mira. You wrong him, his Name is fairly written, as shall appear——You do not remember, Gentlemen, any thing of what that Parchment contained—— [*Undoing the Box.*

Wit. No.

Pet. Not I. I writ, I read nothing.

Mira. Very well, now you shall know——Madam, your Promise.

Lady. Ay, ay, Sir, upon my Honour.

Mira. Mr. *Fainall*, it is now Time that you shou'd know, that your Lady, while she was at her own Disposal, and before you had by your Insinuations wheadl'd her out of a pretended Settlement of the greatest Part of her Fortune——

Fain. Sir! pretended!

Mira. Yes, Sir. I say that this Lady while a Widow, having it seems receiv'd some Cautions respecting your Inconstancy and Tyranny of Temper, which from her own partial Opinion and Fondness of you she cou'd never have suspected——she did, I say, by the wholesome Advice of Friends and of Sages learn'd in the Laws of this Land, deliver this same as her Act and Deed to me in Trust, and to the Uses within mention'd. You may read if you please—[*Holding out the Parchment.*] tho' perhaps what is written on the Back may serve your Occasions.

Fain. Very likely, Sir. What's here? Damnation?

[*Reads.*] *A Deed of Conveyance of the whole Estate real of* Arabella Languish, *Widow, in Trust to* Edward Mirabell. Confusion!

Mira. Even so, Sir, 'tis *the Way of the World,* Sir; of the Widows of the World. I suppose this Deed may bear an elder Date than what you have obtain'd from your Lady.

Fain. Perfidious Fiend! then thus I'll be reveng'd.—

[*Offers to run at Mrs.* Fain.

Sir *Wil.* Hold, Sir, now you may make your *Bear-Garden* Flourish somewhere else, Sir.

Fain. Mirabell, you shall hear of this, Sir, be sure you shall.——Let me pass, Oaf.

Mrs. *Fain.* Madam, you seem to stifle your Resentment: You had better give it Vent.

Mrs. *Mar.* Yes, it shall have Vent——and to your Confusion, or I'll perish in the Attempt.

SCENE *the Last.*

Lady Wishfort, Millamant, Mirabell, *Mrs.* Fainall, *Sir* Wilfull, Petulant, Witwoud, Foible, Mincing, Waitwell.

Lady. O Daughter, Daughter, 'tis plain thou hast inherited thy Mother's Prudence.

Mrs. *Fain.* Thank Mr. *Mirabell,* a cautious Friend, to whose Advice all is owing.

Lady. Well Mr. *Mirabell,* you have kept your Promise——and I must perform mine.——First I pardon for your sake Sir *Rowland* there and *Foible*——The next thing is to break the Matter to my Nephew—and how to do that——

Mira. For that, Madam, give your self no Trouble,—let me have your Consent——Sir *Wilfull* is my Friend; he has had Compassion upon Lovers, and generously engag'd a Volunteer in this Action, for our Service; and now designs to prosecute his Travels.

Sir *Wil.* 'Sheart, Aunt, I have no mind to marry. My Cousin's a fine Lady, and the Gentleman loves her, and she loves him, and they deserve one an-

other; my Resolution is to see Foreign Parts——I have set on't——and when
I'm set on't, I must do't. And if these two Gentlemen wou'd travel too, I
think they may be spar'd.

Pet. For my part, I say little—I think things are best off or on.

Wit. I gad I understand nothing of the matter,—I'm in a Maze yet, like a
Dog in a Dancing-School.

Lady. Well Sir, take her, and with her all the Joy I can give you.

Milla. Why does not the Man take me? Wou'd you have me give my self
to you over again?

Mira. Ay, and over and over again;   [*Kisses her Hand.*
I wou'd have you as often as possibly I can. Well, Heav'n grant I love you
not too well, that's all my Fear.

Sir *Wil.* 'Sheart you'll have time enough to toy after you're marry'd; or
if you will toy now, let us have a Dance in the mean time; that we who
are not Lovers may have some other Employment, besides looking on.

Mira. With all my Heart, dear Sir *Wilfull.* What shall we do for Musick?

Foib. O Sir, some that were provided for Sir *Rowland's* Entertainment
are yet within Call.   [*A Dance.*

Lady. As I am a Person I can hold out no longer;——I have wasted my
Spirits so to Day already, that I am ready to sink under the Fatigue; and
I cannot but have some Fears upon me yet, that my Son *Fainall* will pursue
some desperate Course.

Mira. Madam, disquiet not your self on that account; to my Knowledge
his Circumstances are such, he must of Force comply. For my part I will contribute all that in me lyes to a Reunion: In the mean time, Madam [*To Mrs.
Fain.*], let me before these Witnesses restore to you this Deed of Trust; it
may be a Means, well manag'd, to make you live easily together.

From hence let those be warn'd, who mean to wed;
Lest mutual Falsehood stain the Bridal-Bed:
For each Deceiver to his Cost may find,
That Marriage Frauds too oft are paid in kind.   [Exeunt Omnes.

EPILOGUE

Spoken by Mrs. *Bracegirdle.*

After our Epilogue *this Crowd dismisses,*
I'm thinking how this Play'll be pull'd to Pieces.
But pray consider, e'er you doom its Fall,
How hard a thing 'twou'd be, to please you all.
There are some Criticks so with Spleen diseas'd,
They scarcely come inclining to be Pleas'd:
And sure he must have more than mortal Skill,
Who pleases any one against his Will.

Then, all bad Poets we are sure are Foes,
And how their Number's swell'd the Town well knows:
In Shoals, I've mark'd 'em judging in the Pit; }
Tho' they're on no Pretence for Judgment fit, }
But that they have been Damn'd for Want of Wit. }
Since when, they by their own Offences taught,
Set up for Spies on Plays, and finding Fault.
Others there are, whose Malice we'd prevent; }
Such, who watch Plays, with scurrilous Intent }
To mark out who by Characters *are meant.* }
And tho' no perfect Likeness they can trace;
Yet each pretends to know the Copy'd Face.
These, with false Glosses feed their own Ill-nature,
And turn to Libel, *what was meant a* Satire.
May such malicious Fops *this Fortune find,*
To think themselves alone the Fools *design'd:*
If any are so arrogantly Vain, }
To think they singly *can support a* Scene, }
And furnish Fool *enough to entertain.* }
For well the Learn'd and the Judicious know, }
That Satire *scorns to stoop so meanly low,* }
As any one abstracted Fop *to show.* }
For, as when Painters form a matchless Face,
They from each Fair *one* catch *some diff'rent Grace;*
And shining Features in one Portrait blend,
To which no single Beauty must pretend:
So Poets oft, do in one Piece expose
Whole Belles Assemblées *of* Cocquets *and* Beaux.

THE BEGGAR'S OPERA

by John Gay

——Nos hæc noviffimus effe nihil.   Mart.

DRAMATIS PERSONÆ.

MEN.

Peachum.
Lockit.
Macheath.
Filch.
Jemmy Twitcher.
Crook-finger'd Jack.
Wat Dreary.
Robin *of* Bagshot.   } *Macheath's* Gang.
Nimming Ned.
Harry Paddington.
Matt *of the* Mint.
Ben Budge.
Beggar.
Player.
  Constables, *Drawer, Turnkey,* &c.

WOMEN.

Mrs. Peachum.
Polly Peachum.
Lucy Lockit.
Diana Trapes.
Mrs. Coaxer.
Dolly Trull.
Mrs. Vixen.
Betty Doxy.   } *Women of the Town.*
Jenny Diver.
Mrs. Slammekin.
Suky Tawdry.
Molly Brazen.

INTRODUCTION.

Beggar. Player.

Beggar. If Poverty be a title to Poetry, I am sure no-body can dispute mine. I own myself of the company of Beggars; and I make one at their weekly festivals at St. *Giles's,* I have a small yearly Salary for my Catches, and am welcome to a dinner there whenever I please, which is more than most Poets can say.

Player. As we live by the Muses, it is but gratitude in us to encourage poetical merit where-ever we find it. The Muses, contrary to all other ladies, pay no distinction to dress, and never partially mistake the pertness of embroidery for wit, nor the modesty of want for dulness. Be the author who he will, we push his Play as far as it will go. So (though you are in want) I wish you success heartily.

Beggar. This piece I own was originally writ for the celebrating the marriage of *James Chanter* and *Moll Lay,* two most excellent ballad-singers. I have introduc'd the Similes that are in all your celebrated *Operas:* The *Swallow,* the *Moth,* the *Bee,* the *Ship,* the *Flower,* &c. Besides, I have a Prison Scene, which the ladies always reckon charmingly pathetick. As to the parts, I have observ'd such a nice impartiality to our two ladies, that it is impossible for either of them to take offence. I hope I may be forgiven, that I have not made my Opera throughout unnatural, like those in vogue; for I have no Recitative: excepting this, as I have consented to have neither Prologue nor Epilogue, it must be allow'd an Opera in all its forms. The piece indeed hath been heretofore frequently represented by ourselves in our great room at St. *Giles's* so that I cannot too often acknowledge your charity in bringing it now on the stage.

Player. But I see 'tis time for us to withdraw; the Actors are preparing to begin. Play away the Ouverture.   [*Exeunt.*

THE BEGGAR'S OPERA

ACT I.

SCENE I.—SCENE Peachum's *House*.

Peachum *sitting at a Table with a large Book of Accounts before him.*

AIR I. An old woman cloathed in gray.

> *Through all the employments of life*
> *Each neighbour abuses his brother;*
> *Whore and Rogue they call Husband and Wife:*
> *All professions be-rogue one another.*
> *The Priest calls the Lawyer a cheat,*
> *The Lawyer be-knaves the Divine;*
> *And the Statesman, because he's so great,*
> *Thinks his trade as honest as mine.*

A Lawyer is an honest employment, so is mine. Like me too he acts in a double capacity, both against Rogues and for 'em; for 'tis but fitting that we should protect and encourage Cheats, since we live by 'em.

SCENE II.

Peachum, Filch.

Filch. Sir, black *Moll* hath sent word her tryal comes on in the afternoon, and she hopes you will order matters so as to bring her off.

Peach. Why, she may plead her belly at worst; to my knowledge she hath taken care of that security. But as the wench is very active and industrious, you may satisfy her that I'll soften the evidence.

Filch. Tom *Gagg*, Sir, is found guilty.

Peach. A lazy dog! When I took him the time before, I told him what he would come to if he did not mend his hand. This is death without reprieve. I may venture to book him. [*Writes.*] For *Tom Gagg*, forty pounds. Let *Betty Sly* know that I'll save her from Transportation, for I can get more by her staying in *England*.

Filch. Betty hath brought more goods into our Lock to-year than any five of the gang; and in truth, 'tis a pity to lose so good a customer.

Peach. If none of the gang take her off, she may, in the common course of business, live a twelve-month longer. I love to let women scape. A good sportsman always lets the Hen-Partridges fly, because the breed of the game depends upon them. Besides, here the Law allows us no reward; there is nothing to be got by the death of women——except our wives.

Filch. Without dispute, she is a fine woman! 'Twas to her I was oblig'd for my education, and (to say a bold word) she hath train'd up more young fellows to the business than the Gaming-table.

Peach. Truly, *Filch*, thy observation is right. We and the Surgeons are more beholden to women than all the professions besides.

AIR II. The bonny gray-ey'd morn, *&c.*

Filch. *'Tis woman that seduces all mankind,*
By her we first were taught the wheedling arts:
Her very eyes can cheat; when most she's kind,
She tricks us of our money with our hearts.
For her, like Wolves by night we roam for prey,
And practise ev'ry fraud to bribe her charms;
For suits of love, like law, are won by pay,
And Beauty must be fee'd into our arms.

Peach. But make haste to *Newgate*, boy, and let my friends know what I intend; for I love to make them easy one way or other.

Filch. When a gentleman is long kept in suspence, penitence may break his spirit ever after. Besides, certainty gives a man a good air upon his tryal, and makes him risque another without fear or scruple. But I'll away, for 'tis a pleasure to be the messenger of comfort to friends in affliction.

SCENE III.

Peachum.

But 'tis now high time to look about me for a decent Execution against next Sessions. I hate a lazy rogue, by whom one can get nothing 'till he is hang'd. A Register of the Gang. [*Reading.*] Crook-finger'd *Jack*. A year and a half in the service: Let me see how much the stock owes to his industry; one, two, three, four, five gold Watches, and seven silver ones. A mighty clean-handed fellow! sixteen Snuff-boxes, five of them of true gold. Six dozen of Handkerchiefs, four silver-hilted Swords, half a dozen of Shirts, three Tye-perriwigs, and a piece of Broad Cloth. Considering these are only the fruits of his leisure hours, I don't know a prettier fellow, for no man alive hath a more engaging presence of mind upon the road. *Wat Dreary*, alias *Brown Will*, an irregular dog, who hath an underhand way of disposing his goods. I'll try him only for a Sessions or two longer upon his good behaviour. *Harry Paddington*, a poor petty-larceny rascal, without the least genius; that fellow, though he were to live six months, will never come to the gallows with any credit. *Slippery Sam*, he goes off the next Sessions, for the villain hath the impudence to have views of following his trade as a Taylor, which he calls an honest employment. *Mat* of the *Mint*; listed not above a month ago, a promising sturdy fellow, and diligent in his way; somewhat too bold and hasty, and may raise good contributions on the publick, if he does not cut himself short by murder. *Tom Tipple*, a guzzling soaking sot, who is always too drunk to stand himself, or to make others stand. A cart is absolutely necessary for him. *Robin* of *Bagshot*, alias *Gorgon*, alias *Bluff Bob*, alias *Carbuncle*, alias *Bob Booty*.

SCENE IV.

Peachum, Mrs. Peachum.

Mrs. Peach. What of *Bob Booty*, husband? I hope nothing bad hath betided him. You know, my dear, he's a favourite customer of mine. 'Twas he made me a present of this ring.

Peach. I have set his name down in the black-list, that's all my dear; he spends his life among women, and as soon as his money is gone, one or other of the ladies will hang him for the reward, and there's forty pound lost to us for-ever.

Mrs. Peach. You know, my dear, I never meddle in matters of Death; I always leave those affairs to you. Women indeed are bitter bad judges in these cases, for they are so partial to the brave that they think every man handsome who is going to the Camp or the Gallows.

AIR III. Cold and raw, &c.

If any wench Venus's girdle wear,
  Though she be never so ugly,
Lillies and roses will quickly appear,
  And her face look wondr'ous smuggly.
Beneath the left ear, so fit but a cord,
  (A rope so charming a Zone is!)
The youth in his cart hath the air of a lord,
  And we cry, There dies an Adonis!

But really, husband, you should not be too hard-hearted, for you never had a finer, braver set of men than at present. We have not had a murder among them all, these seven months. And truly, my dear, that is a great blessing.

Peach. What a dickens is the woman always a whimpring about murder for? No gentleman is ever look'd upon the worse for killing a man in his own defence; and if business cannot be carried on without it, what would you have a gentleman do?

Mrs. Peach. If I am in the wrong, my dear, you must excuse me, for nobody can help the frailty of an over-scrupulous Conscience.

Peach. Murder is as fashionable a crime as a man can be guilty of. How many fine gentlemen have we in *Newgate* every year, purely upon that article? If they have wherewithal to perswade the jury to bring it in manslaughter, what are they the worse for it? So, my dear, have done upon this subject. Was captain *Macheath* here this morning, for the bank-notes he left with you last week?

Mrs. Peach. Yes, my dear; and though the Bank hath stopt payment, he was so cheerful and so agreeable! Sure there is not a finer gentleman upon the road than the Captain! If he comes from *Bagshot* at any reasonable hour he hath promis'd to make one this evening with *Polly*, and me, and *Bob Booty*, at a party of Quadrille. Pray, my dear, is the Captain rich?

Peach. The Captain keeps too good company ever to grow rich. *Marybone* and the Chocolate-houses are his undoing. The man that proposes to get money by play should have the education of a fine gentleman, and be train'd up to it from his youth.

Mrs. Peach. Really, I am sorry upon *Polly's* account the Captain hath not more discretion. What business hath he to keep company with lords and gentlemen? he should leave them to prey upon one another.

Peach. Upon *Polly's* account! What, a plague, does the woman mean?—Upon *Polly's* account!

Mrs. Peach. Captain *Macheath* is very fond of the girl.

Peach. And what then?

Mrs. Peach. If I have any skill in the ways of women, I am sure *Polly* thinks him a very pretty man.

Peach. And what then? you would not be so mad to have the wench marry him? Gamesters and highwaymen are generally very good to their whores, but they are very devils to their wives.

Mrs. Peach. But if *Polly* should be in love, how should we help her, or how can she help herself? Poor girl, I am in the utmost concern about her.

AIR IV. Why is your faithful slave disdain'd?

> *If love the virgin's heart invade,*
> *How, like a Moth, the simple maid*
> *Still plays about the flame!*
> *If soon she be not made a wife,*
> *Her honour's sing'd, and then for life,*
> *She's —what I dare not name.*

Peach. Look ye, wife. A handsome wench in our way of business, is as profitable as at the bar of a *Temple* coffee-house, who looks upon it as her livelihood to grant every liberty but one. You see I would indulge the girl as far as prudently we can. In any thing, but marriage! after that, my dear, how shall we be safe? are we not then in her husband's power? for a husband hath the absolute power over all a wife's secrets but her own. If the girl had the discretion of a court lady, who can have a dozen young fellows at her ear without complying with one, I should not matter it; but *Polly* is tinder, and a spark will at once set her on a flame. Married! If the wench does not know her own profit, sure she knows her own pleasure better than to make herself a property! My daughter to me should be, like a court lady to a minister of state, a key to the whole gang. Married! If the affair is not already done, I'll terrify her from it, by the example of our neighbours.

Mrs. Peach. May-hap, my dear, you may injure the girl. She loves to imitate the fine ladies, and she may only allow the Captain liberties in the view of interest.

Peach. But 'tis your duty, my dear, to warn the girl against her ruin, and to instruct her how to make the most of her beauty. I'll go to her this moment, and sift her. In the mean time, wife, rip out the coronets and marks of these dozen of cambric handkerchiefs, for I can dispose of them this afternoon to a chap in the city.

SCENE V.

Mrs. Peachum

Never was a man more out of the way in an argument, than my husband! Why must our *Polly*, forsooth, differ from her sex, and love only her husband? And why must our *Polly's* marriage, contrary to all observation, make her the less followed by other men? All men are thieves in love, and like a woman the better for being another's property.

AIR V. Of all the simple things we do, &c.

A Maid is like the golden ore,
Which hath guineas intrinsical in't,
  Whose worth is never known, before
It is try'd and imprest in the mint.
A Wife's like a guinea in gold,
Stampt with the name of her spouse;
  Now here, now there; is bought, or is sold;
And is current in every house.

SCENE VI.

Mrs. Peachum, Filch.

Mrs. Peach. Come hither, *Filch.* I am as fond of this child, as though my mind misgave me he were my own. He hath as fine a hand at picking a pocket as a woman, and is as nimble-finger'd as a juggler. If an unlucky session does not cut the rope of thy life, I pronounce, boy, thou wilt be a great man in history. Where was your post last night, my boy?

Filch. I ply'd at the Opera, madam; and considering 'twas neither dark nor rainy, so that there was no great hurry in getting chairs and coaches, made a tolerable hand on't. These seven handkerchiefs, madam.

Mrs. Peach. Colour'd ones, I see. They are of sure sale from our warehouse at *Redriff* among the seamen.

Filch. And this snuff-box.

Mrs. Peach. Set in gold! A pretty encouragement this to a young beginner.

Filch. I had a fair tug at a charming gold watch. Pox take the Taylors for making the fobs so deep and narrow! It stuck by the way, and I was forc'd to make my escape under a coach. Really, madam, I fear I shall be cut off in the flower of my youth, so that every now and then (since I was pumpt) I have thoughts of taking up and going to Sea.

Mrs. Peach. You should go to *Hockley in the hole*, and to *Marybone*, child, to learn valour. These are the schools that have bred so many brave men. I thought, boy, by this time, thou hadst lost fear as well as shame. Poor lad! how little does he know yet of the *Old-Baily!* For the first fact I'll ensure thee from being hang'd; and going to Sea, *Filch*, will come time enough upon a sentence of transportation. But now, since you have nothing better to do, ev'n go to your book, and learn your catechism; for really a man makes but an ill figure in the Ordinary's paper, who cannot give a satisfactory answer to his questions. But, hark you, my lad, don't tell me a lye; for you know I hate a lyar. Do you know of any thing that hath past between captain *Macheath* and our *Polly?*

Filch. I beg you, madam, don't ask me: for I must either tell a lye to you or to Miss *Polly;* for I promis'd her I would not tell.

Mrs. Peach. But when the honour of our family is concern'd—

Filch. I shall lead a sad life with Miss *Polly*, if ever she come to know that I told you. Besides, I would not willingly forfeit my own honour by betraying any body.

Mrs. Peach. Yonder comes my husband and *Polly*. Come, *Filch*, you shall go with me into my own room, and tell me the whole story. I'll give thee a glass of a most delicious cordial that I keep for my own drinking.

SCENE VII.

Peachum, Polly.

Polly. I know as well as any of the fine ladies how to make the most of my self and of my man too. A woman knows how to be mercenary, though she hath never been in a court or at an assembly. We have it in our natures, papa. If I allow captain *Macheath* some trifling liberties, I have this watch and other visible marks of his favour to show for it. A girl who cannot grant some things, and refuse what is most material, will make a poor hand of her beauty, and soon be thrown upon the common.

AIR VI. What shall I do to show how much I love her?

Virgins are like the fair flower in its lustre,
Which in the garden enamels the ground;
Near it the Bees in play flutter and cluster,
And gaudy Butterflies frolick around.
But, when once pluck'd, 'tis no longer alluring,
To Covent-garden 'tis sent, (as yet sweet),
There fades, and shrinks, and grows past all enduring,
Rots, stinks, and dies, and is trod under feet.

Peach. You know, *Polly,* I am not against your toying and trifling with a customer in the way of business, or to get out a secret, or so. But if I find out that you have play'd the fool and are married, you jade you, I'll cut your throat, hussy. Now you know my mind.

SCENE VIII.

Peachum, Polly, Mrs. Peachum.

AIR VII. Oh *London* is a fine Town.

Mrs. Peachum [*in a very great passion.*]

Our Polly is a sad slut! nor heeds what we have taught her.
I wonder any man alive will ever rear a daughter!
For she must have both hoods and gowns, and hoops to swell her pride,
With scarfs and stays, and gloves and lace; and she will have men beside;
And when she's drest with care and cost, all-tempting, fine and gay.
As men should serve a Cowcumber, she flings herself away.

You baggage! you hussy! you inconsiderate jade! had you been hang'd, it would not have vex'd me, for that might have been your misfortune; but to do such a mad thing by choice! The wench is married, husband.
Peach. Married? the Captain is a bold man, and will risque any thing for money; to be sure he believes her a fortune. Do you think your mother and I should have liv'd comfortably so long together, if ever we had been married? Baggage!
Mrs. Peach. I knew she was always a proud slut; and now the wench hath play'd the fool and married, because forsooth she would do like the Gentry. Can you support the expence of a husband, hussy, in gaming, drinking and whoring? have you money enough to carry on the daily quarrels of man and wife about who shall squander most? There are not many husbands and wives, who can bear the charges of plaguing one another in a handsome

way. If you must be married, could you introduce no-body into our family, but a highwayman! Why, thou foolish jade, thou wilt be as ill us'd, and as much neglected, as if thou hadst married a Lord!

Peach. Let not your anger, my dear, break through the rules of decency, for the Captain looks upon himself in the military capacity, as a gentleman by his profession. Besides what he hath already, I know he is in a fair way of getting, or of dying; and both these ways, let me tell you, are most excellent chances for a wife. Tell me hussy, are you ruin'd, or no?

Mrs. Peach. With *Polly's* fortune, she might very well have gone off to a person of distinction. Yes, that you might, you pouting slut!

Peach. What, is the wench dumb! Speak, or I'll make you plead by squeezing out an answer from you. Are you really bound wife to him, or are you only upon liking?   *[Pinches her.*

Polly. Oh!   *[Screaming.*

Mrs. Peach. How the mother is to be pitied who hath handsome daughters! Locks, bolts, bars, and lectures of morality are nothing to them: they break through them all. They have as much pleasure in cheating a father and mother, as in cheating at cards.

Peach. Why, *Polly,* I shall soon know if you are married, by *Macheath's* keeping from our house.

AIR VIII. Grim King of the Ghosts, &c.

Polly. *Can Love be controul'd by advice?*
    Will Cupid our mothers obey?
    Though my heart were as frozen as Ice,
        At his flame 'twould have melted away.
    When he kist me so closely he prest,
        'Twas so sweet, that I must have comply'd:
    So I thought it both safest and best
        To marry, for fear you should chide.

Mrs. Peach. Then all the hopes of our family are gone for ever and ever!

Peach. And *Macheath* may hang his father and mother-in-law, in hope to get into their daughter's fortune.

Polly. I did not marry him (as 'tis the fashion) cooly and deliberately for honour or money. But, I love him.

Mrs. Peach. Love him! worse and worse! I thought the girl had been better bred. Oh husband! husband! her folly makes me mad! my head swims! I'm distracted! I can't support myself—Oh!   *[Faints.*

Peach. See, wench, to what a condition you have reduced your poor mother! a glass of cordial, this instant. How the poor woman takes it to heart!   *[Polly goes out, and returns with it.*
Ah, hussy, now this is the only comfort your mother has left!

Polly. Give her another glass, Sir; my Mamma drinks double the quantity whenever she is out of order. This, you see, fetches her.

Mrs. Peach. The girl shows such a readiness, and so much concern, that I could almost find in my heart to forgive her.

AIR IX. *O Jenny, O Jenny, where hast thou been.*

Polly.
> *O Polly, you might have toy'd and kist.*
> *By keeping men off, you keep them on.*
> *   But he so teaz'd me,*
> *   And he so pleas'd me,*
> *What I did, you must have done.*

Mrs. Peach. Not with a highwayman.——You sorry slut!

Peach. A word with you, wife. 'Tis no new thing for a wench to take man without consent of Parents. You know 'tis the frailty of woman, my dear.

Mrs. Peach. Yes, indeed, the sex is frail. But the first time a woman is frail, she should be somewhat nice methinks, for then or never is the time to make her fortune. After that, she hath nothing to do but to guard herself from being found out, and she may do what she pleases.

Peach. Make your self a little easy; I have a thought shall soon set all matters again to rights. Why so melancholy, *Polly?* since what is done cannot be undone, we must all endeavour to make the best of it.

Mrs. Peach. Well, Polly; as far as one woman can forgive another, I forgive thee.—Your father is too fond of you, hussy.

Polly. Then all my sorrows are at an end.

Mrs. Peach. A mighty likely speech, in troth, for a wench who is just married!

AIR X. *Thomas, I cannot, &c.*

Polly.
> *I, like a ship in storms, was tost;*
> *Yet afraid to put into Land;*
> *For seiz'd in the port the vessel's lost,*
> *Whose treasure is contreband.*
> *   The waves are laid,*
> *   My duty's paid.*
> *O joy beyond expression!*
> *   Thus, safe a-shore,*
> *   I ask no more,*
> *My all is in my possession.*

Peach. I hear customers in t'other room; go, talk with 'em, Polly; but come to us again, as soon as they are gone.—But, heark ye, child, if 'tis the gentleman who was here yesterday about the repeating watch, say, you believe we can't get intelligence of it, till to-morrow. For I lent it to *Suky Straddle,* to make a figure with to-night at a tavern in *Drury-Lane.* If t'other gentleman calls for the silver-hilted sword; you know beetle-brow'd *Jemmy* hath it on, and he doth not come from *Tunbridge* till *Tuesday* night; so that it cannot be had till then.

SCENE IX.

Peachum, Mrs. Peachum.

Peach. Dear wife, be a little pacified. Don't let your passion run away with your senses. *Polly*, I grant you, hath done a rash thing.

Mrs. Peach. If she had had only an intrigue with the fellow, why the very best families have excus'd and huddled up a frailty of that sort. 'Tis marriage, husband, that makes it a blemish.

Peach. But money, wife, is the true fuller's earth for reputations, there is not a spot or a stain but what it can take out. A rich rogue now-a-days is fit company for any gentleman; and the world, my dear, hath not such a contempt for roguery as you imagine. I tell you, wife, I can make this match turn to our advantage.

Mrs. Peach. I am very sensible husband, that captain *Macheath* is worth money, but I am in doubt whether he hath not two or three wives already, and then if he should die in a Session or two, *Polly's* dower would come into dispute.

Peach. That, indeed, is a point which ought to be consider'd.

AIR XI. A Soldier and a Sailor.

A Fox may steal your hens, sir,
A whore your health and pence, sir,
Your daughter rob your chest, sir,
Your wife may steal your rest, sir,
　A thief your goods and plate.
But this is all but picking,
With rest, pence, chest and chicken;
It ever was decreed, sir,
If Lawyer's hand is fee'd, sir,
　He steals your whole estate.

The Lawyers are bitter enemies to those in our way. They don't care that any body should get a clandestine livelihood but themselves.

SCENE X.

Mrs. Peachum, Peachum, Polly.

Polly. 'Twas only Nimming *Ned.* He brought in a damask window-curtain, a hoop-petticoat, a pair of silver candlesticks, a perriwig, and one silk stocking, from the fire that happen'd last night.

Peach. There is not a fellow that is cleverer in his way, and saves more goods out of the fire than *Ned*. But now, *Polly*, to your affair; for matters must not be left as they are. You are married then, it seems?

Polly. Yes, Sir.

Peach. And how do you propose to live, child?

Polly. Like other women, Sir, upon the industry of my husband.

Mrs. Peach. What, is the wench turn'd fool? A highwayman's wife, like a soldier's, hath as little of his pay, as of his company.

Peach. And had not you the common views of a gentlewoman in your marriage, *Polly?*

Polly. I don't know what you mean, Sir.

Peach. Of a jointure, and of being a widow.

Polly. But I love him, Sir: how then could I have thoughts of parting with him?

Peach. Parting with him! Why, that is the whole scheme and intention of all Marriage-articles. The comfortable estate of widowhood is the only hope that keeps up a wife's spirits. Where is the woman who would scruple to be a wife, if she had it in her power to be a widow whenever she pleas'd? If you have any views of this sort, *Polly*, I shall think the match not so very unreasonable.

Polly. How I dread to hear your advice! Yet I must beg you to explain yourself.

Peach. Secure what he hath got, have him peach'd the next Sessions, and then at once you are made a rich widow.

Polly. What, murder the man I love! The blood runs cold at my heart with the very thought of it.

Peach. Fye, *Polly!* what hath murder to do in the affair? Since the thing sooner or later must happen, I dare say, the Captain himself would like that we should get the reward for his death sooner than a stranger. Why, *Polly*, the Captain knows, that as 'tis his employment to rob, so 'tis ours to take Robbers; every man in his business. So that there is no malice in the case.

Mrs. Peach. Ay, husband, now you have nick'd the matter. To have him peach'd is the only thing could ever make me forgive her.

AIR XII. Now ponder well, ye parents dear.

Polly.   *Oh, ponder well! be not severe;*
          So save a wretched wife!
     For on the rope that hangs my dear
          Depends poor Polly's *life.*

Mrs. Peach. But your duty to your parents, hussy, obliges you to hang him. What would many a wife give for such an opportunity!

Polly. What is a jointure, what is widowhood to me? I know my heart. I cannot survive him.

AIR XIII. Le printemps rappelle aux armes.

The Turtle thus with plaintive crying,
  Her lover dying,
The turtle thus with plaintive crying
  Laments her Dove.
Down she drops quite spent with sighing,
Pair'd in death, as pair'd in love.

Thus, Sir, it will happen to your poor *Polly*.

Mrs. Peach. What, is the fool in love in earnest then? I hate thee for being particular: Why, wench, thou art a shame to thy very Sex.

Polly. But hear me, mother.—If you ever lov'd—

Mrs Peach. Those cursed Play-books she reads have been her ruin. One word more, hussy, and I shall knock your brains out, if you have any.

Peach. Keep out of the way, Polly, for fear of mischief, and consider of what is propos'd to you.

Mrs. Peach. Away, hussy. Hang your husband, and be dutiful.

SCENE XI.

Mrs. Peachum, Peachum.

[Polly *listning.*

Mrs. Peach. The thing, husband, must and shall be done. For the sake of intelligence we must take other measures, and have him peach'd the next Session without her consent. If she will not know her duty, we know ours.

Peach. But really, my dear, it grieves one's heart to take off a great man. When I consider his personal bravery, his fine stratagem, how much we have already got by him, and how much more we may get, methinks I can't find in my heart to have a hand in his death. I wish you could have made *Polly* undertake it.

Mrs. Peach. But in a case of necessity—our own lives are in danger.

Peach. Then, indeed, we must comply with the customs of the world, and make gratitude give way to interest.—He shall be taken off.

Mrs. Peach. I'll undertake to manage *Polly*.

Peach. And I'll prepare the matters for the Old-Baily.

SCENE XII.

Polly.

Now I'm a wretch, indeed.—Methinks I see him already in the cart, sweeter and more lovely than the nosegay in his hand!—I hear the crowd extolling his resolution and intrepidity!—What vollies of sighs are sent from the windows of *Holborn*, that so comely a youth should be brought to disgrace!—I see him at the tree! the whole Circle are in tears!—even Butchers weep!——*Jack Ketch* himself hesitates to perform his duty, and would be glad to lose his fee, by a reprieve. What then will become of *Polly!*—As yet I may inform him of their design, and aid him in his escape.—It shall be so.—But then he flies, absents himself, and I bar my self from his dear, dear conversation! that too will distract me.—If he keeps out of the way, my Papa and Mamma may in time relent, and we may be happy.—If he stays, he is hang'd, and then he is lost for ever!—He intended to lye conceal'd in my room, 'till the dusk of the evening: If they are abroad I'll this instant let him out, lest some accident should prevent him.

[*Exit, and returns.*

SCENE XIII.

Polly, Macheath.

AIR XIV. Pretty Parrot, say, &c.

Mach.   *Pretty Polly, say,*
        When I was away,
    Did your fancy never stray
      To some newer lover?
Polly.   *Without disguise,*
         Heaving sighs,
         Doating eyes,
    My constant heart discover.
       Fondly let me loll!
Mach.   *O pretty, pretty Poll.*

Polly. And are *you* as fond as ever, my dear?
Mach. Suspect my honour, my courage, suspect any thing but my love.—May my pistols miss fire, and my mare slip her shoulder while I am pursu'd, if I ever forsake thee!
Polly. Nay, my dear, I have no reason to doubt you, for I find in the Romance you lent me, none of the great Heroes were ever false in love.

AIR XV. Pray, fair one, be kind.

Mach.   *My heart was so free,*
        It rov'd like the Bee,
    'Till Polly my passion requited;
      I sipt each flower,
      I chang'd ev'ry hour,
    But here ev'ry flower is united.

Polly. Were you sentenc'd to Transportation, sure, my dear, you could not leave me behind you——could you?

Mach. Is there any power, any force that could tear me from thee? You might sooner tear a pension out of the hands of a Courtier, a fee from a Lawyer, a pretty woman from a looking-glass, or any woman from *Quadrille.*–But to tear me from thee is impossible!

AIR XVI. Over the hills and far away.

Were I laid on Greenland's *coast,*
And in my arms embrac'd my lass;
Warm amidst eternal frost,
Too soon the half year's night would pass.

Polly. *Were I sold on* Indian *soil,*
Soon as the burning day was clos'd,
I could mock the sultry toil,
When on my charmer's breast repos'd.

Mach. *And I would love you all the day,*
Polly. *Every night would kiss and play,*
Mach. *If with me you'd fondly stray*
Polly. *Over the hills and far away.*

Polly. Yes, I would go with thee. But oh!——how shall I speak it? I must be torn from thee. We must part.

Mach. How! Part!

Polly. We must, we must.–My Papa and Mamma are set against thy life. They now, even now are in search after thee. They are preparing evidence against thee. Thy life depends upon a moment.

AIR XVII. Gin thou were mine awn thing.

O what pain it is to part!
Can I leave thee, can I leave thee?
O what pain it is to part!
Can thy Polly ever leave thee?
But lest death my love should thwart,
And bring thee to the fatal cart,
Thus I tear thee from my bleeding heart!
Fly hence, and let me leave thee.

One kiss and then—one kiss—begone—farewell.

Mach. My hand, my heart, my dear, is so riveted to thine, that I cannot unloose my hold.

Polly. But my Papa may intercept thee, and then I should lose the very glimmering of hope. A few weeks, perhaps, may reconcile us all. Shall thy *Polly* hear from thee?

Mach. Must I then go?

Polly. And will not absence change your love?

Mach. If you doubt it, let me stay——and be hang'd.

Polly. O how I fear! how I tremble!—Go—but when safety will give you leave, you will be sure to see me again; for 'till then *Polly* is wretched.

AIR XVIII. O the broom, &c.

Mach. *The Miser thus a shilling sees,*
　　　Which he's oblig'd to pay,
　　With sighs resigns it by degrees,
　　　And fears 'tis gone for aye.

Polly. *The Boy thus, when his Sparrow's flown,*
　　　The bird in silence eyes;
　　But soon as out of sight 'tis gone,
　　Whines, whimpers, sobs and cries.

[Parting, and looking back at each other with fondness; he at one door, she at the other.

ACT II.

SCENE I.—*A Tavern near* Newgate.

Jemmy Twitcher, *Crook-finger'd* Jack, Wat Dreary, Robin *of* Bagshot, Nimming Ned, Henry Paddington, Matt *of the* Mint, Ben Budge, *and the rest of the Gang, at the Table, with Wine, Brandy and Tobacco.*

Ben. But pr'ythee, *Matt*, what is become of thy brother *Tom?* I have not seen him since my return from transportation.

Matt. Poor brother *Tom* had an accident this time twelvemonth, and so clever a made fellow he was, that I could not save him from those fleaing rascals the Surgeons; and now, poor man, he is among the Otamys at *Surgeon's Hall.*

Ben. So it seems, his time was come.

Jem. But the present time is ours, and no body alive hath more. Why are the laws levell'd at us? are we more dishonest than the rest of mankind? what we win, gentlemen, is our own by the law of arms, and the right of conquest.

Crook. Where shall we find such another set of practical philosophers, who to a man are above the fear of Death?

Wat. Sound men, and true!

Robin. Of try'd courage, and indefatigable industry!

Ned. Who is there here that would not dye for his friend?

Harry. Who is there here that would betray him for his interest?

Matt. Show me a gang of Courtiers that can say as much.

Ben. We are for a just partition of the world, for every man hath a right to enjoy life.

Matt. We retrench the superfluities of mankind. The world is avaritious, and I hate avarice. A covetous fellow, like a Jack-daw, steals what he was never made to enjoy, for the sake of hiding it. These are the robbers of mankind, for money was made for the free-hearted and generous, and where is the injury of taking from another, what he hath not the heart to make use of?

Jem. Our several stations for the day are fixt. Good luck attend us all. Fill the glasses.

AIR XIX. Fill ev'ry glass, *&c.*

Matt.   *Fill ev'ry glass, for wine inspires us,*
           And fires us
    With courage, love and joy.
    Women and wine should life employ.
    Is there ought else on earth desirous?
Chorus. *Fill ev'ry glass,* &c.

SCENE II.

To them enter Macheath

Mach. Gentlemen, well met. My heart hath been with you this hour; but an unexpected affair hath detain'd me. No ceremony, I beg you.

Matt. We were just breaking up to go upon duty. Am I to have the honour of taking the air with you, Sir, this evening upon the Heath? I drink a dram now and then with the Stage-coachmen in the way of friendship and intelligence; and I know that about this time there will be passengers upon the western road, who are worth speaking with.

Mach. I was to have been of that party—but——

Matt. But what, Sir?

Mach. Is there any man who suspects my courage?

Matt. We have all been witnesses of it.

Mach. My honour and truth to the gang?

Matt. I'll be answerable for it.

Mach. In the division of our booty, have I ever shown the least marks of avarice or injustice?

Matt. By these questions something seems to have ruffled you. Are any of us suspected?

Mach. I have a fixt confidence, gentlemen, in you all, as men of honour, and as such I value and respect you. *Peachum* is a man that is useful to us.

Matt. Is he about to play us any foul play? I'll shoot him through the head.

Mach. I beg you, gentlemen, act with conduct and discretion. A pistol is your last resort.

Matt. He knows nothing of this meeting.

Mach. Business cannot go on without him. He is a man who knows the world, and is a necessary agent to us. We have had a slight difference, and till it is accommodated I shall be oblig'd to keep out of his way. Any private dispute of mine shall be of no ill consequence to my friends. You must continue to act under his direction, for the moment we break loose from him, our gang is ruin'd.

Matt. As a bawd to a whore, I grant you, he is to us of great convenience.

Mach. Make him believe I have quitted the gang, which I can never do but with life. At our private quarters I will continue to meet you. A week or so will probably reconcile us.

Matt. Your instructions shall be observ'd. 'Tis now high time for us to repair to our several duties; so till the evening, at our quarters in *Moorfields*, we bid you farewell.

Mach. I shall wish my self with you. Success attend you.

[*Sits down melancholy at the Table.*

AIR XX. March in *Rinaldo*, with Drums and Trumpets.

Matt. *Let us take the road.*
> *Hark! I hear the sound of coaches!*
> *The hour of attack approaches,*
> *To your arms, brave boys, and load.*
> *See the ball I hold!*
> *Let the Chymists toil like asses,*
> *Our fire their fire surpasses,*
> *And turns all our lead to gold.*

[The Gang rang'd in the front of the Stage, load their pistols, and stick them under their girdles; then go off singing the first part in Chorus.

SCENE III.

Macheath, Drawer.

Mach. What a fool is a fond wench! Polly is most confoundedly bit.——I love the sex. And a man who loves money, might as well be contented with one guinea, as I with one woman. The town perhaps hath been as much oblig'd to me, for recruiting it with free-hearted ladies, as to any recruiting Officer in the army. If it were not for us and the other gentlemen of the sword, *Drury-lane* would be uninhabited.

AIR XXI. Would you have a young Virgin, &c.

> *If the heart of a man is deprest with cares,*
> *The mist is dispell'd when a woman appears;*
> *Like the notes of a fiddle, she sweetly, sweetly*
> *Raises the spirits, and charms our ears.*
> *Roses and lillies her cheeks disclose,*
> *But her ripe lips are more sweet than those.*

> *Press her,*
> *Caress her,*
> *With blisses,*
> *Her kisses*
> *Dissolve us in pleasure, and soft repose.*

I must have women. There is nothing unbends the mind like them. Money is not so strong a cordial for the time.——Drawer.——[*Enter* Drawer.] Is the Porter gone for all the ladies, according to my directions?

Draw. I expect him back every minute. But you know, Sir, you sent him as far as *Hockley in the Hole*, for three of the ladies, for one in *Vinegar Yard*, and for the rest of them somewhere about *Lewkner's Lane*. Sure some of them are below, for I hear the barr bell. As they come I will show them up.——Coming, coming.

SCENE IV.

Macheath, Mrs. Coaxer, Dolly Trull, Mrs. Vixen, Betty Doxy, Jenny Diver, Mrs. Slammekin, Suky Tawdry, *and* Molly Brazen.

Mach. Dear Mrs. *Coaxer*, you are welcome. You look charmingly to-day. I hope you don't want the repairs of quality, and lay on paint.——*Dolly Trull!* kiss me, you slut; are you as amorous as ever, hussy? You are always so taken up with stealing hearts, that you don't allow your self time to steal any thing else.—Ah *Dolly*, thou wilt ever be a Coquette!——Mrs. *Vixen*, I'm yours, I always lov'd a woman of wit and spirit; they make charming mistresses, but plaguy wives.——*Betty Doxy!* come hither, hussy. Do you drink as hard as ever? You had better stick to good wholesome beer; for in troth, *Betty*, strong-waters will in time ruin your constitution. You should leave those to your betters.——What! and my pretty *Jenny Diver* too! As prim and demure as ever! There is not any Prude, though ever so high bred, hath a more sanctify'd look, with a more mischievous heart. Ah! thou art a dear artful hypocrite.——Mrs. *Slammekin!* as careless and genteel as ever! all you fine ladies, who know your own beauty, affect an undress.——But see, here's *Suky Tawdry* come to contradict what I was saying. Every thing she gets one way she lays out upon her back. Why, *Suky*, you must keep at least a dozen Tally-men. *Molly Brazen!* [*She kisses him.*] That's well done. I love a free-hearted wench. Thou hast a most agreeable assurance, girl, and art as willing as a Turtle.——But hark! I hear musick. The Harper is at the door. If *musick be the food of Love, play on.* E'er you seat your selves, ladies, what think you of a dance? Come in. [*Enter Harper.*] Play the *French* Tune, that Mrs. *Slammekin* was so fond of.

> [*A Dance* à la ronde *in the* French *manner;*
> *near the end of it this Song and Chorus.*

AIR XXII. Cotillon.

Youth's the season made for joys,
  Love is then our duty;
She alone who that employs,
  Well deserves her beauty.
    Let's be gay,
    While we may,
  Beauty's a flower despis'd in decay.
Chorus. *Youth's the season, &c.*
Let us drink and sport to-day,
  Ours is not to-morrow.
Love with youth flies swift away,
  Age is nought but sorrow.
    Dance and sing,
    Time's on the wing,
  Life never knows the return of spring.
Chorus. *Let us drink, &c.*

Mach. Now pray ladies, take your places. Here Fellow. [*Pays the Harper.*]
Bid the Drawer bring us more wine. [*Ex. Harper.*] If any of the ladies chuse
gin, I hope they will be so free to call for it.

Jenny. You look as if you meant me. Wine is strong enough for me. Indeed, Sir, I never drink strong-waters, but when I have the Cholic.

Mach. Just the excuse of the fine ladies! Why, a lady of quality is never
without the Cholic. I hope, Mrs. *Coaxer*, you have had good success of late
in your visits among the Mercers.

Coax. We have so many interlopers——Yet with industry, one may still
have a little picking. I carried a silver-flower'd lutestring and a piece of black
padesoy to Mr. *Peachum's* Lock but last week.

Vix. There's *Molly Brazen* hath the ogle of a Rattlesnake. She rivitted
a Linnen-draper's eye so fast upon her, that he was nick'd of three pieces of
cambric before he could look off.

Braz. O dear madam!——But sure nothing can come up to your handling
of laces! And then you have such a sweet deluding tongue! To cheat a
man is nothing; but the woman must have fine parts indeed who cheats a
woman!

Vix. Lace, madam, lyes in a small compass, and is of easy conveyance.
But you are apt, madam, to think too well of your friends.

Coax. If any woman hath more art than another, to be sure, 'tis *Jenny
Diver*. Though her fellow be never so agreeable, she can pick his pocket as
cooly, as if money were her only pleasure. Now that is a command of the
passions uncommon in a woman!

Jenny. I never go to the tavern with a man, but in the view of business. I
have other hours, and other sort of men for my pleasure. But had I your
address, madam——

Mach. Have done with your compliments, ladies; and drink about: You are not so fond of me, *Jenny*, as you use to be.

Jenny. 'Tis not convenient, Sir, to show my fondness among so many rivals. 'Tis your own choice, and not the warmth of my inclination, that will determine you.

AIR XXIII. All in a misty morning.

Before the barn-door crowing,
  The Cock by Hens attended,
His eyes around him throwing,
  Stands for a while suspended:
Then one he singles from the crew,
  And cheers the happy Hen;
With how do you do, and how do you do,
And how do you do again.

Mach. Ah *Jenny!* thou art a dear slut.

Trull. Pray, madam, were you ever in keeping?

Tawd. I hope, madam, I ha'nt been so long upon the town, but I have met with some good fortune as well as my neighbours.

Trull. Pardon me, madam, I meant no harm by the question; 'twas only in the way of conversation.

Tawd. Indeed, madam, if I had not been a fool, I might have liv'd very handsomely with my last friend. But upon his missing five guineas, he turn'd me off. Now I never suspected he had counted them.

Slam. Who do you look upon, madam, as your best sort of keepers?

Trull. That, madam, is thereafter as they be.

Slam. I, madam, was once kept by a *Jew;* and, bating their religion, to women they are a good sort of people.

Tawd. Now for my part, I own I like an old fellow: for we always make them pay for what they can't do.

Vix. A spruce Prentice, let me tell you, ladies, is no ill thing, they bleed freely. I have sent at least two or three dozen of them, in my time, to the Plantations.

Jenny. But to be sure, Sir, with so much good fortune as you have had upon the road, you must be grown immensely rich.

Mach. The road, indeed, hath done me justice, but the gaming-table hath been my ruin.

AIR XXIV. When once I lay with another man's wife.

Jen. *The Gamesters and Lawyers are jugglers alike,*
  If they meddle your all is in danger:
Like Gypsies, if once they can finger a souse,
Your pockets they pick, and they pilfer your house,
  And give your estate to a stranger.

A man of courage should never put any thing to the risque, but his life. These are the tools of a man of honour. Cards and Dice are only fit for cowardly cheats, who prey upon their friends.

[*She takes up his Pistol.* Tawdry *takes up the other.*

Tawd. This, Sir, is fitter for your hand. Besides your loss of money, 'tis a loss to the ladies. Gaming takes you off from women. How fond could I be of you! but before company, 'tis ill bred.

Mach. Wanton hussies!

Jen. I must and will have a kiss to give my wine a zest.

[*They take him about the neck, and make signs to* Peachum *and Constables; who rush in upon him.*

SCENE V.

To them Peachum *and Constables.*

Peach. I seize you, Sir, as my prisoner.

Mach. Was this well done, *Jenny?*——Women are decoy Ducks; who can trust them! Beasts, Jades, Jilts, Harpies, Furies, Whores!

Peach. Your case, Mr. *Macheath,* is not particular. The greatest Heroes have been ruin'd by women. But, to do them justice, I must own they are a pretty sort of creatures, if we could trust them. You must now, Sir, take your leave of the ladies, and if they have a mind to make you a visit, they will be sure to find you at home. The gentleman, ladies, lodges in *Newgate.* Constables, wait upon the Captain to his lodgings.

AIR XXV. When first I laid siege to my *Chloris.*

Mach. *At the Tree I shall suffer with pleasure,*
At the Tree I shall suffer with pleasure,
Let me go where I will,
In all kinds of ill,
I shall find no such Furies as these are.

Peach. Ladies, I'll take care the reckoning shall be discharg'd.

[*Exit* Macheath, *guarded with* Peachum *and Constables.*

SCENE VI.

The Women remain.

Vix. Look ye, Mrs. *Jenny,* though Mr. *Peachum* may have made a private bargain with you and *Suky Tawdry* for betraying the Captain, as we were all assisting, we ought all to share alike.

Coax. I think, Mr. *Peachum,* after so long an acquaintance, might have trusted me as well as *Jenny Diver.*

Slam. I am sure at least three men of his hanging, and in a year's time too,
(if he did me justice) should be set down to my account.

Trull. Mrs. *Slammekin*, that is not fair. For you know one of them was
taken in bed with me.

Jenny. As far as a bowl of punch or a treat, I believe Mrs. *Suky* will join
with me.——As for any thing else, ladies, you cannot in conscience expect it.

Slam. Dear madam——

Trull. I would not for the world——

Slam. 'Tis impossible for me——

Trull. As I hope to be sav'd, madam——

Slam. Nay, then I must stay here all night——

Trull. Since you command me.   [*Exeunt with great Ceremony.*

SCENE VII. *Newgate.*

Lockit, *Turnkeys*, Macheath, *Constables.*

Lock. Noble Captain, you are welcome. You have not been a lodger of
mine this year and half. You know the custom, Sir. Garnish, Captain,
garnish. Hand me down those fetters there.

Mach. Those, Mr. *Lockit*, seem to be the heaviest of the whole set. With
your leave, I should like the further pair better.

Lock. Look ye, Captain, we know what is fittest for our prisoners. When
a gentleman uses me with civility, I always do the best I can to please him—
Hand them down I say—We have them of all prices, from one guinea to ten,
and 'tis fitting every gentleman should please himself.

Mach. I understand you, Sir. [*Gives money.*] The fees here are so many,
and so exorbitant, that few fortunes can bear the expence of getting off handsomly, or of dying like a gentleman.

Lock. Those, I see, will fit the Captain better.——Take down the further
pair. Do but examine them, Sir—Never was better work.——How genteely
they are made!——They will fit as easy as a glove, and the nicest man in
England might not be asham'd to wear them. [*He puts on the chains.*] If I
had the best gentleman in the land in my custody I could not equip him
more handsomly. And so, Sir—I now leave you to your private meditations.

SCENE VIII.

Macheath.

AIR XXVI. Courtiers, courtiers think it no harm.

> *Man may escape from rope and gun;*
> *Nay, some have out-liv'd the Doctor's pill:*
> *Who takes a woman must be undone,*
> *That Basilisk is sure to kill.*

The Fly that sips treacle is lost in the sweets,
So he that tastes woman, woman, woman,
He that tastes woman, ruin meets.

To what a woful plight have I brought my self! Here must I (all day long, 'till I am hang'd) be confin'd to hear the reproaches of a wench who lays her ruin at my door.——I am in the custody of her father, and to be sure if he knows of the matter, I shall have a fine time on't betwixt this and my execution.——But I promis'd the wench marriage.——What signifies a promise to a woman? does not man in marriage itself promise a hundred things that he never means to perform? Do all we can, women will believe us; for they look upon a promise as an excuse for following their own inclinations.—— But here comes *Lucy*, and I cannot get from her——wou'd I were deaf!

SCENE IX.

Macheath, Lucy.

Lucy. You base man, you,——how can you look me in the face after what hath past between us?——See here, perfidious wretch, how I am forc'd to bear about the load of Infamy you have laid upon me——O *Macheath!* thou hast robb'd me of my quiet——to see thee tortur'd would give me pleasure.

AIR XXVII. A lovely Lass to a Friar came.

Thus when a good huswife sees a Rat
In her trap in the morning taken,
With pleasure her heart goes pit a pat,
In revenge for her loss of bacon.
Then she throws him
To the Dog or Cat,
To be worried, crush'd and shaken.

Mach. Have you no bowels, no tenderness, my dear *Lucy*, to see a husband in these circumstances?
Lucy. A husband!
Mach. In ev'ry respect but the form, and that, my dear, may be said over us at any time.——Friends should not insist upon ceremonies. From a man of honour, his word is as good as his bond.
Lucy. 'Tis the pleasure of all you fine men to insult the women you have ruin'd.

AIR XXVIII. 'Twas when the Sea was roaring.

How cruel are the traytors,
Who lye and swear in jest,
To cheat unguarded creatures
Of virtue, fame, and rest!

> *Whoever steals a shilling,*
>   *Thro' shame the guilt conceals:*
> *In love the perjur'd villain*
>   *With boasts the theft reveals.*

Mach. The very first opportunity, my dear, (have but patience) you shall be my wife in whatever manner you please.

Lucy. Insinuating monster! And so you think I know nothing of the affair of Miss *Polly Peachum*.——I could tear thy eyes out!

Mach. Sure, *Lucy*, you can't be such a fool as to be jealous of *Polly!*

Lucy. Are you not married to her, you brute, you?

Mach. Married! Very good. The wench gives it out only to vex thee, and to ruin me in thy good opinion. 'Tis true, I go to the house; I chat with the girl, I kiss her, I say a thousand things to her (as all gentlemen do) that mean nothing, to divert myself; and now the silly jade hath set it about that I am married to her, to let me know what she would be at. Indeed, my dear *Lucy*, these violent passions may be of ill consequence to a woman in your condition.

Lucy. Come, come, Captain, for all your assurance, you know that Miss *Polly* hath put it out of your power to do me the justice you promis'd me.

Mach. A jealous woman believes ev'ry thing her passion suggests. To convince you of my sincerity, if we can find the Ordinary, I shall have no scruples of making you my wife; and I know the consequence of having two at a time.

Lucy. That you are only to be hang'd, and so get rid of them both.

Mach. I am ready, my dear *Lucy*, to give you satisfaction——if you think there is any in marriage.——What can a man of honour say more?

Lucy. So then it seems you are not married to Miss *Polly*.

Mach. You know, *Lucy*, the girl is prodigiously conceited. No man can say a civil thing to her, but (like other fine ladies) her vanity makes her think he's her own for ever and ever.

AIR XXIX. The Sun had loos'd his weary teams.

> *The first time at the looking-glass*
>   *The mother sets her daughter,*
> *The Image strikes the smiling lass*
>   *With self-love ever after.*
> *Each time she looks, she, fonder grown,*
>   *Thinks ev'ry charm grows stronger:*
> *But alas, vain maid, all eyes but your own*
>   *Can see you are not younger.*

When women consider their own beauties, they are all alike unreasonable in their demands; for they expect their lovers should like them as long as they like themselves.

Lucy. Yonder is my father——perhaps this way we may light upon the Ordinary, who shall try if you will be as good as your word.——For I long to be made an honest woman.

SCENE X.

Peachum, Lockit *with an Account-Book.*

Lock. In this last affair, brother *Peachum,* we are agreed. You have consented to go halves in *Macheath.*

Peach. We shall never fall out about an execution.—But as to that article, pray how stands our last year's account?

Lock. If you will run your eye over it, you'll find 'tis fair and clearly stated.

Peach. This long arrear of the government is very hard upon us! Can it be expected that we should hang our acquaintance for nothing, when our betters will hardly save theirs without being paid for it. Unless the people in employment pay better, I promise them for the future, I shall let other rogues live besides their own.

Lock. Perhaps, brother, they are afraid these matters may be carried too far. We are treated too by them with contempt, as if our profession were not reputable.

Peach. In one respect indeed, our employment may be reckoned dishonest, because, like great Statesmen, we encourage those who betray their friends.

Lock. Such language, brother, any where else, might turn to your prejudice. Learn to be more guarded, I beg you.

AIR XXX. How happy are we, *&c.*

> *When you censure the age,*
> *Be cautious and sage,*
> *Lest the Courtiers offended should be:*
> *If you mention vice or bribe,*
> *'Tis so pat to all the tribe;*
> *Each cries—That was levell'd at me.*

Peach. Here's poor *Ned Clincher's* name, I see. Sure, brother *Lockit,* there was a little unfair proceeding in *Ned's* case: for he told me in the condemn'd hold, that for value receiv'd, you had promis'd him a Session or two longer without molestation.

Lock. Mr. *Peachum,*—this is the first time my honour was ever call'd in question.

Peach. Business is at an end—if once we act dishonourably.

Lock. Who accuses me?

Peach. You are warm, brother.

Lock. He that attacks my honour, attacks my livelyhood.—And this usage —Sir—is not to be borne.

Peach. Since you provoke me to speak—I must tell you too, that Mrs. *Coaxer* charges you with defrauding her of her information-money, for the apprehending of curl-pated *Hugh.* Indeed, indeed, brother, we must punctually pay our Spies, or we shall have no Information.

Lock. Is this language to me, Sirrah——who have sav'd you from the gallows, Sirrah!   [*Collaring each other.*

Peach. If I am hang'd, it shall be for ridding the world of an arrant rascal.

Lock. This hand shall do the office of the halter you deserve, and throttle you—you dog!—

Peach. Brother, brother,—we are both in the wrong—we shall be both losers in the dispute—for you know we have it in our power to hang each other. You should not be so passionate.

Lock. Nor you so provoking.

Peach. 'Tis our mutual interest; 'tis for the interest of the world we should agree. If I said any thing, brother, to the prejudice of your character, I ask pardon.

Lock. Brother *Peachum*—I can forgive as well as resent.—Give me your hand. Suspicion does not become a friend.

Peach. I only meant to give you occasion to justifie yourself: But I must now step home, for I expect the gentleman about this Snuff-box, that *Filch* nimm'd two nights ago in the Park. I appointed him at this hour.

SCENE XI.

Lockit, Lucy.

Lock. Whence come you, hussy?

Lucy. My tears might answer that question.

Lock. You have then been whimpering and fondling, like a Spaniel, over that fellow that hath abus'd you.

Lucy. One can't help love; one can't cure it. 'Tis not in my power to obey you, and hate him.

Lock. Learn to bear your husband's death like a reasonable woman. 'Tis not the fashion, now-a-days, so much as to affect sorrow upon these occasions. No woman would ever marry, if she had not the chance of mortality for a release. Act like a woman of spirit, hussy, and thank your father for what he is doing.

AIR XXXI. Of a noble Race was *Shenkin.*

Lucy. *Is then his fate decreed, Sir,*
        Such a man can I think of quitting?
        When first we met, so moves me yet,
        O see how my heart is splitting!

Lock. Look ye, *Lucy*—there is no saving him.——So, I think, you must ev'n do like other widows—buy your self weeds, and be cheerful.

AIR XXXII.

You'll think, e'er many days ensue,
This sentence not severe;
I hang your husband, child, 'tis true,
But with him hang your care.
Twang dang dillo dee.

Like a good wife, go moan over your dying husband. That, child, is your duty—consider girl, you can't have the man and the money too—so make yourself as easy as you can by getting all you can from him.

SCENE XII.

Lucy, Macheath.

Lucy. Though the Ordinary was out of the way to day, I hope, my dear, you will, upon the first opportunity, quiet my scruples—Oh Sir!—my father's hard heart is not to be soften'd, and I am in the utmost despair.

Mach. But if I could raise a small sum—would not twenty Guineas, think you, move him?—Of all the arguments in the way of business, the perquisite is the most prevailing.——Your father's perquisites for the escape of prisoners must amount to a considerable sum in the year. Money well tim'd, and properly apply'd, will do any thing.

AIR XXXIII. *London* Ladies.

If you at an Office solicit your due,
And would not have matters neglected;
You must quicken the Clerk with the perquisite too,
To do what his duty directed.
Or would you the frowns of a lady prevent,
She too has this palpable failing,
The perquisite softens her into consent;
That reason with all is prevailing.

Lucy. What love or money can do shall be done: for all my comfort depends upon your safety.

SCENE XIII.

Lucy, Macheath, Polly.

Polly. Where is my dear husband?—Was a rope ever intended for this neck!—O let me throw my arms about it, and throttle thee with love!—Why dost thou turn away from me?—'Tis thy *Polly*—'tis thy wife.

Mach. Was ever such an unfortunate rascal as I am!

Lucy. Was there ever such another villain!

Polly. O *Macheath!* was it for this we parted? Taken! Imprison'd! Try'd! Hang'd!—cruel reflection! I'll stay with thee 'till death—no force shall tear thy dear wife from thee now.—What means my love?—Not one kind word! not one kind look! think what thy *Polly* suffers to see thee in this condition.

AIR XXXIV. All in the Downs, &c.

Thus when the Swallow, seeking prey,
Within the sash is closely pent,
His consort with bemoaning lay,
Without sits pining for th' event.
Her chatt'ring lovers all around her skim;
She heeds them not (poor bird) her soul's with him.

Mach. I must disown her. [*Aside.*] The wench is distracted.

Lucy. Am I then bilk'd of my virtue? Can I have no reparation? Sure men were born to lye, and women to believe them! O Villain! Villain!

Polly. Am I not thy wife?—Thy neglect of me, thy aversion to me too severely proves it.—Look on me.—Tell me, am I not thy wife?

Lucy. Perfidious wretch!

Polly. Barbarous husband!

Lucy. Hadst thou been hang'd five months ago, I had been happy.

Polly. And I too—If you had been kind to me 'till death, it would not have vex'd me—And that's no very unreasonable request (though from a wife) to a man who hath not above seven or eight days to live.

Lucy. Art thou then married to another? Hast thou two wives, monster?

Mach. If women's tongues can cease for an answer—hear me.

Lucy. I won't.—Flesh and blood can't bear my usage.

Polly. Shall I not claim my own? Justice bids me speak.

AIR XXXV. Have you heard of a frolicksome ditty.

Mach. *How happy could I be with either,*
Were t'other dear charmer away!
But while you thus teaze me together,
To neither a word will I say,
But tol de rol, &c.

Polly. Sure, my dear, there ought to be some preference shown to a wife! At least she may claim the appearance of it. He must be distracted with his misfortunes, or he cou'd not use me thus!

Lucy. O Villain, Villain! thou hast deceiv'd me—I could even inform against thee with pleasure. Not a Prude wishes more heartily to have facts against her intimate acquaintance, than I now wish to have facts against thee. I would have her satisfaction, and they should all out.

AIR XXXVI. Irish Trot.

Polly. *I'm bubbled.*
Lucy. ――――*I'm bubbled.*
Polly. *Oh how I am troubled!*
Lucy. *Bambouzled, and bit!*
Polly. ――――*My distresses are doubled.*
Lucy. *When you come to the Tree, should the Hangman refuse,*
　　　These fingers, with pleasure, could fasten the noose.
Polly. *I'm bubbled,* &c.

Mach. Be pacified, my dear *Lucy*—This is all a fetch of *Polly's* to make me desperate with you in case I get off. If I am hang'd, she would fain have the credit of being thought my widow—Really, *Polly*, this is no time for a dispute of this sort; for whenever you are talking of marriage, I am thinking of hanging.

Polly. And hast thou the heart to persist in disowning me?

Mach. And hast thou the heart to persist in persuading me that I am married? Why, *Polly*, dost thou seek to aggravate my misfortunes?

Lucy. Really, Miss *Peachum*, you but expose yourself. Besides, 'tis barbarous in you to worry a gentleman in his circumstances.

AIR XXXVII.

Polly.　　　　　*Cease your funning;*
　　　　　　　Force or cunning
　　　　Never shall my heart trapan.
　　　　　　All these sallies
　　　　　　Are but malice
　　　To seduce my constant man.
　　　　　　'Tis most certain,
　　　　　　By their flirting
　　Women oft have envy shown:
　　　　　Pleas'd, to ruin
　　　　　Others wooing;
　　Never happy in their own!

Polly. Decency, madam, methinks might teach you to behave yourself with some reserve with the husband, while his wife is present.

Mach. But seriously, *Polly*, this is carrying the joke a little too far.

Lucy. If you are determin'd, madam, to raise a disturbance in the prison, I shall be oblig'd to send for the Turnkey to shew you the door. I am sorry, madam, you force me to be so ill bred.

Polly. Give me leave to tell you, madam; these forward Airs don't become you in the least, madam. And my duty, madam, obliges me to stay with my husband, madam.

AIR XXXVIII. Good-morrow, Gossip *Joan*.

Lucy. *Why how now, madam* Flirt?
    If you thus must chatter,
    And are for flinging dirt,
    Let's try who best can spatter;
        Madam Flirt!
Polly. *Why how now, saucy Jade;*
    Sure the wench is tipsy!
    How can you see me made   [To him.
    The scoff of such a Gipsy?
        Saucy Jade!   [To her.

SCENE XIV.

Lucy, Macheath, Polly, Peachum.

Peach. Where's my wench? Ah hussy! hussy!—Come you home, you slut; and when your fellow is hang'd, hang yourself, to make your family some amends.

Polly. Dear, dear father, do not tear me from him—I must speak; I have more to say to him—Oh! twist thy fetters about me, that he may not haul me from thee!

Peach. Sure all women are alike! If ever they commit the folly, they are sure to commit another by exposing themselves—Away—Not a word more—You are my prisoner now, hussy.

AIR XXXIX. Irish Howl.

Polly. *No power on earth can e'er divide*
    The knot that sacred Love hath ty'd.
    When parents draw against our mind,
    The true-love's knot they faster bind.
    Oh, oh ray, oh Amborah—oh, oh, &c.
      [*Holding* Macheath, Peachum, *pulling her.*

SCENE XV.

Lucy, Macheath.

Mach. I am naturally compassionate, wife; so that I could not use the wench as she deserv'd; which made you at first suspect there was something in what she said.

Lucy. Indeed, my dear, I was strangely puzzled.

Mach. If that had been the case, her father would never have brought me into this circumstance—No, *Lucy*,—I had rather dye than be false to thee.

Lucy. How happy am I, if you say this from your heart! For I love thee so, that I could sooner bear to see thee hang'd than in the arms of another.

Mach. But couldst thou bear to see me hang'd?

Lucy. O *Macheath*, I can never live to see that day.

Mach. You see, *Lucy*, in the account of Love you are in my debt; and you must now be convinc'd, that I rather chuse to die than be another's.—Make me, if possible, love thee more, and let me owe my life to thee—If you refuse to assist me, *Peachum* and your father will immediately put me beyond all means of escape.

Lucy. My father, I know, hath been drinking hard with the Prisoners: and I fancy he is now taking his nap in his own room—If I can procure the keys, shall I go off with thee, my dear?

Mach. If we are together, 'twill be impossible to lye conceal'd. As soon as the search begins to be a little cool, I will send to thee—'Till then my heart is thy prisoner.

Lucy. Come then, my dear husband—owe thy life to me—and though you love me not—be grateful—But that *Polly* runs in my head strangely.

Mach. A moment of time may make us unhappy forever.

AIR XL. The Lass of *Patie's* Mill.

Lucy.

I like the Fox shall grieve,
  Whose mate hath left her side,
Whom Hounds, from morn to eve,
  Chase o'er the country wide.
Where can my lover hide?
  Where cheat the wary pack?
If Love be not his guide,
  He never will come back!

ACT III.

SCENE I.—SCENE *Newgate*.

Lockit, Lucy.

Lock. To be sure, wench, you must have been aiding and abetting to help him to this escape.

Lucy. Sir, here hath been *Peachum* and his daughter *Polly*, and to be sure they know the ways of *Newgate* as well as if they had been born and bred in the place all their lives. Why must all your suspicion light upon me?

Lock. *Lucy*, *Lucy*, I will have none of these shuffling answers.

Lucy. Well then——If I know any thing of him I wish I may be burnt!

Lock. Keep your temper, *Lucy*, or I shall pronounce you guilty.

Lucy. Keep yours, Sir,——I do wish I may be burnt. I do——And what can I say more to convince you?

Lock. Did he tip handsomely?——How much did he come down with? Come hussy, don't cheat your father; and I shall not be angry with you—— Perhaps, you have made a better bargain with him than I could have done—— How much, my good girl?

Lucy. You know, Sir, I am fond of him, and would have given money to have kept him with me.

Lock. Ah, *Lucy!* thy education might have put thee more upon thy guard; for a girl in the bar of an Alehouse is always besieg'd.

Lucy. Dear Sir, mention not my education——for 'twas to that I owe my ruin.

AIR XLI. If Love's a sweet passion, *&c.*

> *When young at the bar you first taught me to score,*
> *And bid me be free with my lips, and no more;*
> *I was kiss'd by the Parson, the Squire, and the Sot:*
> *When the guest was departed, the kiss was forgot.*
> *But his kiss was so sweet, and so closely he prest,*
> *That I languish'd and pin'd 'till I granted the rest.*

If you can forgive me, Sir, I will make a fair confession, for to be sure he hath been a most barbarous villain to me.

Lock. And so you have let him escape, hussy——have you?

Lucy. When a woman loves; a kind look, a tender word can persuade her to any thing——and I could ask no other bribe.

Lock. Thou wilt always be a vulgar slut, *Lucy*——If you would not be look'd upon as a fool, you should never do any thing but upon the foot of interest. Those that act otherwise are their own bubbles.

Lucy. But Love, Sir, is a misfortune that may happen to the most discreet woman, and in love we are all fools alike.——Notwithstanding all he swore, I am now fully convinc'd that *Polly Peachum* is actually his wife.——Did I let him escape (fool that I was!) to go to her?—*Polly* will wheedle her self into his money, and then *Peachum* will hang him, and cheat us both.

Lock. So I am to be ruin'd, because, forsooth, you must be in love!——a very pretty excuse!

Lucy. I could murder that impudent happy strumpet:——I gave him his life, and that creature enjoys the sweets of it.——Ungrateful *Macheath!*

AIR XLII. *South-Sea* Ballad.

> *My love is all madness and folly,*
> *Alone I lye,*
> *Toss, tumble, and cry,*
> *What a happy creature is* Polly!
> *Was e'er such a wretch as I!*

With rage I redden like scarlet,
That my dear inconstant Varlet,
    Stark blind to my charms,
    Is lost in the arms
Of that Jilt, that inveigling Harlot!
    Stark blind to my charms,
    Is lost in the arms
Of that Jilt, that inveigling Harlot!
This, this my resentment alarms.

Lock. And so, after all this mischief, I must stay here to be entertain'd with your catterwauling, mistress Puss!——Out of my sight, wanton Strumpet! you shall fast and mortify yourself into reason, with now and then a little handsome discipline to bring you to your senses.——Go.

SCENE II.

Lockit.

Peachum then intends to outwit me in this affair; but I'll be even with him.——The dog is leaky in his liquor, so I'll ply him that way, get the secret from him, and turn this affair to my own advantage.——Lions, Wolves, and Vulturs don't live together in herds, droves or flocks.——Of all animals of prey, man is the only sociable one. Every one of us preys upon his neighbour, and yet we herd together.——*Peachum* is my companion, my friend——According to the custom of the world, indeed, he may quote thousands of Precedents for cheating me——And shall not I make use of the privilege of friendship to make him a return?

AIR XLIII. *Packington's* Pound.

Thus Gamesters united in friendship are found,
Though they know that their industry all is a cheat;
They flock to their prey at the Dice-box's sound,
And join to promote one another's deceit.
    But if by mishap
    They fail of a chap,
To keep in their hands, they each other entrap.
Like Pikes, lank with hunger, who miss of their ends,
They bite their companions, and prey on their friends.

Now, *Peachum,* you and I, like honest Tradesmen, are to have a fair tryal which of us two can over-reach the other.——*Lucy*——[*Enter* Lucy.] Are there any of *Peachum's* people now in the house?

Lucy. Filch, Sir, is drinking a quartern of strong-waters in the next room with black *Moll.*

Lock. Bid him come to me.

SCENE III.

Lockit, Filch.

Lock. Why, boy, thou lookest as if thou wert half starv'd; like a shotten Herring.

Filch. One had need have the constitution of a horse to go through the business.——Since the favourite Child-getter was disabled by a mis-hap, I have pick'd up a little money by helping the ladies to a pregnancy against their being call'd down to sentence.——But if a man cannot get an honest livelihood any easier way, I am sure, 'tis what I can't undertake for another Session.

Lock. Truly, if that great man should tip off, 'twould be an irreparable loss. The vigor and prowess of a Knight-errant never sav'd half the ladies in distress that he hath done.——But, boy, can'st thou tell me where thy master is to be found?

Filch. At his Lock, Sir, at the *Crooked Billet*.

Lock. Very well.——I have nothing more with you. [*Ex.* Filch.] I'll go to him there, for I have many important affairs to settle with him; and in the way of those transactions, I'll artfully get into his secret.——So that *Macheath* shall not remain a day longer out of my clutches.

SCENE IV. *A Gaming-House.*

Macheath, *in a fine tarnish'd Coat*, Ben Budge, Matt *of the* Mint.

Mach. I am sorry, gentlemen, the road was so barren of money. When my friends are in difficulties, I am always glad that my fortune can be serviceable to them. [*Gives them money*.] You see, gentlemen, I am not a meer Court friend, who professes every thing and will do nothing.

AIR XLIV. Lillibulero.

> *The modes of the Court so common are grown,*
> *That a true friend can hardly be met;*
> *Friendship for interest is but a loan,*
> *Which they let out for what they can get.*
> *'Tis true, you find*
> *Some friends so kind,*
> *Who will give you good counsel themselves to defend.*
> *In sorrowful ditty,*
> *They promise, they pity,*
> *But shift you for money, from friend to friend.*

But we, gentlemen, have still honour enough to break through the corruptions of the world.—And while I can serve you, you may command me.

Ben. It grieves my heart that so generous a man should be involv'd in such difficulties, as oblige him to live with such ill company, and herd with gamesters.

Matt. See the partiality of mankind!—One man may steal a horse, better than another look over a hedge.—Of all mechanics, of all servile handycrafts-men, a gamester is the vilest. But yet, as many of the Quality are of the pro-fession, he is admitted amongst the politest company. I wonder we are not more respected.

Mach. There will be deep play tonight at *Marybone,* and consequently money may be pick'd up upon the road. Meet me there, and I'll give you the hint who is worth setting.

Matt. The fellow with a brown coat with a narrow gold binding, I am told, is never without money.

Mach. What do you mean, *Matt?*—Sure you will not think of meddling with him!—He's a good honest kind of a fellow, and one of us.

Ben. To be sure, Sir, we will put our selves under your direction.

Mach. Have an eye upon the money-lenders.—A *Rouleau,* or two, would prove a pretty sort of an expedition. I hate extortion.

Matt. Those *Rouleaus* are very pretty things.—I hate your Bank bills—there is such a hazard in putting them off.

Mach. There is a certain man of distinction, who in his time hath nick'd me out of a great deal of the ready. He is in my cash, *Ben;*—I'll point him out to you this evening, and you shall draw upon him for the debt.—The company are met; I hear the Dice-box in the other room. So, gentlemen, your servant. You'll meet me at *Marybone.*

SCENE V. Peachum's *Lock.*

A Table with Wine, Brandy, Pipes and Tobacco.
Peachum, Lockit.

Lock. The Coronation account, brother *Peachum,* is of so intricate a nature, that I believe it will never be settled.

Peach. It consists indeed of a great variety of articles.—It was worth to our people, in fees of different kinds, above ten instalments.—This is part of the account, brother, that lies open before us.

Lock. A lady's tail of rich Brocade—that, I see, is dispos'd of.

Peach. To Mrs. *Diana Trapes,* the Tally-woman, and she will make a good hand on't in shoes and slippers, to trick out young ladies, upon their going into keeping.—

Lock. But I don't see any article of the Jewels.

Peach. Those are so well known, that they must be sent abroad—you'll find them enter'd under the article of Exportation.—As for the Snuff-boxes, Watches, Swords, &c.—I thought it best to enter them under their several heads.

Lock. Seven and twenty women's pockets compleat; with the several things therein contain'd; all seal'd, number'd, and enter'd.

Peach. But, brother, it is impossible for us now to enter upon this affair.—We should have the whole day before us.—Besides, the account of the last half year's Plate is a book by it self, which lies at the other Office.

Lock. Bring us then more liquor.—To-day shall be for pleasure—to-morrow for business.—Ah brother, those daughters of ours are two slippery hussies—keep a watchful eye upon *Polly*, and *Macheath* in a day or two shall be our own again.

AIR XLV. Down in the North Country.

Lock. *What Gudgeons are we men!*
Ev'ry woman's easy prey.
Though we have felt the hook, agen
We bite, and they betray.

The bird that hath been trapt,
When he hears his calling mate,
To her he flies, again he's clapt
Within the wiry grate.

Peach. But what signifies catching the Bird, if your daughter *Lucy* will set open the door of the Cage?

Lock. If men were answerable for the follies and frailties of their wives and daughters, no friends could keep a good correspondence together for two days.—This is unkind of you, brother; for among good friends, what they say or do goes for nothing.

Enter a Servant.

Serv. Sir, here's Mrs. *Diana Trapes* wants to speak with you.

Peach. Shall we admit her, brother *Lockit?*

Lock. By all means—she's a good customer, and a fine-spoken woman—and a woman who drinks and talks so freely will enliven the conversation.

Peach. Desire her to walk in. [*Exit Servant.*

SCENE VI.

Peachum, Lockit, Mrs. Trapes.

Peach. Dear Mrs. *Dye*, your servant—one may know by your kiss, that your Ginn is excellent.

Trap. I was always very curious in my liquors.

Lock. There is no perfum'd breath like it—I have been long acquainted with the flavour of those lips—han't I, Mrs. *Dye?*

Trap. Fill it up.—I take as large draughts of liquor, as I did of love.—I hate a Flincher in either.

AIR XLVI. A Shepherd kept sheep, &c.

In the days of my youth I could bill like a Dove, fa, la, la, &c.
Like a Sparrow at all times was ready for love, fa, la, la, &c.
The life of all mortals in kissing should pass,
Lip to lip while we're young—then the lip to the glass, fa, la, &c.

But now, Mr. *Peachum,* to our business.—If you have blacks of any kind, brought in of late; Mantoes—Velvet Scarfs—Petticoats—let it be what it will —I am your chap—for all my ladies are very fond of mourning.

Peach. Why, look ye, Mrs. *Dye*—you deal so hard with us, that we can afford to give the gentlemen, who venture their lives for the goods, little or nothing.

Trap. The hard times oblige me to go very near in my dealing.—To be sure, of late years I have been a great sufferer by the Parliament.—Three thousand pounds would hardly make me amends.—The Act for destroying the Mint was a severe cut upon our business—'till then, if a customer stept out of the way—we knew where to have her—no doubt you know Mrs. *Coaxer*—there's a wench now ('till to-day) with a good suit of cloaths of mine upon her back, and I could never set eyes upon her for three months together.—Since the Act too against imprisonment for small sums, my loss there too hath been very considerable, and it must be so, when a lady can borrow a handsome petticoat, or a clean gown, and I not have the least hank upon her! And, o' my conscience, now-a-days most ladies take a delight in cheating, when they can do it with safety.

Peach. Madam, you had a handsome gold watch of us t'other day for seven Guineas.—Considering we must have our profit—to a gentleman upon the road, a gold watch will be scarce worth the taking.

Trap. Consider, Mr. *Peachum,* that watch was remarkable, and not of very safe sale.—If you have any black Velvet Scarfs—they are a handsome winter wear; and take with most gentlemen who deal with my customers.—'Tis I that put the ladies upon a good foot. 'Tis not youth or beauty that fixes their price. The gentlemen always pay according to their dress, from half a crown to two guineas; and yet those hussies make nothing of bilking of me.—Then too, allowing for accidents.—I have eleven fine customers now down under the Surgeon's hands,—what with fees and other expences, there are great goings-out, and no comings-in, and not a farthing to pay for at least a month's cloathing.—We run great risques—great risques indeed.

Peach. As I remember, you said something just now of Mrs. *Coaxer.*

Trap. Yes, Sir.—To be sure I stript her of a suit of my own cloaths about two hours ago; and have left her as she should be, in her shift, with a lover of hers at my house. She call'd him up stairs, as he was going to *Marybone* in a hackney-coach.—And I hope, for her own sake and mine, she will per-swade the Captain to redeem her, for the Captain is very generous to the ladies.

Lock. What Captain?

Trap. He thought I did not know him.—An intimate acquaintance of yours, Mr. *Peachum*—only captain *Macheath*—as fine as a Lord.

Peach. To-morrow, dear Mrs. *Dye*, you shall set your own price upon any of the goods you like—we have at least half a dozen Velvet Scarfs, and all at your service. Will you give me leave to make you a present of this suit of night-cloaths for your own wearing?—But are you sure it is captain *Macheath*?

Trap. Though he thinks I have forgot him; no body knows him better. I have taken a great deal of the Captain's money in my time at second-hand, for he always lov'd to have his ladies well drest.

Peach. Mr. *Lockit* and I have a little business with the Captain;—you understand me—and we will satisfie you for Mrs. *Coaxer's* debt.

Lock. Depend upon it—we will deal like men of honour.

Trap. I don't enquire after your affairs—so whatever happens, I wash my hands on't.—It hath always been my Maxim, that one friend should assist another.—But if you please—I'll take one of the Scarfs home with me, 'tis always good to have something in hand.

SCENE VII. *Newgate.*

Lucy.

Jealousy, rage, love and fear are at once tearing me to pieces. How I am weather-beaten and shatter'd with distresses!

AIR XLVII. One evening having lost my way.

I'm like a skiff on the Ocean tost,
 Now high, now low, with each billow born,
With her rudder broke, and her anchor lost,
 Deserted and all forlorn.
While thus I lie rolling and tossing all night,
That Polly lyes sporting on seas of delight!
 Revenge, revenge, revenge,
Shall appease my restless sprite.

I have the Rats-bane ready.—I run no risque; for I can lay her death upon the Ginn, and so many dye of that naturally that I shall never be call'd in question.—But say I were to be hang'd—I never could be hang'd for any thing that would give me greater comfort, than the poysoning that slut.

Enter Filch.

Filch. Madam, here's our Miss *Polly* come to wait upon you.

Lucy. Show her in.

SCENE VIII.

Lucy, Polly.

Lucy. Dear madam, your servant.—I hope you will pardon my passion, when I was so happy to see you last.—I was so over-run with the spleen, that I was perfectly out of my self. And really when one hath the spleen, every thing is to be excus'd by a friend.

AIR XLVIII. Now *Roger*, I'll tell thee, because thou'rt my son.

> *When a wife's in her pout,*
> *(As she's sometimes, no doubt)*
>   *The good husband as meek as a lamb,*
>   *Her vapours to still,*
>   *First grants her her will,*
> *And the quieting draught is a dram.*
> *Poor man! And the quieting draught is a dram.*

—I wish all our quarrels might have so comfortable a reconciliation.

Polly. I have no excuse for my own behaviour, madam, but my misfortunes.—And really, madam, I suffer too upon your account.

Lucy. But, Miss *Polly*—in the way of friendship, will you give me leave to propose a glass of Cordial to you?

Polly. Strong-waters are apt to give me the headache—I hope, Madam, you will excuse me.

Lucy. Not the greatest lady in the land could have better in her closet, for her own private drinking.—You seem mighty low in Spirits, my dear.

Polly. I am sorry, madam, my health will not allow me to accept of your offer.—I should not have left you in the rude manner I did when we met last, madam, had not my Papa haul'd me away so unexpectedly.—I was indeed somewhat provok'd, and perhaps might use some expressions that were disrespectful.—But really, madam, the Captain treated me with so much contempt and cruelty, that I deserv'd your pity, rather than your resentment.

Lucy. But since his escape, no doubt all matters are made up again.—Ah *Polly! Polly!* 'tis I am the unhappy wife; and he loves you as if you were only his mistress.

Polly. Sure, madam, you cannot think me so happy as to be the object of your jealousy.—A man is always afraid of a woman who loves him too well—so that I must expect to be neglected and avoided.

Lucy. Then our cases, my dear *Polly*, are exactly alike. Both of us indeed have been too fond.

AIR XLIX. *O Bessy Bell*, &c.

Polly. *A curse attends that woman's love,*
Who always would be pleasing.
Lucy. *The pertness of the billing Dove,*
Like tickling, is but teazing.
Polly. *What then in love can woman do?*
Lucy. *If we grow fond they shun us.*
Polly. *And when we fly them, they pursue:*
Lucy. *But leave us when they've won us.*

Lucy. Love is so very whimsical in both sexes, that it is impossible to be lasting.—But my heart is particular, and contradicts my own observation.
Polly. But really, mistress *Lucy*, by his last behaviour, I think I ought to envy you.—When I was forc'd from him, he did not shew the least tenderness.—But perhaps, he hath a heart not capable of it.

AIR L. Wou'd Fate to me *Belinda* give.

Among the men, Coquets we find,
Who court by turns all woman-kind;
And we grant all their hearts desir'd,
When they are flattered and admir'd.

The Coquets of both sexes are self-lovers, and that is a love no other whatever can dispossess. I fear, my dear *Lucy*, our husband is one of those.
Lucy. Away with these melancholy reflections,——indeed, my dear *Polly*, we are both of us a cup too low.—Let me prevail upon you, to accept of my offer.

AIR LI. Come, sweet lass.

Come, sweet lass,
Let's banish sorrow
'Till to-morrow;
Come sweet lass,
Let's take a chirping glass.
Wine can clear
The vapours of despair;
And make us light as air;
Then drink, and banish care.

I can't bear, child, to see you in such low spirits.—And I must persuade you to what I know will do you good.—I shall now soon be even with the hypocritical Strumpet. [*Aside.*

SCENE IX.

Polly.

Polly. All this wheedling of *Lucy* cannot be for nothing.—At this time too! when I know she hates me!—The dissembling of a woman is always the forerunner of mischief.—By pouring Strong-waters down my throat, she thinks to pump some secrets out of me—I'll be upon my guard, and won't taste a drop of her liquor, I'm resolv'd.

SCENE X.

Lucy, *with Strong-waters*. Polly.

Lucy. Come, Miss *Polly*.

Polly. Indeed, child, you have given yourself trouble to no purpose.—You must, my dear, excuse me.

Lucy. Really, Miss *Polly*, you are so squeamishly affected about taking a cup of Strong-waters, as a lady before company. I vow, *Polly*, I shall take it monstrously ill if you refuse me.—Brandy and Men (though women love them never so well) are always taken by us with some reluctance—unless 'tis in private.

Polly. I protest, madam, it goes against me.—What do I see! *Macheath* again in custody!—Now every glimmering of happiness is lost.

[*Drops the glass of liquor on the ground.*

Lucy. Since things are thus, I'm glad the wench hath escap'd: for by this event, 'tis plain, she was not happy enough to deserve to be poison'd.

SCENE XI.

Lockit, Macheath, Peachum, Lucy, Polly.

Lock. Set your heart to rest, Captain.—You have neither the chance of Love or Money for another escape—for you are order'd to be call'd down upon your Tryal immediately.

Peach. Away, hussies!—This is not a time for a man to be hamper'd with his wives.—You see, the gentleman is in chains already.

Lucy. O husband, husband, my heart long'd to see thee; but to see thee thus distracts me!

Polly. Will not my dear husband look upon his *Polly?* Why hadst thou not flown to me for protection? with me thou hadst been safe.

AIR LII. The last time I went o'er the Moor.

Polly. *Hither, dear husband, turn your eyes.*
Lucy.   *Bestow one glance to cheer me.*
Polly. *Think with that look, thy* Polly *dyes.*
Lucy.   *O shun me not,—but hear me.*
Polly. 'Tis Polly *sues.*
Lucy.   ——————*'Tis* Lucy *speaks.*
Polly. *Is thus true love requited?*
Lucy.   *My heart is bursting.*
Polly.   ——————*Mine too breaks.*
Lucy. *Must I,*
Polly.   ——————*Must I be slighted?*

Mach. What would you have me say, ladies?——You see, this affair will soon be at an end, without my disobliging either of you.

Peach. But the settling this point, Captain, might prevent a Law-suit between your two widows.

AIR LIII. *Tom Tinker's* my true love, &c.

Mach. *Which way shall I turn me—how can I decide?*
    Wives, the day of our death, are as fond as a bride.
    One wife is too much for most husbands to hear,
    But two at a time there's no mortal can bear.
    This way, and that way, and which way I will,
    What would comfort the one, t'other wife would take ill.

Polly. But if his own misfortunes have made him insensible to mine—a Father sure will be more compassionate.—Dear, dear Sir, sink the material evidence, and bring him off at his Tryal—*Polly* upon her knees begs it of you.

AIR LIV. I am a poor Shepherd undone.

    When my Hero in court appears,
      And stands arraign'd for his life,
    Then think of poor Polly's *tears;*
      For ah! poor Polly's *his wife.*
    Like the Sailor he holds up his hand,
      Distrest on the dashing wave.
    To die a dry death at land,
      Is as bad as a watry grave.
    And alas, poor Polly!
    Alack, and well-a-day!
    Before I was in love,
      Oh! every month was May.

Lucy. If *Peachum's* heart is harden'd; sure you, Sir, will have more compassion on a daughter.——I know the evidence is in your power.——How then can you be a tyrant to me?   [*Kneeling.*

AIR LV. *Ianthe* the lovely, *&c.*

When he holds up his hand arraign'd for his life,
O think of your daughter, and think I'm his wife!
What are cannons, or bombs, or clashing of swords?
For death is more certain by witnesses words.
Then nail up their lips; that dread thunder allay;
And each month of my life will hereafter be May.

Lock. Macheath's time is come, *Lucy.*—We know our own affairs, therefore let us have no more whimpering or whining.

AIR LVI. A Cobler there was, *&c.*

Our selves, like the Great, to secure a retreat,
When matters require it, must give up our gang:
        And good reason why,
        Or, instead of the fry,
        Ev'n Peachum and I,
Like poor petty rascals, might hang, hang;
Like poor petty rascals, might hang.

Peach. Set your heart at rest, *Polly.*——Your husband is to dye to day.—— Therefore, if you are not already provided, 'tis high time to look about for another. There's comfort for you, you slut.

Lock. We are ready, Sir, to conduct you to the *Old Baily.*

AIR LVII. Bonny *Dundee.*

Mach. The charge is prepar'd; the Lawyers are met;
        The Judges all rang'd (a terrible show!)
        I go, undismay'd.—For death is a debt,
        A debt on demand.—So, take what I owe.
Then, farewell, my love—dear charmers, adieu.
Contented I die—'tis the better for you.
Here ends all dispute the rest of our lives,
For this way at once I please all my wives.

Now, Gentlemen, I am ready to attend you.

SCENE XII.

Lucy, Polly, Filch.

Polly. Follow them, *Filch*, to the Court. And when the Tryal is over, bring me a particular account of his behaviour, and of every thing that happen'd.— You'll find me here with Miss *Lucy.* [*Ex.* Filch.] But why is all this Musick?

Lucy. The Prisoners, whose tryals are put off till next Session, are diverting themselves.

Polly. Sure there is nothing so charming as Musick! I'm fond of it to distraction—But alas!—now, all mirth seems an insult upon my affliction.——Let us retire, my dear *Lucy*, and indulge our sorrows.—The noisy crew, you see, are coming upon us.   [*Exeunt.*

A Dance of Prisoners in chains, &c.

SCENE XIII. *The Condemn'd Hold.*

Macheath, *in a melancholy posture.*

AIR LVIII. Happy Groves.

O cruel, cruel, cruel case!
Must I suffer this disgrace?

AIR LIX. Of all the girls that are so smart.

Of all the friends in time of grief,
When threat'ning Death looks grimmer,
Not one so sure can bring relief,
As this best friend a brimmer.   [Drinks.

AIR LX. *Britons* strike home.

Since I must swing,—I scorn, I scorn to wince or whine.
        [Rises.

AIR LXI. Chevy Chase.

But now again my spirits sink;
I'll raise them high with wine.
        [Drinks a glass of wine.

AIR LXII. To old Sir *Simon* the King.

But valour the stronger grows,
  The stronger liquor we're drinking.
And how can we feel our woes,
  When we've lost the trouble of thinking?   [Drinks.

AIR LXIII. Joy to great *Caesar.*

If thus—A man can die
Much bolder with brandy.
                    [Pours out a bumper of brandy.

AIR LXIV. There was an old woman, *&c.*

So I drink off this bumper—And now I can stand the test,
And my Comrades shall see, that I die as brave as the best.
                                              [Drinks.

AIR LXV. Did you ever hear of a gallant sailor.

But can I leave my pretty hussies,
Without one tear, or tender sigh?

AIR LXVI. Why are mine eyes still flowing.

Their eyes, their lips, their busses
Recall my love—Ah must I die!

AIR LXVII. Green sleeves.

Since laws were made for ev'ry degree,
To curb vice in others, as well as me,
I wonder we han't better company
  Upon Tyburn tree!
But gold from law can take out the sting;
And if rich men like us were to swing,
'Twould thin the land, such numbers to string
  Upon Tyburn tree!

Jailor. Some friends of yours, Captain, desire to be admitted—I leave you
together.

SCENE XIV.

Macheath, Ben Budge, Matt *of the* Mint.

Mach. For my having broke Prison, you see, gentlemen, I am ordered immediate execution.——The Sheriff's officers, I believe, are now at the door.——That *Jemmy Twitcher* should peach me, I own surpriz'd me!—'Tis a plain proof that the world is all alike, and that even our Gang can no more trust one another than other people. Therefore, I beg you, gentlemen, look well to your selves, for in all probability you may live some months longer.

Matt. We are heartily sorry, Captain, for your misfortune.—But 'tis what we must all come to.

Mach. *Peachum* and *Lockit*, you know, are infamous Scoundrels. Their lives are as much in your power, as yours are in theirs——Remember your dying friend!——'Tis my last request.——Bring those villains to the Gallows before you, and I am satisfied.

Matt. We'll do't.

Jailor. Miss *Polly* and Miss *Lucy* intreat a word with you.

Mach. Gentlemen, adieu.

SCENE XV.

Lucy, Macheath, Polly.

Mach. My dear *Lucy*——my dear *Polly*——Whatsoever hath past between us, is now at an end.—If you are fond of marrying again, the best advice I can give you, is to ship yourselves off for the *West-Indies*, where you'll have a fair chance of getting a husband a-piece; or by good luck, two or three, as you like best.

Polly. How can I support this sight!

Lucy. There is nothing moves one so much as a great man in distress.

AIR LXVIII. All you that must take a leap, &c.

Lucy. *Wou'd I might be hang'd!*
Polly. ———————— *And I would so too!*
Lucy. *To be hang'd with you,*
Polly. ——————*My dear, with you.*
Mach. *O leave me to thought! I fear! I doubt!*
 I tremble! I droop!——See my courage is out.
         [Turns up the empty bottle.
Polly. *No token of love?*
Mach. ——————*See my courage is out.*
         [Turns up the empty pot.

Lucy. *No token of love?*
Polly. ——————*Adieu.*
Lucy. ————————*Farewell.*
Mach. *But hark! I hear the toll of the bell.*
Chorus.   *Tol de rol lol,* &c.

Jailor. Four women more, Captain, with a child a-piece! See, here they come.   [*Enter women and children.*
Mach. What—four wives more!—This is too much.—Here—tell the Sheriff's Officers I am ready.   [*Exit* Macheath *guarded.*

SCENE XVI.

To them, Enter Player *and* Beggar.

Play. But honest friend, I hope you don't intend that *Macheath* shall be really executed.

Beg. Most certainly, Sir.—To make the piece perfect, I was for doing strict poetical Justice.—*Macheath* is to be hang'd; and for the other personages of the Drama, the Audience must have suppos'd they were all either hang'd or transported.

Play. Why then, friend, this is a down-right deep Tragedy. The catastrophe is manifestly wrong, for an Opera must end happily.

Beg. Your objection, Sir, is very just; and is easily remov'd. For you must allow, that in this kind of Drama, 'tis no matter how absurdly things are brought about—So—you rabble there—run and cry a Reprieve—let the prisoner be brought back to his wives in triumph.

Play. All this we must do, to comply with the taste of the town.

Beg. Through the whole piece you may observe such a similitude of manners in high and low life, that it is difficult to determine whether (in the fashionable vices) the fine gentlemen imitate the gentlemen of the road, or the gentlemen of the road the fine gentlemen.——Had the Play remain'd, as I at first intended, it would have carried a most excellent moral. 'Twould have shown that the lower sort of people have their vices in a degree as well as the rich: And that they are punish'd for them.

SCENE XVII.

To them Macheath *with Rabble, &c.*

Mach. So, it seems, I am not left to my choice, but must have a wife at last.——Look ye, my dears, we will have no controversie now. Let us give this day to mirth, and I am sure she who thinks her self my wife will testifie her joy by a dance.

All. Come, a Dance——a Dance.

Mach. Ladies, I hope you will give me leave to present a Partner to each of you. And (if I may without offence) for this time, I take *Polly* for mine.—And for life, you Slut,—for we were really marry'd.——As for the rest.——But at present keep your own secret.   [*To Polly.*

A DANCE.

AIR LXIX. Lumps of Pudding, &c.

Thus I stand like a Turk, *with his doxies around;*
From all sides their glances his passion confound;
For black, brown, and fair, his inconstancy burns,
And the different beauties subdue him by turns:
Each calls forth her charms, to provoke his desires:
Though willing to all; with but one he retires.
But think of this maxim, and put off your sorrow,
The wretch of to-day, may be happy to morrow.

Chorus.   *But think of this maxim,* &c.

THE RIVALS

A COMEDY
by Richard Brinsley Sheridan

PREFACE

A PREFACE to a play seems generally to be considered as a kind of closet-prologue, in which—if his piece has been successful—the author solicits that indulgence from the reader which he had before experienced from the audience: but as the scope and immediate object of a play is to please a mixed assembly in *representation* (whose judgment in the theatre at least is decisive), its degree of reputation is usually as determined as public, before it can be prepared for the cooler tribunal of the study. Thus any farther solicitude on the part of the writer becomes unnecessary at least, if not an intrusion: and if the piece has been condemned in the performance, I fear an address to the closet, like an appeal to posterity, is constantly regarded as the procrastination of a suit, from a consciousness of the weakness of the cause. From these considerations, the following comedy would certainly have been submitted to the reader, without any farther introduction than what it had in the representation, but that its success has probably been founded on a circumstance which the author is informed has not before attended a theatrical trial, and which consequently ought not to pass unnoticed.

I need scarcely add, that the circumstance alluded to was the withdrawing of the piece, to remove those imperfections in the first representation which were too obvious to escape reprehension, and too numerous to admit of a hasty correction. There are few writers, I believe, who, even in the fullest consciousness of error, do not wish to palliate the faults which they acknowledge; and, however trifling the performance, to second their confession of its deficiencies, by whatever plea seems least disgraceful to their ability. In the present instance, it cannot be said to amount either to candour or modesty in me, to acknowledge an extreme inexperience and want of judgment on matters, in which, without guidance from practice, or spur from success, a young man should scarcely boast of being an adept. If it be said, that under such disadvantages no one should attempt to write a play, I must beg leave to dissent from the position, while the first point of experience that I have gained on the subject is, a knowledge of the candour and judgment with which an impartial public distinguishes between the errors of inexperience and incapacity, and the indulgence which it shows even to a disposition to remedy the defects of either.

It were unnecessary to enter into any further extenuation of what was thought exceptionable in this play, but that it has been said, that the managers should have prevented some of the defects before its appearance to the public—and in particular the uncommon length of the piece as represented the first night. It were an ill return for the most liberal and gentlemanly conduct on their side, to suffer any censure to rest where none was deserved.

Hurry in writing has long been exploded as an excuse for an author;—however, in the dramatic line, it may happen, that both an author and a manager may wish to fill a chasm in the entertainment of the public with a hastiness not altogether culpable. The season was advanced when I first put the play into Mr. Harris's hands: it was at that time at least double the length of any acting comedy. I profited by his judgment and experience in the curtailing of it—till, I believe, his feeling for the vanity of a young author got the better of his desire for correctness, and he left many excrescences remaining, because he had assisted in pruning so many more. Hence, though I was not uninformed that the acts were still too long, I flattered myself that, after the first trial, I might with safer judgment proceed to remove what should appear to have been most dissatisfactory. Many other errors there were, which might in part have arisen from my being by no means conversant with plays in general, either in reading or at the theatre. Yet I own that, in one respect, I did not regret my ignorance: for as my first wish in attempting a play was to avoid every appearance of plagiary, I thought I should stand a better chance of effecting this from being in a walk which I had not frequented, and where, consequently, the progress of invention was less likely to be interrupted by starts of recollection: for on subjects on which the mind has been much informed, invention is slow of exerting itself. Faded ideas float in the fancy like half-forgotten dreams; and the imagination in its fullest enjoyments becomes suspicious of its offspring, and doubts whether it has created or adopted.

With regard to some particular passages which on the first night's representation seemed generally disliked, I confess, that if I felt any emotion of surprise at the disapprobation, it was not that they were disapproved of, but that I had not before perceived that they deserved it. As some part of the attack on the piece was begun too early to pass for the sentence of *judgment*, which is ever tardy in condemning, it has been suggested to me, that much of the disapprobation must have arisen from virulence of malice, rather than severity of criticism: but as I was more apprehensive of there being just grounds to excite the latter than conscious of having deserved the former, I continue not to believe that probable, which I am sure must have been unprovoked. However, if it was so, and I could even mark the quarter from whence it came, it would be ungenerous to retort: for no passion suffers more than malice from disappointment. For my own part, I see no reason why the author of a play should not regard a first night's audience as a candid and judicious friend attending, in behalf of the public, at his last rehearsal. If he can dispense with flattery, he is sure at least of sincerity, and even though the annotation be rude, he may rely upon the justness of the comment. Considered in this light, that audience, whose *fiat* is essential to the poet's claim, whether his object be fame or profit, has surely a right to expect some deference to its opinion, from principles of politeness at least, if not from gratitude.

As for the little puny critics, who scatter their peevish strictures in private circles, and scribble at every author who has the eminence of being unconnected with them, as they are usually spleen-swoln from a vain idea of increasing their consequence, there will always be found a petulance and illiberality in their remarks, which should place them as far beneath the notice of a gentleman, as their original dulness had sunk them from the level of the most unsuccessful author.

It is not without pleasure that I catch at an opportunity of justifying myself from the charge of intending any national reflection in the character of Sir Lucius O'Trigger. If any gentlemen opposed the piece from that idea, I thank them sincerely for their opposition; and if the condemnation of this comedy (however misconceived the provocation) could have added one spark to the decaying flame of national attachment to the country supposed to be reflected on, I should have been happy in its fate; and might with truth have boasted, that it had done more real service in its failure, than the successful morality of a thousand stage-novels will ever effect.

It is usual, I believe, to thank the performers in a new play, for the exertion of their several abilities. But where (as in this instance) their merit has been so striking and uncontroverted, as to call for the warmest and truest applause from a number of judicious audiences, the poet's after-praise comes like the feeble acclamation of a child to close the shouts of a multitude. The conduct, however, of the principals in a theatre cannot be so apparent to the public. I think it therefore but justice to declare, that from this theatre (the only one I can speak of from experience) those writers who wish to try the dramatic line will meet with that candour and liberal attention, which are generally allowed to be better calculated to lead genius into excellence, than either the precepts of judgment, or the guidance of experience.

THE AUTHOR.

DRAMATIS PERSONÆ

AS ORIGINALLY ACTED AT COVENT-GARDEN THEATRE IN 1775.

SIR ANTHONY ABSOLUTE	DAVID
CAPTAIN ABSOLUTE	THOMAS
FAULKLAND	MRS. MALAPROP
ACRES	LYDIA LANGUISH
SIR LUCIUS O'TRIGGER	JULIA
FAG	LUCY

Maid, Boy, Servants, &c.

SCENE—BATH.

Time of Action—Five Hours.

PROLOGUE

BY THE AUTHOR

Enter SERJEANT-AT-LAW, *and* ATTORNEY *following, and giving a paper.*

Serj. WHAT's here!—a vile cramp hand! I cannot see
Without my spectacles.
    Att.   He means his fee.
Nay, Mr. Serjeant, good sir, try again.   [*Gives money.*
    Serj. The scrawl improves! [*more*] O come, 'tis pretty plain
Hey! how's this? Dibble!—sure it cannot be!
A poet's brief! a poet and a fee!
    Att. Yes, sir! though you without reward, I know,
Would gladly plead the Muse's cause.
    Serj.   So!—so!
    Att. And if the fee offends, your wrath should fall
On me.
    Serj.   Dear Dibble, no offence at all.
    Att. Some sons of Phœbus in the courts we meet,
    Serj. And fifty sons of Phœbus in the Fleet!
    Att. Nor pleads he worse, who with a decent sprig
Of bays adorns his legal waste of wig.
    Serj. Full-bottom'd heroes thus, on signs, unfurl
A leaf of laurel in a grove of curl!
Yet tell your client, that, in adverse days,
This wig is warmer than a bush of bays.
    Att. Do you, then, sir, my client's place supply,
Profuse of robe, and prodigal of tie——
Do you, with all those blushing powers of face,
And wonted bashful hesitating grace,
Rise in the court, and flourish on the case.   [*Exit.*
    Serj. For practice then suppose—this brief will show it,—
Me, Serjeant Woodward,—counsel for the poet.
Used to the ground, I know 'tis hard to deal
With this dread court, from whence there's no appeal;
No tricking here, to blunt the edge of law,
Or, damn'd in equity, escape by flaw:
But judgment given, your sentence must remain;
No writ of error lies—to Drury-lane:
    Yet when so kind you seem, 'tis past dispute
We gain some favour, if not costs of suit.

No spleen is here! I see no hoarded fury;—
I think I never faced a milder jury!
Sad else our plight! where frowns are transportation.
A hiss the gallows, and a groan damnation!
But such the public candour, without fear
My client waves all right of challenge here.
No newsman from our session is dismiss'd,
Nor wit nor critic we scratch off the list;
His faults can never hurt another's ease,
His crime, at worst, a bad attempt to please:
Thus, all respecting, he appeals to all,
And by the general voice will stand or fall.

PROLOGUE
BY THE AUTHOR

SPOKEN ON THE TENTH NIGHT, BY MRS. BULKLEY.

GRANTED our cause, our suit and trial o'er,
The worthy serjeant need appear no more:
In pleasing I a different client choose,
He served the Poet—I would serve the Muse:
Like him, I'll try to merit your applause,
A female counsel in a female's cause.

    Look on this form,—where humour, quaint and sly,
Dimples the cheek, and points the beaming eye;
Where gay invention seems to boast its wiles
In amorous hint, and half-triumphant smiles;
While her light mask or covers satire's strokes,
Or hides the conscious blush her wit provokes.
Look on her well—does she seem form'd to teach?
Should you expect to hear this lady preach?
Is grey experience suited to her youth?
Do solemn sentiments become that mouth?
Bid her be grave, those lips should rebel prove
To every theme that slanders mirth or love.

    Yet, thus adorn'd with every graceful art
To charm the fancy and yet reach the heart—
Must we displace her? And instead advance
The goddess of the woful countenance—
The sentimental Muse!—Her emblems view,
The Pilgrim's Progress, and a sprig of rue!
View her—too chaste to look like flesh and blood—
Primly portray'd on emblematic wood!
There, fix'd in usurpation, should she stand,
She'll snatch the dagger from her sister's hand:
And having made her votaries weep a flood,
Good heaven! she'll end her comedies in blood—
Bid Harry Woodward break poor Dunstal's crown!
Imprison Quick, and knock Ned Shuter down;
While sad Barsanti, weeping o'er the scene,
Shall stab herself—or poison Mrs. Green.

    Such dire encroachments to prevent in time,
Demands the critic's voice—the poet's rhyme.

Can our light scenes add strength to holy laws!
Such puny patronage but hurts the cause:
Fair virtue scorns our feeble aid to ask;
And moral truth disdains the trickster's mask
For here their favourite stands, whose brow severe
And sad, claims youth's respect, and pity's tear;
Who, when oppress'd by foes her worth creates,
Can point a poniard at the guilt she hates.

THE RIVALS

ACT I.

SCENE I.—*A Street.*

Enter THOMAS; *he crosses the Stage;* FAG *follows, looking after him.*

Fag. What! Thomas! sure 'tis he?—What! Thomas! Thomas!

Thos. Hey!—Odd's life! Mr. Fag!—give us your hand, my old fellow-servant.

Fag. Excuse my glove, Thomas:—I'm devilish glad to see you, my lad. Why, my prince of charioteers, you look as hearty!—but who the deuce thought of seeing you in Bath?

Thos. Sure, master, Madam Julia, **Harry, Mrs. Kate,** and the postillion, be all come.

Fag. Indeed!

Thos. Ay, master thought another fit of the gout was coming to make him a visit;—so he'd a mind to gi't the slip, and whip! we were all off at an hour's warning.

Fag. Ay, ay, hasty in every thing, or it would not be Sir Anthony Absolute!

Thos. But tell us, Mr. Fag, how does young master? Odd! Sir Anthony will stare to see the Captain here!

Fag. I do not serve Captain Absolute now.

Thos. Why sure!

Fag. At present I am employed by Ensign Beverley.

Thos. I doubt, Mr. Fag, you ha'n't changed for the better.

Fag. I have not changed, Thomas.

Thos. No! Why didn't you say you had left young master?

Fag. No.—Well, honest Thomas, I must puzzle you no farther:—briefly then—Captain Absolute and Ensign Beverley are one and the same person.

Thos. The devil they are!

Fag. So it is indeed, Thomas; and the ensign half of my master being on guard at present—the captain has nothing to do with me.

Thos. So, so!—What, this is some freak, I warrant!—Do tell us, Mr. Fag, the meaning o't—you know I ha' trusted you.

Fag. You'll be secret, Thomas?

Thos. As a coach-horse.

Fag. Why then the cause of all this is—Love,—Love, Thomas, who (as you may get read to you) has been a masquerader ever since the days of Jupiter.

221

Thos. Ay, ay;—I guessed there was a lady in the case:—but pray, why does your master pass only for ensign?—Now if he had shammed general indeed——

Fag. Ah! Thomas, there lies the mystery o' the matter. Hark'ee, Thomas, my master is in love with a lady of a very singular taste: a lady who likes him better as a half pay ensign than if she knew he was son and heir to Sir Anthony Absolute, a baronet of three thousand a year.

Thos. That is an odd taste indeed!—But has she got the stuff, Mr. Fag? Is she rich, hey?

Fag. Rich!—Why, I believe she owns half the stocks! Zounds! Thomas, she could pay the national debt as easily as I could my washerwoman! She has a lapdog that eats out of gold,—she feeds her parrot with small pearls,—and all her thread-papers are made of bank-notes!

Thos. Bravo, faith!—Odd! I warrant she has a set of thousands at least:—but does she draw kindly with the captain?

Fag. As fond as pigeons.

Thos. May one hear her name?

Fag. Miss Lydia Languish.—But there is an old tough aunt in the way; though, by the by, she has never seen my master—for we got acquainted with miss while on a visit in Gloucestershire.

Thos. Well—I wish they were once harnessed together in matrimony.— But pray, Mr. Fag, what kind of a place is this Bath?—I ha' heard a deal of it—here's a mort o' merrymaking, hey?

Fag. Pretty well, Thomas, pretty well—'tis a good lounge; in the morning we go to the pump-room (though neither my master nor I drink the waters); after breakfast we saunter on the parades, or play a game at billiards; at night we dance; but damn the place, I'm tired of it: their regular hours stupify me—not a fiddle nor a card after eleven!—However, Mr. Faulkland's gentleman and I keep it up a little in private parties;—I'll introduce you there, Thomas—you'll like him much.

Thos. Sure I know Mr. Du-Peigne—you know his master is to marry Madam Julia.

Fag. I had forgot.—But, Thomas, you must polish a little—indeed you must.—Here now—this wig!—What the devil do you do with a wig, Thomas? —None of the London whips of any degree of *ton* wear wigs now.

Thos. More's the pity! more's the pity! I say.—Odd's life! when I heard how the lawyers and doctors had took to their own hair, I thought how 'twould go next:—odd rabbit it! when the fashion had got foot on the bar, I guessed 'twould mount to the box!—but 'tis all out of character, believe me, Mr. Fag: and look'ee, I'll never gi' up mine—the lawyers and doctors may do as they will.

Fag. Well, Thomas, we'll not quarrel about that.

Thos. Why, bless you, the gentlemen of the professions ben't all of a mind —for in our village now, thoff Jack Gauge, the exciseman, has ta'en to his carrots, there's little Dick the farrier swears he'll never forsake his bob, though all the college should appear with their own heads!

Fag. Indeed! well said, Dick!—But hold—mark! mark! Thomas.

Thos. Zooks! 'tis the captain.—Is that the lady with him?

Fag. No, no, that is Madam Lucy, my master's mistress's maid. They lodge at that house—but I must after him to tell him the news.

Thos. Odd! he's giving her money!—Well, Mr. Fag——

Fag. Good-bye, Thomas. I have an appointment in Gyde's Porch this evening at eight; meet me there, and we'll make a little party. [*Exeunt severally.*

SCENE II.—*A Dressing-room in* MRS. MALAPROP'S *Lodgings.*

LYDIA *sitting on a sofa, with a book in her hand.* LUCY, *as just returned from a message.*

Lucy. Indeed, ma'am, I traversed half the town in search of it: I don't believe there's a circulating library in Bath I ha'n't been at.

Lyd. And could not you get *The Reward of Constancy?*

Lucy. No, indeed, ma'am.

Lyd. Nor *The Fatal Connexion?*

Lucy. No, indeed, ma'am.

Lyd. Nor *The Mistakes of the Heart?*

Lucy. Ma'am, as ill luck would have it, Mr. Bull said Miss Sukey Saunter had just fetched it away.

Lyd. Heigh-ho!—Did you inquire for *The Delicate Distress?*

Lucy. Or, *The Memoirs of Lady Woodford?* Yes, indeed, ma'am. I asked every where for it; and I might have brought it from Mr. Frederick's, but Lady Slattern Lounger, who had just sent it home, had so soiled and dog's-eared it, it wa'n't fit for a Christian to read.

Lyd. Heigh-ho!—Yes, I always know when Lady Slattern has been before me. She has a most observing thumb; and, I believe, cherishes her nails for the convenience of making marginal notes.—Well, child, what have you brought me?

Lucy. Oh! here, ma'am.—[*Taking books from under her cloak, and from her pockets.*] This is *The Gordian Knot,*—and this *Peregrine Pickle.* Here are *The Tears of Sensibility,* and *Humphrey Clinker.* This is *The Memoirs of a Lady of Quality, written by herself,* and here the second volume of *The Sentimental Journey.*

Lyd. Heigh-ho!—What are those books by the glass?

Lucy. The great one is only *The Whole Duty of Man,* where I press a few blonds, ma'am.

Lyd. Very well—give me the sal volatile.

Lucy. Is it in a blue cover, ma'am?

Lyd. My smelling-bottle, you simpleton!

Lucy. Oh, the drops!—here, ma'am.

Lyd. Hold!—here's some one coming—quick, see who it is.—[*Exit* LUCY.] Surely I heard my cousin Julia's voice.

Re-enter LUCY.

Lucy. Lud! ma'am, here is Miss Melville.
Lyd. Is it possible!—

[*Exit* LUCY.

Enter JULIA.

Lyd. My dearest Julia, how delighted am I!—[*Embrace.*] How unexpected was this happiness!

Jul. True, Lydia—and our pleasure is the greater.—But what has been the matter?—you were denied to me at first!

Lyd. Ah, Julia, I have a thousand things to tell you!—But first inform me what has conjured you to Bath?—Is Sir Anthony here?

Jul. He is—we are arrived within this hour—and I suppose he will be here to wait on Mrs. Malaprop as soon as he is dressed.

Lyd. Then before we are interrupted, let me impart to you some of my distress!—I know your gentle nature will sympathize with me, though your prudence may condemn me! My letters have informed you of my whole connection with Beverley; but I have lost him, Julia! My aunt has discovered our intercourse by a note she intercepted, and has confined me ever since! Yet, would you believe it? she has absolutely fallen in love with a tall Irish baronet she met one night since we have been here, at Lady Macshuffle's rout.

Jul. You jest, Lydia!

Lyd. No, upon my word.—She really carries on a kind of correspondence with him, under a feigned name though, till she chooses to be known to him; —but it is a Delia or a Celia, I assure you.

Jul. Then, surely, she is now more indulgent to her niece.

Lyd. Quite the contrary. Since she has discovered her own frailty, she is become more suspicious of mine. Then I must inform you of another plague! —That odius Acres is to be in Bath to-day; so that I protest I shall be teased out of all spirits!

Jul. Come, come, Lydia, hope for the best—Sir Anthony shall use his interest with Mrs. Malaprop.

Lyd. But you have not heard the worst. Unfortunately I had quarrelled with my poor Beverley, just before my aunt made the discovery, and I have not seen him since, to make it up.

Jul. What was his offence?

Lyd. Nothing at all!—But, I don't know how it was, as often as we had been together, we had never had a quarrel, and, somehow, I was afraid he would never give me an opportunity. So, last Thursday, I wrote a letter to myself, to inform myself that Beverley was at that time paying his addresses to another woman. I signed it *your friend unknown,* showed it to Beverley, charged him with his falsehood, put myself in a violent passion, and vowed I'd never see him more.

Jul. And you let him depart so, and have not seen him since?

Lyd. 'Twas the next day my aunt found the matter out. I intended only to have teased him three days and a half, and now I've lost him for ever.

Jul. If he is as deserving and sincere as you have represented him to me, he will never give you up so. Yet consider, Lydia, you tell me he is but an ensign, and you have thirty thousand pounds.

Lyd. But you know I lose most of my fortune if I marry without my aunt's consent, till of age; and that is what I have determined to do, ever since I knew the penalty. Nor could I love the man, who would wish to wait a day for the alternative.

Jul. Nay, this is caprice!

Lyd. What, does Julia tax me with caprice?—I thought her lover Faulkland had inured her to it.

Jul. I do not love even his faults.

Lyd. But apropos—you have sent to him, I suppose?

Jul. Not yet, upon my word—nor has he the least idea of my being in Bath. Sir Anthony's resolution was so sudden, I could not inform him of it.

Lyd. Well, Julia, you are your own mistress, (though under the protection of Sir Anthony), yet have you, for this long year, been a slave to the caprice, the whim, the jealousy of this ungrateful Faulkland, who will ever delay assuming the right of a husband, while you suffer him to be equally imperious as a lover.

Jul. Nay, you are wrong entirely. We were contracted before my father's death. That, and some consequent embarrassments, have delayed what I know to be my Faulkland's most ardent wish. He is too generous to trifle on such a point:—and for his character, you wrong him there too. No, Lydia, he is too proud, too noble to be jealous; if he is captious, 'tis without dissembling; if fretful, without rudeness. Unused to the fopperies of love, he is negligent of the little duties expected from a lover—but being unhackneyed in the passion, his affection is ardent and sincere; and as it engrosses his whole soul, he expects every thought and emotion of his mistress to move in unison with his. Yet, though his pride calls for this full return, his humility makes him undervalue those qualities in him which would entitle him to it; and not feeling why he should be loved to the degree he wishes, he still suspects that he is not loved enough. This temper, I must own, has cost me many unhappy hours; but I have learned to think myself his debtor, for those imperfections which arise from the ardour of his attachment.

Lyd. Well, I cannot blame you for defending him. But tell me candidly, Julia, had he never saved your life, do you think you should have been attached to him as you are?—Believe me, the rude blast that overset your boat was a prosperous gale of love to him.

Jul. Gratitude may have strengthened my attachment to Mr. Faulkland, but I loved him before he had preserved me; yet surely that alone were an obligation sufficient.

Lyd. Obligation! why a water spaniel would have done as much!—Well, I should never think of giving my heart to a man because he could swim.

Jul. Come, Lydia, you are too inconsiderate.

Lyd. Nay, I do but jest.—What's here?

Re-enter LUCY *in a hurry.*

Lucy. O ma'am, here is Sir Anthony Absolute just come home with your aunt.

Lyd. They'll not come here.—Lucy, do you watch.   [*Exit* LUCY.

Jul. Yet I must go. Sir Anthony does not know I am here, and if he meet, he'll detain me, to show me the town. I'll take another opportunity of paying my respects to Mrs. Malaprop, when she shall treat me, as long as she chooses, with her select words so ingeniously misapplied, without being mispronounced.

Re-enter LUCY.

Lucy. O Lud! ma'am, they are both coming up stairs.

Lyd. Well, I'll not detain you, coz.—Adieu, my dear Julia, I'm sure you are in haste to send to Faulkland.—There—through my room you'll find another staircase.

Jul. Adieu!   [*Embraces* LYDIA, *and exit.*

Lyd. Here, my dear Lucy, hide these books. Quick, quick.—Fling *Peregrine Pickle* under the toilet—throw *Roderick Random* into the closet—put *The Innocent Adultery* into *The Whole Duty of Man*—thrust *Lord Aimworth* under the sofa—cram *Ovid* behind the bolster—there—put *The Man of Feeling* into your pocket—so, so—now lay *Mrs. Chapone* in sight, and leave *Fordyce's Sermons* open on the table.

Lucy. O burn it, ma'am! the hair-dresser has torn away as far as *Proper Pride.*

Lyd. Never mind—open at *Sobriety.*—Fling me *Lord Chesterfield's Letters.* —Now for 'em.   [*Exit* LUCY.

Enter Mrs. MALAPROP, *and* Sir ANTHONY ABSOLUTE.

Mrs. Mal. There, Sir Anthony, there sits the deliberate simpleton who wants to disgrace her family, and lavish herself on a fellow not worth a shilling.

Lyd. Madam, I thought you once——

Mrs. Mal. You thought, miss! I don't know any business you have to think at all—thought does not become a young woman. But the point we would request of you is, that you will promise to forget this fellow—to illiterate him, I say, quite from your memory.

Lyd. Ah, madam! our memories are independent of our wills. It is not so easy to forget.

Mrs. Mal. But I say it is, miss; there is nothing on earth so easy as to forget, if a person chooses to set about it. I'm sure I have as much forgot your poor dear uncle as if he had never existed—and I thought it my duty so to do; and let me tell you, Lydia, these violent memories don't become a young woman.

Sir Anth. Why sure she won't pretend to remember what she's ordered not!—ay, this comes of her reading!

Lyd. What crime, madam, have I committed, to be treated thus?

Mrs. Mal. Now don't attempt to extirpate yourself from the matter; you know I have proof controvertible of it.—But tell me, will you promise to do as you're bid? Will you take a husband of your friends' choosing?

Lyd. Madam, I must tell you plainly, that had I no preference for any one else, the choice you have made would be my aversion.

Mrs. Mal. What business have you, miss, with preference and aversion? They don't become a young woman; and you ought to know, that as both always wear off, 'tis safest in matrimony to begin with a little aversion. I am sure I hated your poor dear uncle before marriage as if he'd been a blacka-moor—and yet, miss, you are sensible what a wife I made!—and when it pleased Heaven to release me from him, 'tis unknown what tears I shed!—But suppose we were going to give you another choice, will you promise us to give up this Beverley?

Lyd. Could I belie my thoughts so far as to give that promise, my actions would certainly as far belie my words.

Mrs. Mal. Take yourself to your room.—You are fit company for nothing but your own ill-humours.

Lyd. Willingly, ma'am—I cannot change for the worse. [*Exit.*

Mrs. Mal. There's a little intricate hussy for you!

Sir Anth. It is not to be wondered at, ma'am,—all this is the natural conse-quence of teaching girls to read. Had I a thousand daughters, by Heaven! I'd as soon have them taught the black art as their alphabet!

Mrs. Mal. Nay, nay, Sir Anthony, you are an absolute misanthropy.

Sir Anth. In my way hither, Mrs. Malaprop, I observed your niece's maid coming forth from a circulating library!—She had a book in each hand—they were half-bound volumes, with marble covers!—From that moment I guessed how full of duty I should see her mistress!

Mrs. Mal. Those are vile places, indeed!

Sir Anth. Madam, a circulating library in a town is as an evergreen tree of diabolical knowledge! It blossoms through the year!—And depend on it, Mrs. Malaprop, that they who are so fond of handling the leaves, will long for the fruit at last.

Mrs. Mal. Fy, fy, Sir Anthony! you surely speak laconically.

Sir Anth. Why, Mrs. Malaprop, in moderation now, what would you have a woman know?

Mrs. Mal. Observe me, Sir Anthony. I would by no means wish a daughter of mine to be a progeny of learning; I don't think so much learning becomes a young woman; for instance, I would never let her meddle with Greek, or Hebrew, or algebra, or simony, or fluxions, or paradoxes, or such inflamma-tory branches of learning—neither would it be necessary for her to handle any of your mathematical, astronomical, diabolical instruments.—But, Sir Anthony, I would send her, at nine years old, to a boarding-school, in order to learn a little ingenuity and artifice. Then, sir, she should have a supercilious knowledge in accounts;—and as she grew up, I would have her instructed in geometry, that she might know something of the contagious countries;— but above all, Sir Anthony, she should be mistress of orthodoxy, that she might not mis-spell, and mis-pronounce words so shamefully as girls usually do; and likewise that she might reprehend the true meaning of what she is saying. This, Sir Anthony, is what I would have a woman know;—and I don't think there is a superstitious article in it.

Sir Anth. Well, well, Mrs. Malaprop, I will dispute the point no further with you; though I must confess, that you are a truly moderate and polite arguer, for almost every third word you say is on my side of the question. But, Mrs. Malaprop, to the more important point in debate—you say you have no objection to my proposal?

Mrs. Mal. None, I assure you. I am under no positive engagement with Mr. Acres, and as Lydia is so obstinate against him, perhaps your son may have better success.

Sir. Anth. Well, madam, I will write for the boy directly. He knows not a syllable of this yet, though I have for some time had the proposal in my head. He is at present with his regiment.

Mrs. Mal. We have never seen your son, Sir Anthony; but I hope no objection on his side.

Sir Anth. Objection!—let him object if he dare!—No, no, Mrs. Malaprop, Jack knows that the least demur puts me in a frenzy directly. My process was always very simple—in their younger days, 'twas "Jack, do this";—if he demurred, I knocked him down—and if he grumbled at that, I always sent him out of the room.

Mrs. Mal. Ay, and the properest way, o' my conscience!—nothing is so conciliating to young people as severity.—Well, Sir Anthony, I shall give Mr. Acres his discharge, and prepare Lydia to receive your son's invocations; —and I hope you will represent her to the captain as an object not altogether illegible.

Sir Anth. Madam, I will handle the subject prudently.—Well, I must leave you; and let me beg you, Mrs. Malaprop, to enforce this matter roundly to the girl.—Take my advice—keep a tight hand: if she rejects this proposal, clap her under lock and key; and if you were just to let the servants forget to bring her dinner for three or four days, you can't conceive how she'd come about. [*Exit.*

Mrs. Mal. Well, at any rate I shall be glad to get her from under my intuition. She has somehow discovered my partiality for Sir Lucius O'Trigger —sure, Lucy can't have betrayed me!—No, the girl is such a simpleton, I should have made her confess it.—Lucy!—Lucy!—[*Calls.*] Had she been one of your artificial ones, I should never have trusted her.

Re-enter LUCY.

Lucy. Did you call, ma'am?

Mrs. Mal. Yes, girl.—Did you see Sir Lucius while you was out?

Lucy. No, indeed, ma'am, not a glimpse of him.

Mrs. Mal. You are sure, Lucy, that you never mentioned——

Lucy. Oh gemini! I'd sooner cut my tongue out.

Mrs. Mal. Well, don't let your simplicity be imposed on.

Lucy. No, ma'am.

Mrs. Mal. So, come to me presently, and I'll give you another letter to Sir Lucius; but mind, Lucy—if ever you betray what you are entrusted with (unless it be other people's secrets to me), you forfeit my malevolence for ever; and your being a simpleton shall be no excuse for your locality.   [*Exit.*

Lucy. Ha! ha! ha!—So, my dear Simplicity, let me give you a little respite. —[*Altering her manner.*] Let girls in my station be as fond as they please of appearing expert, and knowing in their trusts; commend me to a mask of silliness, and a pair of sharp eyes for my own interest under it!—Let me see to what account have I turned my simplicity lately.—[*Looks at a paper.*] *For abetting Miss Lydia Languish in a design of running away with an ensign!— in money, sundry times, twelve pound twelve; gowns, five; hats, ruffles, caps, &c. &c., numberless!—From the said ensign, within this last month, six guineas and a half.*—About a quarter's pay!—Item, *from Mrs. Malaprop, for betraying the young people to her*—when I found matters were likely to be discovered—*two guineas, and a black paduasoy.*—Item, *from Mr. Acres, for carrying divers letters*—which I never delivered—*two guineas, and a pair of buckles.*—Item, *from Sir Lucius O'Trigger, three crowns, two gold pocket-pieces, and a silver snuff-box!*—Well done, Simplicity!—Yet I was forced to make my Hibernian believe, that he was corresponding, not with the aunt, but with the niece: for though not over rich, I found he had too much pride and delicacy to sacrifice the feelings of a gentleman to the necessities of his fortune.   [*Exit.*

ACT II.

Scene I.—Captain Absolute's *Lodgings.*

Captain Absolute *and* Fag.

Fag. Sir, while I was there Sir Anthony came in: I told him, you had sent me to inquire after his health, and to know if he was at leisure to see you.

Abs. And what did he say, on hearing I was at Bath?

Fag. Sir, in my life I never saw an elderly gentleman more astonished! He started back two or three paces, rapped out a dozen interjectural oaths, and asked, what the devil had brought you here.

Abs. Well, sir, and what did you say?

Fag. Oh, I lied, sir—I forget the precise lie; but you may depend on't, he got no truth from me. Yet, with submission, for fear of blunders in future, I should be glad to fix what has brought us to Bath; in order that we may lie a little consistently. Sir Anthony's servants were curious, sir, very curious indeed.

Abs. You have said nothing to them?

Fag. Oh, not a word, sir,—not a word! Mr. Thomas, indeed, the coachman (whom I take to be the discreetest of whips)——

Abs. 'Sdeath!—you rascal! you have not trusted him!

Fag. Oh, no, sir—no—no—not a syllable, upon my veracity!—He was, indeed, a little inquisitive; but I was sly, sir—devilish sly! My master (said I), honest Thomas (you know, sir, one says honest to one's inferiors), is come to Bath to recruit—Yes, sir, I said to recruit—and whether for men, money, or constitution, you know, sir, is nothing to him, nor any one else.

Abs. Well, recruit will do—let it be so.

Fag. Oh, sir, recruit will do surprisingly—indeed, to give the thing an air, I told Thomas, that your honour had already enlisted five disbanded chairmen, seven minority waiters, and thirteen billiard-markers.

Abs. You blockhead, never say more than is necessary.

Fag. I beg pardon, sir—I beg pardon—but, with submission, a lie is nothing unless one supports it. Sir, whenever I draw on my invention for a good current lie, I always forge indorsements as well as the bill.

Abs. Well, take care you don't hurt your credit, by offering too much security.—Is Mr. Faulkland returned?

Fag. He is above, sir, changing his dress.

Abs. Can you tell whether he has been informed of Sir Anthony and Miss Melville's arrival?

Fag. I fancy not, sir; he has seen no one since he came in but his gentleman, who was with him at Bristol.—I think, sir, I hear Mr. Faulkland coming down——

Abs. Go, tell him I am here.

Fag. Yes, sir.—[*Going.*] I beg pardon, sir, but should Sir Anthony call, you will do me the favour to remember that we are recruiting, if you please.

Abs. Well, well.

Fag. And, in tenderness to my character, if your honour could bring in the chairmen and waiters, I should esteem it as an obligation; for though I never scruple a lie to serve my master, yet it hurts one's conscience to be found out.   [*Exit.*

Abs. Now for my whimsical friend—if he does not know that his mistress is here, I'll tease him a little before I tell him—

Enter FAULKLAND.

Faulkland, you're welcome to Bath again; you are punctual in your return.

Faulk. Yes; I had nothing to detain me, when I had finished the business I went on. Well, what news since I left you? how stand matters between you and Lydia?

Abs. Faith, much as they were; I have not seen her since our quarrel; however, I expect to be recalled every hour.

Faulk. Why don't you persuade her to go off with you at once?

Abs. What, and lose two-thirds of her fortune? you forget that, my friend.—No, no, I could have brought her to that long ago.

Faulk. Nay then, you trifle too long—if you are sure of her, propose to the aunt in your own character, and write to Sir Anthony for his consent.

Abs. Softly, softly; for though I am convinced my little Lydia would elope with me as Ensign Beverley, yet am I by no means certain that she would take me with the impediment of our friends' consent, a regular humdrum wedding, and the reversion of a good fortune on my side: no, no; I must prepare her gradually for the discovery, and make myself necessary to her, before I risk it.—Well, but Faulkland, you'll dine with us to-day at the hotel?

Faulk. Indeed I cannot; I am not in spirits to be of such a party.

Abs. By heavens! I shall forswear your company. You are the most teasing, captious, incorrigible lover!—Do love like a man.

Faulk. I own I am unfit for company.

Abs. Am not I a lover; ay, and a romantic one too? Yet do I carry every where with me such a confounded farrago of doubts, fears, hopes, wishes, and all the flimsy furniture of a country miss's brain!

Faulk. Ah! Jack, your heart and soul are not, like mine, fixed immutably on one only object. You throw for a large stake, but losing, you could stake and throw again;—but I have set my sum of happiness on this cast, and not to succeed, were to be stripped of all.

Abs. But, for Heaven's sake! what grounds for apprehension can your whimsical brain conjure up at present?

Faulk. What grounds for apprehension, did you say? Heavens! are there not a thousand! I fear for her spirits—her health—her life.—My absence may fret her; her anxiety for my return, her fears for me may oppress her gentle temper: and for her health, does not every hour bring me cause to be alarmed? If it rains, some shower may even then have chilled her delicate frame! If the wind be keen, some rude blast may have affected her! The heat of noon, the dews of the evening, may endanger the life of her, for whom only I value mine. O Jack! when delicate and feeling souls are separated, there is not a feature in the sky, not a movement of the elements, not an aspiration of the breeze, but hints some cause for a lover's apprehension!

Abs. Ay, but we may choose whether we will take the hint or not.—So, then, Faulkland, if you were convinced that Julia were well and in spirits, you would be entirely content?

Faulk. I should be happy beyond measure—I am anxious only for that.

Abs. Then to cure your anxiety at once—Miss Melville is in perfect health, and is at this moment in Bath.

Faulk. Nay, Jack—don't trifle with me.

Abs. She is arrived here with my father within this hour.

Faulk. Can you be serious?

Abs. I thought you knew Sir Anthony better than to be surprised at a sudden whim of this kind.—Seriously, then, it is as I tell you—upon my honour.

Faulk. My dear friend!—Hollo, Du Peigne! my hat.—My dear Jack—now nothing on earth can give me a moment's uneasiness.

Re-enter FAG.

Fag. Sir, Mr. Acres, just arrived, is below.

Abs. Stay, Faulkland, this Acres lives within a mile of Sir Anthony, and he shall tell you how your mistress has been ever since you left her.—Fag, show the gentleman up.   [*Exit* FAG.

Faulk. What, is he much acquainted in the family?

Abs. Oh, very intimate: I insist on your not going: besides, his character will divert you.

Faulk. Well, I should like to ask him a few questions.

Abs. He is likewise a rival of mine—that is, of my other self's, for he does not think his friend Captain Absolute ever saw the lady in question; and it is ridiculous enough to hear him complain to me of one Beverley, a concealed skulking rival, who——

Faulk. Hush!—he's here.

Enter ACRES.

Acres. Ha! my dear friend, noble captain, and honest Jack, how do'st thou? just arrived, faith, as you see.—Sir, your humble servant.—Warm work on the roads, Jack!—Odds whips and wheels! I've travelled like a comet, with a tail of dust all the way as long as the Mall.

Abs. Ah! Bob, you are indeed an eccentric planet, but we know your attraction hither.—Give me leave to introduce Mr. Faulkland to you; Mr. Faulkland, Mr. Acres.

Acres. Sir, I am most heartily glad to see you: sir, I solicit your connections.—Hey, Jack—what, this is Mr. Faulkland, who——

Abs. Ay, Bob, Miss Melville's Mr. Faulkland.

Acres. Odso! she and your father can be but just arrived before me:—I suppose you have seen them. Ah! Mr. Faulkland, you are indeed a happy man.

Faulk. I have not seen Miss Melville, yet, sir;—I hope she enjoyed full health and spirits in Devonshire?

Acres. Never knew her better in my life, sir,—never better. Odds blushes and blooms! she has been as healthy as the German Spa.

Faulk. Indeed!—I did hear that she had been a little indisposed.

Acres. False, false, sir—only said to vex you: quite the reverse, I assure you.

Faulk. There, Jack, you see she has the advantage of me; I had almost fretted myself ill.

Abs. Now are you angry with your mistress for not having been sick?

Faulk. No, no, you misunderstand me: yet surely a little trifling indisposition is not an unnatural consequence of absence from those we love.—Now confess—isn't there something unkind in this violent, robust, unfeeling health?

Abs. Oh, it was very unkind of her to be well in your absence, to be sure!

Acres. Good apartments, Jack.

Faulk. Well, sir, but you was saying that Miss Melville has been so exceedingly well—what then she has been merry and gay, I suppose?—Always in spirits—hey?

Acres. Merry, odds crickets! she has been the belle and spirit of the company wherever she has been—so lively and entertaining! so full of wit and humour!

Faulk. There, Jack, there.—Oh, by my soul! there is an innate levity in woman, that nothing can overcome.—What! happy, and I away!

Abs. Have done.—How foolish this is! just now you were only apprehensive for your mistress' spirits.

Faulk. Why, Jack, have I been the joy and spirit of the company?

Abs. No indeed, you have not.

Faulk. Have I been lively and entertaining?

Abs. Oh, upon my word, I acquit you.

Faulk. Have I been full of wit and humour?

Abs. No, faith, to do you justice, you have been confoundedly stupid indeed.

Acres. What's the matter with the gentleman?

Abs. He is only expressing his great satisfaction at hearing that Julia has been so well and happy—that's all—hey, Faulkland?

Faulk. Oh! I am rejoiced to hear it—yes, yes, she has a happy disposition!

Acres. That she has indeed—then she is so accomplished—so sweet a voice —so expert at her harpsichord—such a mistress of flat and sharp, squallante, rumblante, and quiverante!—There was this time month—odds minims and crotchets! how she did chirrup at Mrs. Piano's concert!

Faulk. There again, what say you to this? you see she has been all mirth and song—not a thought of me!

Abs. Pho! man, is not music the food of love?

Faulk. Well, well, it may be so.—Pray, Mr. ——, what's his damned name?— Do you remember what songs Miss Melville sung?

Acres. Not I indeed.

Abs. Stay, now, they were some pretty melancholy purling-stream airs, I warrant; perhaps you may recollect;—did she sing, *When absent from my soul's delight?*

Acres. No, that wa'n't it.

Abs. Or, *Go, gentle gales!* [*Sings.*

Acres. Oh, no! nothing like it. Odds! now I recollect one of them—*My heart's my own, my will is free.* [*Sings.*

Faulk. Fool! fool that I am! to fix all my happiness on such a trifler! 'Sdeath! to make herself the pipe and ballad-monger of a circle! to soothe her light heart with catches and glees!—What can you say to this, sir?

Abs. Why, that I should be glad to hear my mistress had been so merry, sir.

Faulk. Nay, nay, nay—I'm not sorry that she has been happy—no, no, I am glad of that—I would not have had her sad or sick—yet surely a sympathetic heart would have shown itself even in the choice of a song—she might have been temperately healthy, and somehow, plaintively gay;—but she has been dancing too, I doubt not!

Acres. What does the gentleman say about dancing?

Abs. He says the lady we speak of dances as well as she sings.

Acres. Ay, truly, does she—there was at our last race ball——

Faulk. Hell and the devil! There!—there—I told you so! I told you so! Oh! she thrives in my absence!—Dancing! but her whole feelings have been in opposition with mine;—I have been anxious, silent, pensive, sedentary—my days have been hours of care, my nights of watchfulness.—She has been all health! spirit! laugh! song! dance!—Oh! damned, damned levity!

Abs. For Heaven's sake, Faulkland, don't expose yourself so!—Suppose she has danced, what then?—does not the ceremony of society often oblige——

Faulk. Well, well, I'll contain myself—perhaps as you say—for form sake.— What, Mr. Acres, you were praising Miss Melville's manner of dancing a minuet—hey?

Acres. Oh, I dare insure her for that—but what I was going to speak of was her country-dancing. Odds swimmings! she has such an air with her!

Faulk. Now disappointment on her!—Defend this, Absolute; why don't you defend this?—Country-dances! jigs and reels! am I to blame now? A minuet I could have forgiven—I should not have minded that—I say I should not have regarded a minuet—but country-dances!—Zounds! had she made one in a cotillion—I believe I could have forgiven even that—but to be monkey-led for a night!—to run the gauntlet through a string of amorous palming puppies!—to show paces like a managed filly!—Oh, Jack, there never can be but one man in the world whom a truly modest and delicate woman ought to pair with in a country-dance; and, even then, the rest of the couples should be her great-uncles and aunts!

Abs. Ay, to be sure!—grandfathers and grandmothers!

Faulk. If there be but one vicious mind in the set, 'twill spread like a contagion—the action of their pulse beats to the lascivious movement of the jig—their quivering, warm-breathed sighs impregnate the very air—the atmosphere becomes electrical to love, and each amorous spark darts through every link of the chain!—I must leave you—I own I am somewhat flurried—and that confounded looby has perceived it.   [*Going.*

Abs. Nay, but stay, Faulkland, and thank Mr. Acres for his good news.

Faulk. Damn his news!   [*Exit.*

Abs. Ha! ha! ha! poor Faulkland five minutes since—"nothing on earth could give him a moment's uneasiness!"

Acres. The gentleman wa'n't angry at my praising his mistress, was he?

Abs. A little jealous, I believe, Bob.

Acres. You don't say so? Ha! ha! jealous of me—that's a good joke.

Abs. There's nothing strange in that, Bob; let me tell you, that sprightly grace and insinuating manner of yours will do some mischief among the girls here.

Acres. Ah! you joke—ha! ha! mischief—ha! ha! but you know I am not my own property, my dear Lydia has forestalled me. She could never abide me in the country, because I used to dress so badly—but odds frogs and tambours! I shan't take matters so here, now ancient madam has no voice in it: I'll make my old clothes know who's master. I shall straightway cashier the hunting-frock, and render my leather breeches incapable. My hair has been in training some time.

Abs. Indeed!

Acres. Ay—and tho'ff the side curls are a little restive, my hind-part takes it very kindly.

Abs. Ah, you'll polish, I doubt not.

Acres. Absolutely I propose so—then if I can find out this Ensign Beverley, odds triggers and flints! I'll make him know the difference o't.

Abs. Spoke like a man! But pray, Bob, I observe you have got an odd kind of a new method of swearing——

Acres. Ha! ha! you've taken notice of it—'tis genteel, isn't it!—I didn't invent it myself though; but a commander in our militia, a great scholar, I assure you, says that there is no meaning in the common oaths, and that nothing but their antiquity makes them respectable;—because, he says, the ancients would never stick to an oath or two, but would say, by Jove! or by Bacchus! or by Mars! or by Venus! or by Pallas, according to the sentiment: so that to swear with propriety, says my little major, the oath should be an echo to the sense; and this we call the *oath referential* or *sentimental swearing*—ha! ha! 'tis genteel, isn't it?

Abs. Very genteel, and very new, indeed!—and I dare say will supplant all other figures of imprecation.

Acres. Ay, ay, the best terms will grow obsolete.—Damns have had their day.

Re-enter FAG.

Fag. Sir, there is a gentleman below desires to see you.—Shall I show him into the parlour?

Abs. Ay—you may.

Acres. Well, I must be gone——

Abs. Stay; who is it, Fag?

Fag. Your father, sir.

Abs. You puppy, why didn't you show him up directly?   [*Exit* FAG.

Acres. You have business with Sir Anthony.—I expect a message from Mrs. Malaprop at my lodgings. I have sent also to my dear friend Sir Lucius O'Trigger. Adieu, Jack! we must meet at night, when you shall give me a dozen bumpers to little Lydia.

Abs. That I will with all my heart.—[*Exit* ACRES.] Now for a parental lecture—I hope he has heard nothing of the business that has brought me here —I wish the gout had held him fast in Devonshire, with all my soul!

Enter Sir ANTHONY ABSOLUTE.

Sir, I am delighted to see you here; looking so well! your sudden arrival at Bath made me apprehensive for your health.

Sir Anth. Very apprehensive, I dare say, Jack.—What, you are recruiting here, hey?

Abs. Yes, sir, I am on duty.

Sir Anth. Well, Jack, I am glad to see you, though I did not expect it, for I was going to write to you on a little matter of business.—Jack, I have been considering that I grow old and infirm, and shall probably not trouble you long.

Abs. Pardon me, sir, I never saw you look more strong and hearty; and I pray frequently that you may continue so.

Sir Anth. I hope your prayers may be heard, with all my heart. Well then, Jack, I have been considering that I am so strong and hearty I may continue to plague you a long time. Now, Jack, I am sensible that the income of your commission, and what I have hitherto allowed you, is but a small pittance for a lad of your spirit.

Abs. Sir, you are very good.

Sir Anth. And it is my wish, while yet I live, to have my boy make some figure in the world. I have resolved, therefore, to fix you at once in a noble independence.

Abs. Sir, your kindness overpowers me—such generosity makes the gratitude of reason more lively than the sensations even of filial affection.

Sir Anth. I am glad you are so sensible of my attention—and you shall be master of a large estate in a few weeks.

Abs. Let my future life, sir, speak my gratitude; I cannot express the sense I have of your munificence.—Yet, sir, I presume you would not wish me to quit the army?

Sir Anth. Oh, that shall be as your wife chooses.

Abs. My wife, sir!

Sir Anth. Ay, ay, settle that between you—settle that between you.

Abs. A wife, sir, did you say?

Sir Anth. Ay, a wife—why, did not I mention her before?

Abs. Not a word of her, sir.

Sir Anth. Odd so!—I mustn't forget her though.—Yes, Jack, the independence I was talking of is by a marriage—the fortune is saddled with a wife—but I suppose that makes no difference.

Abs. Sir! sir!—you amaze me!

Sir Anth. Why, what the devil's the matter with the fool? Just now you were all gratitude and duty.

Abs. I was, sir,—you talked to me of independence and a fortune, but not a word of a wife.

Sir Anth. Why—what difference does that make? Odds life, sir! if you have the estate, you must take it with the live stock on it, as it stands.

Abs. If my happiness is to be the price, I must beg leave to decline the purchase.—Pray, sir, who is the lady?

Sir Anth. What's that to you, sir?—Come, give me your promise to love, and to marry her directly.

Abs. Sure, sir, this is not very reasonable, to summon my affections for a lady I know nothing of!

Sir Anth. I am sure, sir, 'tis more unreasonable in you to object to a lady you know nothing of.

Abs. Then, sir, I must tell you plainly that my inclinations are fixed on another—my heart is engaged to an angel.

Sir Anth. Then pray let it send an excuse. It is very sorry—but business prevents its waiting on her.

Abs. But my vows are pledged to her.

Sir Anth. Let her foreclose, Jack; let her foreclose; they are not worth redeeming; besides, you have the angel's vows in exchange, I suppose; so there can be no loss there.

Abs. You must excuse me, sir, if I tell you, once for all, that in this point I cannot obey you.

Sir Anth. Hark'ee, Jack;—I have heard you for some time with patience—I have been cool—quite cool; but take care—you know I am compliance itself—when I am not thwarted;—no one more easily led—when I have my own way;—but don't put me in a frenzy.

Abs. Sir, I must repeat it—in this I cannot obey you.

Sir Anth. Now damn me! if ever I call you Jack again while I live!

Abs. Nay, sir, but hear me.

Sir Anth. Sir, I won't hear a word—not a word! not one word! so give me your promise by a nod—and I'll tell you what, Jack—I mean, you dog—if you don't, by——

Abs. What, sir, promise to link myself to some mass of ugliness! to——

Sir Anth. Zounds! sirrah! the lady shall be as ugly as I choose: she shall have a hump on each shoulder; she shall be as crooked as the crescent; her one eye shall roll like the bull's in Cox's Museum; she shall have a skin like a mummy, and the beard of a Jew—she shall be all this, sirrah!—yet I will make you ogle her all day, and sit up all night to write sonnets on her beauty.

Abs. This is reason and moderation indeed!

Sir Anth. None of your sneering, puppy! no grinning, jackanapes!

Abs. Indeed, sir, I never was in a worse humour for mirth in my life.

Sir Anth. 'Tis false, sir, I know you are laughing in your sleeve; I know you'll grin when I am gone, sirrah!

Abs. Sir, I hope I know my duty better.

Sir Anth. None of your passion, sir! none of your violence, if you please! —It won't do with me, I promise you.

Abs. Indeed, sir, I never was cooler in my life.

Sir Anth. 'Tis a confounded lie!—I know you are in a passion in your heart; I know you are, you hypocritical young dog! but it won't do.

Abs. Nay, sir, upon my word——

Sir Anth. So you will fly out! can't you be cool like me? What the devil good can passion do?—Passion is of no service, you impudent, insolent, overbearing reprobate!—There, you sneer again! don't provoke me!—but you rely upon the mildness of my temper—you do, you dog! you play upon the meekness of my disposition!—Yet take care—the patience of a saint may be overcome at last!—but mark! I give you six hours and a half to consider of this: if you then agree, without any condition, to do every thing on earth that I choose, why—confound you! I may in time forgive you.—If not, zounds! don't enter the same hemisphere with me! don't dare to breathe the same air, or use the same light with me; but get an atmosphere and a sun of your own! I'll strip you of your commission; I'll lodge a five-and-threepence in the hands of trustees, and you shall live on the interest.—I'll disown you, I'll disinherit you, I'll unget you! and damn me! if ever I call you Jack again!

[*Exit.*

Abs. Mild, gentle, considerate father—I kiss your hands!—What a tender method of giving his opinion in these matters Sir Anthony has! I dare not trust him with the truth.—I wonder what old wealthy hag it is that he wants to bestow on me!—Yet he married himself for love! and was in his youth a bold intriguer, and a gay companion!

Re-enter FAG.

Fag. Assuredly, sir, your father is wrath to a degree; he comes down stairs eight or ten steps at a time—muttering, growling, and thumping the banisters all the way: I and the cook's dog stand bowing at the door—rap! he gives me a stroke on the head with his cane; bids me carry that to my master; then kicking the poor turnspit into the area, damns us all, for a puppy triumvirate! —Upon my credit, sir, were I in your place, and found my father such very bad company, I should certainly drop his acquaintance.

Abs. Cease your impertinence, sir, at present.—Did you come in for nothing more?—Stand out of the way!   [*Pushes him aside, and exit.*

Fag. So! Sir Anthony trims my master: he is afraid to reply to his father— then vents his spleen on poor Fag!—When one is vexed by one person, to revenge one's self on another, who happens to come in the way, is the vilest injustice! Ah! it shows the worst temper—the basest——

Enter BOY.

Boy. Mr. Fag! Mr. Fag! your master calls you.

Fag. Well, you little dirty puppy, you need not bawl so!—The meanest disposition! the——

Boy. Quick, quick, Mr. Fag!

Fag. Quick! quick! you impudent jackanapes! am I to be commanded by you too? you little impertinent, insolent, kitchen-bred——

[*Exit kicking and beating him.*

SCENE II.—*The North Parade.*

Enter LUCY.

Lucy. So—I shall have another rival to add to my mistress's list—Captain Absolute. However, I shall not enter his name till my purse has received notice in form. Poor Acres is dismissed!—Well, I have done him a last friendly office, in letting him know that Beverley was here before him.—Sir Lucius is generally more punctual, when he expects to hear from his *dear Dalia*, as he calls her: I wonder he's not here!—I have a little scruple of conscience from this deceit; though I should not be paid so well, if my hero knew that Delia was near fifty, and her own mistress.

Enter SIR LUCIUS O'TRIGGER.

Sir Luc. Ha! my little ambassadress—upon my conscience, I have been looking for you; I have been on the South Parade this half hour.

Lucy. [*Speaking simply.*] O gemini! and I have been waiting for your worship here on the North.

Sir Luc. Faith!—may be that was the reason we did not meet; and it is very comical too, how you could go out and I not see you—for I was only taking a nap at the Parade Coffee-house, and I chose the window on purpose that I might not miss you.

Lucy. My stars! Now I'd wager a sixpence I went by while you were asleep.

Sir Luc. Sure enough it must have been so—and I never dreamt it was so late, till I waked. Well, but my little girl, have you got nothing for me?

Lucy. Yes, but I have—I've got a letter for you in my pocket.

Sir Luc. O faith! I guessed you weren't come empty-handed—Well—let me see what the dear creature says.

Lucy. There, Sir Lucius. [*Gives him a letter.*

Sir Luc. [Reads.] *Sir—there is often a sudden incentive impulse in love, that has a greater induction than years of domestic combination: such was the commotion I felt at the first superfluous view of Sir Lucius O'Trigger.*—Very pretty, upon my word.—*Female punctuation forbids me to say more, yet let me add, that it will give me joy infallible to find Sir Lucius worthy the last criterion of my affections.* DELIA.

Upon my conscience! Lucy, your lady is a great mistress of language. Faith, she's quite the queen of the dictionary!—for the devil a word dare refuse coming at her call—though one would think it was quite out of hearing.

Lucy. Ay, sir, a lady of her experience——

Sir Luc. Experience! what, at seventeen?

Lucy. O true, sir—but then she reads so—my stars! how she will read off hand!

Sir Luc. Faith, she must be very deep read to write this way—though she is rather an arbitrary writer too—for here are a great many poor words pressed into the service of this note, that would get their *habeas corpus* from any court in Christendom.

Lucy. Ah! Sir Lucius, if you were to hear how she talks of you!

Sir Luc. Oh, tell her I'll make her the best husband in the world, and Lady O'Trigger into the bargain!—But we must get the old gentlewoman's consent—and do every thing fairly.

Lucy. Nay, Sir Lucius, I thought you wa'n't rich enough to be so nice!

Sir Luc. Upon my word, young woman, you have hit it:—I am so poor, that I can't afford to do a dirty action.—If I did not want money, I'd steal your mistress and her fortune with a great deal of pleasure.—However, my pretty girl [*Gives her money*], here's a little something to buy you a ribbon; and meet me in the evening, and I'll give you an answer to this. So, hussy, take a kiss beforehand to put you in mind.   [*Kisses her.*

Lucy. O Lud! Sir Lucius—I never seed such a gemman! My lady won't like you if you're so impudent.

Sir Luc. Faith she will, Lucy!—That same—pho! what's the name of it?—modesty—is a quality in a lover more praised by the women than liked; so, if your mistress asks you whether Sir Lucius ever gave you a kiss, tell her fifty—my dear.

Lucy. What, would you have me tell her a lie?

Sir Luc. Ah, then, you baggage! I'll make it a truth presently.

Lucy. For shame now! here is some one coming.

Sir Luc. Oh, faith, I'll quiet your conscience!   [*Exit, humming a tune.*

Enter FAG.

Fag. So, so, ma'am! I humbly beg pardon.

Lucy. O Lud! now, Mr. Fag—you flurry one so.

Fag. Come, come, Lucy, here's no one by—so a little less simplicity, with a grain or two more sincerity, if you please.—You play false with us, madam.—I saw you give the baronet a letter.—My master shall know this—and if he don't call him out, I will.

Lucy. Ha! ha! ha! you gentlemen's gentlemen are so hasty.—That letter was from Mrs. Malaprop, simpleton.—She is taken with Sir Lucius's address.

Fag. How! what tastes some people have!—Why, I suppose I have walked by her window a hundred times.—But what says our young lady? any message to my master?

Lucy. Sad news, Mr. Fag.—A worse rival than Acres! Sir Anthony Absolute has proposed his son.

Fag. What, Captain Absolute?

Lucy. Even so—I overheard it all.

Fag. Ha! ha! ha! very good, faith. Good-bye, Lucy, I must away with this news.

Lucy. Well, you may laugh—but it is true, I assure you.—[*Going.*] But, Mr. Fag, tell your master not to be cast down by this.

Fag. Oh, he'll be so disconsolate!

Lucy. And charge him not to think of quarrelling with young Absolute.

Fag. Never fear! never fear!

Lucy. Be sure—bid him keep up his spirits.

Fag. We will—we will.   [*Exeunt severally.*

ACT III.

Scene I.—*The North Parade.*

Enter Captain Absolute.

Abs. 'Tis just as Fag told me, indeed. Whimsical enough, faith! My father wants to force me to marry the very girl I am plotting to run away with! He must not know of my connection with her yet awhile. He has too summary a method of proceeding in these matters. However, I'll read my recantation instantly. My conversion is something sudden, indeed—but I can assure him it is very sincere. So, so—here he comes. He looks plaguy gruff.

[*Steps aside.*

Enter Sir Anthony Absolute.

Sir Anth. No—I'll die sooner than forgive him. Die, did I say? I'll live these fifty years to plague him. At our last meeting, his impudence had almost put me out of temper. An obstinate, passionate, self-willed boy! Who can he take after? This is my return for getting him before all his brothers and sisters!—for putting him, at twelve years old, into a marching regiment, and allowing him fifty pounds a year, besides his pay, ever since! But I have done with him; he's anybody's son for me. I never will see him more, never—never—never.

Abs. [*Aside, coming forward.*] Now for a penitential face.

Sir Anth. Fellow, get out of my way!

Abs. Sir, you see a penitent before you.

Sir Anth. I see an impudent scoundrel before me.

Abs. A sincere penitent. I am come, sir, to acknowledge my error, and to submit entirely to your will.

Sir Anth. What's that?

Abs. I have been revolving, and reflecting, and considering on your past goodness, and kindness, and condescension to me.

Sir Anth. Well, sir?

Abs. I have been likewise weighing and balancing what you were pleased to mention concerning duty, and obedience, and authority.

Sir Anth. Well, puppy?

Abs. Why then, sir, the result of my reflections is—a resolution to sacrifice every inclination of my own to your satisfaction.

Sir Anth. Why now you talk sense—absolute sense—I never heard any thing more sensible in my life. Confound you! you shall be Jack again.

Abs. I am happy in the appellation.

Sir Anth. Why then, Jack, my dear Jack, I will now inform you who the lady really is. Nothing but your passion and violence, you silly fellow, pre-

vented my telling you at first. Prepare, Jack, for wonder and rapture—pre
pare. What think you of Miss Lydia Languish?

Abs. Languish! What, the Languishes of Worcestershire?

Sir Anth. Worcestershire! no. Did you never meet Mrs. Malaprop and he
niece, Miss Languish, who came into our country just before you were las
ordered to your regiment?

Abs. Malaprop! Languish! I don't remember ever to have heard the name
before. Yet, stay—I think I do recollect something. Languish! Languish! Sh
squints, don't she? A little red-haired girl?

Sir Anth. Squints! A red-haired girl! Zounds! no.

Abs. Then I must have forgot; it can't be the same person.

Sir Anth. Jack! Jack! what think you of blooming, love-breathing seven
teen?

Abs. As to that, sir, I am quite indifferent. If I can please you in th
matter, 'tis all I desire.

Sir Anth. Nay, but Jack, such eyes! such eyes! so innocently wild! sc
bashfully irresolute! not a glance but speaks and kindles some thought ot
love! Then, Jack, her cheeks! her cheeks, Jack! so deeply blushing at the
insinuations of her tell-tale eyes! Then, Jack, her lips! O Jack, lips smiling
at their own discretion; and if not smiling, more sweetly pouting; more
lovely in sullenness!

Abs. That's she indeed. Well done, old gentleman.   [*Aside*

Sir Anth. Then, Jack, her neck! O Jack! Jack!

Abs. And which is to be mine, sir, the niece, or the aunt?

Sir Anth. Why, you unfeeling, insensible puppy, I despise you! When I
was of your age, such a description would have made me fly like a rocket!
The aunt indeed! Odds life! when I ran away with your mother, I would
not have touched any thing old or ugly to gain an empire.

Abs. Not to please your father, sir?

Sir Anth. To please my father! zounds! not to please—Oh, my father—odd
so!—yes—yes; if my father indeed had desired—that's quite another matter
Though he wa'n't the indulgent father that I am, Jack.

Abs. I dare say not, sir.

Sir Anth. But, Jack, you are not sorry to find your mistress is so beautiful?

Abs. Sir, I repeat it—if I please you in this affair, 'tis all I desire. Not that I
think a woman the worse for being handsome; but, sir, if you please to recollect, you before hinted something about a hump or two, one eye, and a few
more graces of that kind—now, without being very nice, I own I should
rather choose a wife of mine to have the usual number of limbs, and a limited
quantity of back: and though one eye may be very agreeable, yet as the
prejudice has always run in favour of two, I would not wish to affect a
singularity in that article.

Sir Anth. What a phlegmatic sot it is! Why, sirrah, you're an anchorite!—
a vile, insensible stock. You a soldier!—you're a walking block, fit only tc
dust the company's regimentals on! Odds life! I have a great mind to marry
the girl myself.

Abs. I am entirely at your disposal, sir: if you should think of addressing Miss Languish yourself, I suppose you would have me marry the aunt; or if you should change your mind, and take the old lady—'tis the same to me—I'll marry the niece.

Sir Anth. Upon my word, Jack, thou'rt either a very great hypocrite, or—but, come, I know your indifference on such a subject must be all a lie—I'm sure it must—come, now—damn your demure face!—come, confess Jack—you have been lying—ha'n't you? You have been playing the hypocrite, hey! —I'll never forgive you, if you ha'n't been lying and playing the hypocrite.

Abs. I'm sorry, sir, that the respect and duty which I bear to you should be so mistaken.

Sir Anth. Hang your respect and duty! But come along with me, I'll write a note to Mrs. Malaprop, and you shall visit the lady directly. Her eyes shall be the Promethean torch to you—come along, I'll never forgive you, if you don't come back stark mad with rapture and impatience—if you don't, egad, I will marry the girl myself! [*Exeunt.*

SCENE II.—JULIA's *Dressing-room.*

FAULKLAND *discovered alone.*

Faulk. They told me Julia would return directly; I wonder she is not yet come! How mean does this captious, unsatisfied temper of mine appear to my cooler judgment! Yet I know not that I indulge it in any other point: but on this one subject, and to this one subject, whom I think I love beyond my life, I am ever ungenerously fretful and madly capricious! I am conscious of it—yet I cannot correct myself! What tender honest joy sparkled in her eyes when we met! how delicate was the warmth of her expressions! I was ashamed to appear less happy—though I had come resolved to wear a face of coolness and upbraiding. Sir Anthony's presence prevented my proposed expostulations: yet I must be satisfied that she has not been so very happy in my absence. She is coming! Yes!—I know the nimbleness of her tread, when she thinks her impatient Faulkland counts the moments of her stay.

Enter JULIA.

Jul. I had not hoped to see you again so soon.

Faulk. Could I, Julia, be contented with my first welcome—restrained as we were by the presence of a third person?

Jul. O Faulkland, when your kindness can make me thus happy, let me not think that I discovered something of coldness in your first salutation.

Faulk. 'Twas but your fancy, Julia. I was rejoiced to see you—to see you in such health. Sure I had no cause for coldness?

Jul. Nay then, I see you have taken something ill. You must not conceal from me what it is.

Faulk. Well, then—shall I own to you that my joy at hearing of your healt and arrival here, by your neighbour Acres, was somewhat damped by hi dwelling much on the high spirits you had enjoyed in Devonshire—on you mirth—your singing—dancing, and I know not what! For such is my temper Julia, that I should regard every mirthful moment in your absence as a treason to constancy. The mutual tear that steals down the cheek of parting lovers is a compact, that no smile shall live there till they meet again.

Jul. Must I never cease to tax my Faulkland with this teasing minute caprice? Can the idle reports of a silly boor weigh in your breast against my tried affection?

Faulk. They have no weight with me, Julia: No, no—I am happy if you have been so—yet only say, that you did not sing with mirth—say that you thought of Faulkland in the dance.

Jul. I never can be happy in your absence. If I wear a countenance of con tent, it is to show that my mind holds no doubt of my Faulkland's truth. I I seemed sad, it were to make malice triumph; and say, that I had fixed my heart on one, who left me to lament his roving, and my own credulity. Be lieve me, Faulkland, I mean not to upbraid you, when I say, that I have ofter dressed sorrow in smiles, lest my friends should guess whose unkindness hac caused my tears.

Faulk. You were ever all goodness to me. Oh, I am a brute, when I bu admit a doubt of your true constancy!

Jul. If ever without such cause from you, as I will not suppose possible you find my affections veering but a point, may I become a proverbial scof for levity and base ingratitude.

Faulk. Ah! Julia, that last word is grating to me. I would I had no title to your gratitude! Search your heart, Julia; perhaps what you have mistaker for love, is but the warm effusion of a too thankful heart.

Jul. For what quality must I love you?

Faulk. For no quality! To regard me for any quality of mind or under standing, were only to esteem me. And for person—I have often wished my self deformed, to be convinced that I owed no obligation there for any part of your affection.

Jul. Where nature has bestowed a show of nice attention in the features of a man, he should laugh at it as misplaced. I have seen men, who in this vain article, perhaps, might rank above you; but my heart has never asked my eyes if it were so or not.

Faulk. Now this is not well from you, Julia—I despise person in a man— yet if you loved me as I wish, though I were an Æthiop, you'd thing none so fair.

Jul. I see you are determined to be unkind! The contract which my poor father bound us in gives you more than a lover's privilege.

Faulk. Again, Julia, you raise ideas that feed and justify my doubts. I would not have been more free—no—I am proud of my restraint. Yet—yet— perhaps your high respect alone for this solemn compact has fettered your inclinations, which else had made a worthier choice. How shall I be sure, had you remained unbound in thought and promise, that I should still have been the object of your persevering love?

Jul. Then try me now. Let us be free as strangers as to what is past: my heart will not feel more liberty!

Faulk. There now! so hasty, Julia! so anxious to be free! If your love for me were fixed and ardent, you would not lose your hold, even though I wished it!

Jul. Oh! you torture me to the heart! I cannot bear it.

Faulk. I do not mean to distress you. If I loved you less I should never give you an uneasy moment. But hear me. All my fretful doubts arise from this. Women are not used to weigh and separate the motives of their affections: the cold dictates of prudence, gratitude, or filial duty, may sometimes be mistaken for the pleadings of the heart. I would not boast—yet let me say, that I have neither age, person, nor character, to found dislike on; my fortune such as few ladies could be charged with indiscretion in the match. O Julia! when love receives such countenance from prudence, nice minds will be suspicious of its birth.

Jul. I know not whither your insinuations would tend:—but as they seem pressing to insult me, I will spare you the regret of having done so.—I have given you no cause for this! [*Exit in tears.*

Faulk. In tears! Stay, Julia: stay but for a moment.—The door is fastened! —Julia!—my soul—but for one moment!—I hear her sobbing!—'Sdeath! what a brute am I to use her thus! Yet stay.—Ay—she is coming now:—how little resolution there is in woman!—how a few soft words can turn them!—No, faith!—she is not coming either.—Why, Julia—my love—say but that you forgive me—come but to tell me that—now this is being too resentful. Stay! she is coming too—I thought she would—no steadiness in any thing: her going away must have been a mere trick then—she shan't see that I was hurt by it.— I'll affect indifference—[*Hums a tune: then listens.*] No—zounds! she's not coming!—nor don't intend it, I suppose.—This is not steadiness, but obstinacy! Yet I deserve it.—What, after so long an absence to quarrel with her tenderness!—'twas barbarous and unmanly!—I should be ashamed to see her now.— I'll wait till her just resentment is abated—and when I distress her so again, may I lose her for ever! and be linked instead to some antique virago, whose gnawing passions, and long hoarded spleen, shall make me curse my folly half the day and all the night. [*Exit.*

SCENE III. MRS. MALAPROP'S *Lodgings.*

MRS. MALAPROP, *with a letter in her hand, and* CAPTAIN ABSOLUTE.

Mrs. Mal. Your being Sir Anthony's son, captain, would itself be a sufficient accommodation; but from the ingenuity of your appearance, I am convinced you deserve the character here given of you.

Abs. Permit me to say, madam, that as I never yet have had the pleasure of seeing Miss Languish, my principal inducement in this affair at present is the honour of being allied to Mrs. Malaprop; of whose intellectual accomplishments, elegant manners, and unaffected learning, no tongue is silent.

Mrs. Mal. Sir, you do me infinite honour! I beg, captain, you'll be seated. —[*They sit.*] Ah! few gentlemen, now-a-days, know how to value the ineffectual qualities in a woman! few think how a little knowledge becomes a gentlewoman!—Men have no sense now but for the worthless flower of beauty!

Abs. It is but too true, indeed, ma'am;—yet I fear our ladies should share the blame—they think our admiration of beauty so great, that knowledge in them would be superfluous. Thus, like garden-trees, they seldom show fruit, till time has robbed them of the more specious blossom.—Few, like Mrs. Malaprop and the orange-tree, are rich in both at once!

Mrs. Mal. Sir, you overpower me with good-breeding.—He is the very pine-apple of politeness!—You are not ignorant, captain, that this giddy girl has somehow contrived to fix her affections on a beggarly, strolling, eavesdropping ensign, whom none of us have seen, and nobody knows anything of.

Abs. Oh, I have heard the silly affair before.—I'm not at all prejudiced against her on that account.

Mrs. Mal. You are very good and very considerate, captain. I am sure I have done every thing in my power since I exploded the affair; long ago I laid my positive conjunctions on her, never to think on the fellow again;—I have since laid Sir Anthony's preposition before her; but, I am sorry to say, she seems resolved to decline every particle that I enjoin her.

Abs. It must be very distressing, indeed, ma'am.

Mrs. Mal. Oh! it gives me the hydrostatics to such a degree.—I thought she had persisted from corresponding with him; but, behold, this very day, I have interceded another letter from the fellow; I believe I have it in my pocket.

Abs. Oh, the devil! my last note. [*Aside.*

Mrs. Mal. Ay, here it is.

Abs. Ay, my note indeed! O the little traitress Lucy. [*Aside.*

Mrs. Mal. There, perhaps you may know the writing. [*Gives him the letter.*

Abs. I think I have seen the hand before—yes, I certainly must have seen this hand before—

Mrs. Mal. Nay, but read it, captain.

Abs. [Reads.] *My soul's idol, my adored Lydia!*—Very tender indeed!

Mrs. Mal. Tender! ay, and profane too, o' my conscience.

Abs. [Reads.] *I am excessively alarmed at the intelligence you send me, the more so as my new rival*——

Mrs. Mal. That's you, sir.

Abs. [Reads.] *Has universally the character of being an accomplished gentleman and a man of honour.*—Well, that's handsome enough.

Mrs. Mal. Oh, the fellow has some design in writing so.

Abs. That he had, I'll answer for him, ma'am.

Mrs. Mal. But go on, sir—you'll see presently.

Abs. [Reads.] *As for the old weather-beaten she-dragon who guards you*—Who can he mean by that?

Mrs. Mal. Me, sir!—me!—he means me!—There—what do you think now?—but go on a little further.

Abs. Impudent scoundrel!—[Reads.] *it shall go hard but I will elude her vigilance, as I am told that the same ridiculous vanity, which makes her dress up her coarse features, and deck her dull chat with hard words which she don't understand*——

Mrs. Mal. There, sir, an attack upon my language! what do you think of that?—an aspersion upon my parts of speech! was ever such a brute! Sure, if I reprehend any thing in this world, it is the use of my oracular tongue, and a nice derangement of epitaphs!

Abs. He deserves to be hanged and quartered! let me see—[Reads.] *same ridiculous vanity*——

Mrs. Mal. You need not read it again, sir.

Abs. I beg pardon, ma'am.—[Reads.] *does also lay her open to the grossest deceptions from flattery and pretended admiration*—an impudent coxcomb!—*so that I have a scheme to see you shortly with the old harridan's consent, and even to make her a go-between in our interview.*—Was ever such assurance!

Mrs. Mal. Did you ever hear any thing like it?—he'll elude my vigilance, will he—yes, yes! ha! ha! he's very likely to enter these doors;—we'll try who can plot best!

Abs. So we will, ma'am—so we will! Ha! ha! ha! a conceited puppy, ha! ha! ha!—Well, but Mrs. Malaprop, as the girl seems so infatuated by this fellow, suppose you were to wink at her corresponding with him for a little time—let her even plot an elopement with him—then do you connive at her escape—while I, just in the nick, will have the fellow laid by the heels, and fairly contrive to carry her off in his stead.

Mrs. Mal. I am delighted with the scheme; never was anything better perpetrated!

Abs. But, pray, could not I see the lady for a few minutes now?—I should like to try her temper a little.

Mrs. Mal. Why, I don't know—I doubt she is not prepared for a visit of this kind. There is a decorum in these matters.

Abs. O Lord! she won't mind me—only tell her Beverley——

Mrs. Mal. Sir!

Abs. Gently, good tongue. [*Aside.*

Mrs. Mal. What did you say of Beverley?

Abs. Oh, I was going to propose that you should tell her, by way of jest, that it was Beverley who was below; she'd come down fast enough then—ha! ha! ha!

Mrs. Mal. 'Twould be a trick she well deserves; besides, you know the fellow tells her he'll get my consent to see her—ha! ha! Let him if he can, I say again. Lydia, come down here!—[*Calling.*] He'll make me a go-between

in their interviews!—ha! ha! ha! Come down, I say, Lydia! I don't wonder at
your laughing, ha! ha! ha! his impudence is truly ridiculous.

Abs. 'Tis very ridiculous, upon my soul, ma'am, ha! ha! ha!

Mrs. Mal. The little hussy won't hear. Well, I'll go and tell her at once
who it is—she shall know that Captain Absolute is come to wait on her. And
I'll make her behave as becomes a young woman.

Abs. As you please, ma'am.

Mrs. Mal. For the present, captain, your servant. Ah! you've not done
laughing yet, I see—elude my vigilance; yes, yes; ha! ha! ha!   [*Exit*

Abs. Ha! ha! ha! one would think now that I might throw off all disguise at once, and seize my prize with security; but such is Lydia's caprice
that to undeceive were probably to lose her. I'll see whether she knows me
       [*Walks aside, and seems engaged in looking at the pictures*

Enter LYDIA.

Lyd. What a scene am I now to go through! surely nothing can be more
dreadful than to be obliged to listen to the loathsome addresses of a stranger
to one's heart. I have heard of girls persecuted as I am, who have appealed in
behalf of their favoured lover to the generosity of his rival—suppose I were
to try it—there stands the hated rival—an officer too!—but oh, how unlike my
Beverley! I wonder he don't begin—truly he seems a very negligent wooer
—quite at his ease, upon my word!—I'll speak first—Mr. Absolute.

Abs. Ma'am.   [*Turns round*

Lyd. O heavens! Beverley!

Abs. Hush!—hush, my life! softly! be not surprised!

Lyd. I am so astonished! and so terrified! and so overjoyed!—for Heaven's
sake! how came you here?

Abs. Briefly, I have deceived your aunt—I was informed that my new rival
was to visit here this evening, and contriving to have him kept away, have
passed myself on her for Captain Absolute.

Lyd. O charming! And she really takes you for young Absolute?

Abs. Oh, she's convinced of it.

Lyd. Ha! ha! ha! I can't forbear laughing to think how her sagacity is
overreached!

Abs. But we trifle with our precious moments—such another opportunity
may not occur; then let me now conjure my kind, my condescending angel,
to fix the time when I may rescue her from undeserving persecution, and
with a licensed warmth plead for my reward.

Lyd. Will you then, Beverley, consent to forfeit that portion of my paltry
wealth?—that burden on the wings of love?

Abs. Oh, come to me—rich only thus—in loveliness! Bring no portion to
me but thy love—'twill be generous in you, Lydia—for well you know, it is
the only dower your poor Beverley can repay.

Lyd. How persuasive are his words!—how charming will poverty be with
him!   [*Aside*

Abs. Ah! my soul, what a life will we then live! Love shall be our idol

nd support! we will worship him with a monastic strictness; abjuring all
orldly toys, to centre every thought and action there. Proud of calamity,
e will enjoy the wreck of wealth; while the surrounding gloom of adver-
ty shall make the flame of our pure love show doubly bright. By Heavens!
would fling all goods of fortune from me with a prodigal hand, to enjoy
he scene where I might clasp my Lydia to my bosom, and say, the world
fords no smile to me but here—[*Embracing her.*] If she holds out now,
he devil is in it!   [*Aside.*

Lyd. Now could I fly with him to the antipodes! but my persecution is
ot yet come to a crisis.   [*Aside.*

Re-enter MRS. MALAPROP, *listening.*

Mrs. Mal. I am impatient to know how the little hussy deports herself.
                                                                     [*Aside.*
Abs. So pensive, Lydia!—is then your warmth abated?
Mrs. Mal. Warmth abated!—so!—she has been in a passion, I suppose.
                                                                     [*Aside.*
Lyd. No—nor ever can while I have life.
Mrs. Mal. An ill tempered little devil! She'll be in a passion all her life—
ill she?   [*Aside.*
Lyd. Think not the idle threats of my ridiculous aunt can ever have any
eight with me.
Mrs. Mal. Very dutiful, upon my word!   [*Aside.*
Lyd. Let her choice be Captain Absolute, but Beverley is mine.
Mrs. Mal. I am astonished at her assurance!—to his face—this is to his face!
                                                                     [*Aside.*
Abs. Thus then let me enforce my suit.   [*Kneeling.*
Mrs. Mal. [*Aside.*] Ay, poor young man!—down on his knees entreating
r pity!—I can contain no longer.—[*Coming forward.*] Why, thou vixen!—
have overheard you.
Abs. Oh, confound her vigilance!   [*Aside.*
Mrs. Mal. Captain Absolute, I know not how to apologize for her shocking
deness.
Abs. [*Aside.*] So all's safe, I find.—[*Aloud.*] I have hopes, madam, that
me will bring the young lady——
Mrs. Mal. Oh, there's nothing to be hoped for from her! she's as head-
rong as an allegory on the banks of Nile.
Lyd. Nay, madam, what do you charge me with now?
Mrs. Mal. Why, thou unblushing rebel—didn't you tell this gentleman to
s face that you loved another better?—didn't you say you never would be
s?
Lyd. No, madam—I did not.
Mrs. Mal. Good Heavens! what assurance!—Lydia, Lydia, you ought to
now that lying don't become a young woman!—Didn't you boast that
everley, that stroller Beverley, possessed your heart?—Tell me that, I say.
Lyd. 'Tis true, ma'am, and none but Beverley——

Mrs. Mal. Hold!—hold, Assurance!—you shall not be so rude.

Abs. Nay, pray, Mrs. Malaprop, don't stop the young lady's speech: sh‹ very welcome to talk thus—it does not hurt me in the least, I assure you.

Mrs. Mal. You are too good, captain—too amiably patient—but come wi me, miss.—Let us see you again soon, captain—remember what we have fixe‹

Abs. I shall ma'am.

Mrs. Mal. Come, take a graceful leave of the gentleman.

Lyd. May every blessing wait on my Beverley, my loved Bev——

Mrs. Mal. Hussy! I'll choke the word in your throat!—come along—con‹ along.

[*Exeunt severally;* Captain Absolute *kissing his hand to* Lydia—M‹ Malaprop *stopping her from speaking.*]

Scene IV.— Acres' *Lodgings.*

Acres, *as just dressed, and* David.

Acres. Indeed, David—do you think I become it so?

Dav. You are quite another creature, believe me, master, by the mass! a we've any luck we shall see the Devon mon kerony in all the print-shops : Bath!

Acres. Dress does make a difference, David.

Dav. 'Tis all in all, I think.—Difference! why, an' you were to go now ‹ Clod-hall, I am certain the old lady wouldn't know you: master Butl‹ wouldn't believe his own eyes, and Mrs. Pickle would cry, Lard presarve m‹ our dairy-maid would come giggling to the door, and I warrant Doll Tester, your honour's favourite, would blush like my waistcoat.—Oons! I hold a gallon, there ain't a dog in the house but would bark, and I questic whether Phillis would wag a hair of her tail!

Acres. Ay, David, there's nothing like polishing.

Dav. So I says of your honour's boots; but the boy never heeds me!

Acres. But, David, has Mr. De-la-grace been here? I must rub up m‹ balancing, and chasing, and boring.

Dav. I'll call again, sir.

Acres. Do—and see if there are any letters for me at the post-office.

Dav. I will.—By the mass, I can't help looking at your head!—if I hadn been by at the cooking, I wish I may die if I should have known the dis‹ again myself! [*Exi*

Acres. [*Practising a dancing-step.*] Sink, slide—coupee.—Confound the fir‹ inventors of cotillons! say I—they are as bad as algebra to us country gentl‹ men—I can walk a minuet easy enough when I am forced!—and I have bee‹ accounted a good stick in a country-dance.—Odds jigs and tabors! I nev‹ valued your cross-over to couple—figure in—right and left—and I'd foot with e'er a captain in the county!—but these outlandish heathen allemand‹ and cotillons are quite beyond me!—I shall never prosper at 'em, that's sure mine are true-born English legs—they don't understand their curst French lingo!—their *pas* this, and *pas* that, and *pas* t'other!—damn me! my feet don't like to be called paws! no, 'tis certain I have most Antigallican toes!

Enter SERVANT.

Serv. Here is Sir Lucius O'Trigger to wait on you, sir.
Acres. Show him in.   [*Exit* SERVANT.

Enter SIR LUCIUS O'TRIGGER.

Sir Luc. Mr. Acres, I am delighted to embrace you.

Acres. My dear Sir Lucius, I kiss your hands.

Sir Luc. Pray, my friend, what has brought you so suddenly to Bath?

Acres. Faith! I have followed Cupid's Jack-a-lantern, and find myself in a quagmire at last.—In short, I have been very ill used, Sir Lucius.—I don't choose to mention names, but look on me as on a very ill-used gentleman.

Sir Luc. Pray what is the case?—I ask no names.

Acres. Mark me, Sir Lucius, I fall as deep as need be in love with a young lady—her friends take my part—I follow her to Bath—send word of my arrival; and receive answer, that the lady is to be otherwise disposed of.—This, Sir Lucius, I call being ill used.

Sir Luc. Very ill, upon my conscience.—Pray, can you divine the cause of it?

Acres. Why, there's the matter; she has another lover, one Beverley, who, I am told, is now in Bath.—Odds slanders and lies! he must be at the bottom of it.

Sir Luc. A rival in the case, is there?—and you think he has supplanted you unfairly?

Acres. Unfairly! to be sure he has. He never could have done it fairly.

Sir Luc. Then sure you know what is to be done!

Acres. Not I, upon my soul!

Sir Luc. We wear no swords here, but you understand me.

Acres. What! fight him!

Sir Luc. Ay, to be sure: what can I mean else?

Acres. But he has given me no provocation.

Sir Luc. Now, I think he has given you the greatest provocation in the world. Can a man commit a more heinous offence against another than to fall in love with the same woman? Oh, by my soul! it is the most unpardonable breach of friendship.

Acres. Breach of friendship! ay, ay; but I have no acquaintance with this man. I never saw him in my life.

Sir Luc. That's no argument at all—he has the less right then to take such a liberty.

Acres. Gad, that's true—I grow full of anger, Sir Lucius!—I fire apace! Odds hilts and blades! I find a man may have a deal of valour in him, and not know it! But couldn't I contrive to have a little right of my side?

Sir Luc. What the devil signifies right, when your honour is concerned? Do you think Achilles, or my little Alexander the Great, ever inquired where the right lay? No, by my soul, they drew their broad-swords, and left the lazy sons of peace to settle the justice of it.

Acres. Your words are a grenadier's march to my heart! I believe courage must be catching! I certainly do feel a kind of valour rising as it were—a kind of courage, as I may say.—Odds flints, pans, and triggers! I'll challenge him directly.

Sir Luc. Ah, my little friend, if I had Blunderbuss Hall here, I could show you a range of ancestry, in the O'Trigger line, that would furnish the new room; every one of whom had killed his man!—For though the mansion-house and dirty acres have slipped through my fingers, I thank heaven our honour and the family-pictures are as fresh as ever.

Acres. O, Sir Lucius! I have had ancestors too!—every man of 'em colonel or captain in the militia!—Odds balls and barrels! say no more—I'm braced for it. The thunder of your words has soured the milk of human kindness in my breast;—Zounds! as the man in the play says, *I could do such deeds!*

Sir Luc. Come, come, there must be no passion at all in the case—these things should always be done civilly.

Acres. I must be in a passion, Sir Lucius—I must be in a rage.—Dear Sir Lucius, let me be in a rage, if you love me. Come, here's pen and paper.—[*Sits down to write.*] I would the ink were red!—Indite, I say indite!—How shall I begin? Odds bullets and blades! I'll write a good bold hand, however.

Sir Luc. Pray compose yourself.

Acres. Come—now, shall I begin with an oath? Do, Sir Lucius, let me begin with a damme.

Sir Luc. Pho! pho! do the thing decently, and like a Christian. Begin now —*Sir*—

Acres. That's too civil by half.

Sir Luc. To prevent the confusion that might arise——

Acres. Well——

Sir. Luc. From our both addressing the same lady——

Acres. Ay, there's the reason—*same lady*—well——

Sir Luc. I shall expect the honour of your company——

Acres. Zounds! I'm not asking him to dinner.

Sir Luc. Pray be easy.

Acres. Well then, *honour of your company*——

Sir Luc. To settle our pretensions——

Acres. Well.

Sir Luc. Let me see, ay, King's-Mead-Fields will do—*in King's-Mead-Fields.*

Acres. So, that's done—Well, I'll fold it up presently; my own crest—a hand and dagger shall be the seal.

Sir Luc. You see now this little explanation will put a stop at once to all confusion or misunderstanding that might arise between you.

Acres. Ay, we fight to prevent any misunderstanding.

Sir Luc. Now, I'll leave you to fix your own time.—Take my advice, and you'll decide it this evening if you can; then let the worst come of it, 'twill be off your mind to-morrow.

Acres. Very true.

Sir Luc. So I shall see nothing more of you, unless it be by letter, till the evening.—I would do myself the honour to carry your message; but, to tell you a secret, I believe I shall have just such another affair on my own hands. There is a gay captain here, who put a jest on me lately, at the expense of my country, and I only want to fall in with the gentleman, to call him out.

Acres. By my valour, I should like to see you fight first! Odds life! I should like to see you kill him if it was only to get a little lesson.

Sir Luc. I shall be very proud of instructing you.—Well for the present—but remember now, when you meet your antagonist, do everything in a mild and agreeable manner.—Let your courage be as keen, but at the same time as polished, as your sword. [*Exeunt severally.*

ACT IV.

SCENE I.—ACRES' *Lodgings.*

ACRES *and* DAVID.

Dav. Then, by the mass, sir! I would do no such thing—ne'er a Sir Lucius O'Trigger in the kingdom should make me fight, when I wa'n't so minded. Oons! what will the old lady say, when she hears o't?

Acres. Ah! David, if you had heard Sir Lucius!—Odds sparks and flames! he would have roused your valour.

Dav. Not he, indeed. I hate such bloodthirsty cormorants. Look'ee, master, if you'd wanted a bout at boxing, quarter-staff, or short-staff, I should never be the man to bid you cry off: but for your curst sharps and snaps, I never knew any good come of 'em.

Acres. But my honour, David, my honour! I must be very careful of my honour.

Dav. Ay, by the mass! and I would be very careful of it; and I think in return my honour couldn't do less than to be very careful of me.

Acres. Odds blades! David, no gentleman will ever risk the loss of his honour!

Dav. I say then, it would be but civil in honour never to risk the loss of a gentleman.—Look'ee, master, this honour seems to me to be a marvellous false friend: ay, truly, a very courtier-like servant.—Put the case, I was a gentleman (which, thank God, no one can say of me); well—my honour makes me quarrel with another gentleman of my acquaintance.—So—we fight. (Pleasant enough that!) Boh!—I kill him—(the more's my luck!) now, pray who gets the profit of it?—Why, my honour. But put the case that he kills me!—by the mass! I go to the worms, and my honour whips over to my enemy.

Acres. No, David—in that case!—Odds crowns and laurels! your honour follows you to the grave.

Dav. Now, that's just the place where I could make a shift to do without it.

Acres. Zounds! David, you are a coward!—It doesn't become my valour to listen to you.—What, shall I disgrace my ancestors?—Think of that, David—think what it would be to disgrace my ancestors!

Dav. Under favour, the surest way of not disgracing them, is to keep as long as you can out of their company. Look'ee now, master, to go to them in such haste—with an ounce of lead in your brains—I should think might as well be let alone. Our ancestors are very good kind of folks; but they are the last people I should choose to have a visiting acquaintance with.

Acres. But, David, now, you don't think there is such very, very, very great danger, hey?—Odds life! people often fight without any mischief done!

Dav. By the mass, I think 'tis ten to one against you!—Oons! here to meet some lion-headed fellow, I warrant, with his damned double-barrelled swords, and cut-and-thrust pistols!—Lord bless us! it makes me tremble to think o't!—Those be such desperate bloody-minded weapons! Well, I never could abide 'em—from a child I never could fancy 'em!—I suppose there a'nt been so merciless a beast in the world as your loaded pistol!

Acres. Zounds! I won't be afraid!—Odds fire and fury! you shan't make me afraid.—Here is the challenge, and I have sent for my dear friend Jack Absolute to carry it for me.

Dav. Ay, i'the name of mischief, let him be the messenger.—For my part, I wouldn't lend a hand to it for the best horse in your stable. By the mass! it don't look like another letter! It is, as I may say, a designing and malicious-looking letter; and I warrant smells of gunpowder like a soldier's pouch!—Oons! I wouldn't swear it mayn't go off!

Acres. Out, you poltroon! you ha'nt the valour of a grasshopper.

Dav. Well, I say no more—'twill be sad news, to be sure, at Clod-Hall! but I ha' done.—How Phillis will howl when she hears of it!—Ay, poor bitch, she little thinks what shooting her master's going after! And I warrant old Crop, who has carried your honour, field and road, these ten years, will curse the hour he was born. [*Whimpering.*

Acres. It won't do, David—I am determined to fight—so get along you coward, while I'm in the mind.

Enter SERVANT.

Ser. Captain Absolute, sir.

Acres. Oh! show him up. [*Exit* SERVANT.

Dav. Well, Heaven send we be all alive this time to-morrow.

Acres. What's that?—Don't provoke me, David!

Dav. Good-bye, master. [*Whimpering.*

Acres. Get along, you cowardly, dastardly, croaking raven! [*Exit* DAVID.

Enter CAPTAIN ABSOLUTE.

Abs. What's the matter, Bob?

Acres. A vile, sheep-hearted blockhead! If I hadn't the valour of St. George and the dragon to boot——

Abs. But what did you want with me, Bob?

Acres. Oh!—There——   [*Gives him the challenge.*

Abs. [*Aside.*] *To Ensign Beverley.*—So, what's going on now!—[*Aloud.*] Well, what's this?

Acres. A challenge!

Abs. Indeed! Why, you won't fight him; will you, Bob?

Acres. Egad, but I will, Jack. Sir Lucius has wrought me to it. He has left me full of rage—and I'll fight this evening, that so much good passion mayn't be wasted.

Abs. But what have I to do with this?

Acres. Why, as I think you know something of this fellow, I want you to find him out for me, and give him this mortal defiance.

Abs. Well, give it to me, and trust me he gets it.

Acres. Thank you, my dear friend, my dear Jack; but it is giving you a great deal of trouble.

Abs. Not in the least—I beg you won't mention it.—No trouble in the world, I assure you.

Acres. You are very kind.—What it is to have a friend!—You couldn't be my second, could you, Jack?

Abs. Why no, Bob—not in this affair—it would not be quite so proper.

Acres. Well, then, I must get my friend Sir Lucius. I shall have your good wishes, however, Jack?

Abs. Whenever he meets you, believe me.

Re-enter SERVANT.

Ser. Sir Anthony Absolute is below, inquiring for the captain.

Abs. I'll come instantly.—[*Exit* SERVANT.] Well, my little hero, success attend you.   [*Going.*

Acres.—Stay—stay, Jack.—If Beverley should ask you what kind of a man your friend Acres is, do tell him I am a devil of a fellow—will you, Jack?

Abs. To be sure I shall. I'll say you are a determined dog—hey, Bob!

Acres. Ay, do, do—and if that frightens him, egad, perhaps he mayn't come. So tell him I generally kill a man a week; will you, Jack?

Abs. I will, I will; I'll say you are called in the country Fighting Bob.

Acres. Right—right—'tis all to prevent mischief; for I don't want to take his life if I clear my honour.

Abs. No!—that's very kind of you.

Acres. Why, you don't wish me to kill him—do you, Jack?

Abs. No, upon my soul, I do not. But a devil of a fellow, hey?   [*Going.*

Acres. True, true—but stay—stay, Jack—you may add, that you never saw me in such a rage before—a most devouring rage!

Abs. I will, I will.

Acres. Remember, Jack—a determined dog!

Abs. Ay, ay, Fighting Bob!   [*Exeunt severally.*

Scene II.—Mrs. Malaprop's *Lodgings.*

Mrs. Malaprop *and* Lydia.

Mrs. Mal. Why, thou perverse one!—tell me what you can object to him? Isn't he a handsome man?—tell me that. A genteel man? a pretty figure of a man?

Lyd. [*Aside.*] She little thinks whom she is praising!—[*Aloud.*] So is Beverley, ma'am.

Mrs. Mal. No caparisons, miss, if you please. Caparisons don't become a young woman. No! Captain Absolute is indeed a fine gentleman!

Lyd. Ay, the Captain Absolute you have seen.   [*Aside.*

Mrs. Mal. Then he's so well bred;—so full of alacrity, and adulation!—and has so much to say for himself:—in such good language too! His physiognomy so grammatical! Then his presence is so noble! I protest, when I saw him, I thought of what Hamlet says in the play:—

> "Hesperian curls—the front of Job himself!—
> An eye, like March, to threaten at command!—
> A station, like Harry Mercury, new—"

Something about kissing—on a hill—however, the similitude struck me directly.

Lyd. How enraged she'll be presently, when she discovers her mistake!   [*Aside.*

Enter Servant.

Ser. Sir Anthony and Captain Absolute are below, ma'am.

Mrs. Mal. Show them up here.—[*Exit* Servant.] Now, Lydia, I insist on your behaving as becomes a young woman. Show your good breeding, at least, though you have forgot your duty.

Lyd. Madam, I have told you my resolution!—I shall not only give him no encouragement, but I won't even speak to, or look at him.

[*Flings herself into a chair, with her face from the door.*

Enter Sir Anthony Absolute *and* Captain Absolute.

Sir Anth. Here we are, Mrs. Malaprop; come to mitigate the frowns of unrelenting beauty,—and difficulty enough I had to bring this fellow.—I don't know what's the matter; but if I had not held him by force, he'd have given me the slip.

Mrs. Mal. You have infinite trouble, Sir Anthony, in the affair. I am ashamed for the cause!—[*Aside to* LYDIA.] Lydia, Lydia, rise, I beseech you! —pay your respects!

Sir Anth. I hope, madam, that Miss Languish has reflected on the worth of this gentleman, and the regard due to her aunt's choice, and my alliance.— [*Aside to* CAPTAIN ABSOLUTE.] Now, Jack, speak to her.

Abs. [*Aside.*] What the devil shall I do!—[*Aside to* SIR ANTHONY.] You see, sir, she won't even look at me whilst you are here. I knew she wouldn't! I told you so. Let me entreat you, sir, to leave us together!

[*Seems to expostulate with his father.*

Lyd. [*Aside.*] I wonder I ha'n't heard my aunt exclaim yet! sure she can't have looked at him!—perhaps their regimentals are alike, and she is something blind.

Sir Anth. I say, sir, I won't stir a foot yet!

Mrs. Mal. I am sorry to say, Sir Anthony, that my affluence over my niece is very small.—[*Aside to* LYDIA.] Turn round, Lydia: I blush for you!

Sir Anth. May I not flatter myself, that Miss Languish will assign what cause of dislike she can have to my son!—[*Aside to* CAPTAIN ABSOLUTE.] Why don't you begin, Jack?—Speak, you puppy—speak!

Mrs. Mal. It is impossible, Sir Anthony, she can have any. She will not say she has.—[*Aside to* LYDIA.] Answer, hussy! why don't you answer?

Sir Anth. Then, madam, I trust that a childish and hasty predilection will be no bar to Jack's happiness.—[*Aside to* CAPTAIN ABSOLUTE.]—Zounds! sirrah! why don't you speak!

Lyd. [*Aside.*] I think my lover seems as little inclined to conversation as myself.—How strangely blind my aunt must be!

Abs. Hem! hem! madam—hem!—[*Attempts to speak, then returns to* SIR ANTHONY.] Faith! sir, I am so confounded!—and—so—so—confused!—I told you I should be so, sir—I knew it.—The—the—tremor of my passion entirely takes away my presence of mind.

Sir Anth. But it don't take away your voice, fool, does it?—Go up, and speak to her directly!

[CAPTAIN ABSOLUTE *makes signs to* MRS. MALAPROP *to leave them together.*

Mrs. Mal. Sir Anthony, shall we leave them together?—[*Aside to* LYDIA.] Ah! you stubborn little vixen!

Sir Anth. Not yet, ma'am, not yet!—[*Aside to* CAPTAIN ABSOLUTE.] What the devil are you at? unlock your jaws, sirrah, or——

Abs. [*Aside.*] Now Heaven send she may be too sullen to look round!—I must disguise my voice.—[*Draws near* LYDIA, *and speaks in a low hoarse tone.*] Will not Miss Languish lend an ear to the mild accents of true love? Will not——

Sir Anth. What the devil ails the fellow? Why don't you speak out?—not stand croaking like a frog in a quinsy!

Abs. The—the—excess of my awe, and my—my—my modesty, quite choke me!

Sir Anth. Ah! your modesty again!—I'll tell you what, Jack; if you don't speak out directly, and glibly too, I shall be in such a rage!—Mrs. Malaprop, I wish the lady would favour us with something more than a side-front.

[MRS. MALAPROP *seems to chide* LYDIA.

Abs. [*Aside.*] So all will out, I see!—[*Goes up to* LYDIA, *speaks softly.*] Be not surprised, my Lydia, suppress all surprise at present.

Lyd. [*Aside.*] Heavens! 'tis Beverley's voice! Sure he can't have imposed on Sir Anthony too!—[*Looks round by degrees, then starts up.*] Is this possible!—my Beverley!—how can this be?—my Beverley?

Abs. Ah! 'tis all over. [*Aside.*

Sir Anth. Beverley!—the devil—Beverley!—What can the girl mean?—This is my son, Jack Absolute.

Mrs. Mal. For shame, hussy! for shame! your head runs so on that fellow, that you have him always in your eyes!—beg Captain Absolute's pardon directly.

Lyd. I see no Captain Absolute, but my loved Beverley!

Sir Anth. Zounds! the girl's mad!—her brain's turned by reading.

Mrs. Mal. O' my conscience, I believe so!—What do you mean by Beverley, hussy?—You saw Captain Absolute before to-day; there he is—your husband that shall be.

Lyd. With all my soul, ma'am—when I refuse my Beverley——

Sir Anth. Oh! she's as mad as Bedlam!—or has this fellow been playing us a rogue's trick!—Come here, sirrah, who the devil are you?

Abs. Faith, sir, I am not quite clear myself; but I'll endeavour to recollect.

Sir Anth. Are you my son or not?—answer for your mother, you dog, if you won't for me.

Mrs. Mal. Ay, sir, who are you? O mercy! I begin to suspect!—

Abs. [*Aside.*] Ye powers of impudence, befriend me!—[*Aloud.*] Sir Anthony, most assuredly I am your wife's son: and that I sincerely believe myself to be yours also, I hope my duty has always shown.—Mrs. Malaprop, I am your most respectful admirer, and shall be proud to add affectionate nephew.—I need not tell my Lydia, that she sees her faithful Beverley, who, knowing the singular generosity of her temper, assumed that name and station, which has proved a test of the most disinterested love, which he now hopes to enjoy in a more elevated character.

Lyd. So!—there will be no elopement after all! [*Sullenly.*

Sir Anth. Upon my soul, Jack, thou art a very impudent fellow! to do you justice, I think I never saw a piece of more consummate assurance!

Abs. Oh, you flatter me, sir—you compliment—'tis my modesty you know, sir,—my modesty that has stood in my way.

Sir Anth. Well, I am glad you are not the dull, insensible varlet you pretended to be, however!—I'm glad you have made a fool of your father, you dog—I am. So this was your *penitence*, your *duty* and *obedience!*—I thought it was damned sudden!—*You never heard their names before,* not you!—*what the Languishes of Worcestershire,* hey?—*if you could please me in the affair it was all you desired!*—Ah! you dissembling villain!—What!—[*Pointing to* LYDIA.] *She squints, don't she?—a little red-haired girl!*—hey?—Why, you hypocritical young rascal!—I wonder you an't ashamed to hold up your head!

Abs. 'Tis with difficulty, sir.—I am confused—very much confused, as you must perceive.

Mrs. Mal. O Lud! Sir Anthony!—a new light breaks in upon me!—hey!—how! what! captain, did you write the letters then?—What—am I to thank you for the elegant compilation of *an old weather-beaten she-dragon*—hey! —O mercy!—was it you that reflected on my parts of speech?

Abs. Dear sir! my modesty will be overpowered at last, if you don't assist me—I shall certainly not be able to stand it!

Sir Anth. Come, come, Mrs. Malaprop, we must forget and forgive;—odds life! matters have taken so clever a turn all of a sudden, that I could find in my heart to be so good-humoured! and so gallant! hey! Mrs. Malaprop!

Mrs. Mal. Well, Sir Anthony, since you desire it, we will not anticipate the past!—so mind, young people—our retrospection will be all to the future.

Sir Anth. Come, we must leave them together; Mrs. Malaprop, they long to fly into each other's arms, I warrant!—Jack—isn't the cheek as I said, hey? —and the eye, you rogue!—and the lip—hey? Come, Mrs. Malaprop, we'll not disturb their tenderness—theirs is the time of life for happiness!—*Youth's the season made for joy*—[*Sings*]—hey!—Odds life! I'm in such spirits,—I don't know what I could not do!—Permit me, ma'am—[*Gives his hand to* Mrs. MALAPROP.] Tol-de-rol—'gad, I should like to have a little fooling my-self—Tol-de-rol! de-rol.

[*Exit, singing and handing* Mrs. MALAPROP.—LYDIA *sits sullenly in her chair.*

Abs. [*Aside.*] So much thought bodes me no good.—[*Aloud.*] So grave, Lydia!

Lyd. Sir!

Abs. [*Aside.*] So!—egad! I thought as much!—that damned monosyllable has froze me!—[*Aloud.*] What, Lydia, now that we are as happy in our friends' consent, as in our mutual vows——

Lyd. Friends' consent indeed! [*Peevishly.*

Abs. Come, come, we must lay aside some of our romance—a little wealth and comfort may be endured after all. And for your fortune, the lawyers shall make such settlements as——

Lyd. Lawyers! I hate lawyers!

Abs. Nay, then, we will not wait for their lingering forms, but instantly procure the licence, and——

Lyd. The licence!—I hate licence!

Abs. Oh my love! be not so unkind!—thus let me entreat—— [*Kneeling.*

Lyd. Psha!—what signifies kneeling, when you know I must have you?

Abs. [*Rising.*] Nay, madam, there shall be no constraint upon your in-clinations, I promise you.—If I have lost your heart—I resign the rest— [*Aside.*] 'Gad, I must try what a little spirit will do.

Lyd. [*Rising.*] Then, sir, let me tell you, the interest you had there was acquired by a mean, unmanly imposition, and deserves the punishment of fraud.—What, you have been treating me like a child!—humouring my romance! and laughing, I suppose, at your success!

Abs. You wrong me, Lydia, you wrong me—only hear——

Lyd. So, while I fondly imagined we were deceiving my relations, and flattered myself that I should outwit and incense them all—behold my hopes are to be crushed at once, by my aunt's consent and approbation—and I am myself the only dupe at last!—[*Walking about in a heat.*] But here, sir, here is the picture—Beverley's picture! [*taking a miniature from her bosom*] which I have worn, night and day, in spite of threats and entreaties!—There, sir [*flings it to him*]; and be assured I throw the original from my heart as easily.

Abs. Nay, nay, ma'am, we will not differ as to that.—Here [*taking out a picture*], here is Miss Lydia Languish.—What a difference!—ay, there is the heavenly assenting smile that first gave soul and spirit to my hopes!—those are the lips which sealed a vow, as yet scarce dry in Cupid's calendar! and there the half-resentful blush, that would have checked the ardour of my thanks!—Well, all that's past!—all over indeed!—There, madam—in beauty, that copy is not equal to you, but in my mind its merit over the original, in being still the same, is such—that—I cannot find in my heart to part with it.   [*Puts it up again.*

Lyd. [*Softening.*] 'Tis your own doing, sir—I, I, I suppose you are perfectly satisfied.

Abs. O, most certainly—sure, now, this is much better than being in love! —ha! ha! ha!—there's some spirit in this!—What signifies breaking some scores of solemn promises:—all that's of no consequence, you know.—To be sure people will say, that miss don't know her own mind—but never mind that! Or, perhaps, they may be ill-natured enough to hint, that the gentleman grew tired of the lady and forsook her—but don't let that fret you.

Lyd. There is no bearing his insolence.   [*Bursts into tears.*

Re-enter MRS. MALAPROP *and* SIR ANTHONY ABSOLUTE.

Mrs. Mal. Come, we must interrupt your billing and cooing awhile.

Lyd. This is worse than your treachery and deceit, you base ingrate!
                                                      [*Sobbing.*

Sir Anth. What the devil's the matter now!—Zounds. Mrs. Malaprop, this is the oddest billing and cooing I ever heard!—but what the deuce is the meaning of it?—I am quite astonished!

Abs. Ask the lady, sir.

Mrs. Mal. Oh mercy!—I'm quite analysed, for my part!—Why, Lydia, what is the reason of this?

Lyd. Ask the gentleman, ma'am.

Sir Anth. Zounds! I shall be in a frenzy!—Why, Jack, you are not come out to be any one else, are you?

Mrs. Mal. Ay, sir, there's no more trick, is there?—you are not like Cerberus, three gentlemen at once, are you?

Abs. You'll not let me speak—I say the lady can account for this much much better than I can.

Lyd. Ma'am, you once commanded me never to think of Beverley again—there is the man—I now obey you: for, from this moment, I renounce him for ever. [*Exit.*

Mrs. Mal. O mercy! and miracles! what a turn here is—why sure, captain, you haven't behaved disrespectfully to my niece.

Sir Anth. Ha! ha! ha!—ha! ha! ha!—now I see it. Ha! ha! ha!—now I see it—you have been too lively, Jack.

Abs. Nay, sir, upon my word——

Sir Anth. Come, no lying, Jack—I'm sure 'twas so.

Mrs. Mal. O Lud! Sir Anthony!—O fy, captain!

Abs. Upon my soul, ma'am——

Sir Anth. Come, no excuses, Jack; why, your father, you rogue, was so before you:—the blood of the Absolutes was always impatient.—Ha! ha! ha! poor little Lydia! why, you've frightened her, you dog, you have.

Abs. By all that's good, sir——

Sir Anth. Zounds! say no more, I tell you—Mrs. Malaprop shall make your peace.—You must make his peace, Mrs. Malaprop:—you must tell her 'tis Jack's way—tell her 'tis all our ways—it runs in the blood of our family!—Come away, Jack—Ha! ha! ha! Mrs. Malaprop—a young villain!

[*Pushing him out.*

Mrs. Mal. O! Sir Anthony!—O fy, captain! [*Exeunt severally.*

Scene III.—*The North Parade.*

Enter Sir Lucius O'Trigger.

Sir Luc. I wonder where this Captain Absolute hides himself! Upon my conscience! these officers are always in one's way in love affairs:—I remember I might have married lady Dorothy Carmine, if it had not been for a little rogue of a major, who ran away with her before she could get a sight of me! And I wonder too what it is the ladies can see in them to be so fond of them —unless it be a touch of the old serpent in 'em, that makes the little creatures be caught, like vipers, with a bit of red cloth. Ha! isn't this the captain coming?—faith it is!—There is a probability of succeeding about that fellow, that is mighty provoking! Who the devil is he talking to? [*Steps aside.*

Enter Captain Absolute.

Abs. [*Aside.*] To what fine purpose I have been plotting! a noble reward for all my schemes, upon my soul!—a little gipsy!—I did not think her romance could have made her so damned absurd either. 'Sdeath, I never was in a worse humour in my life!—I could cut my own throat, or any other person's, with the greatest pleasure in the world!

Sir Luc. Oh, faith! I'm in the luck of it. I never could have found him in a sweeter temper for my purpose—to be sure I'm just come in the nick! Now to enter into conversation with him, and so quarrel genteelly.—[*Goes up to* CAPTAIN ABSOLUTE.] With regard to that matter, captain, I must beg leave to differ in opinion with you.

Abs. Upon my word, then, you must be a very subtle disputant:—because, sir, I happened just then to be giving no opinion at all.

Sir Luc. That's no reason. For give me leave to tell you, a man may think an untruth as well as speak one.

Abs. Very true, sir; but if a man never utters his thoughts, I should think they might stand a chance of escaping controversy.

Sir Luc. Then, sir, you differ in opinion with me, which amounts to the same thing.

Abs. Hark'ee, Sir Lucius; if I had not before known you to be a gentleman, upon my soul, I should not have discovered it at this interview: for what you can drive at, unless you mean to quarrel with me, I cannot conceive!

Sir Luc. I humbly thank you, sir, for the quickness of your apprehension.— [*Bowing.*] You have named the very thing I would be at.

Abs. Very well, sir; I shall certainly not balk your inclinations.—But I should be glad you would please to explain your motives.

Sir Luc. Pray sir, be easy; the quarrel is a very pretty quarrel as it stands; we should only spoil it by trying to explain it. However, your memory is very short, or you could not have forgot an affront you passed on me within this week. So, no more, but name your time and place.

Abs. Well, sir, since you are so bent on it, the sooner the better; let it be this evening—here, by the Spring Gardens. We shall scarcely be interrupted.

Sir Luc. Faith! that same interruption in affairs of this nature shows very great ill-breeding. I don't know what's the reason, but in England, if a thing of this kind gets wind, people make such a pother, that a gentleman can never fight in peace and quietness. However, if it's the same to you, captain, I should take it as a particular kindness if you'd let us meet in King's-Mead-Fields, as a little business will call me there about six o'clock, and I may despatch both matters at once.

Abs. 'Tis the same to me exactly. A little after six, then, we will discuss this matter more seriously.

Sir Luc. If you please, sir; there will be very pretty small-sword light, though it won't do for a long shot. So that matter's settled, and my mind's at ease! [*Exit.*

Enter FAULKLAND.

Abs. Well met! I was going to look for you. O Faulkland! all the demons of spite and disappointment have conspired against me! I'm so vexed, that if I had not the prospect of a resource in being knocked o' the head by-and-by, I should scarce have spirits to tell you the cause.

Faulk. What can you mean?—Has Lydia changed her mind?—I should have thought her duty and inclination would now have pointed to the same object.

Abs. Ay, just as the eyes do of a person who squints: when her love-eye was fixed on me, t'other, her eye of duty, was finely obliqued: but when duty bid her point that the same way, off t'other turned on a swivel, and secured its retreat with a frown!

Faulk. But what's the resource you——

Abs. Oh, to wind up the whole, a good-natured Irishman here has—[*Mimicking* Sir Lucius]—begged leave to have the pleasure of cutting my throat; and I mean to indulge him—that's all.

Faulk. Prithee, be serious!

Abs. 'Tis fact, upon my soul! Sir Lucius O'Trigger—you know him by sight—for some affront, which I am sure I never intended, has obliged me to meet him this evening at six o'clock: 'tis on that account I wished to see you; you must go with me.

Faulk. Nay, there must be some mistake, sure. Sir Lucius shall explain himself, and I dare say matters may be accommodated. But this evening did you say? I wish it had been any other time.

Abs. Why? there will be light enough: there will (as Sir Lucius says) be very pretty small-sword light, though it will not do for a long shot. Confound his long shots.

Faulk. But I am myself a good deal ruffled by a difference I have had with Julia. My vile tormenting temper has made me treat her so cruelly, that I shall not be myself till we are reconciled.

Abs. By heavens! Faulkland, you don't deserve her!

Enter Servant, *gives* Faulkland *a letter, and exit.*

Faulk. Oh, Jack! this is from Julia. I dread to open it! I fear it may be to take a last leave!—perhaps to bid me return her letters, and restore——Oh, how I suffer for my folly!

Abs. Here, let me see.—[*Takes the letter and opens it.*] Ay, a final sentence, indeed!—'tis all over with you, faith!

Faulk. Nay, Jack, don't keep me in suspense!

Abs. Hear then.—[Reads.] *As I am convinced that my dear Faulkland's own reflections have already upbraided him for his last unkindness to me, I will not add a word on the subject. I wish to speak with you as soon as possible. Yours ever and truly,* Julia. There's stubbornness and resentment for you!—[*Gives him the letter.*] Why, man, you don't seem one whit the happier at this!

Faulk. O yes, I am; but—but——

Abs. Confound your buts! you never hear any thing that would make another man bless himself, but you immediately damn it with a but!

Faulk. Now, Jack, as you are my friend, own honestly—don't you think there is something forward, something indelicate, in this haste to forgive? Women should never sue for reconciliation: that should always come from us. They should retain their coldness till wooed to kindness; and their pardon, like their love, should "not unsought be won."

Abs. I have not patience to listen to you! thou'rt incorrigible! so say no more on the subject. I must go to settle a few matters. Let me see you before six, remember, at my lodgings. A poor industrious devil like me, who have toiled, and drudged, and plotted to gain my ends, and am at last disappointed by other people's folly, may in pity be allowed to swear and grumble a little; but a captious sceptic in love, a slave to fretfulness and whim, who has no difficulties but of his own creating, is a subject more fit for ridicule than compassion! [*Exit.*

Faulk. I feel his reproaches; yet I would not change this too exquisite nicety for the gross content with which he tramples on the thorns of love! His engaging me in this duel has started an idea in my head, which I will instantly pursue. I'll use it as the touchstone of Julia's sincerity and disinterestedness. If her love prove pure and sterling ore, my name will rest on it with honour; and once I've stamped it there, I lay aside my doubts for ever! But if the dross of selfishness, the alloy of pride, predominate, 'twill be best to leave her as a toy for some less cautious fool to sigh for! [*Exit.*

ACT V.

SCENE I.—JULIA's *Dressing-Room.*

JULIA *discovered alone.*

Jul. How this message has alarmed me! what dreadful accident can he mean? why such charge to be alone?—O Faulkland!—how many unhappy moments—how many tears have you cost me.

Enter FAULKLAND.

Jul. What means this?—why this caution, Faulkland?

Faulk. Alas! Julia, I am come to take a long farewell.

Jul. Heavens! what do you mean?

Faulk. You see before you a wretch, whose life is forfeited. Nay, start not! —the infirmity of my temper has drawn all this misery on me. I left you fretful and passionate—an untoward accident drew me into a quarrel—the event is, that I must fly this kingdom instantly. O Julia, had I been so fortunate as to have called you mine entirely, before this mischance had fallen on me, I should not so deeply dread my banishment!

Jul. My soul is oppressed with sorrow at the nature of your misfortune: had these adverse circumstances arisen from a less fatal cause, I should have felt strong comfort in the thought that I could now chase from your bosom every doubt of the warm sincerity of my love. My heart has long known no other guardian—I now entrust my person to your honour—we will fly together. When safe from pursuit, my father's will may be fulfilled—and I receive a legal claim to be the partner of your sorrows, and tenderest comforter. Then on the bosom of your wedded Julia, you may lull your keen regret to slumbering; while virtuous love, with a cherub's hand, shall smooth the brow of upbraiding thought, and pluck the thorn from compunction.

Faulk. O Julia! I am bankrupt in gratitude! but the time is so pressing, it calls on you for so hasty a resolution.—Would you not wish some hours to weigh the advantages you forego, and what little compensation poor Faulkland can make you beside his solitary love?

Jul. I ask not a moment. No, Faulkland, I have loved you for yourself: and if I now, more than ever, prize the solemn engagement which so long has pledged us to each other, it is because it leaves no room for hard aspersions on my fame, and puts the seal of duty to an act of love. But let us not linger. Perhaps this delay——

Faulk. 'Twill be better I should not venture out again till dark. Yet am I grieved to think what numberless distresses will press heavy on your gentle disposition!

Jul. Perhaps your fortune may be forfeited by this unhappy act.—I know not whether 'tis so; but sure that alone can never make us unhappy. The little I have will be sufficient to support us; and exile never should be splendid.

Faulk. Ay, but in such an abject state of life, my wounded pride perhaps may increase the natural fretfulness of my temper, till I become a rude, morose companion, beyond your patience to endure. Perhaps the recollection of a deed my conscience cannot justify may haunt me in such gloomy and unsocial fits, that I shall hate the tenderness that would relieve me, break from your arms, and quarrel with your fondness!

Jul. If your thoughts should assume so unhappy a bent, you will the more want some mild and affectionate spirit to watch over and console you: one who, by bearing your infirmities with gentleness and resignation, may teach you so to bear the evils of your fortune.

Faulk. Julia, I have proved you to the quick! and with this useless device I throw away all my doubts. How shall I plead to be forgiven this last unworthy effect of my restless, unsatisfied disposition?

Jul. Has no such disaster happened as you related?

Faulk. I am ashamed to own that it was pretended; yet in pity, Julia, do not kill me with resenting a fault which never can be repeated: but sealing, this once, my pardon, let me to-morrow, in the face of Heaven, receive my future guide and monitress, and expiate my past folly by years of tender adoration.

Jul. Hold, Faulkland!—that you are free from a crime, which I before feared to name, Heaven knows how sincerely I rejoice! These are tears of thankfulness for that! But that your cruel doubts should have urged you to an imposition that has wrung my heart, gives me now a pang more keen than I can express!

Faulk. By Heavens! Julia——

Jul. Yet hear me.—My father loved you, Faulkland! and you preserved the life that tender parent gave me; in his presence I pledged my hand—joyfully pledged it—where before I had given my heart. When, soon after, I lost that parent, it seemed to me that Providence had, in Faulkland, shown me whither to transfer without a pause, my grateful duty, as well as my affection: hence I have been content to bear from you what pride and delicacy would have forbid me from another. I will not upbraid you, by repeating how you have trifled with my sincerity——

Faulk. I confess it all! yet hear——

Jul. After such a year of trial, I might have flattered myself that I should not have been insulted with a new probation of my sincerity, as cruel as unnecessary! I now see it is not in your nature to be content or confident in love. With this conviction—I never will be yours. While I had hopes that my persevering attention, and unreproaching kindness, might in time reform your temper, I should have been happy to have gained a dearer influence over you; but I will not furnish you with a licensed power to keep alive an incorrigible fault, at the expense of one who never would contend with you.

Faulk. Nay, but, Julia, by my soul and honour, if after this——

Jul. But one word more.—As my faith has once been given to you, I never will barter it with another.—I shall pray for your happiness with the truest sincerity; and the dearest blessing I can ask of Heaven to send you will be to charm you from that unhappy temper, which alone has prevented the performance of our solemn engagement. All I request of you is, that you will yourself reflect upon this infirmity, and when you number up the many true delights it has deprived you of, let it not be your least regret, that it lost you the love of one who would have followed you in beggary through the world! [*Exit.*

Faulk. She's gone—for ever!—There was an awful resolution in her manner, that riveted me to my place.—O fool!—dolt!—barbarian! Cursed as I am, with more imperfections than my fellow wretches, kind Fortune sent a heaven-gifted cherub to my aid, and, like a ruffian, I have driven her from my side! —I must now haste to my appointment. Well, my mind is tuned for such a scene. I shall wish only to become a principal in it, and reverse the tale my cursed folly put me upon forging here.—O Love!—tormentor!—fiend!—whose influence, like the moon's, acting on men of dull souls, makes idiots of them, but meeting subtler spirits, betrays their course, and urges sensibility to madness! [*Exit.*

Enter Lydia and Maid.

Maid. My mistress, ma'am, I know, was here just now—perhaps she is only in the next room. [*Exit.*

Lyd. Heigh-ho! Though he has used me so, this fellow runs strangely in my head. I believe one lecture from my grave cousin will make me recall him. [*Re-enter* Julia.] O Julia, I am come to you with such an appetite for consolation.—Lud! child, what's the matter with you? You have been crying! —I'll be hanged if that Faulkland has not been tormenting you!

Jul. You mistake the cause of my uneasiness!—Something has flurried me a little. Nothing that you can guess at.—[*Aside.*] I would not accuse Faulkland to a sister!

Lyd. Ah! whatever vexations you may have, I can assure you mine surpass them. You know who Beverley proves to be?

Jul. I will now own to you, Lydia, that Mr. Faulkland had before informed me of the whole affair. Had young Absolute been the person you took him for, I should not have accepted your confidence on the subject, without a serious endeavour to counteract your caprice.

Lyd. So, then, I see I have been deceived by every one! But I don't care —I'll never have him.

Jul. Nay, Lydia——

Lyd. Why, is it not provoking? when I thought we were coming to the prettiest distress imaginable, to find myself made a mere Smithfield bargain of at last! There, had I projected one of the most sentimental elopements!— so becoming a disguise!—so amiable a ladder of ropes!—Conscious moon— four horses—Scotch parson—with such surprise to Mrs. Malaprop—and such paragraphs in the newspapers!—Oh, I shall die with disappointment!

Jul. I don't wonder at it!

Lyd. Now—sad reverse!—what have I to expect, but, after a deal of flimsy preparation with a bishop's licence, and my aunt's blessing, to go simpering up to the altar; or perhaps be cried three times in a country church, and have an unmannerly fat clerk ask the consent of every butcher in the parish to join John Absolute and Lydia Languish, spinster! Oh that I should live to hear myself called spinster!

Jul. Melancholy indeed!

Lyd. How mortifying, to remember the dear delicious shifts I used to be put to, to gain half a minute's conversation with this fellow! How often have I stole forth, in the coldest night in January, and found him in the garden, stuck like a dripping statue! There would he kneel to me in the snow, and sneeze and cough so pathetically! he shivering with cold and I with apprehension! and while the freezing blast numbed our joints, how warmly would he press me to pity his flame, and glow with mutual ardour!—Ah, Julia, that was something like being in love.

Jul. If I were in spirits, Lydia, I should chide you only by laughing heartily at you; but it suits more the situation of my mind, at present, earnestly to entreat you not to let a man, who loves you with sincerity, suffer that unhappiness from your caprice, which I know too well caprice can inflict.

Lyd. O Lud! what has brought my aunt here?

Enter MRS. MALAPROP, FAG, *and* DAVID.

Mrs. Mal. So! so! here's fine work!—here's fine suicide, parricide, and simulation, going on in the fields! and Sir Anthony not to be found to prevent the antistrophe!

Jul. For Heaven's sake, madam, what's the meaning of this?

Mrs. Mal. That gentleman can tell you—'twas he enveloped the affair to me.

Lyd. Do, sir, will you, inform us?   [*To* FAG.

Fag. Ma'am, I should hold myself very deficient in every requisite that forms the man of breeding, if I delayed a moment to give all the information in my power to a lady so deeply interested in the affair as you are.

Lyd. But quick! quick sir!

Fag. True, ma'am, as you say, one should be quick in divulging matters of this nature; for should we be tedious, perhaps while we are flourishing on the subject, two or three lives may be lost!

Lyd. O patience!—Do, ma'am, for Heaven's sake! tell us what is the matter?

Mrs. Mal. Why, murder's the matter! slaughter's the matter! killing's the matter!—but he can tell you the perpendiculars.

Lyd. Then, prithee, sir, be brief.

Fag. Why then, ma'am, as to murder—I cannot take upon me to say—and as to slaughter, or manslaughter, that will be as the jury finds it.

Lyd. But who, sir—who are engaged in this?

Fag. Faith, ma'am, one is a young gentleman whom I should be very sorry any thing was to happen to—a very pretty behaved gentleman! We have lived much together, and always on terms.

Lyd. But who is this? who! who! who?

Fag. My master, ma'am—my master—I speak of my master.

Lyd. Heavens! What, Captain Absolute!

Mrs. Mal. Oh, to be sure, you are frightened now!

Jul. But who are with him, sir?

Fag. As to the rest, ma'am, this gentleman can inform you better than I.

Jul. Do speak, friend.   [*To* DAVID.

Dav. Look'ee, my lady—by the mass! there's mischief going on. Folks don't use to meet for amusement with firearms, firelocks, fire-engines, fire-screens, fire-office, and the devil knows what other crackers beside!—This, my lady, I say, has an angry favour.

Jul. But who is there beside Captain Absolute, friend?

Dav. My poor master—under favour for mentioning him first. You know me, my lady—I am David—and my master of course is, or was, Squire Acres. Then comes Squire Faulkland.

Jul. Do, ma'am, let us instantly endeavour to prevent mischief.

Mrs. Mal. O fy!—it would be very inelegant in us:—we should only participate things.

Dav. Ah! do, Mrs. Aunt, save a few lives—they are desperately given, believe me.—Above all, there is that blood-thirsty Philistine, Sir Lucius O'Trigger.

Mrs. Mal. Sir Lucius O'Trigger? O mercy! have they drawn poor little dear Sir Lucius into the scrape?—Why, how you stand, girl! you have no more feeling than one of the Derbyshire petrifactions!

Lyd. What are we to do, madam?

Mrs. Mal. Why fly with the utmost felicity, to be sure, to prevent mischief!—Here, friend, you can show us the place?

Fag. If you please, ma'am, I will conduct you.—David, do you look for Sir Anthony.   [*Exit* DAVID.

Mrs. Mal. Come, girls! this gentleman will exhort us.—Come, sir, you're our envoy—lead the way, and we'll precede.

Fag. Not a step before the ladies for the world!

Mrs. Mal. You're sure you know the spot?

Fag. I think I can find it, ma'am; and one good thing is, we shall hear the report of the pistols as we draw near, so we can't well miss them;—never fear, ma'am, never fear.   [*Exeunt, he talking.*

SCENE II.—*The South Parade.*

Enter CAPTAIN ABSOLUTE, *putting his sword under his great coat.*

Abs. A sword seen in the streets of Bath would raise as great an alarm as a mad dog.—How provoking this is in Faulkland!—never punctual! I shall be obliged to go without him at last.—Oh, the devil! here's Sir Anthony! how shall I escape him?   [*Muffles up his face, and takes a circle to go off.*

Enter SIR ANTHONY ABSOLUTE.

Sir Anth. How one may be deceived at a little distance! only that I see he don't know me, I could have sworn that was Jack!—Hey! Gad's life! it is.—Why, Jack, what are you afraid of? hey!—sure I'm right.—Why Jack, Jack Absolute!   [*Goes up to him.*

Abs. Really, sir, you have the advantage of me:—I don't remember ever to have had the honour—my name is Saunderson, at your service.

Sir Anth. Sir, I beg your pardon—I took you—hey?—why, zounds! it is— Stay—[*Looks up to his face.*] So, so—your humble servant, Mr. Saunderson! Why, you scoundrel, what tricks are you after now?

Abs. Oh, a joke, sir, a joke! I came here on purpose to look for you, sir.

Sir Anth. You did! well, I am glad you were so lucky:—but what are you muffled up so for?—what's this for?—hey!

Abs. 'Tis cool, sir; isn't?—rather chilly somehow;—but I shall be late—I have a particular engagement.

Sir Anth. Stay!—Why, I thought you were looking for me?—Pray, Jack, where is't you are going?

Abs. Going, sir?

Sir Anth. Ay, where are you going?

Abs. Where am I going?

Sir Anth. You unmannerly puppy!

Abs. I was going, sir, to—to—to—to Lydia—sir, to Lydia—to make matters up if I could;—and I was looking for you, sir, to—to—

Sir Anth. To go with you, I suppose.—Well, come along.

Abs. Oh! zounds! no, sir, not for the world!—I wished to meet with you, sir,—to—to—to—You find it cool, I'm sure, sir—you'd better not stay out.

Sir Anth. Cool!—not at all.—Well, Jack—and what will you say to Lydia?

Abs. Oh, sir, beg her pardon, humour her—promise and vow: but I detain you, sir—consider the cold air on your gout.

Sir Anth. Oh, not at all!—Not at all! I'm in no hurry.—Ah! Jack, you youngsters, when once you are wounded here [*Putting his hand to* Captain Absolute's *breast.*] Hey! what the deuce have you got here?

Abs. Nothing, sir—nothing.

Sir Anth. What's this?—here's something damned hard.

Abs. Oh, trinkets, sir! trinkets!—a bauble for Lydia!

Sir Anth. Nay, let me see your taste.—[*Pulls his coat open, the sword falls.*] Trinkets!—a bauble for Lydia!—Zounds! sirrah, you are not going to cut her throat, are you?

Abs. Ha! ha! ha!—I thought it would divert you, sir, though I didn't mean to tell you till afterwards.

Sir Anth. You didn't?—Yes, this is a very diverting trinket, truly!

Abs. Sir, I'll explain to you.—You know, sir, Lydia is romantic, devilish romantic, and very absurd of course: now, sir, I intend, if she refuses to forgive me, to unsheath this sword, and swear—I'll fall upon its point, and expire at her feet!

Sir Anth. Fall upon a fiddlestick's end!—why, I suppose it is the very thing that would please her.—Get along, you fool!

Abs. Well, sir, you shall hear of my success—you shall hear.—*O Lydia!— forgive me, or this pointed steel*—says I.

Sir Anth. O, *booby! stab away and welcome*—says she.—Get along! and damn your trinkets!   [*Exit* Captain Absolute.

Enter David, *running.*

Dav. Stop him! stop him! Murder! Thief! Fire!—Stop fire! Stop fire!—O Sir Anthony—call! call! bid 'm stop! Murder! Fire!

Sir Anth. Fire! Murder!—Where?

Dav. Oons! he's out of sight! and I'm out of breath! for my part! O Sir Anthony, why didn't you stop him? why didn't you stop him?

Sir Anth. Zounds! the fellow's mad!—Stop whom? stop Jack?

Dav. Ay, the captain, sir!—there's murder and slaughter——

Sir Anth. Murder!

Dav. Ay, please you, Sir Anthony, there's all kinds of murder, all sorts of slaughter to be seen in the fields: there's fighting going on, sir—bloody sword-and-gun fighting!

Sir Anth. Who are going to fight, dunce?

Dav. Every body that I know of, Sir Anthony:—every body is going to fight, my poor master, Sir Lucius O'Trigger, your son, the captain——

Sir Anth. Oh, the dog! I see his tricks.—Do you know the place?

Dav. King's-Mead-Fields.

Sir Anth. You know the way?

Dav. Not an inch; but I'll call the mayor—aldermen—constables—church-wardens—and beadles—we can't be too many to part them.

Sir Anth. Come along—give me your shoulder! we'll get assistance as we go—the lying villain!—Well, I shall be in such a frenzy!—So—this was the history of his trinkets! I'll bauble him!   [*Exeunt.*

SCENE III.—*King's-Mead-Fields.*

Enter Sir Lucius O'Trigger *and* Acres, *with pistols.*

Acres. By my valour! then, Sir Lucius, forty yards is a good distance. Odds levels and aims!—I say it is a good distance.

Sir Luc. Is it for muskets or small field-pieces? Upon my conscience, Mr. Acres, you must leave those things to me.—Stay now—I'll show you.— [*Measures paces along the stage.*] There now, that is a very pretty distance— a pretty gentleman's distance.

Acres. Zounds! we might as well fight in a sentry-box! I tell you, Sir Lucius, the farther he is off, the cooler I shall take my aim.

Sir Luc. Faith! then I suppose you would aim at him best of all if he was out of sight!

Acres. No, Sir Lucius; but I should think forty or eight-and-thirty yards——

Sir Luc. Pho! pho! nonsense! three or four feet between the mouths of your pistols is as good as a mile.

Acres. Odds bullets, no!—by my valour! there is no merit in killing him so near: do, my dear Sir Lucius, let me bring him down at a long shot:—a long shot, Sir Lucius, if you love me!

Sir Luc. Well, the gentleman's friend and I must settle that.—But tell me now, Mr. Acres, in case of an accident, is there any little will or commission I could execute for you?

Acres. I am much obliged to you, Sir Lucius—but I don't understand——

Sir Luc. Why, you may think there's no being shot at without a little risk—and if an unlucky bullet should carry a quietus with it—I say it will be no time then to be bothering you about family matters.

Acres. A quietus!

Sir Luc. For instance, now—if that should be the case—would you choose to be pickled and sent home?—or would it be the same to you to lie here in the Abbey?—I'm told there is very snug lying in the Abbey.

Acres. Pickled!—Snug lying in the Abbey!—Odds tremors! Sir Lucius, don't talk so!

Sir Luc. I suppose, Mr. Acres, you never were engaged in an affair of this kind before?

Acres. No, Sir Lucius, never before.

Sir Luc. Ah! that's a pity!—there's nothing like being used to a thing.— Pray now, how would you receive the gentleman's shot?

Acres. Odds files!—I've practised that—there, Sir Lucius—there.—[*Puts himself in an attitude.*] A side-front, hey? Odd! I'll make myself small enough: I'll stand edgeways.

Sir Luc. Now—you're quite out—for if you stand so when I take my aim—— [*Levelling at him.*

Acres. Zounds! Sir Lucius—are you sure it is not cocked?

Sir Luc. Never fear.

Acres. But—but—you don't know—it may go off of its own head!

Sir Luc. Pho! be easy.—Well, now if I hit you in the body, my bullet has a double chance—for if it misses a vital part of your right side—'twill be very hard if it don't succeed on the left!

Acres. A vital part!

Sir Luc. But, there—fix yourself so—[*Placing him*]—let him see the broad-side of your full front—there—now a ball or two may pass clean through your body, and never do any harm at all.

Acres. Clean through me!—a ball or two clean through me!

Sir Luc. Ay—may they—and it is much the genteelest attitude into the bargain.

Acres. Look'ee! Sir Lucius—I'd just as lieve be shot in an awkward posture as a genteel one; so, by my valour! I will stand edgeways.

Sir Luc. [*Looking at his watch.*] Sure they don't mean to disappoint us—Hah!—no, faith—I think I see them coming.

Acres. Hey!—what!—coming!——

Sir Luc. Ay.—Who are those yonder getting over the stile?

Acres. There are two of them indeed!—well—let them come—hey, Sir Lucius!—we—we—we—we—won't run.

Sir Luc. Run!

Acres. No—I say—we won't run, by my valour!

Sir Luc. What the devil's the matter with you?

Acres. Nothing—nothing—my dear friend—my dear Sir Lucius—but I—I—I don't feel quite so bold, somehow, as I did.

Sir Luc. O fy!—consider your honour.

Acres. Ay—true—my honour. Do, Sir Lucius, edge in a word or two every now and then about my honour.

Sir Luc. Well, here they're coming. [*Looking.*

Acres. Sir Lucius—if I wa'n't with you, I should almost think I was afraid.—If my valour should leave me!—Valour will come and go.

Sir Luc. Then pray keep it fast, while you have it.

Acres. Sir Lucius—I doubt it is going—yes—my valour is certainly going!—it is sneaking off!—I feel it oozing out as it were at the palms of my hands!

Sir Luc. Your honour—your honour.—Here they are.

Acres. O mercy!—now—that I was safe at Clod-Hall! or could be shot before I was aware!

Enter FAULKLAND *and* CAPTAIN ABSOLUTE.

Sir Luc. Gentlemen, your most obedient.—Hah!—what, Captain Absolute!—So, I suppose, sir, you are come here, just like myself—to do a kind office, first for your friend—then to proceed to business on your own account.

Acres. What, Jack!—my dear Jack!—my dear friend!

Abs. Hark'ee, Bob, Beverley's at hand.

Sir Luc. Well, Mr. Acres—I don't blame your saluting the gentleman civilly. —[*To* FAULKLAND.] So, Mr. Beverley, if you'll choose your weapons, the captain and I will measure the ground.

Faulk. My weapons, sir!

Acres. Odds life! Sir Lucius, I'm not going to fight Mr. Faulkland; these are my particular friends.

Sir Luc. What, sir, did you not come here to fight Mr. Acres?

Faulk. Not I, upon my word, sir.

Sir Luc. Well, now, that's mighty provoking! But I hope, Mr. Faulkland, as there are three of us come on purpose for the game, you won't be so cantanckerous as to spoil the party by sitting out.

Abs. O pray, Faulkland, fight to oblige Sir Lucius.

Faulk. Nay, if Mr. Acres is so bent on the matter——

Acres. No, no, Mr. Faulkland;—I'll bear my disappointment like a Christian.—Look'ee, Sir Lucius, there's no occasion at all for me to fight; and if it is the same to you, I'd as lieve let it alone.

Sir Luc. Observe me, Mr. Acres—I must not be trifled with. You have certainly challenged somebody—and you came here to fight him. Now, if that gentleman is willing to represent him—I can't see, for my soul, why it isn't just the same thing.

Acres. Why no—Sir Lucius—I tell you, 'tis one Beverley I've challenged— a fellow, you see, that dare not show his face!—If he were here, I'd make him give up his pretensions directly!

Abs. Hold, Bob—let me set you right—there is no such man as Beverley in the case.—The person who assumed that name is before you; and as his pretensions are the same in both characters, he is ready to support them in whatever way you please.

Sir Luc. Well, this is lucky.—Now you have an opportunity——

Acres. What, quarrel with my dear friend Jack Absolute?—not if he were fifty Beverleys! Zounds! Sir Lucius, you would not have me so unnatural.

Sir Luc. Upon my conscience, Mr. Acres, your valour has oozed away with a vengeance!

Acres. Not in the least! Odds backs and abettors! I'll be your second with all my heart—and if you should get a quietus, you may command me entirely. I'll get you snug lying in the Abbey here; or pickle you, and send you over to Blunderbuss-hall, or any thing of the kind, with the greatest pleasure.

Sir Luc. Pho! pho! you are little better than a coward.

Acres. Mind, gentlemen, he calls me a coward; coward was the word, by my valour!

Sir Luc. Well, sir?

Acres. Look'ee, Sir Lucius, 'tisn't that I mind the word coward—coward may be said in joke—But if you had called me a poltroon, odds daggers and balls——

Sir Luc. Well, sir?

Acres. I should have thought you a very ill-bred man.

Sir Luc. Pho! you are beneath my notice.

Abs. Nay, Sir Lucius, you can't have a better second than my friend Acres —He is a most determined dog—called in the country, Fighting Bob.—He generally kills a man a week—don't you, Bob?

Acres. Ay—at home!

Sir Luc. Well, then, captain, 'tis we must begin—so come out, my little counsellor—[*Draws his sword*]—and ask the gentleman, whether he will resign the lady, without forcing you to proceed against him?

Abs. Come on then, sir—[*Draws*]; since you won't let it be an amicable suit, here's my reply.

Enter SIR ANTHONY ABSOLUTE, DAVID, MRS. MALAPROP, LYDIA, *and* JULIA.

Dav. Knock 'em all down, sweet Sir Anthony; knock down my master in particular; and bind his hands over to their good behaviour!

Sir Anth. Put up, Jack, put up, or I shall be in a frenzy—how came you in a duel, sir?

Abs. Faith, sir, that gentleman can tell you better than I; 'twas he called on me, and you know, sir, I serve his majesty.

Sir Anth. Here's a pretty fellow; I catch him going to cut a man's throat, and he tells me, he serves his majesty!—Zounds! sirrah, then how durst you draw the king's sword against one of his subjects?

Abs. Sir, I tell you! that gentleman called me out, without explaining his reasons.

Sir Anth. Gad! sir, how came you to call my son out, without explaining your reasons?

Sir Luc. Your son, sir, insulted me in a manner which my honour could not brook.

Sir Anth. Zounds! Jack, how durst you insult the gentleman in a manner which his honour could not brook?

Mrs. Mal. Come, come, let's have no honour before ladies—Captain Absolute, come here—How could you intimidate us so?—Here's Lydia has been terrified to death for you.

Abs. For fear I should be killed, or escape, ma'am?

Mrs. Mal. Nay, no delusions to the past—Lydia is convinced; speak, child.

Sir Luc. With your leave, ma'am, I must put in a word here: I believe I could interpret the young lady's silence. Now mark——

Lyd. What is it you mean, sir?

Sir Luc. Come, come, Delia, we must be serious now—this is no time for trifling.

Lyd. 'Tis true, sir; and your reproof bids me offer this gentleman my hand, and solicit the return of his affections.

Abs. O! my little angel, say you so!—Sir Lucius—I perceive there must be some mistake here, with regard to the affront which you affirm I have given you. I can only say, that it could not have been intentional. And as you must be convinced, that I should not fear to support a real injury—you shall now see that I am not ashamed to atone for an inadvertency—I ask your pardon.—

But for this lady, while honoured with her approbation, I will support my
claim against any man whatever.

Sir Anth. Well said, Jack, and I'll stand by you, my boy.

Acres. Mind, I give up all my claim—I make no pretensions to any thing
in the world; and if I can't get a wife without fighting for her, by my valour!
I'll live a bachelor.

Sir Luc. Captain, give me your hand: an affront handsomely acknowledged becomes an obligation; and as for the lady, if she chooses to deny her
own hand-writing, here——   [*Takes out letters.*

Mrs. Mal. O, he will dissolve my mystery!—Sir Lucius, perhaps there's
some mistake—perhaps I can illuminate——

Sir Luc. Pray, old gentlewoman, don't interfere where you have no business.—Miss Languish, are you my Delia, or not?

Lyd. Indeed, Sir Lucius, I am not.   [*Walks aside with* CAPTAIN ABSOLUTE.

Mrs. Mal. Sir Lucius O'Trigger—ungrateful as you are—I own the soft
impeachment—pardon my blushes, I am Delia.

Sir Luc. You Delia—pho! pho! be easy.

Mrs. Mal. Why, thou barbarous Vandyke—those letters are mine—When
you are more sensible of my benignity—perhaps I may be brought to encourage your addresses.

Sir Luc. Mrs. Malaprop, I am extremely sensible of your condescension;
and whether you or Lucy have put this trick on me, I am equally beholden
to you.—And, to show you I am not ungrateful, Captain Absolute, since you
have taken that lady from me, I'll give you my Delia into the bargain.

Abs. I am much obliged to you, Sir Lucius; but here's my friend, Fighting
Bob, unprovided for.

Sir Luc. Hah! little Valour—here, will you make your fortune?

Acres. Odds wrinkles! No.—But give me your hand, Sir Lucius, forget and
forgive; but if ever I give you a chance of pickling me again, say Bob Acres
is a dunce, that's all.

Sir Anth. Come, Mrs. Malaprop, don't be cast down—you are in your
bloom yet.

Mrs. Mal. O Sir Anthony—men are all barbarians.

                              [*All retire but* JULIA *and* FAULKLAND.

Jul. [*Aside.*] He seems dejected and unhappy—not sullen; there was some
foundation, however, for the tale he told me—O woman! how true should be
your judgment, when your resolution is so weak!

Faulk. Julia!—how can I sue for what I so little deserve? I dare not presume—yet Hope is the child of Penitence.

Jul. Oh! Faulkland, you have not been more faulty in your unkind treatment of me, than I am now in wanting inclination to resent it. As my heart
honestly bids me place my weakness to the account of love, I should be ungenerous not to admit the same plea for yours.

Faulk. Now I shall be blest indeed!

Sir Anth. [*Coming forward.*] What's going on here?—So you have been
quarrelling too, I warrant! Come, Julia, I never interfered before; but let

me have a hand in the matter at last.—All the faults I have ever seen in m
friend Faulkland seemed to proceed from what he calls the delicacy an
warmth of his affection for you—There, marry him directly, Julia; you
find he'll mend surprisingly!   [*The rest come forwar*

Sir Luc. Come, now, I hope there is no dissatisfied person, but what
content; for as I have been disappointed myself, it will be very hard if
have not the satisfaction of seeing other people succeed better.

Acres. You are right, Sir Lucius.—So Jack, I wish you joy—Mr. Faulklan
the same.—Ladies,—come now, to show you I'm neither vexed nor angr
odds tabors and pipes! I'll order the fiddles in half an hour to the Ne
Rooms—and I insist on your all meeting me there.

Sir Anth. 'Gad! sir, I like your spirit; and at night we single lads wi
drink a health to the young couples, and a husband to Mrs. Malaprop.

Faulk. Our partners are stolen from us, Jack—I hope to be congratulate
by each other—yours for having checked in time the errors of an ill-directe
imagination, which might have betrayed an innocent heart; and mine, fo
having, by her gentleness and candour, reformed the unhappy temper of on
who by it made wretched whom he loved most, and tortured the heart h
ought to have adored.

Abs. Well, Jack, we have both tasted the bitters, as well as the sweets o
love; with this difference only, that you always prepared the bitter cup fo
yourself, while I——

Lyd. Was always obliged to me for it, hey! Mr. Modesty?——But, come
no more of that—our happiness is now as unalloyed as general.

Jul. Then let us study to preserve it so: and while Hope pictures to us
flattering scene of future bliss, let us deny its pencil those colours which ar
too bright to be lasting.—When hearts deserving happiness would unite thei
fortunes, Virtue would crown them with an unfading garland of modes
hurtless flowers; but ill-judging Passion will force the gaudier rose into th
wreath, whose thorn offends them when its leaves are dropped!

                                              [*Exeunt omnes*

EPILOGUE

BY THE AUTHOR

SPOKEN BY MRS. BULKLEY.

LADIES, for you—I heard our poet say—
He'd try to coax some moral from his play:
"One moral's plain," cried I, "without more fuss;
Man's social happiness all rests on us:
Through all the drama—whether damn'd or not—
Love gilds the scene, and women guide the plot.
From every rank obedience is our due—
D'ye doubt?—The world's great stage shall prove it true."
　　The cit, well skill'd to shun domestic strife,
Will sup abroad; but first he'll ask his wife:
John Trot, his friend, for once will do the same,
But then—he'll just step home to tell his dame.
　　The surly squire at noon resolves to rule,
And half the day—Zounds! madam is a fool!
Convinced at night, the vanquish'd victor says,
Ah, Kate! you women have such coaxing ways.
　　The jolly toper chides each tardy blade,
Till reeling Bacchus calls on Love for aid:
Then with each toast he sees fair bumpers swim,
And kisses Chloe on the sparkling brim!
　　Nay, I have heard that statesmen—great and wise—
Will sometimes counsel with a lady's eyes!
The servile suitors watch her various face,
She smiles preferment, or she frowns disgrace,
Curtsies a pension here—there nods a place.
　　Nor with less awe, in scenes of humbler life,
Is view'd the mistress, or is heard the wife.
The poorest peasant of the poorest soil,
The child of poverty, and heir to toil,
Early from radiant Love's impartial light
Steals one small spark to cheer this world of night:
Dear spark! that oft through winter's chilling woes
Is all the warmth his little cottage knows!
　　The wandering tar, who not for years has press'd,
The widow'd partner of his day of rest,
On the cold deck, far from her arms removed,
Still hums the ditty which his Susan loved;
And while around the cadence rude is blown,
The boatswain whistles in a softer tone.

The soldier, fairly proud of wounds and toil,
Pants for the triumph of his Nancy's smile;
But ere the battle should he list her cries,
The lover trembles—and the hero dies!
That heart, by war and honour steel'd to fear,
Droops on a sigh, and sickens at a tear!
But ye more cautious, ye nice-judging few,
Who give to beauty only beauty's due,
Though friends to love—ye view with deep regret
Our conquests marr'd, our triumphs incomplete,
Till polish'd wit more lasting charms disclose,
And judgment fix the darts which beauty throws!
In female breasts did sense and merit rule,
The lover's mind would ask no other school;
Shamed into sense, the scholars of our eyes,
Our beaux from gallantry would soon be wise;
Would gladly light, their homage to improve,
The lamp of knowledge at the torch of love!

THE SCHOOL FOR SCANDAL

A COMEDY

by Richard Brinsley Sheridan

DRAMATIS PERSONÆ

Sir Peter Teazle

Sir Oliver Surface

Sir Harry Bumper

Sir Benjamin Backbite

Joseph Surface

Charles Surface

Careless

Snake

Crabtree

Rowley

Moses

Trip

Lady Teazle

Lady Sneerwell

Mrs. Candour

Maria

Gentlemen, Maid, *and* Servants.

SCENE.—London.

A PORTRAIT;

ADDRESSED TO MRS. CREWE, WITH THE COMEDY OF THE SCHOOL FOR SCANDAL.

BY R. B. SHERIDAN, ESQ.

TELL me, ye prim adepts in Scandal's school,
Who rail by precept, and detract by rule,
Lives there no character, so tried, so known,
So deck'd with grace, and so unlike your own,
That even you assist her fame to raise,
Approve by envy, and by silence praise!
Attend!—a model shall attract your view—
Daughters of calumny, I summon you!
You shall decide if this a portrait prove,
Or fond creation of the Muse and Love.
Attend, ye virgin critics, shrewd and sage,
Ye matron censors of this childish age,
Whose peering eye and wrinkled front declare
A fix'd antipathy to young and fair;
By cunning, cautious; or by nature, cold,
In maiden madness, virulently bold!—
Attend, ye skill'd to coin the precious tale,
Creating proof, where inuendos fail!
Whose practised memories, cruelly exact,
Omit no circumstance, except the fact!—
Attend, all ye who boast,—or old or young,—
The living libel of a slanderous tongue!
So shall my theme as far contrasted be,
As saints by fiends, or hymns by calumny.
Come, gentle Amoret (for 'neath that name
In worthier verse is sung thy beauty's fame);
Come—for but thee who seeks the Muse? and while
Celestial blushes check thy conscious smile,
With timid grace, and hesitating eye,
The perfect model, which I boast, supply:—
Vain Muse! couldst thou the humblest sketch create
Of her, or slightest charm couldst imitate—
Could thy blest strain in kindred colours trace
The faintest wonder of her form and face—
Poets would study the immortal line,
And Reynolds own his art subdued by thine;

That art, which well might added lustre give
To Nature's best, and Heaven's superlative:
On Granby's cheek might bid new glories rise,
Or point a purer beam from Devon's eyes!
Hard is the task to shape that beauty's praise,
Whose judgment scorns the homage flattery pays!
But praising Amoret we cannot err,
No tongue o'ervalues Heaven, or flatters her!
Yet she by fate's perverseness—she alone
Would doubt our truth, nor deem such praise her own
Adorning fashion, unadorn'd by dress,
Simple from taste, and not from carelessness;
Discreet in gesture, in deportment mild,
Not stiff with prudence, nor uncouthly wild:
No state has Amoret; no studied mien;
She frowns no goddess, and she moves no queen.
The softer charm that in her manner lies
Is framed to captivate, yet not surprise;
It justly suits the expression of her face,—
'Tis less than dignity, and more than grace!
On her pure cheek the native hue is such,
That, form'd by Heaven to be admired so much,
The hand divine, with a less partial care,
Might well have fix'd a fainter crimson there,
And bade the gentle inmate of her breast—
Inshrined Modesty—supply the rest.
But who the peril of her lips shall paint?
Strip them of smiles—still, still all words are faint.
But moving Love himself appears to teach
Their action, though denied to rule her speech;
And thou who seest her speak, and dost not hear,
Mourn not her distant accents 'scape thine ear;
Viewing those lips, thou still may'st make pretence
To judge of what she says, and swear 'tis sense:
Clothed with such grace, with such expression fraught,
They move in meaning, and they pause in thought!
But dost thou farther watch, with charm'd surprise,
The mild irresolution of her eyes,
Curious to mark how frequent they repose,
In brief eclipse and momentary close—
Ah! seest thou not an ambush'd Cupid there,
Too tim'rous of his charge, with jealous care
Veils and unveils those beams of heavenly light,
Too full, too fatal else, for mortal sight?
Nor yet, such pleasing vengeance fond to meet,
In pard'ning dimples hope a safe retreat.

What though her peaceful breast should ne'er allow
Subduing frowns to arm her alter'd brow,
By Love, I swear, and by his gentle wiles,
More fatal still the mercy of her smiles!
Thus lovely, thus adorn'd, possessing all
Of bright or fair that can to woman fall,
The height of vanity might well be thought
Prerogative in her, and Nature's fault.
Yet gentle Amoret, in mind supreme
As well as charms, rejects the vainer theme;
And, half mistrustful of her beauty's store,
She barbs with wit those darts too keen before:—
Read in all knowledge that her sex should reach,
Though Greville, or the Muse, should deign to teach,
Fond to improve, nor timorous to discern
How far it is a woman's grace to learn;
In Millar's dialect she would not prove
Apollo's priestess, but Apollo's love,
Graced by those signs which truth delights to own,
The timid blush, and mild submitted tone:
Whate'er she says, though sense appear throughout,
Displays the tender hue of female doubt;
Deck'd with that charm, how lovely wit appears,
How graceful science, when that robe she wears!
Such too her talents, and her bent of mind,
As speak a sprightly heart by thought refined:
A taste for mirth, by contemplation school'd,
A turn for ridicule, by candour ruled,
A scorn of folly, which she tries to hide;
An awe of talent, which she owns with pride!
  Peace, idle Muse! no more thy strain prolong,
But yield a theme, thy warmest praises wrong;
Just to her merit, though thou canst not raise
Thy feeble verse, behold th' acknowledged praise
Has spread conviction through the envious train,
And cast a fatal gloom o'er Scandal's reign!
And lo! each pallid hag, with blister'd tongue,
Mutters assent to all thy zeal has sung—
Owns all the colours just—the outline true;
Thee my inspirer, and my model—CREWE!

PROLOGUE

WRITTEN BY MR. GARRICK.

A SCHOOL for Scandal! tell me, I beseech you,
Needs there a school this modish art to teach you?
No need of lessons now, the knowing think;
We might as well be taught to eat and drink.
Caused by a dearth of scandal, should the vapours
Distress our fair ones—let them read the papers;
Their powerful mixtures such disorders hit;
Crave what you will—there's *quantum sufficit.*
"Lord!" cries my Lady Wormwood (who loves tattle,
And puts much salt and pepper in her prattle),
Just risen at noon, all night at cards when threshing
Strong tea and scandal—"Bless me, how refreshing!
Give me the papers, Lisp—how bold and free!   [*Sips.*
Last night Lord L. [*Sips*] *was caught with Lady D.*
For aching heads what charming sal volatile!   [*Sips.*
If Mrs. B. will still continue flirting,
We hope she'll DRAW, *or we'll* UNDRAW *the curtain.*
Fine satire, poz—in public all abuse it,
But, by ourselves [*Sips*], our praise we can't refuse it.
Now, Lisp, read you—there, at that dash and star."
"Yes, ma'am—*A certain lord had best beware,*
Who lives not twenty miles from Grosvenor Square;
For, should he Lady W. find willing,
Wormwood is bitter"——"Oh! that's me! the villain!
Throw it behind the fire, and never more
Let that vile paper come within my door."
Thus at our friends we laugh, who feel the dart;
To reach our feelings, we ourselves must smart.
Is our young bard so young, to think that he
Can stop the full spring-tide of calumny?
Knows he the world so little, and its trade?
Alas! the devil's sooner raised than laid.
So strong, so swift, the monster there's no gagging:
Cut Scandal's head off, still the tongue is wagging.
Proud of your smiles once lavishly bestow'd,
Again our young Don Quixote takes the road;
To show his gratitude he draws his pen,
And seeks this hydra, Scandal, in his den.
For your applause all perils he would through—
He'll fight—that's write—a cavalliero true,
Till every drop of blood—that's ink—is spilt for you.

THE SCHOOL FOR SCANDAL

ACT I.

SCENE I.—LADY SNEERWELL'S *Dressing-room.*

LADY SNEERWELL *discovered at her toilet;* SNAKE *drinking chocolate.*

Lady Sneer. The paragraphs, you say, Mr. Snake, were all inserted?

Snake. They were, madam; and, as I copied them myself in a feigned hand, there can be no suspicion whence they came.

Lady Sneer. Did you circulate the report of Lady Brittle's intrigue with Captain Boastall?

Snake. That's in as fine a train as your ladyship could wish. In the common course of things, I think it must reach Mrs. Clackitt's ears within four-and-twenty hours; and then, you know, the business is as good as done.

Lady Sneer. Why, truly, Mrs. Clackitt has a very pretty talent, and a great deal of industry.

Snake. True, madam, and has been tolerably successful in her day. To my knowledge, she has been the cause of six matches being broken off, and three sons being disinherited; of four forced elopements, and as many close confinements; nine separate maintenances, and two divorces. Nay, I have more than once traced her causing a *tête-à-tête* in the "Town and Country Magazine," when the parties, perhaps, had never seen each other's face before in the course of their lives.

Lady Sneer. She certainly has talents, but her manner is gross.

Snake. 'Tis very true. She generally designs well, has a free tongue and a bold invention; but her colouring is too dark, and her outlines often extravagant. She wants that delicacy of tint, and mellowness of sneer, which distinguish your ladyship's scandal.

Lady Sneer. You are partial, Snake.

Snake. Not in the least; every body allows that Lady Sneerwell can do more with a word or look than many can with the most laboured detail, even when they happen to have a little truth on their side to support it.

Lady Sneer. Yes, my dear Snake; and I am no hypocrite to deny the satisfaction I reap from the success of my efforts. Wounded myself, in the early part of my life, by the envenomed tongue of slander, I confess I have since known no pleasure equal to the reducing others to the level of my own reputation.

Snake. Nothing can be more natural. But, Lady Sneerwell, there is one affair in which you have lately employed me, wherein, I confess, I am at a loss to guess your motives.

Lady Sneer. I conceive you mean with respect to my neighbour, Sir Peter Teazle, and his family?

Snake. I do. Here are two young men, to whom Sir Peter has acted as a kind of guardian since their father's death; the eldest possessing the most amiable character, and universally well spoken of—the youngest, the most dissipated and extravagant young fellow in the kingdom, without friends or character: the former an avowed admirer of your ladyship, and apparently your favourite; the latter attached to Maria, Sir Peter's ward, and confessedly beloved by her. Now, on the face of these circumstances, it is utterly unaccountable to me, why you, the widow of a city knight, with a good jointure, should not close with the passion of a man of such character and expectations as Mr. Surface; and more so why you should be so uncommonly earnest to destroy the mutual attachment subsisting between his brother Charles and Maria.

Lady Sneer. Then, at once to unravel this mystery, I must inform you that love has no share whatever in the intercourse between Mr. Surface and me.

Snake. No!

Lady Sneer. His real attachment is to Maria, or her fortune; but, finding in his brother a favoured rival, he has been obliged to mask his pretensions, and profit by my assistance.

Snake. Yet still I am more puzzled why you should interest yourself in his success.

Lady Sneer. Heavens! how dull you are! Cannot you surmise the weakness which I hitherto, through shame, have concealed even from you? Must I confess that Charles—that libertine, that extravagant, that bankrupt in fortune and reputation—that he it is for whom I am thus anxious and malicious, and to gain whom I would sacrifice every thing?

Snake. Now, indeed, your conduct appears consistent: but how came you and Mr. Surface so confidential?

Lady Sneer. For our mutual interest. I have found him out a long time since. I know him to be artful, selfish, and malicious—in short, a sentimental knave; while with Sir Peter, and indeed with all his acquaintance, he passes for a youthful miracle of prudence, good sense, and benevolence.

Snake. Yes; yet Sir Peter vows he has not his equal in England; and, above all, he praises him as a man of sentiment.

Lady Sneer. True; and with the assistance of his sentiment and hypocrisy he has brought Sir Peter entirely into his interest with regard to Maria; while poor Charles has no friend in the house—though, I fear, he has a powerful one in Maria's heart, against whom we must direct our schemes.

Enter SERVANT.

Ser. Mr. Surface.

Lady Sneer. Show him up. [*Exit* SERVANT.] He generally calls about this time. I don't wonder at people giving him to me for a lover.

Enter JOSEPH SURFACE.

Jos. Surf. My dear Lady Sneerwell, how do you do to-day? Mr. Snake, your most obedient.

Lady Sneer. Snake has just been rallying me on our mutual attachment; but I have informed him of our real views. You know how useful he has been to us; and, believe me, the confidence is not ill placed.

Jos. Surf. Madam, it is impossible for me to suspect a man of Mr. Snake's sensibility and discernment.

Lady Sneer. Well, well, no compliments now; but tell me when you saw your mistress, Maria—or, what is more material to me, your brother.

Jos. Surf. I have not seen either since I left you; but I can inform you that they never meet. Some of your stories have taken a good effect on Maria.

Lady Sneer. Ah, my dear Snake! the merit of this belongs to you. But do your brother's distresses increase?

Jos. Surf. Every hour. I am told he has had another execution in the house yesterday. In short, his dissipation and extravagance exceed any thing I have ever heard of.

Lady Sneer. Poor Charles!

Jos. Surf. True, madam; notwithstanding his vices, one can't help feeling for him. Poor Charles! I'm sure I wish it were in my power to be of any essential service to him; for the man who does not share in the distresses of a brother, even though merited by his own misconduct, deserves——

Lady Sneer. O Lud! you are going to be moral, and forget that you are among friends.

Jos. Surf. Egad, that's true! I'll keep that sentiment till I see Sir Peter. However, it is certainly a charity to rescue Maria from such a libertine, who, if he is to be reclaimed, can be so only by a person of your ladyship's superior accomplishments and understanding.

Snake. I believe, Lady Sneerwell, here's company coming; I'll go and copy the letter I mentioned to you. Mr. Surface, your most obedient.

Jos. Surf. Sir, your very devoted.—[*Exit* SNAKE.] Lady Sneerwell, I am very sorry you have put any farther confidence in that fellow.

Lady Sneer. Why so?

Jos. Surf. I have lately detected him in frequent conference with old Rowley, who was formerly my father's steward, and has never, you know, been a friend of mine.

Lady Sneer. And do you think he would betray us?

Jos. Surf. Nothing more likely: take my word for't, Lady Sneerwell, that fellow hasn't virtue enough to be faithful even to his own villainy. Ah, Maria!

Enter MARIA.

Lady Sneer. Maria, my dear, how do you do? What's the matter?

Mar. Oh! there's that disagreeable lover of mine, Sir Benjamin Backbite, has just called at my guardian's, with his odious uncle, Crabtree; so I slipped out, and ran hither to avoid them.

Lady Sneer. Is that all?

Jos. Surf. If my brother Charles had been of the party, madam, perhaps you would not have been so much alarmed.

Lady Sneer. Nay, now you are severe; for I dare swear the truth of the matter is, Maria heard you were here. But, my dear, what has Sir Benjamin done, that you should avoid him so?

Mar. Oh, he has done nothing—but 'tis for what he has said: his conversation is a perpetual libel on all his acquaintance.

Jos. Surf. Ay, and the worst of it is, there is no advantage in not knowing him; for he'll abuse a stranger just as soon as his best friend: and his uncle's as bad.

Lady Sneer. Nay, but we should make allowance; Sir Benjamin is a wit and a poet.

Mar. For my part, I own, madam, wit loses its respect with me, when I see it in company with malice. What do you think, Mr. Surface?

Jos. Surf. Certainly, madam; to smile at the jest which plants a thorn in another's breast is to become a principal in the mischief.

Lady Sneer. Psha! there's no possibility of being witty without a little ill nature: the malice of a good thing is the barb that makes it stick. What's your opinion, Mr. Surface?

Jos. Surf. To be sure, madam; that conversation, where the spirit of raillery is suppressed, will ever appear tedious and insipid.

Mar. Well, I'll not debate how far scandal may be allowable; but in a man, I am sure, it is always contemptible. We have pride, envy, rivalship, and a thousand motives to depreciate each other; but the male slanderer must have the cowardice of a woman before he can traduce one.

Re-enter SERVANT.

Ser. Madam, Mrs. Candour is below, and, if your ladyship's at leisure, will leave her carriage.

Lady Sneer. Beg her to walk in.—[*Exit* SERVANT.] Now, Maria, here is a character to your taste; for, though Mrs. Candour is a little talkative, every body allows her to be the best natured and best sort of woman.

Mar. Yes, with a very gross affectation of good nature and benevolence, she does more mischief than the direct malice of old Crabtree.

Jos. Surf. I' faith that's true, Lady Sneerwell: whenever I hear the current running against the characters of my friends, I never think them in such danger as when Candour undertakes their defence.

Lady Sneer. Hush!—here she is!

Enter MRS. CANDOUR.

Mrs. Can. My dear Lady Sneerwell, how have you been this century?—Mr. Surface, what news do you hear?—though indeed it is no matter, for I think one hears nothing else but scandal.

Jos. Surf. Just so, indeed, ma'am.

Mrs. Can. Oh, Maria! child—what, is the whole affair off between you and Charles? His extravagance, I presume—the town talks of nothing else.

Mar. I am very sorry, ma'am, the town has so little to do.

Mrs. Can. True, true, child: but there's no stopping people's tongues. I own I was hurt to hear it, as I indeed was to learn, from the same quarter, that your guardian, Sir Peter, and Lady Teazle have not agreed lately as well as could be wished.

Mar. 'Tis strangely impertinent for people to busy themselves so.

Mrs. Can. Very true, child: but what's to be done? People will talk—there's no preventing it. Why, it was but yesterday I was told that Miss Gadabout had eloped with Sir Filigree Flirt. But, Lord! there's no minding what one hears; though, to be sure, I had this from very good authority.

Mar. Such reports are highly scandalous.

Mrs. Can. So they are, child—shameful, shameful! But the world is so censorious, no character escapes. Lord, now who would have suspected your friend, Miss Prim, of an indiscretion? Yet such is the ill nature of people, that they say her uncle stopped her last week, just as she was stepping into the York Mail with her dancing-master.

Mar. I'll answer for't there are no grounds for that report.

Mrs. Can. Ah, no foundation in the world, I dare swear; no more, probably, than for the story circulated last month, of Mrs. Festino's affair with Colonel Cassino—though, to be sure, that matter was never rightly cleared up.

Jos. Surf. The licence of invention some people take is monstrous indeed.

Mar. 'Tis so; but, in my opinion, those who report such things are equally culpable.

Mrs. Can. To be sure they are; tale-bearers are as bad as the tale-makers—'tis an old observation, and a very true one: but what's to be done, as I said before? how will you prevent people from talking? To-day, Mrs. Clackitt assured me, Mr. and Mrs. Honeymoon were at last become mere man and wife, like the rest of their acquaintance. She likewise hinted that a certain widow, in the next street, had got rid of her dropsy and recovered her shape in a most surprising manner. And at the same time Miss Tattle, who was by, affirmed, that Lord Buffalo had discovered his lady at a house of no extraordinary fame; and that Sir Harry Bouquet and Tom Saunter were to measure swords on a similar provocation. But, Lord, do you think I would report these things! No, no! tale-bearers, as I said before, are just as bad as the tale-makers.

Jos. Surf. Ah! Mrs. Candour, if every body had your forbearance and good nature!

Mrs. Can. I confess, Mr. Surface, I cannot bear to hear people attacked behind their backs; and when ugly circumstances come out against our acquaintance I own I always love to think the best. By the by, I hope 'tis not true that your brother is absolutely ruined?

Jos. Surf. I am afraid his circumstances are very bad indeed, ma'am.

Mrs. Can. Ah! I heard so—but you must tell him to keep up his spirits;

every body almost is in the same way: Lord Spindle, Sir Thomas Splint, Captain Quinze, and Mr. Nickit—all up, I hear, within this week; so, if Charles is undone, he'll find half his acquaintance ruined too, and that, you know, is a consolation.

Jos. Surf. Doubtless, ma'am—a very great one.

Re-enter SERVANT.

Ser. Mr. Crabtree and Sir Benjamin Backbite. [*Exit.*

Lady Sneer. So, Maria, you see your lover pursues you; positively you sha'n't escape.

Enter CRABTREE *and* SIR BENJAMIN BACKBITE.

Crab. Lady Sneerwell, I kiss your hand. Mrs. Candour, I don't believe you are acquainted with my nephew, Sir Benjamin Backbite? Egad, ma'am, he has a pretty wit, and is a pretty poet too. Isn't he, Lady Sneerwell?

Sir. Ben. Oh, fie, uncle!

Crab. Nay, egad it's true; I back him at a rebus or a charade against the best rhymer in the kingdom. Has your ladyship heard the epigram he wrote last week on Lady Frizzle's feather catching fire?—Do, Benjamin, repeat it, or the charade you made last night extempore at Mrs. Drowzie's conversazione. Come now; your first is the name of a fish, your second a great naval commander, and——

Sir. Ben. Uncle, now—pr'ythee——

Crab. I' faith, ma'am, 'twould surprise you to hear how ready he is at all these sort of things.

Lady Sneer. I wonder, Sir Benjamin, you never publish any thing.

Sir Ben. To say truth, ma'am, 'tis very vulgar to print; and as my little productions are mostly satires and lampoons on particular people, I find they circulate more by giving copies in confidence to the friends of the parties. However, I have some love elegies, which, when favoured with this lady's smiles, I mean to give the public. [*Pointing to* MARIA.

Crab. [*To* MARIA.] 'Fore heaven, ma'am, they'll immortalize you!—you will be handed down to posterity, like Petrarch's Laura, or Waller's Sacharissa.

Sir Ben. [*To* MARIA.] Yes, madam, I think you will like them, when you shall see them on a beautiful quarto page, where a neat rivulet of text shall meander through a meadow of margin. 'Fore Gad they will be the most elegant things of their kind!

Crab. But, ladies, that's true—have you heard the news?

Mrs. Can. What, sir, do you mean the report of——

Crab. No, ma'am, that's not it.—Miss Nicely is going to be married to her own footman.

Mrs. Can. Impossible.

Crab. Ask Sir Benjamin.

Sir Ben. 'Tis very true, ma'am: every thing is fixed, and the wedding liveries bespoke.

Crab. Yes—and they do say there were pressing reasons for it.

Lady Sneer. Why, I have heard something of this before.

Mrs. Can. It can't be—and I wonder any one should believe such a story of so prudent a lady as Miss Nicely.

Sir Ben. O Lud! ma'am, that's the very reason 'twas believed at once. She has always been so cautious and so reserved, that every body was sure there was some reason for it at bottom.

Mrs. Can. Why, to be sure, a tale of scandal is as fatal to the credit of a prudent lady of her stamp as a fever is generally to those of the strongest constitutions. But there is a sort of puny sickly reputation, that is always ailing, yet will outlive the robuster characters of a hundred prudes.

Sir Ben. True, madam, there are valetudinarians in reputation as well as constitution, who, being conscious of their weak part, avoid the least breath of air, and supply their want of stamina by care and circumspection.

Mrs. Can. Well, but this may be all a mistake. You know, Sir Benjamin, very trifling circumstances often give rise to the most injurious tales.

Crab. That they do, I'll be sworn, ma'am. Did you ever hear how Miss Piper came to lose her lover and her character last summer at Tunbridge?— Sir Benjamin, you remember it?

Sir Ben. Oh, to be sure!—the most whimsical circumstance.

Lady Sneer. How was it, pray?

Crab. Why, one evening, at Mrs. Ponto's assembly, the conversation happened to turn on the breeding Nova Scotia sheep in this country. Says a young lady in company, I have known instances of it; for Miss Letitia Piper, a first cousin of mine, had a Nova Scotia sheep that produced her twins. "What!" cries the Lady Dowager Dundizzy (who you know is as deaf as a post), "has Miss Piper had twins?" This mistake, as you may imagine, threw the whole company into a fit of laughter. However, 'twas the next morning every where reported, and in a few days believed by the whole town, that Miss Letitia Piper had actually been brought to bed of a fine boy and a girl: and in less than a week there were some people who could name the father, and the farm-house where the babies were put to nurse.

Lady Sneer. Strange, indeed!

Crab. Matter of fact, I assure you. O Lud! Mr. Surface, pray is it true that your uncle, Sir Oliver, is coming home?

Jos. Surf. Not that I know of, indeed, sir.

Crab. He has been in the East Indies a long time. You can scarcely remember him, I believe? Sad comfort, whenever he returns, to hear how your brother has gone on!

Jos. Surf. Charles has been imprudent, sir, to be sure; but I hope no busy people have already prejudiced Sir Oliver against him. He may reform.

Sir Ben. To be sure he may: for my part, I never believed him to be so utterly void of principle as people say; and, though he has lost all his friends, I am told nobody is better spoken of by the Jews.

Crab. That's true, egad, nephew. If the Old Jewry was a ward, I believe Charles would be an alderman: no man more popular there, 'fore Gad! I hear he pays as many annuities as the Irish tontine; and that, whenever he is sick, they have prayers for the recovery of his health in all the synagogues.

Sir Ben. Yet no man lives in greater splendour. They tell me, when he entertains his friends he will sit down to dinner with a dozen of his own securities; have a score of tradesmen waiting in the antechamber, and an officer behind every guest's chair.

Jos. Surf. This may be entertainment to you, gentlemen, but you pay very little regard to the feelings of a brother.

Mar. [*Aside.*] Their malice is intolerable!—[*Aloud.*] Lady Sneerwell, I must wish you a good morning: I'm not very well. [*Exit.*

Mrs. Can. O dear! she changes colour very much.

Lady Sneer. Do, Mrs. Candour, follow her: she may want your assistance.

Mrs. Can. That I will, with all my soul, ma'am.—Poor dear girl, who knows what her situation may be! [*Exit.*

Lady Sneer. 'Twas nothing but that she could not bear to hear Charles reflected on, notwithstanding their difference.

Sir Ben. The young lady's *penchant* is obvious.

Crab. But, Benjamin, you must not give up the pursuit for that: follow her, and put her into good humour. Repeat her some of your own verses. Come, I'll assist you.

Sir Ben. Mr. Surface, I did not mean to hurt you; but depend on't your brother is utterly undone.

Crab. O Lud, ay! undone as ever man was—can't raise a guinea!

Sir. Ben. And every thing sold, I'm told, that was movable.

Crab. I have seen one that was at his house. Not a thing left but some empty bottles that were overlooked, and the family pictures, which I believe are framed in the wainscots.

Sir Ben. And I'm very sorry also to hear some bad stories against him.

[*Going.*

Crab. Oh, he has done many mean things, that's certain.

Sir Ben. But, however, as he's your brother—— [*Going.*

Crab. We'll tell you all another opportunity.

[*Exeunt* CRABTREE *and* SIR BENJAMIN.

Lady Sneer. Ha! ha! 'tis very hard for them to leave a subject they have not quite run down.

Jos. Surf. And I believe the abuse was no more acceptable to your ladyship than Maria.

Lady Sneer. I doubt her affections are farther engaged than we imagine. But the family are to be here this evening, so you may as well dine where you are, and we shall have an opportunity of observing farther; in the meantime, I'll go and plot mischief, and you shall study sentiment. [*Exeunt.*

SCENE II.—*A Room in* SIR PETER TEAZLE'S *House.*

Enter SIR PETER TEAZLE.

Sir. Pet. When an old bachelor marries a young wife, what is he to expect? 'Tis now six months since Lady Teazle made me the happiest of men—and I have been the most miserable dog ever since! We tift a little going to church, and fairly quarrelled before the bells had done ringing, I was more than once nearly choked with gall during the honeymoon, and had lost all comfort in life before my friends had done wishing me joy. Yet I chose with caution—a girl bred wholly in the country, who never knew luxury beyond one silk gown, nor dissipation above the annual gala of a race ball. Yet she now plays her part in all the extravagant fopperies of fashion and the town, with as ready a grace as if she never had seen a bush or a grass-plot out of Grosvenor Square! I am sneered at by all my acquaintance, and paragraphed in the newspapers. She dissipates my fortune, and contradicts all my humours; yet the worst of it is, I doubt I love her, or I should never bear all this. However, I'll never be weak enough to own it.

Enter ROWLEY.

Row. Oh! Sir Peter, your servant: how is it with you, sir?

Sir Pet. Very bad, Master Rowley, very bad. I meet with nothing but crosses and vexations.

Row. What can have happened since yesterday?

Sir Pet. A good question to a married man!

Row. Nay, I'm sure, Sir Peter, your lady can't be the cause of your uneasiness.

Sir Pet. Why, has any body told you she was dead?

Row. Come, come, Sir Peter, you love her, notwithstanding your tempers don't exactly agree.

Sir Pet. But the fault is entirely hers, Master Rowley. I am, myself, the sweetest-tempered man alive, and hate a teasing temper; and so I tell her a hundred times a day.

Row. Indeed!

Sir Pet. Ay; and what is very extraordinary, in all our disputes she is always in the wrong! But Lady Sneerwell, and the set she meets at her house, encourage the perverseness of her disposition. Then, to complete my vexation, Maria, my ward, whom I ought to have the power of a father over, is determined to turn rebel too, and absolutely refuses the man whom I have long resolved on for her husband; meaning, I suppose, to bestow herself on his profligate brother.

Row. You know, Sir Peter, I have always taken the liberty to differ with you on the subject of these two young gentlemen. I only wish you may not be deceived in your opinion of the elder. For Charles, my life on't! he will retrieve his errors yet. Their worthy father, once my honoured master, was, at his years, nearly as wild a spark; yet, when he died, he did not leave a more benevolent heart to lament his loss.

Sir Pet. You are wrong, Master Rowley. On their father's death, you know, I acted as a kind of guardian to them both, till their uncle Sir Oliver's liberality gave them an early independence: of course, no person could have more opportunities of judging of their hearts, and I was never mistaken in my life. Joseph is indeed a model for the young men of the age. He is a man of sentiment, and acts up to the sentiments he professes; but, for the other, take my word for't, if he had any grain of virtue by descent, he has dissipated it with the rest of his inheritance. Ah! my old friend, Sir Oliver, will be deeply mortified when he finds how part of his bounty has been misapplied.

Row. I am sorry to find you so violent against the young man, because this may be the most critical period of his fortune. I came hither with news that will surprise you.

Sir Pet. What! let me hear.

Row. Sir Oliver is arrived, and at this moment in town.

Sir Pet. How! you astonish me! I thought you did not expect him this month.

Row. I did not: but his passage has been remarkably quick.

Sir Pet. Egad, I shall rejoice to see my old friend. 'Tis sixteen years since we met. We have had many a day together:—but does he still enjoin us not to inform his nephews of his arrival?

Row. Most strictly. He means, before it is known, to make some trial of their dispositions.

Sir Pet. Ah! there needs no art to discover their merits—however he shall have his way; but, pray, does he know I am married?

Row. Yes, and will soon wish you joy.

Sir Pet. What, as we drink health to a friend in a consumption! Ah! Oliver will laugh at me. We used to rail at matrimony together, but he has been steady to his text. Well, he must be soon at my house, though—I'll instantly give orders for his reception. But, Master Rowley, don't drop a word that Lady Teazle and I ever disagree.

Row. By no means.

Sir Pet. For I should never be able to stand Noll's jokes; so I'll have him think, Lord forgive me! that we are a very happy couple.

Row. I understand you:—but then you must be very careful not to differ while he is in the house with you.

Sir Pet. Egad, and so we must—and that's impossible. Ah! Master Rowley, when an old bachelor marries a young wife, he deserves—no—the crime carries its punishment along with it.   [*Exeunt.*

ACT II.

SCENE I.—*A Room in* SIR PETER TEAZLE'S *House.*

Enter SIR PETER *and* LADY TEAZLE.

Sir. Pet. Lady Teazle, Lady Teazle, I'll not bear it!

Lady Teaz. Sir Peter, Sir Peter, you may bear it or not, as you please; but I ought to have my own way in every thing, and, what's more, I will too. What! though I was educated in the country, I know very well that women of fashion in London are accountable to nobody after they are married.

Sir. Pet. Very well, ma'am, very well; so a husband is to have no influence, no authority?

Lady Teaz. Authority! No, to be sure:—if you wanted authority over me, you should have adopted me, and not married me: I am sure you were old enough.

Sir Pet. Old enough!—ay, there it is. Well, well, Lady Teazle, though my life may be made unhappy by your temper, I'll not be ruined by your extravagance!

Lady Teaz. My extravagance! I'm sure I'm not more extravagant than a woman of fashion ought to be.

Sir Pet. No, no, madam, you shall throw away no more sums on such unmeaning luxury. 'Slife! to spend as much to furnish your dressing-room with flowers in winter as would suffice to turn the Pantheon into a greenhouse, and give a *fête champêtre* at Christmas.

Lady Teaz. And am I to blame, Sir Peter, because flowers are dear in cold weather? You should find fault with the climate, and not with me. For my part, I'm sure I wish it was spring all the year round, and that roses grew under our feet!

Sir Pet. Oons! madam—if you had been born to this, I shouldn't wonder at your talking thus; but you forget what your situation was when I married you.

Lady Teaz. No, no, I don't; 'twas a very disagreeable one, or I should never have married you.

Sir Pet. Yes, yes, madam, you were then in somewhat a humbler style—the daughter of a plain country squire. Recollect, Lady Teazle, when I saw you first sitting at your tambour, in a pretty figured linen gown, with a bunch of keys at your side, your hair combed smooth over a roll, and your apartment hung round with fruits in worsted, of your own working.

Lady Teaz. Oh, yes! I remember it very well, and a curious life I led. My daily occupation to inspect the dairy, superintend the poultry, make extracts from the family receipt-book, and comb my aunt Deborah's lapdog.

Sir Pet. Yes, yes, ma'am, 'twas so indeed.

Lady Teaz. And then you know, my evening amusements! To draw patterns for ruffles, which I had not materials to make up; to play Pope Joan with the curate; to read a sermon to my aunt; or to be stuck down to an old spinnet to strum my father to sleep after a fox-chase.

Sir Pet. I am glad you have so good a memory. Yes, madam, these were the recreations I took you from; but now you must have your coach—*vis-à-vis*—and three powdered footmen before your chair; and, in the summer, a pair of white cats to draw you to Kensington Gardens. No recollection, I suppose, when you were content to ride double, behind the butler, on a docked coach-horse.

Lady Teaz. No—I swear I never did that: I deny the butler and the coach-horse.

Sir Pet. This, madam, was your situation; and what have I done for you? I have made you a woman of fashion, of fortune, of rank—in short, I have made you my wife.

Lady Teaz. Well, then, and there is but one thing more you can make me to add to the obligation, that is——

Sir Pet. My widow, I suppose?

Lady Teaz. Hem! hem!

Sir Pet. I thank you, madam—but don't flatter yourself; for, though your ill conduct may disturb my peace of mind, it shall never break my heart, I promise you: however, I am equally obliged to you for the hint.

Lady Teaz. Then why will you endeavour to make yourself so disagreeable to me, and thwart me in every little elegant expense?

Sir Pet. 'Slife, madam, I say, had you any of these little elegant expenses when you married me?

Lady Teaz. Lud, Sir Peter! would you have me be out of the fashion?

Sir Pet. The fashion, indeed! what had you to do with the fashion before you married me?

Lady Teaz. For my part, I should think you would like to have your wife thought a woman of taste.

Sir Pet. Ay—there again—taste! Zounds! madam, you had no taste when you married me!

Lady Teaz. That's very true, indeed, Sir Peter! and, after having married you, I should never pretend to taste again, I allow. But now, Sir Peter, since we have finished our daily jangle, I presume I may go to my engagement at Lady Sneerwell's.

Sir Pet. Ay, there's another precious circumstance—a charming set of acquaintance you have made there!

Lady Teaz. Nay, Sir Peter, they are all people of rank and fortune, and remarkably tenacious of reputation.

Sir Pet. Yes, egad, they are tenacious of reputation with a vengeance; for they don't choose any body should have a character but themselves! Such a crew! Ah! many a wretch has rid on a hurdle who has done less mischief than these utterers of forged tales, coiners of scandal, and clippers of reputation.

Lady Teaz. What, would you restrain the freedom of speech?

Sir Pet. Ah! they have made you just as bad as any one of the society.

Lady Teaz. Why, I believe I do bear a part with a tolerable grace.

Sir Pet. Grace indeed!

Lady Teaz. But I vow I bear no malice against the people I abuse: when I say an ill-natured thing, 'tis out of pure good humour; and I take it for granted they deal exactly in the same manner with me. But, Sir Peter, you know you promised to come to Lady Sneerwell's too.

Sir Pet. Well, well, I'll call in, just to look after my own character.

Lady Teaz. Then, indeed, you must make haste after me, or you'll be too late. So good-bye to ye. [*Exit.*

Sir Pet. So—I have gained much by my intended expostulation! Yet with what a charming air she contradicts every thing I say, and how pleasantly she shows her contempt for my authority! Well, though I can't make her love me, there is great satisfaction in quarrelling with her; and I think she never appears to such advantage as when she is doing every thing in her power to plague me. [*Exit.*

SCENE II.—*A Room in* LADY SNEERWELL'S *House.*

LADY SNEERWELL, MRS. CANDOUR, CRABTREE, SIR BENJAMIN BACKBITE, *and* JOSEPH SURFACE, *discovered.*

Lady Sneer. Nay, positively, we will hear it.

Jos. Surf. Yes, yes, the epigram, by all means.

Sir Ben. O plague on't, uncle! 'tis mere nonsense.

Crab. No, no; 'fore Gad, very clever for an extempore!

Sir Ben. But, ladies, you should be acquainted with the circumstance. You must know, that one day last week, as Lady Betty Curricle was taking the dust in Hyde Park, in a sort of duodecimo phaeton, she desired me to write some verses on her ponies; upon which, I took out my pocket-book, and in one moment produced the following:—

> Sure never were seen two such beautiful ponies;
> Other horses are clowns, but these macaronies:
> To give them this title I'm sure can't be wrong,
> Their legs are so slim, and their tails are so long.

Crab. There, ladies, done in the smack of a whip, and on horseback too.

Jos. Surf. A very Phœbus, mounted—indeed, Sir Benjamin!

Sir Ben. Oh dear, sir! trifles—trifles.

Enter LADY TEAZLE *and* MARIA.

Mrs. Can. I must have a copy.

Lady Sneer. Lady Teazle, I hope we shall see Sir Peter?

Lady Teaz. I believe he'll wait on your ladyship presently.

Lady Sneer. Maria, my love, you look grave. Come, you shall sit down to piquet with Mr. Surface.

Mar. I take very little pleasure in cards—however, I'll do as your ladyship pleases.

Lady Teaz. I am surprised Mr. Surface should sit down with her; I thought he would have embraced this opportunity of speaking to me before Sir Peter came. [*Aside.*

Mrs. Can. Now, I'll die; but you are so scandalous, I'll forswear your society.

Lady Teaz. What's the matter, Mrs. Candour?

Mrs. Can. They'll not allow our friend Miss Vermilion to be handsome.

Lady Sneer. Oh, surely she is a pretty woman.

Crab. I am very glad you think so, ma'am.

Mrs. Can. She has a charming fresh colour.

Lady Teaz. Yes, when it is fresh put on.

Mrs. Can. Oh, fie! I'll swear her colour is natural: I have seen it come and go!

Lady Teaz. I dare swear you have, ma'am: it goes off at night, and comes again in the morning.

Sir Ben. True, ma'am, it not only comes and goes; but, what's more, egad, her maid can fetch and carry it!

Mrs. Can. Ha! ha! ha! how I hate to hear you talk so! But surely, now, her sister is, or was, very handsome.

Crab. Who? Mrs. Evergreen? O Lord! she's six-and-fifty if she's an hour!

Mrs. Can. Now positively you wrong her; fifty-two or fifty-three is the utmost—and I don't think she looks more.

Sir Ben. Ah! there's no judging by her looks, unless one could see her face.

Lady Sneer. Well, well, if Mrs. Evergreen does take some pains to repair the ravages of time, you must allow she effects it with great ingenuity; and surely that's better than the careless manner in which the widow Ochre caulks her wrinkles.

Sir Ben. Nay, now, Lady Sneerwell, you are severe upon the widow. Come, come, 'tis not that she paints so ill—but, when she has finished her face, she joins it on so badly to her neck, that she looks like a mended statue, in which the connoisseur may see at once that the head is modern, though the trunk's antique.

Crab. Ha! ha! ha! Well said, nephew!

Mrs. Can. Ha! ha! ha! Well, you make me laugh; but I vow I hate you for it. What do you think of Miss Simper?

Sir Ben. Why, she has very pretty teeth.

Lady Teaz. Yes; and on that account, when she is neither speaking nor laughing (which very seldom happens), she never absolutely shuts her mouth, but leaves it always on a-jar, as it were—thus. [*Shows her teeth.*

Mrs. Can. How can you be so ill-natured?

Lady Teaz. Nay, I allow even that's better than the pains Mrs. Prim takes to conceal her losses in front. She draws her mouth till it positively resembles the aperture of a poor's-box, and all her words appear to slide out edgewise, as it were—thus: *How do you do, madam? Yes, madam.* [*Mimics.*

Lady Sneer. Very well, Lady Teazle; I see you can be a little severe.

Lady Teaz. In defence of a friend it is but justice. But here comes Sir Peter to spoil our pleasantry.

Enter SIR PETER TEAZLE.

Sir Pet. Ladies, your most obedient.—[*Aside.*] Mercy on me, here is the whole set! a character dead at every word, I suppose.

Mrs. Can. I am rejoiced you are come, Sir Peter. They have been so censorious—and Lady Teazle as bad as any one.

Sir Pet. That must be very distressing to you, indeed, Mrs. Candour.

Mrs. Can. Oh, they will allow good qualities to nobody; not even good nature to our friend Mrs. Pursy.

Lady Teaz. What, the fat dowager who was at Mrs. Quadrille's last night?

Mrs. Can. Nay, her bulk is her misfortune; and, when she takes so much pains to get rid of it, you ought not to reflect on her.

Lady Sneer. That's very true, indeed.

Lady Teaz. Yes, I know she almost lives on acids and small whey; laces herself by pulleys; and often, in the hottest noon in summer, you may see her on a little squat pony, with her hair plaited up behind like a drummer's and puffing round the Ring on a full trot.

Mrs. Can. I thank you, Lady Teazle, for defending her.

Sir Pet. Yes, a good defence, truly.

Mrs. Can. Truly, Lady Teazle is as censorious as Miss Sallow.

Crab. Yes, and she is a curious being to pretend to be censorious—an awkward gawky, without any one good point under heaven.

Mrs. Can. Positively you shall not be so very severe. Miss Sallow is a near relation of mine by marriage, and, as for her person, great allowance is to be made; for, let me tell you, a woman labours under many disadvantages who tries to pass for a girl of six-and-thirty.

Lady Sneer. Though, surely, she is handsome still—and for the weakness in her eyes, considering how much she reads by candlelight, it is not to be wondered at.

Mrs. Can. True, and then as to her manner; upon my word I think it is particularly graceful, considering she never had the least education: for you know her mother was a Welsh milliner, and her father a sugar-baker at Bristol.

Sir Ben. Ah! you are both of you too good-natured!

Sir Pet. Yes, damned good-natured! This their own relation! mercy on me! [*Aside.*]

Mrs. Can. For my part, I own I cannot bear to hear a friend ill spoken of.

Sir Pet. No, to be sure!

Sir Ben. Oh! you are of a moral turn. Mrs. Candour and I can sit for an hour and hear Lady Stucco talk sentiment.

Lady Teaz. Nay, I vow Lady Stucco is very well with the dessert after dinner; for she's just like the French fruit one cracks for mottoes—made up of paint and proverb.

Mrs. Can. Well, I will never join in ridiculing a friend; and so I constantly tell my cousin Ogle, and you all know what pretensions she has to be critical on beauty.

Crab. Oh, to be sure! she has herself the oddest countenance that ever was seen; 'tis a collection of features from all the different countries of the globe.

Sir Ben. So she has, indeed—an Irish front——

Crab. Caledonian locks——

Sir Ben. Dutch nose——

Crab. Austrian lips——

Sir Ben. Complexion of a Spaniard——

Crab. And teeth *à la Chinoise*——

Sir Ben. In short, her face resembles a *table d'hôte* at Spa—where no two guests are of a nation——

Crab. Or a congress at the close of a general war—wherein all the members, even to her eyes, appear to have a different interest, and her nose and chin are the only parties likely to join issue.

Mrs. Can. Ha! ha! ha!

Sir Pet. Mercy on my life!—a person they dine with twice a week! [*Aside.*

Mrs. Can. Nay, but I vow you shall not carry the laugh off so—for give me leave to say, that Mrs. Ogle——

Sir Pet. Madam, madam, I beg your pardon—there's no stopping these good gentlemen's tongues. But when I tell you, Mrs. Candour, that the lady they are abusing is a particular friend of mine, I hope you'll not take her part.

Lady Sneer. Ha! ha! ha! well said, Sir Peter! but you are a cruel creature —too phlegmatic yourself for a jest, and too peevish to allow wit in others.

Sir Pet. Ah, madam, true wit is more nearly allied to good nature than your ladyship is aware of.

Lady Teaz. True, Sir Peter: I believe they are so near akin that they can never be united.

Sir Ben. Or rather, suppose them man and wife, because one seldom sees them together.

Lady Teaz. But Sir Peter is such an enemy to scandal, I believe he would have it put down by parliament.

Sir Pet. 'Fore heaven, madam, if they were to consider the sporting with reputation of as much importance as poaching on manors, and pass an act for the preservation of fame, as well as game, I believe many would thank them for the bill.

Lady Sneer. O Lud! Sir Peter; would you deprive us of our privileges?

Sir Pet. Ay, madam; and then no person should be permitted to kill characters and run down reputations, but qualified old maids and disappointed widows.

Lady Sneer. Go, you monster!

Mrs. Can. But, surely, you would not be quite so severe on those who only report what they hear?

Sir Pet. Yes, madam, I would have law merchant for them too; and in all cases of slander currency, whenever the drawer of the lie was not to be found, the injured parties should have a right to come on any of the indorsers.

Crab. Well, for my part, I believe there never was a scandalous tale without some foundation.

Lady Sneer. Come, ladies, shall we sit down to cards in the next room?

Enter SERVANT, *who whispers* SIR PETER.

Sir Pet. I'll be with them directly.—[*Exit* SERVANT.] I'll get away unperceived.   [*Aside.*

Lady Sneer. Sir Peter, you are not going to leave us?

Sir Pet. Your ladyship must excuse me; I'm called away by particular business. But I leave my character behind me.   [*Exit.*

Sir Ben. Well—certainly, Lady Teazle, that lord of yours is a strange being: I could tell you some stories of him would make you laugh heartily if he were not your husband.

Lady Teaz. Oh, pray don't mind that; come, do let's hear them.

[*Exeunt all but* JOSEPH SURFACE *and* MARIA.

Jos. Surf. Maria, I see you have no satisfaction in this society.

Mar. How is it possible I should? If to raise malicious smiles at the infirmities or misfortunes of those who have never injured us be the province of wit or humour, Heaven grant me a double portion of dulness!

Jos. Surf. Yet they appear more ill-natured than they are; they have no malice at heart.

Mar. Then is their conduct still more contemptible; for, in my opinion, nothing could excuse the intemperance of their tongues but a natural and uncontrollable bitterness of mind.

Jos. Surf. Undoubtedly, madam; and it has always been a sentiment of mine, that to propagate a malicious truth wantonly is more despicable than to falsify from revenge. But can you, Maria, feel thus for others, and be unkind to me alone? Is hope to be denied the tenderest passion?

Mar. Why will you distress me by renewing this subject?

Jos. Surf. Ah, Maria! you would not treat me thus, and oppose your guardian, Sir Peter's will, but that I see that profligate Charles is still a favoured rival.

Mar. Ungenerously urged! But, whatever my sentiments are for that unfortunate young man, be assured I shall not feel more bound to give him up, because his distresses have lost him the regard even of a brother.

Jos. Surf. Nay, but, Maria, do not leave me with a frown: by all that's honest, I swear——   [*Kneels.*

Re-enter LADY TEAZLE *behind.*

[*Aside.*] Gad's life, here's Lady Teazle.—[*Aloud to* MARIA.] You must not—no, you shall not—for, though I have the greatest regard for Lady Teazle——

Mar. Lady Teazle!

Jos. Surf. Yet were Sir Peter to suspect——

Lady Teaz. [*Coming forward.*] What is this, pray? Does he take her for me?—Child, you are wanted in the next room.—[*Exit* MARIA.] What is all this, pray?

Jos. Surf. Oh, the most unlucky circumstance in nature! Maria has some-how suspected the tender concern I have for your happiness, and threatened to acquaint Sir Peter with her suspicions, and I was just endeavouring to reason with her when you came in.

Lady Teaz. Indeed! but you seemed to adopt a very tender mode of rea-soning—do you usually argue on your knees?

Jos. Surf. Oh, she's a child, and I thought a little bombast——But, Lady Teazle, when are you to give me your judgment on my library, as you promised?

Lady Teaz. No, no; I begin to think it would be imprudent, and you know I admit you as a lover no farther than fashion requires.

Jos. Surf. True—a mere Platonic cicisbeo, what every wife is entitled to.

Lady Teaz. Certainly, one must not be out of the fashion. However, I have so many of my country prejudices left, that, though Sir Peter's ill humour may vex me ever so, it never shall provoke me to——

Jos. Surf. The only revenge in your power. Well, I applaud your modera-tion.

Lady Teaz. Go—you are an insinuating wretch! But we shall be missed—let us join the company.

Jos. Surf. But we had best not return together.

Lady Teaz. Well, don't stay; for Maria sha'n't come to hear any more of your reasoning, I promise you. [*Exit.*

Jos. Surf. A curious dilemma, truly, my politics have run me into! I wanted, at first, only to ingratiate myself with Lady Teazle, that she might not be my enemy with Maria; and I have, I don't know how, become her serious lover. Sincerely I begin to wish I had never made such a point of gaining so very good a character, for it has led me into so many cursed rogueries that I doubt I shall be exposed at last. [*Exit.*

SCENE III.—*A Room in* SIR PETER TEAZLE'S *House.*

Enter SIR OLIVER SURFACE *and* ROWLEY.

Sir Oliv. Ha! ha! ha! so my old friend is married, hey?—a young wife out of the country. Ha! ha! ha! that he should have stood bluff to old bachelor so long, and sink into a husband at last!

Row. But you must not rally him on the subject, Sir Oliver; 'tis a tender point, I assure you, though he has been married only seven months.

Sir Oliv. Then he has been just half a year on the stool of repentance!—Poor Peter! But you say he has entirely given up Charles—never sees him, hey?

Row. His prejudice against him is astonishing, and I am sure greatly increased by a jealousy of him with Lady Teazle, which he has industriously been led into by a scandalous society in the neighbourhood, who have contributed not a little to Charles's ill name. Whereas the truth is, I believe, if the lady is partial to either of them, his brother is the favourite.

Sir Oliv. Ay, I know there are a set of malicious, prating, prudent gossips, both male and female, who murder characters to kill time, and will rob a young fellow of his good name before he has years to know the value of it. But I am not to be prejudiced against my nephew by such, I promise you! No, no; if Charles has done nothing false or mean, I shall compound for his extravagance.

Row. Then, my life on't, you will reclaim him. Ah, sir, it gives me new life to find that your heart is not turned against him, and that the son of my good old master has one friend, however, left.

Sir Oliv. What! shall I forget, Master Rowley, when I was at his years myself? Egad, my brother and I were neither of us very prudent youths; and yet, I believe, you have not seen many better men than your old master was?

Row. Sir, 'tis this reflection gives me assurance that Charles may yet be a credit to his family. But here comes Sir Peter.

Sir Oliv. Egad, so he does! Mercy on me! he's greatly altered, and seems to have a settled married look! One may read husband in his face at this distance!

Enter SIR PETER TEAZLE.

Sir Pet. Ha! Sir Oliver—my old friend! Welcome to England a thousand times!

Sir Oliv. Thank you, thank you, Sir Peter! and i' faith I am glad to find you well, believe me!

Sir Pet. Oh! 'tis a long time since we met—fifteen years, I doubt, Sir Oliver, and many a cross accident in the time.

Sir Oliv. Ay, I have had my share. But, what! I find you are married, hey, my old boy? Well, well, it can't be helped; and so—I wish you joy with all my heart!

Sir Pet. Thank you, thank you, Sir Oliver.—Yes, I have entered into—the happy state; but we'll not talk of that now.

Sir Oliv. True, true, Sir Peter; old friends should not begin on grievances at first meeting. No, no, no.

Row. [*Aside to* SIR OLIVER.] Take care, pray, sir.

Sir Oliv. Well, so one of my nephews is a wild rogue, hey?

Sir Pet. Wild! Ah! my old friend, I grieve for your disappointment there; he's a lost young man, indeed. However, his brother will make you amends; Joseph is, indeed, what a youth should be—every body in the world speaks well of him.

Sir Oliv. I am sorry to hear it; he has too good a character to be an honest fellow. Every body speaks well of him! Psha! then he has bowed as low to knaves and fools as to the honest dignity of genius and virtue.

Sir Pet. What, Sir Oliver! do you blame him for not making enemies?

Sir Oliv. Yes, if he has merit enough to deserve them.

Sir Pet. Well, well—you'll be convinced when you know him. 'Tis edification to hear him converse; he professes the noblest sentiments.

Sir Oliv. Oh, plague of his sentiments! If he salutes me with a scrap of morality in his mouth, I shall be sick directly. But, however, don't mistake me, Sir Peter; I don't mean to defend Charles's errors: but, before I form my judgment of either of them, I intend to make a trial of their hearts; and my friend Rowley and I have planned something for the purpose.

Row. And Sir Peter shall own for once he has been mistaken.

Sir Pet. Oh, my life on Joseph's honour!

Sir Oliv. Well—come, give us a bottle of good wine, and we'll drink the lads' health, and tell you our scheme.

Sir Pet. Allons, then!

Sir Oliv. And don't, Sir Peter, be so severe against your old friend's son. Odds my life! I am not sorry that he has run out of the course a little: for my part, I hate to see prudence clinging to the green suckers of youth; 'tis like ivy round a sapling, and spoils the growth of the tree.   [*Exeunt.*

ACT III.

Scene I.—*A Room in* Sir Peter Teazle's *House.*

Enter Sir Peter Teazle, Sir Oliver Surface, *and* Rowley.

Sir Pet. Well, then, we will see this fellow first, and have our wine afterwards. But how is this, Master Rowley? I don't see the jet of your scheme.

Row. Why, sir, this Mr. Stanley, whom I was speaking of, is nearly related to them by their mother. He was once a merchant in Dublin, but has been ruined by a series of undeserved misfortunes. He has applied, by letter, since his confinement, both to Mr. Surface and Charles: from the former he has received nothing but evasive promises of future service, while Charles has done all that his extravagance has left him powered to do; and he is, at this time, endeavouring to raise a sum of money, part of which, in the midst of his own distresses, I know he intends for the service of poor Stanley.

Sir Oliv. Ah! he is my brother's son.

Sir Pet. Well, but how is Sir Oliver personally to——

Row. Why, sir, I will inform Charles and his brother that Stanley has obtained permission to apply personally to his friends; and, as they have neither of them ever seen him, let Sir Oliver assume his character, and he will have a fair opportunity of judging, at least, of the benevolence of their dispositions: and believe me, sir, you will find in the youngest brother one who, in the midst of folly and dissipation, has still, as our immortal bard expresses it,—

"a heart to pity, and a hand,
Open as day, for melting charity."

Sir Pet. Psha! What signifies his having an open hand or purse either, when he has nothing left to give? Well, well, make the trial, if you please. But where is the fellow whom you brought for Sir Oliver to examine, relative to Charles's affairs?

Row. Below, waiting his commands, and no one can give him better intelligence.—This, Sir Oliver, is a friendly Jew, who, to do him justice, has done every thing in his power to bring your nephew to a proper sense of his extravagance.

Sir Pet. Pray let us have him in.

Row. Desire Mr. Moses to walk up stairs.   [*Calls to* SERVANT.

Sir Pet. But, pray, why should you suppose he will speak the truth?

Row. Oh, I have convinced him that he has no chance of recovering certain sums advanced to Charles but through the bounty of Sir Oliver, who he knows is arrived; so that you may depend on his fidelity to his own interests. I have also another evidence in my power, one Snake, whom I have detected in a matter little short of forgery, and shall shortly produce to remove some of your prejudices, Sir Peter, relative to Charles and Lady Teazle.

Sir Pet. I have heard too much on that subject.

Row. Here comes the honest Israelite.

Enter MOSES.

—This is Sir Oliver.

Sir Oliv. Sir, I understand you have lately had great dealings with my nephew Charles.

Mos. Yes, Sir Oliver, I have done all I could for him; but he was ruined before he came to me for assistance.

Sir Oliv. That was unlucky, truly; for you have had no opportunity of showing your talents.

Mos. None at all; I hadn't the pleasure of knowing his distresses till he was some thousands worse than nothing.

Sir Oliv. Unfortunate, indeed! But I suppose you have done all in your power for him, honest Moses?

Mos. Yes, he knows that. This very evening I was to have brought him a gentleman from the city, who does not know him, and will, I believe, advance him some money.

Sir Pet. What, one Charles has never had money from before?

Mos. Yes, Mr. Premium, of Crutched Friars, formerly a broker.

Sir Pet. Egad, Sir Oliver, a thought strikes me!—Charles, you say, does not know Mr. Premium?

Mos. Not at all.

Sir Pet. Now then, Sir Oliver, you may have a better opportunity of satisfying yourself than by an old romancing tale of a poor relation: go with my friend Moses, and represent Premium, and then, I'll answer for it, you'll see your nephew in all his glory.

Sir Oliv. Egad, I like this idea better than the other, and I may visit Joseph afterwards as old Stanley.

Sir Pet. True—so you may.

Row. Well, this is taking Charles rather at a disadvantage, to be sure. However, Moses, you understand Sir Peter, and will be faithful?

Mos. You may depend upon me.—[*Looks at his watch.*] This is near the time I was to have gone.

Sir Oliv. I'll accompany you as soon as you please, Moses——But hold! I have forgot one thing—how the plague shall I be able to pass for a Jew?

Mos. There's no need—the principal is Christian.

Sir Oliv. Is he? I'm very sorry to hear it. But, then again, an't I rather too smartly dressed to look like a money lender?

Sir Pet. Not at all; 'twould not be out of character, if you went in your own carriage—would it, Moses?

Mos. Not in the least.

Sir Oliv. Well, but how must I talk? there's certainly some cant of usury and mode of treating that I ought to know.

Sir Pet. Oh, there's not much to learn. The great point, as I take it, is to be exorbitant enough in your demands. Hey, Moses?

Mos. Yes, that's a very great point.

Sir Oliv. I'll answer for 't I'll not be wanting in that. I'll ask him eight or ten per cent. on the loan, at least.

Mos. If you ask him no more than that, you'll be discovered immediately.

Sir Oliv. Hey! what, the plague! how much then?

Mos. That depends upon the circumstances. If he appears not very anxious for the supply, you should require only forty or fifty per cent.; but if you find him in great distress, and want the moneys very bad, you may ask double.

Sir Pet. A good honest trade you're learning, Sir Oliver!

Sir Oliv. Truly, I think so—and not unprofitable.

Mos. Then, you know, you haven't the moneys yourself, but are forced to borrow them for him of a friend.

Sir Oliv. Oh! I borrow it of a friend, do I?

Mos. And your friend is an unconscionable dog: but you can't help that,

Sir Oliv. My friend an unconscionable dog, is he?

Mos. Yes, and he himself has not the moneys by him, but is forced to sell stock at a great loss.

Sir Oliv. He is forced to sell stock at a great loss, is he? Well, that's very kind of him.

Sir Pet. I' faith, Sir Oliver—Mr. Premium, I mean—you'll soon be master of the trade. But, Moses! would not you have him run out a little against the annuity bill? That would be in character, I should think.

Mos. Very much.

Row. And lament that a young man now must be at years of discretion before he is suffered to ruin himself?

Mos. Ay, great pity!

Sir Pet. And abuse the public for allowing merit to an act whose only object is to snatch misfortune and imprudence from the rapacious gripe of usury, and give the minor a chance of inheriting his estate without being undone by coming into possession.

Sir Oliv. So, so—Moses shall give me farther instructions as we go together.

Sir Pet. You will not have much time, for your nephew lives hard by.

Sir Oliv. Oh, never fear! my tutor appears so able, that though Charles lived in the next street, it must be my own fault if I am not a complete rogue before I turn the corner.   [*Exit with* MOSES.

Sir Pet. So, now, I think Sir Oliver will be convinced: you are partial, Rowley, and would have prepared Charles for the other plot.

Row. No, upon my word, Sir Peter.

Sir Pet. Well, go bring me this Snake, and I'll hear what he has to say presently. I see Maria, and want to speak with her.—[*Exit* ROWLEY.] I should be glad to be convinced my suspicions of Lady Teazle and Charles were unjust. I have never yet opened my mind on this subject to my friend Joseph—I am determined I will do it—he will give me his opinion sincerely.

Enter MARIA.

So, child, has Mr. Surface returned with you?

Mar. No, sir; he was engaged.

Sir Pet. Well, Maria, do you not reflect, the more you converse with that amiable young man, what return his partiality for you deserves?

Mar. Indeed, Sir Peter, your frequent importunity on this subject distresses me extremely—you compel me to declare, that I know no man who has ever paid me a particular attention whom I would not prefer to Mr. Surface.

Sir Pet. So—here's perverseness! No, no, Maria, 'tis Charles only whom you would prefer. 'Tis evident his vices and follies have won your heart.

Mar. This is unkind, sir. You know I have obeyed you in neither seeing nor corresponding with him: I have heard enough to convince me that he is unworthy my regard. Yet I cannot think it culpable, if, while my understanding severely condemns his vices, my heart suggests some pity for his distresses.

Sir Pet. Well, well, pity him as much as you please; but give your heart and hand to a worthier object.

Mar. Never to his brother!

Sir Pet. Go, perverse and obstinate! But take care, madam; you have never yet known what the authority of a guardian is: don't compel me to inform you of it.

Mar. I can only say, you shall not have just reason. 'Tis true, by my father's will, I am for a short period bound to regard you as his substitute; but must cease to think you so, when you would compel me to be miserable.   [*Exit.*

Sir Pet. Was ever man so crossed as I am, every thing conspiring to fret me! I had not been involved in matrimony a fortnight, before her father, a hale and hearty man, died, on purpose, I believe, for the pleasure of plaguing me with the care of his daughter.—[*Lady Teazle sings without.*] But here comes my helpmate! She appears in great good humour. How happy I should be if I could tease her into loving me, though but a little!

Enter LADY TEAZLE.

Lady Teaz. Lud! Sir Peter, I hope you haven't been quarrelling with Maria? It is not using me well to be ill-humoured when I am not by.

Sir Pet. Ah, Lady Teazle, you might have the power to make me good-humoured at all times.

Lady Teaz. I am sure I wish I had; for I want you to be in a charming sweet temper at this moment. Do be good-humoured now, and let me have two hundred pounds, will you?

Sir Pet. Two hundred pounds; what an't I to be in a good humour without paying for it! But speak to me thus, and i'faith there's nothing I could refuse you. You shall have it; but seal me a bond for the repayment.

Lady Teaz. Oh, no—there—my note of hand will do as well.

[*Offering her hand.*

Sir Pet. And you shall no longer reproach me with not giving you an independent settlement. I mean shortly to surprise you: but shall we always live thus, hey?

Lady Teaz. If you please. I'm sure I don't care how soon we leave off quarrelling, provided you'll own you were tired first.

Sir Pet. Well—then let our future contest be, who shall be most obliging.

Lady Teaz. I assure you, Sir Peter, good nature becomes you. You look now as you did before we were married, when you used to walk with me under the elms, and tell me stories of what a gallant you were in your youth, and chuck me under the chin, you would; and ask me if I thought I could love an old fellow, who would deny me nothing—didn't you?

Sir Pet. Yes, yes, and you were as kind and attentive——

Lady Teaz. Ay, so I was, and would always take your part, when my acquaintance used to abuse you, and turn you into ridicule.

Sir Pet. Indeed!

Lady Teaz. Ay, and when my cousin Sophy has called you a stiff, peevish old bachelor, and laughed at me for thinking of marrying one who might be my father, I have always defended you, and said, I didn't think you so ugly by any means.

Sir Pet. Thank you.

Lady Teaz. And I dared say you'd make a very good sort of a husband.

Sir Pet. And you prophesied right; and we shall now be the happiest couple——

Lady Teaz. And never differ again?

Sir Pet. No, never!—though at the same time, indeed, my dear Lady Teazle, you must watch your temper very seriously; for in all our little quarrels, my dear, if you recollect, my love, you always began first.

Lady Teaz. I beg your pardon, my dear Sir Peter: indeed, you always gave the provocation.

Sir Pet. Now see, my angel! take care—contradicting isn't the way to keep friends.

Lady Teaz. Then don't you begin it, my love!

Sir Pet. There, now! you—you are going on. You don't perceive, my life, that you are just doing the very thing which you know always makes me angry.

Lady Teaz. Nay, you know if you will be angry without any reason, my dear——

Sir Pet. There! now you want to quarrel again.

Lady Teaz. No, I'm sure I don't: but, if you will be so peevish——

Sir Pet. There now! who begins first?

Lady Teaz. Why, you, to be sure. I said nothing—but there's no bearing your temper.

Sir Pet. No, no, madam: the fault's in your own temper.

Lady Teaz. Ay, you are just what my cousin Sophy said you would be.

Sir Pet. Your cousin Sophy is a forward, impertinent gipsy.

Lady Teaz. You are a great bear, I'm sure, to abuse my relations.

Sir Pet. Now may all the plagues of marriage be doubled on me, if ever I try to be friends with you any more!

Lady Teaz. So much the better.

Sir Pet. No, no, madam: 'tis evident you never cared a pin for me, and I was a madman to marry you—a pert, rural coquette, that had refused half the honest 'squires in the neighbourhood!

Lady Teaz. And I am sure I was a fool to marry you—an old dangling bachelor, who was single at fifty, only because he never could meet with any one who would have him.

Sir Pet. Ay, ay, madam; but you were pleased enough to listen to me: you never had such an offer before.

Lady Teaz. No! didn't I refuse Sir Tivy Terrier, who every body said would have been a better match? for his estate is just as good as yours, and he has broke his neck since we have been married.

Sir Pet. I have done with you, madam! You are an unfeeling, ungrateful— but there's an end of every thing. I believe you capable of every thing that is bad. Yes, madam, I now believe the reports relative to you and Charles, madam. Yes, madam, you and Charles are, not without grounds——

Lady Teaz. Take care, Sir Peter! you had better not insinuate any such thing! I'll not be suspected without cause, I promise you.

Sir Pet. Very well, madam! very well! A separate maintenance as soon as you please. Yes, madam, or a divorce! I'll make an example of myself for the benefit of all old bachelors. Let us separate, madam.

Lady Teaz. Agreed! agreed! And now, my dear Sir Peter, we are of a mind once more, we may be the happiest couple, and never differ again, you know: ha! ha! ha! Well, you are going to be in a passion, I see, and I shall only interrupt you—so, bye! bye!   [*Exit.*

Sir Pet. Plagues and tortures! can't I make her angry either! Oh, I am the most miserable fellow! But I'll not bear her presuming to keep her temper: no! she may break my heart, but she shan't keep her temper. [*Exit.*

Scene II.—*A Room in* Charles Surface's *House.*

Enter Trip, Moses, *and* Sir Oliver Surface.

Trip. Here, Master Moses! if you'll stay a moment, I'll try whether—what's the gentleman's name?

Sir Oliv. Mr. Moses, what is my name?　　　　　　[*Aside to* Moses.

Mos. Mr. Premium.

Trip. Premium—very well.　　　　　　　　　[*Exit, taking snuff.*

Sir Oliv. To judge by the servants, one wouldn't believe the master was ruined. But what!—sure, this was my brother's house?

Mos. Yes, sir; Mr. Charles bought it of Mr. Joseph, with the furniture, pictures, &c., just as the old gentleman left it. Sir Peter thought it a piece of extravagance in him.

Sir Oliv. In my mind, the other's economy in selling it to him was more reprehensible by half.

Re-enter Trip.

Trip. My master says you must wait, gentlemen: he has company, and can't speak with you yet.

Sir Oliv. If he knew who it was wanted to see him, perhaps he would not send such a message?

Trip. Yes, yes, sir; he knows you are here—I did not forget little Premium: no, no, no.

Sir Oliv. Very well; and I pray, sir, what may be your name?

Trip. Trip, sir; my name is Trip, at your service.

Sir Oliv. Well, then, Mr. Trip, you have a pleasant sort of place here, I guess?

Trip. Why, yes—here are three or four of us pass our time agreeably enough; but then our wages are sometimes a little in arrear—and not very great either—but fifty pounds a year, and find our own bags and bouquets.

Sir Oliv. Bags and bouquets! halters and bastinadoes!　　　[*Aside.*

Trip. And *à propos*, Moses, have you been able to get me that little bill discounted?

Sir Oliv. Wants to raise money too!—mercy on me! Has his distresses too, I warrant, like a lord, and affects creditors and duns.　　　　[*Aside.*

Mos. 'Twas not to be done, indeed, Mr. Trip.

Trip. Good lack, you surprise me! My friend Brush has indorsed it, and I thought when he put his name at the back of a bill 'twas the same as cash.

Mos. No, 'twouldn't do.

Trip. A small sum—but twenty pounds. Hark'ee, Moses, do you think you couldn't get it me by way of annuity?

Sir Oliv. An annuity! ha! ha! a footman raise money by way of annuity! Well done, luxury, egad!   [*Aside.*

Mos. Well, but you must insure your place.

Trip. Oh, with all my heart! I'll insure my place, and my life too, if you please.

Sir Oliv. It's more than I would your neck.   [*Aside.*

Mos. But is there nothing you could deposit?

Trip. Why, nothing capital of my master's wardrobe has dropped lately; but I could give you a mortgage on some of his winter clothes, with equity of redemption before November—or you shall have the reversion of the French velvet, or a post-obit on the blue and silver;—these, I should think, Moses, with a few pair of point ruffles, as a collateral security—hey, my little fellow?

Mos. Well, well.   [*Bell rings.*

Trip. Egad, I heard the bell! I believe, gentlemen, I can now introduce you. Don't forget the annuity, little Moses! This way, gentlemen, I'll insure my place, you know.

Sir Oliv. [*Aside.*] If the man be a shadow of the master, this is the temple of dissipation indeed!   [*Exeunt.*

SCENE III.—*Another Room in the same.*

CHARLES SURFACE, SIR HARRY BUMPER, CARELESS, *and* GENTLEMEN, *discovered drinking.*

Chas. Surf. 'Fore heaven, 'tis true!—there's the great degeneracy of the age. Many of our acquaintance have taste, spirit, and politeness; but, plague on't, they won't drink.

Care. It is so, indeed, Charles! they give into all the substantial luxuries of the table, and abstain from nothing but wine and wit. Oh, certainly society suffers by it intolerably! for now, instead of the social spirit of raillery that used to mantle over a glass of bright Burgundy, their conversation is become just like the Spa-water they drink, which has all the pertness and flatulency of champagne, without its spirit or flavour.

1 Gent. But what are they to do who love play better than wine?

Care. True! there's Sir Harry diets himself for gaming, and is now under a hazard regimen.

Chas. Surf. Then he'll have the worst of it. What! you wouldn't train a horse for the course by keeping him from corn? For my part, egad, I am never so successful as when I am a little merry: let me throw on a bottle of champagne, and I never lose.

All. Hey, what?

Care. At least I never feel my losses, which is exactly the same thing.

2 Gent. Ay, that I believe.

Chas. Surf. And then, what man can pretend to be a believer in love, who is an abjurer of wine? 'Tis the test by which the lover knows his own heart.

Fill a dozen bumpers to a dozen beauties, and she that floats at the top is the maid that has bewitched you.

Care. Now then, Charles, be honest, and give us your real favourite.

Chas. Surf. Why, I have withheld her only in compassion to you. If I toast her, you must give a round of her peers, which is impossible—on earth.

Care. Oh! then we'll find some canonised vestals or heathen goddesses that will do, I warrant!

Chas. Surf. Here then, bumpers, you rogues! bumpers! Maria! Maria!——

Sir Har. Maria who?

Chas. Surf. Oh, damn the surname!—'tis too formal to be registered in Love's calendar—Maria!

All. Maria!

Chas. Surf. But now, Sir Harry, beware, we must have beauty superlative.

Care. Nay, never study, Sir Harry: we'll stand to the toast, though your mistress should want an eye, and you know you have a song will excuse you.

Sir Har. Egad, so I have! and I'll give him the song instead of the lady.

[*Sings.*

> Here's to the maiden of bashful fifteen;
>   Here's to the widow of fifty;
> Here's to the flaunting extravagant quean,
>   And here's to the housewife that's thrifty.
> *Chorus.* Let the toast pass,—
>   Drink to the lass,
> I'll warrant she'll prove an excuse for the glass.
> Here's to the charmer whose dimples we prize;
>   Now to the maid who has none, sir:
> Here's to the girl with a pair of blue eyes,
>   And here's to the nymph with but one, sir.
> *Chorus.* Let the toast pass, &c.
> Here's to the maid with a bosom of snow:
>   Now to her that's as brown as a berry:
> Here's to the wife with a face full of woe,
>   And now to the damsel that's merry.
> *Chorus.* Let the toast pass, &c.
> For let 'em be clumsy, or let 'em be slim,
>   Young or ancient, I care not a feather;
> So fill a pint bumper quite up to the brim,
> So fill up your glasses, nay, fill to the brim,
>   And let us e'en toast them together.
> *Chorus.* Let the toast pass, &c.

All. Bravo! bravo!

Enter Trip, *and whispers* Charles Surface.

Chas. Surf. Gentlemen, you must excuse me a little.—Careless, take the chair, will you?

Care. Nay, pr'ythee, Charles, what now? This is one of your peerless beauties, I suppose, has dropped in by chance?

Chas. Surf. No, faith! To tell you the truth, 'tis a Jew and a broker, who are come by appointment.

Care. Oh, damn it! let's have the Jew in.

1 *Gent.* Ay, and the broker too, by all means.

2 *Gent.* Yes, yes, the Jew and the broker.

Chas. Surf. Egad, with all my heart!—Trip, bid the gentlemen walk in.— [*Exit* TRIP.] Though there's one of them a stranger, I can tell you.

Care. Charles, let us give them some generous Burgundy, and perhaps they'll grow conscientious.

Chas. Surf. Oh, hang 'em, no! wine does but draw forth a man's natural qualities; and to make them drink would only be to whet their knavery.

Re-enter TRIP, *with* SIR OLIVER SURFACE *and* MOSES.

Chas. Surf. So, honest Moses; walk in, pray, Mr. Premium—that's the gentleman's name, isn't it, Moses?

Mos. Yes, sir.

Chas. Surf. Set chairs, Trip.—Sit down, Mr. Premium.—Glasses, Trip.— [TRIP *gives chairs and glasses, and exit.*] Sit down, Moses.—Come, Mr. Premium, I'll give you a sentiment; here's *Success to usury!*—Moses, fill the gentleman a bumper.

Mos. Success to usury! [*Drinks.*

Care. Right, Moses—usury is prudence and industry, and deserves to succeed.

Sir Oliv. Then here's—All the success it deserves! [*Drinks.*

Care. No, no, that won't do! Mr. Premium, you have demurred at the toast, and must drink it in a pint bumper.

1 *Gent.* A pint bumper, at least.

Mos. Oh, pray, sir, consider—Mr. Premium's a gentleman.

Care. And therefore loves good wine.

2 *Gent.* Give Moses a quart glass—this is mutiny, and a high contempt for the chair.

Care. Here, now for 't! I'll see justice done, to the last drop of my bottle.

Sir Oliv. Nay, pray, gentlemen—I did not expect this usage.

Chas. Surf. No, hang it, you shan't; Mr. Premium's a stranger.

Sir Oliv. Odd! I wish I was well out of their company. [*Aside.*

Care. Plague on 'em then! if they won't drink, we'll not sit down with them. Come, Harry, the dice are in the next room.—Charles, you'll join us when you have finished your business with the gentlemen?

Chas. Surf. I will! I will!—[*Exeunt* SIR HARRY BUMPER *and* GENTLEMEN; CARELESS *following.*] Careless!

Care. [*Returning.*] Well!

Chas. Surf. Perhaps I may want you.

Care. Oh, you know I am always ready: word, note, or bond, 'tis all the same to me. [*Exit.*

Mos. Sir, this is Mr. Premium, a gentleman of the strictest honour and secrecy; and always performs what he undertakes. Mr. Premium, this is——

Chas. Surf. Psha! have done. Sir, my friend Moses is a very honest fellow, but a little slow at expression: he'll be an hour giving us our titles. Mr. Premium, the plain state of the matter is this: I am an extravagant young fellow who wants to borrow money; you I take to be a prudent old fellow, who have got money to lend. I am blockhead enough to give fifty per cent. sooner than not have it; and you, I presume, are rogue enough to take a hundred if you can get it. Now, sir, you see we are acquainted at once, and may proceed to business without farther ceremony.

Sir Oliv. Exceeding frank, upon my word. I see, sir, you are not a man of many compliments.

Chas. Surf. Oh, no, sir! plain dealing in business I always think best.

Sir Oliv. Sir, I like you the better for it. However, you are mistaken in one thing; I have no money to lend, but I believe I could procure some of a friend; but then he's an unconscionable dog. Isn't he, Moses? And must sell stock to accommodate you. Mustn't he, Moses?

Mos. Yes, indeed! You know I always speak the truth, and scorn to tell a lie!

Chas. Surf. Right. People that speak truth generally do. But these are trifles, Mr. Premium. What! I know money isn't to be bought without paying for't!

Sir Oliv. Well, but what security could you give? You have no land, I suppose?

Chas. Surf. Not a mole-hill, nor a twig, but what's in the bough-pots out of the window!

Sir Oliv. Nor any stock, I presume?

Chas. Surf. Nothing but live stock—and that's only a few pointers and ponies. But pray, Mr. Premium, are you acquainted at all with any of my connexions?

Sir Oliv. Why, to say truth, I am.

Chas. Surf. Then you must know that I have a devilish rich uncle in the East Indies, Sir Oliver Surface, from whom I have the greatest expectations?

Sir Oliv. That you have a wealthy uncle, I have heard; but how your expectations will turn out is more, I believe, than you can tell.

Chas. Surf. Oh, no!—there can be no doubt. They tell me I'm a prodigious favourite, and that he talks of leaving me every thing.

Sir Oliv. Indeed! this is the first I've heard of it.

Chas. Surf. Yes, yes, 'tis just so. Moses knows 'tis true; don't you, Moses?

Mos. Oh, yes! I'll swear to 't.

Sir Oliv. Egad, they'll persuade me presently I'm at Bengal.   [*Aside.*

Chas. Surf. Now I propose, Mr. Premium, if it's agreeable to you, a post-obit on Sir Oliver's life: though at the same time the old fellow has been so liberal to me, that I give you my word, I should be very sorry to hear that any thing had happened to him.

Sir Oliv. Not more than I should, I assure you. But the bond you mention happens to be just the worst security you could offer me—for I might live to a hundred and never see the principal.

Chas. Surf. Oh, yes, you would! the moment Sir Oliver dies, you know, you would come on me for the money.

Sir Oliv. Then I believe I should be the most unwelcome dun you ever had in your life.

Chas. Surf. What! I suppose you're afraid that Sir Oliver is too good a life?

Sir Oliv. No, indeed I am not; though I have heard he is as hale and healthy as any man of his years in Christendom.

Chas. Surf. There again, now, you are misinformed. No, no, the climate has hurt him considerably, poor uncle Oliver. Yes, yes, he breaks apace, I'm told—and is so much altered lately that his nearest relations would not know him.

Sir Oliv. No! Ha! ha! ha! so much altered lately that his nearest relations would not know him! Ha! ha! ha! egad—ha! ha! ha!

Chas. Surf. Ha! ha!—you're glad to hear that, little Premium?

Sir Oliv. No, no, I'm not.

Chas. Surf. Yes, yes, you are—ha! ha! ha!—you know that mends your chance.

Sir Oliv. But I'm told Sir Oliver is coming over; nay, some say he is actually arrived.

Chas. Surf. Psha! sure I must know better than you whether he's come or not. No, no, rely on't he's at this moment at Calcutta. Isn't he, Moses?

Mos. Oh, yes, certainly.

Sir Oliv. Very true, as you say, you must know better than I, though I have it from pretty good authority. Haven't I, Moses?

Mos. Yes, most undoubted!

Sir Oliv. But, sir, as I understand you want a few hundreds immediately, is there nothing you could dispose of?

Chas. Surf. How do you mean?

Sir Oliv. For instance, now, I have heard that your father left behind him a great quantity of massy old plate.

Chas. Surf. O Lud! that's gone long ago. Moses can tell you how better than I can.

Sir Oliv. [*Aside.*] Good lack! all the family race-cups and corporation-bowls!—[*Aloud.*] Then it was also supposed that his library was one of the most valuable and compact.

Chas. Surf. Yes, yes, so it was—vastly too much so for a private gentleman. For my part, I was always of a communicative disposition, so I thought it a shame to keep so much knowledge to myself.

Sir Oliv. [*Aside.*] Mercy upon me! learning that had run in the family like an heir-loom!—[*Aloud.*] Pray, what are become of the books?

Chas. Surf. You must inquire of the auctioneer, Master Premium, for I don't believe even Moses can direct you.

Mos. I know nothing of books.

Sir Oliv. So, so, nothing of the family property left, I suppose?

Chas. Surf. Not much, indeed; unless you have a mind to the family pictures. I have got a room full of ancestors above: and if you have a taste for old paintings, egad, you shall have 'em a bargain!

Sir Oliv. Hey! what the devil! sure, you wouldn't sell your forefathers, would you?

Chas. Surf. Every man of them, to the best bidder.

Sir Oliv. What! your great-uncles and aunts?

Chas. Surf. Ay, and my great-grandfathers and grandmothers too.

Sir Oliv. [*Aside.*] Now I give him up!—[*Aloud.*] What the plague, have you no bowels for your own kindred? Odd's life! do you take me for Shylock in the play, that you would raise money of me on your own flesh and blood?

Chas. Surf. Nay, my little broker, don't be angry: what need you care, if you have your money's worth?

Sir Oliv. Well, I'll be the purchaser: I think I can dispose of the family canvas.—[*Aside.*] Oh, I'll never forgive him this! never!

Re-enter CARELESS.

Care. Come, Charles, what keeps you?

Chas. Surf. I can't come yet. I'faith, we are going to have a sale above stairs; here's little Premium will buy all my ancestors!

Care. Oh, burn your ancestors!

Chas. Surf. No, he may do that afterwards, if he pleases. Stay, Careless, we want you: egad, you shall be auctioneer—so come along with us.

Care. Oh, have with you, if that's the case. I can handle a hammer as well as a dice-box! Going! going!

Sir Oliv. Oh, the profligates! [*Aside.*]

Chas. Surf. Come, Moses, you shall be appraiser, if we want one. Gad's life, little Premium, you don't seem to like the business?

Sir Oliv. Oh, yes, I do, vastly! Ha! ha! ha! yes, yes, I think it a rare joke to sell one's family by auction—ha! ha!—[*Aside.*] Oh, the prodigal!

Chas. Surf. To be sure! when a man wants money, where the plague should he get assistance, if he can't make free with his own relations? [*Exeunt.*]

Sir Oliv. I'll never forgive him; never! never!

ACT IV.

SCENE I.—*A Picture Room in* CHARLES SURFACE'S *House.*

Enter CHARLES SURFACE, SIR OLIVER SURFACE, MOSES, *and* CARELESS.

Chas. Surf. Walk in, gentlemen, pray walk in;—here they are, the family of the Surfaces, up to the Conquest.

Sir Oliv. And, in my opinion, a goodly collection.

Chas. Surf. Ay, ay, these are done in the true spirit of portrait-painting; no *volontière grace* or expression. Not like the works of your modern Raphaels, who give you the strongest resemblance, yet contrive to make your portrait independent of you; so that you may sink the original and not hurt the picture. No, no; the merit of these is the inveterate likeness—all stiff and awkward as the originals, and like nothing in human nature besides.

Sir Oliv. Ah! we shall never see such figures of men again.

Chas. Surf. I hope not. Well, you see, Master Premium, what a domestic character I am; here I sit of an evening surrounded by my family. But come, get to your pulpit, Mr. Auctioneer; here's an old gouty chair of my grand-father's will answer the purpose.

Care. Ay, ay, this will do. But, Charles, I haven't a hammer; and what's an auctioneer without his hammer?

Chas. Surf. Egad, that's true. What parchment have we here? Oh, our genealogy in full. [*Taking pedigree down.*] Here, Careless, you shall have no common bit of mahogany, here's the family tree for you, you rogue! This shall be your hammer, and now you may knock down my ancestors with their own pedigree.

Sir Oliv. What an unnatural rogue!—an *ex post facto* parricide!   [*Aside.*

Care. Yes, yes, here's a list of your generation indeed;—faith, Charles, this is the most convenient thing you could have found for the business, for 'twill not only serve as a hammer, but a catalogue into the bargain. Come, begin—A-going, a-going, a-going!

Chas. Surf. Bravo, Careless! Well, here's my great-uncle, Sir Richard Raveline, a marvellous good general in his day, I assure you. He served in all the Duke of Marlborough's wars, and got that cut over his eye at the battle of Malplaquet. What say you, Mr. Premium? look at him—there's a hero! not cut out of his feathers, as your modern clipped captains are, but en-veloped in wig and regimentals, as a general should be. What do you bid?

Sir Oliv. [*Aside to Moses.*] Bid him speak.

Mos. Mr. Premium would have you speak.

Chas. Surf. Why, then, he shall have him for ten pounds, and I'm sure that's not dear for a staff-officer.

Sir Oliv. [*Aside.*] Heaven deliver me! his famous uncle Richard for ten pounds!—[*Aloud.*] Very well, sir, I take him at that.

Chas. Surf. Careless, knock down my uncle Richard.—Here, now, is a maiden sister of his, my great-aunt Deborah, done by Kneller, in his best manner, and esteemed a very formidable likeness. There she is, you see, a shepherdess feeding her flock. You shall have her for five pounds ten—the sheep are worth the money.

Sir Oliv. [*Aside.*] Ah! poor Deborah! a woman who set such a value on herself!—[*Aloud.*] Five pounds ten—she's mine.

Chas. Surf. Knock down my aunt Deborah! Here, now, are two that were a sort of cousins of theirs.—You see, Moses, these pictures were done some time ago, when beaux wore wigs, and the ladies their own hair.

Sir Oliv. Yes, truly, head dresses appear to have been a little lower in those days.

Chas. Surf. Well take that couple for the same.

Mos. 'Tis a good bargain.

Chas. Surf. Careless!—This, now, is a grandfather of my mother's, a learned judge, well known on the western circuit.—What do you rate him at, Moses?

Mos. Four guineas.

Chas. Surf. Four guineas! Gad's life, you don't bid me the price of his wig.—Mr. Premium, you have more respect for the woolsack; do let us knock his lordship down at fifteen.

Sir Oliv. By all means.

Care. Gone!

Chas. Surf. And there are two brothers of his, William and Walter Blunt, Esquires, both members of parliament, and noted speakers; and, what's very extraordinary, I believe, this is the first time they were ever bought or sold.

Sir Oliv. That is very extraordinary, indeed! I'll take them at your own price, for the honour of parliament.

Care. Well said, little Premium! I'll knock them down at forty.

Chas. Surf. Here's a jolly fellow—I don't know what relation, but he was mayor of Norwich: take him at eight pounds.

Sir Oliv. No, no; six will do for the mayor.

Chas. Surf. Come, make it guineas, and I'll throw you the two aldermen there into the bargain.

Sir Oliv. They're mine.

Chas. Surf. Careless, knock down the mayor and aldermen. But, plague on 't! We shall be all day retailing in this manner; do let us deal wholesale: what say you, little Premium? Give me three hundred pounds for the rest of the family in the lump.

Care. Ay, ay, that will be the best way.

Sir Oliv. Well, well, any thing to accommodate you; they are mine. But there is one portrait which you have always passed over.

Care. What, that ill-looking little fellow over the settee?

Sir Oliv. Yes, sir, I mean that; though I don't think him so ill-looking a little fellow, by any means.

Chas. Surf. What, that? Oh; that's my uncle Oliver! 'twas done before he went to India.

Care. Your uncle Oliver! Gad, then you'll never be friends, Charles. That, now, to me, is as stern a looking rogue as ever I saw; an unforgiving eye, and a damned disinheriting countenance! an inveterate knave, depend on 't. Don't you think so, little Premium?

Sir Oliv. Upon my soul, sir, I do not; I think it is as honest a looking face as any in the room, dead or alive. But I suppose uncle Oliver goes with the rest of the lumber?

Chas. Surf. No, hang it! I'll not part with poor Noll. The old fellow has been very good to me, and, egad, I'll keep his picture while I've a room to put it in.

Sir Oliv. [*Aside.*] The rogue's my nephew after all!—[*Aloud.*] But, sir, I have somehow taken a fancy to that picture.

Chas. Surf. I'm sorry for 't, for you certainly will not have it. Oons, haven't you got enough of them?

Sir Oliv. [*Aside.*] I forgive him every thing!—[*Aloud.*] But, sir, when I take a whim in my head, I don't value money. I'll give you as much for that as for all the rest.

Chas. Surf. Don't tease me, master broker; I tell you I'll not part with it, and there's an end of it.

Sir Oliv. [*Aside.*] How like his father the dog is!—[*Aloud.*] Well, well, I have done.—[*Aside.*] I did not perceive it before, but I think I never saw such a striking resemblance.—[*Aloud.*] Here is a draught for your sum.

Chas. Surf. Why, 'tis for eight hundred pounds!

Sir Oliv. You will not let Sir Oliver go?

Chas. Surf. Zounds! no! I tell you, once more.

Sir Oliv. Then never mind the difference, we'll balance that another time. But give me your hand on the bargain; you are an honest fellow, Charles— I beg pardon, sir, for being so free.—Come, Moses.

Chas. Surf. Egad, this is a whimsical old fellow!—But hark'ee, Premium, you'll prepare lodgings for these gentlemen.

Sir Oliv. Yes, yes, I'll send for them in a day or two.

Chas. Surf. But hold; do now send a genteel conveyance for them, for, I assure you, they were most of them used to ride in their own carriages.

Sir Oliv. I will, I will—for all but Oliver.

Chas. Surf. Ay, all but the little nabob.

Sir Oliv. You're fixed on that?

Chas. Surf. Peremptorily.

Sir Oliv. [*Aside.*] A dear extravagant rogue!—[*Aloud.*] Good day!— Come, Moses.—[*Aside.*] Let me hear now who dares call him profligate!

[*Exit with* Moses.

Care. Why, this is the oddest genius of the sort I ever met with!

Chas. Surf. Egad, he's the prince of brokers, I think. I wonder how the devil Moses got acquainted with so honest a fellow.—Ha! here's Rowley.— Do, Careless, say I'll join the company in a few moments.

Care. I will—but don't let that old blockhead persuade you to squander any of that money on old musty debts, or any such nonsense; for tradesmen, Charles, are the most exorbitant fellows.

Chas. Surf. Very true, and paying them is only encouraging them.

Care. Nothing else.

Chas. Surf. Ay, ay, never fear.—[*Exit* Careless.] So! this was an odd old fellow, indeed. Let me see, two-thirds of these five hundred and thirty odd pounds are mine by right. 'Fore Heaven! I find one's ancestors are more valuable relations than I took them for!—Ladies and gentlemen, your most obedient and very grateful servant.   [*Bows ceremoniously to the pictures.*

Enter ROWLEY.

Ha! old Rowley! egad, you are just come in time to take leave of your old acquaintance.

Row. Yes, I heard they were a-going. But I wonder you can have such spirits under so many distresses.

Chas. Surf. Why, there's the point! my distresses are so many, that I can't afford to part with my spirits; but I shall be rich and splenetic, all in good time. However, I suppose you are surprised that I am not more sorrowful at parting with so many near rel. ·ions; to be sure, 'tis very affecting, but you see they never move a muscle, so why should I?

Row. There's no making you serious a moment.

Chas. Surf. Yes, faith, I am so now. Here, my honest Rowley, here, get me this changed directly, and take a hundred pounds of it immediately to old Stanley.

Row. A hundred pounds! Consider only——

Chas. Surf. Gad's life, don't talk about it! poor Stanley's wants pressing, and, if you don't make haste, we shall have some one call that has a better right to the money.

Row. Ah! there's the point! I never will cease dunning you with the old proverb——

Chas. Surf. Be just before you're generous.—Why, so I would if I could; but Justice is an old, hobbling beldame, and I can't get her to keep pace with Generosity, for the soul of me.

Row. Yet, Charles, believe me, one hour's reflection——

Chas. Surf. Ay, ay, it's very true; but, hark'ee, Rowley, while I have, by Heaven I'll give; so, damn your economy! and now for hazard. [*Exeunt.*

SCENE II.—*Another room in the same.*

Enter SIR OLIVER SURFACE *and* MOSES.

Mos. Well, sir, I think, as Sir Peter said, you have seen Mr. Charles in high glory; 'tis great pity he's so extravagant.

Sir Oliv. True, but he would not sell my picture.

Mos. And loves wine and women so much.

Sir Oliv. But he would not sell my picture.

Mos. And games so deep.

Sir Oliv. But he would not sell my picture. Oh, here's Rowley.

Enter ROWLEY.

Row. So, Sir Oliver, I find you have made a purchase——

Sir Oliv. Yes, yes, our young rake has parted with his ancestors like old tapestry.

Row. And here has he commissioned me to re-deliver you part of the purchase money—I mean, though, in your necessitous character of old Stanley.

Mos. Ah! there is the pity of all; he is so damned charitable.

Row. And I left a hosier and two tailors in the hall, who, I'm sure, won't be paid, and this hundred would satisfy them.

Sir Oliv. Well, well, I'll pay his debts, and his benevolence too. But now I am no more a broker, and you shall introduce me to the elder brother as old Stanley.

Row. Not yet awhile; Sir Peter, I know, means to call there about this time.

Enter TRIP.

Trip. Oh, gentlemen, I beg pardon for not showing you out; this way— Moses, a word.   [*Exit with* MOSES.

Sir Oliv. There's a fellow for you! Would you believe it, that puppy intercepted the Jew on our coming, and wanted to raise money before he got to his master!

Row. Indeed!

Sir Oliv. Yes, they are now planning an annuity business. Ah, Master Rowley, in my days servants were content with the follies of their masters, when they were worn a little threadbare; but now they have their vices, like their birthday clothes, with the gloss on.   [*Exeunt.*

SCENE III.—*A Library in* JOSEPH SURFACE's *House.*

Enter JOSEPH SURFACE *and* SERVANT.

Jos. Surf. No letter from Lady Teazle?

Ser. No, sir.

Jos. Surf. [*Aside.*] I am surprised she has not sent, if she is prevented from coming. Sir Peter certainly does not suspect me. Yet I wish I may not lose the heiress, through the scrape I have drawn myself into with the wife; however, Charles's imprudence and bad character are great points in my favour.   [*Knocking without.*

Ser. Sir, I believe that must be Lady Teazle.

Jos. Surf. Hold! See whether it is or not, before you go to the door: I have a particular message for you if it should be my brother.

Ser. 'Tis her ladyship, sir; she always leaves her chair at the milliner's in the next street.

Jos. Surf. Stay, stay; draw that screen before the window—that will do;— my opposite neighbour is a maiden lady of so curious a temper.—[SERVANT *draws the screen, and exit.*] I have a difficult hand to play in this affair. Lady Teazle has lately suspected my views on Maria; but she must by no means be let into that secret,—at least, till I have her more in my power.

Enter LADY TEAZLE.

Lady Teaz. What, sentiment in soliloquy now? Have you been very impatient? O Lud! don't pretend to look grave. I vow I couldn't come before.

Jos. Surf. O madam, punctuality is a species of constancy very unfashionable in a lady of quality.

[*Places chairs, and sits after* LADY TEAZLE *is seated.*

Lady Teaz. Upon my word, you ought to pity me. Do you know Sir Peter is grown so ill-natured to me of late, and so jealous of Charles too—that's the best of the story, isn't it?

Jos. Surf. I am glad my scandalous friends keep that up. [*Aside.*

Lady Teaz. I am sure I wish he would let Maria marry him, and then perhaps he would be convinced; don't you, Mr. Surface?

Jos. Surf. [*Aside.*] Indeed I do not.—[*Aloud.*] Oh, certainly I do! for then my dear Lady Teazle would also be convinced how wrong her suspicions were of my having any design on the silly girl.

Lady Teaz. Well, well, I'm inclined to believe you. But isn't it provoking, to have the most ill-natured things said of one? And there's my friend Lady Sneerwell has circulated I don't know how many scandalous tales of me, and all without any foundation too; that's what vexes me.

Jos. Surf. Ay, madam, to be sure, that is the provoking circumstance—without foundation; yes, yes, there's the mortification, indeed; for, when a scandalous story is believed against one, there certainly is no comfort like the consciousness of having deserved it.

Lady Teaz. No, to be sure, then I'd forgive their malice; but to attack me, who am really so innocent, and who never say an ill-natured thing of any body—that is, of any friend; and then Sir Peter, too, to have him so peevish, and so suspicious, when I know the integrity of my own heart—indeed 'tis monstrous!

Jos. Surf. But, my dear Lady Teazle, 'tis your own fault if you suffer it. When a husband entertains a groundless suspicion of his wife, and withdraws his confidence from her, the original compact is broken, and she owes it to the honour of her sex to endeavour to outwit him.

Lady Teaz. Indeed! So that, if he suspects me without cause, it follows, that the best way of curing his jealousy is to give him reason for't?

Jos. Surf. Undoubtedly—for your husband should never be deceived in you: and in that case it becomes you to be frail in compliment to his discernment.

Lady Teaz. To be sure, what you say is very reasonable, and when the consciousness of my innocence——

Jos. Surf. Ah, my dear madam, there is the great mistake! 'tis this very conscious innocence that is of the greatest prejudice to you. What is it makes you negligent of forms, and careless of the world's opinion? why, the consciousness of your own innocence. What makes you thoughtless in your conduct, and apt to run into a thousand little imprudences? why, the consciousness of your own innocence. What makes you impatient of Sir Peter's temper, and outrageous at his suspicions? why, the consciousness of your innocence.

Lady Teaz. 'Tis very true!

Jos. Surf. Now, my dear Lady Teazle, if you would but once make a trifling *faux pas*, you can't conceive how cautious you would grow, and how ready to humour and agree with your husband.

Lady Teaz. Do you think so?

Jos. Surf. Oh, I am sure on 't; and then you would find all scandal would cease at once, for—in short, your character at present is like a person in a plethora, absolutely dying from too much health.

Lady Teaz. So, so; then I perceive your prescription is, that I must sin in my own defence, and part with my virtue to preserve my reputation?

Jos. Surf. Exactly so, upon my credit, ma'am.

Lady Teaz. Well, certainly this is the oddest doctrine, and the newest receipt for avoiding calumny!

Jos. Surf. An infallible one, believe me. Prudence, like experience, must be paid for.

Lady Teaz. Why, if my understanding were once convinced——

Jos. Surf. Oh, certainly, madam, your understanding should be convinced. Yes, yes—Heaven forbid I should persuade you to do any thing you thought wrong. No, no, I have too much honour to desire it.

Lady Teaz. Don't you think we may as well leave honour out of the argument?   [*Rises.*

Jos. Surf. Ah, the ill effects of your country education, I see, still remain with you.

Lady Teaz. I doubt they do indeed; and I will fairly own to you, that if I could be persuaded to do wrong, it would be by Sir Peter's ill usage sooner than your honourable logic, after all.

Jos. Surf. Then, by this hand, which he is unworthy of——
                                                        [*Taking her hand.*

Re-enter SERVANT.

'Sdeath, you blockhead—what do you want?

Ser. I beg your pardon, sir, but I thought you would not choose Sir Peter to come up without announcing him.

Jos. Surf. Sir Peter!—Oons—the devil!

Lady Teaz. Sir Peter! O Lud! I'm ruined! I'm ruined!

Ser. Sir, 'twasn't I let him in.

Lady Teaz. Oh! I'm quite undone! What will become of me? Now, Mr. Logic—Oh! mercy, sir, he's on the stairs—I'll get behind here—and if ever I'm so imprudent again——   [*Goes behind the screen.*

Jos. Surf. Give me that book.
                              [*Sits down.* SERVANT *pretends to adjust his chair.*

Enter Sir Peter Teazle.

Sir Pet. Ay, ever improving himself—Mr. Surface, Mr. Surface——

[*Pats* Joseph *on the shoulder.*

Jos. Surf. Oh, my dear Sir Peter, I beg your pardon—[*Gaping, throws away the book.*] I have been dozing over a stupid book. Well, I am much obliged to you for this call. You haven't been here, I believe, since I fitted up this room. Books, you know, are the only things I am a coxcomb in.

Sir Pet. 'Tis very neat indeed. Well, well, that's proper; and you can make even your screen a source of knowledge—hung, I perceive, with maps.

Jos. Surf. Oh, yes, I find great use in that screen.

Sir Pet. I dare say you must, certainly, when you want to find any thing in a hurry.

Jos. Surf. Ay, or to hide any thing in a hurry either. [*Aside.*

Sir Pet. Well, I have a little private business——

Jos. Surf. You need not stay. [*To* Servant.

Ser. No, sir. [*Exit.*

Jos. Surf. Here's a chair, Sir Peter—I beg——

Sir Pet. Well, now we are alone, there is a subject, my dear friend, on which I wish to unburden my mind to you—a point of the greatest moment to my peace; in short, my good friend, Lady Teazle's conduct of late has made me very unhappy.

Jos. Surf. Indeed! I am very sorry to hear it.

Sir Pet. Yes, 'tis but too plain she has not the least regard for me; but, what's worse, I have pretty good authority to suppose she has formed an attachment to another.

Jos. Surf. Indeed! you astonish me!

Sir Pet. Yes! and, between ourselves, I think I've discovered the person.

Jos. Surf. How! you alarm me exceedingly.

Sir Pet. Ay, my dear friend, I knew you would sympathise with me!

Jos. Surf. Yes, believe me, Sir Peter, such a discovery would hurt me just as much as it would you.

Sir Pet. I am convinced of it. Ah! it is a happiness to have a friend whom we can trust even with one's family secrets. But have you no guess who I mean?

Jos. Surf. I haven't the most distant idea. It can't be Sir Benjamin Backbite!

Sir Pet. Oh, no! What say you to Charles?

Jos. Surf. My brother! impossible!

Sir Pet. Oh, my dear friend, the goodness of your own heart misleads you. You judge of others by yourself.

Jos. Surf. Certainly, Sir Peter, the heart that is conscious of its own integrity is ever slow to credit another's treachery.

Sir Pet. True; but your brother has no sentiment—you never hear him talk so.

Jos. Surf. Yet I can't but think Lady Teazle herself has too much principle.

Sir Pet. Ay; but what is principle against the flattery of a handsome, lively young fellow?

Jos. Surf. That's very true.

Sir Pet. And then, you know, the difference of our ages makes it very improbable that she should have any great affection for me; and if she were to be frail, and I were to make it public, why the town would only laugh at me, the foolish old bachelor, who had married a girl.

Jos. Surf. That's true, to be sure—they would laugh.

Sir Pet. Laugh! ay, and make ballads, and paragraphs, and the devil knows what of me.

Jos. Surf. No, you must never make it public.

Sir Pet. But then again—that the nephew of my old friend, Sir Oliver, should be the person to attempt such a wrong, hurts me more nearly.

Jos. Surf. Ay, there's the point. When ingratitude barbs the dart of injury, the wound has double danger in it.

Sir Pet. Ay—I, that was, in a manner, left his guardian; in whose house he had been so often entertained; who never in my life denied him—my advice!

Jos. Surf. Oh, 'tis not to be credited! There may be a man capable of such baseness, to be sure; but, for my part, till you can give me positive proofs, I cannot but doubt it. However, if it should be proved on him, he is no longer a brother of mine—I disclaim kindred with him: for the man who can break the laws of hospitality, and tempt the wife of his friend, deserves to be branded as the pest of society.

Sir Pet. What a difference there is between you! What noble sentiments!

Jos. Surf. Yet I cannot suspect Lady Teazle's honour.

Sir Pet. I am sure I wish to think well of her, and to remove all ground of quarrel between us. She has lately reproached me more than once with having made no settlement on her; and, in our last quarrel, she almost hinted that she should not break her heart if I was dead. Now, as we seem to differ in our ideas of expense, I have resolved she shall have her own way, and be her own mistress in that respect for the future; and, if I were to die, she will find I have not been inattentive to her interest while living. Here, my friend, are the drafts of two deeds, which I wish to have your opinion on. By one, she will enjoy eight hundred a year independent while I live; and, by the other, the bulk of my fortune at my death.

Jos. Surf. This conduct, Sir Peter, is indeed truly generous.—[*Aside.*] I wish it may not corrupt my pupil.

Sir Pet. Yes, I am determined she shall have no cause to complain, though I would not have her acquainted with the latter instance of my affection yet awhile.

Jos. Surf. Nor I, if I could help it.   [*Aside.*

Sir Pet. And now, my dear friend, if you please, we will talk over the situation of your hopes with Maria.

Jos. Surf. [*Softly.*] Oh, no, Sir Peter; another time, if you please.

Sir Pet. I am sensibly chagrined at the little progress you seem to make in her affections.

Jos. Surf. [*Softly.*] I beg you will not mention it. What are my disappointments when your happiness is in debate!—[*Aside.*] 'Sdeath, I shall be ruined every way!

Sir Pet. And though you are averse to my acquainting Lady Teazle with your passion, I'm sure she's not your enemy in the affair.

Jos. Surf. Pray, Sir Peter, now oblige me. I am really too much affected by the subject we have been speaking of to bestow a thought on my own concerns. The man who is entrusted with his friend's distresses can never——

Re-enter SERVANT.

Well, sir?

Ser. Your brother, sir, is speaking to a gentleman in the street, and says he knows you are within.

Jos. Surf. 'Sdeath, blockhead, I'm not within—I'm out for the day.

Sir Pet. Stay—hold—a thought has struck me:—you shall be at home.

Jos. Surf. Well, well, let him up.—[*Exit* SERVANT.] He'll interrupt Sir Peter, however. [*Aside.*

Sir Pet. Now, my good friend, oblige me, I entreat you. Before Charles comes, let me conceal myself somewhere, then do you tax him on the point we have been talking, and his answer may satisfy me at once.

Jos. Surf. Oh, fie, Sir Peter! would you have me join in so mean a trick?—to trepan my brother too?

Sir Pet. Nay, you tell me you are sure he is innocent; if so, you do him the greatest service by giving him an opportunity to clear himself, and you will set my heart at rest. Come, you shall not refuse me: [*Going up*] here, behind the screen will be—Hey! what the devil! there seems to be one listener here already—I'll swear I saw a petticoat!

Jos. Surf. Ha! ha! ha! Well, this is ridiculous enough. I'll tell you, Sir Peter, though I hold a man of intrigue to be a most despicable character, yet, you know, it does not follow that one is to be an absolute Joseph either! Hark'ee, 'tis a little French milliner, a silly rogue that plagues me; and having some character to lose, on your coming, sir, she ran behind the screen.

Sir Pet. Ah, Joseph! Joseph! Did I ever think that you——But, egad, she has overheard all I have been saying of my wife.

Jos. Surf. Oh, 'twill never go any farther, you may depend upon it!

Sir Pet. No! then, faith, let her hear it out.—Here's a closet will do as well.

Jos. Surf. Well, go in there.

Sir Pet. Sly rogue! sly rogue! [*Goes into the closet.*

Jos. Surf. A narrow escape, indeed! and a curious situation I'm in, to part man and wife in this manner.

Lady Teaz. [*Peeping.*] Couldn't I steal off?

Jos. Surf. Keep close, my angel!

Sir Pet. [*Peeping.*] Joseph, tax him home.

Jos. Surf. Back, my dear friend!

Lady Teaz. [*Peeping.*] Couldn't you lock Sir Peter in?

Jos. Surf. Be still, my life!

Sir Pet. [*Peeping.*] You're sure the little milliner won't blab?

Jos. Surf. In, in, my dear Sir Peter!—'Fore Gad, I wish I had a key to the door.

Enter CHARLES SURFACE.

Chas. Surf. Holla! brother, what has been the matter? Your fellow would not let me up at first. What! have you had a Jew or a wench with you?

Jos. Surf. Neither, brother, I assure you.

Chas. Surf. But what has made Sir Peter steal off? I thought he had been with you.

Jos. Surf. He was, brother; but, hearing you were coming, he did not choose to stay.

Chas. Surf. What! was the old gentleman afraid I wanted to borrow money of him?

Jos. Surf. No, sir: but I am sorry to find, Charles, you have lately given that worthy man grounds for great uneasiness.

Chas. Surf. Yes, they tell me I do that to a great many worthy men. But how so, pray?

Jos. Surf. To be plain with you, brother, he thinks you are endeavouring to gain Lady Teazle's affections from him.

Chas. Surf. Who, I? O Lud! not I, upon my word.—Ha! ha! ha! ha! so the old fellow has found out that he has got a young wife, has he?—or, what is worse, Lady Teazle has found out she has an old husband?

Jos. Surf. This is no subject to jest on, brother. He who can laugh——

Chas. Surf. True, true, as you were going to say—then, seriously, I never had the least idea of what you charge me with, upon my honour.

Jos. Surf. Well, it will give Sir Peter great satisfaction to hear this.

[*Raising his voice.*

Chas. Surf. To be sure, I once thought the lady seemed to have taken a fancy to me; but, upon my soul, I never gave her the least encouragement. Besides, you know my attachment to Maria.

Jos. Surf. But sure, brother, even if Lady Teazle had betrayed the fondest partiality for you——

Chas. Surf. Why, look'ee, Joseph, I hope I shall never deliberately do a dishonourable action; but if a pretty woman was purposely to throw herself in my way—and that pretty woman married to a man old enough to be her father——

Jos. Surf. Well!

Chas. Surf. Why, I believe I should be obliged to——

Jos. Surf. What?

Chas. Surf. To borrow a little of your morality, that's all. But, brother, do you know now that you surprise me exceedingly, by naming me with Lady Teazle; for, i'faith, I always understood you were her favourite.

Jos. Surf. Oh, for shame, Charles! This retort is foolish.

Chas. Surf. Nay, I swear I have seen you exchange such significant glances——

Jos. Surf. Nay, nay, sir, this is no jest.

Chas. Surf. Egad, I'm serious! Don't you remember one day, when I called here——

Jos. Surf. Nay, pr'ythee, Charles——

Chas. Surf. And found you together——

Jos. Surf. Zounds, sir, I insist——

Chas. Surf. And another time when your servant——

Jos. Surf. Brother, brother, a word with you!—[*Aside.*] Gad, I must stop him.

Chas. Surf. Informed, I say, that——

Jos. Surf. Hush! I beg your pardon, but Sir Peter has overheard all we have been saying. I knew you would clear yourself, or I should not have consented.

Chas. Surf. How, Sir Peter! Where is he?

Jos. Surf. Softly, there!   [*Points to the closet.*

Chas. Surf. Oh, 'fore Heaven, I'll have him out. Sir Peter, come forth!

Jos. Surf. No, no——

Chas. Surf. I say, Sir Peter, come into court.—[*Pulls in* SIR PETER.] What! my old guardian!—What! turn inquisitor, and take evidence incog.? Oh, fie! Oh, fie!

Sir Pet. Give me your hand, Charles—I believe I have suspected you wrongfully; but you mustn't be angry with Joseph—'twas my plan!

Chas. Surf. Indeed!

Sir Pet. But I acquit you. I promise you I don't think near so ill of you as I did: what I have heard has given me great satisfaction.

Chas. Surf. Egad, then, 'twas lucky you didn't hear any more. Wasn't it, Joseph?

Sir Pet. Ah! you would have retorted on him.

Chas. Surf. Ay, ay, that was a joke.

Sir Pet. Yes, yes, I know his honour too well.

Chas. Surf. But you might as well have suspected him as me in this matter, for all that. Mightn't he, Joseph?

Sir Pet. Well, well, I believe you.

Jos. Surf. Would they were both out of the room!   [*Aside.*

Sir Pet. And in future, perhaps, we may not be such strangers.

Re-enter SERVANT, *and whispers* JOSEPH SURFACE.

Serv. Lady Sneerwell is below, and says she will come up.

Jos. Surf. Lady Sneerwell! Gad's life! she must not come here. [*Exit* SERVANT.] Gentlemen, I beg pardon—I must wait on you down stairs: here is a person come on particular business.

Chas. Surf. Well, you can see him in another room. Sir Peter and I have not met a long time, and I have something to say to him.

Jos. Surf. [*Aside.*] They must not be left together.—[*Aloud.*] I'll send Lady Sneerwell away, and return directly.—[*Aside to* SIR PETER.] Sir Peter, not a word of the French milliner.

Sir Pet. [*Aside to* JOSEPH SURFACE.] I! not for the world!—[*Exit* JOSEPH SURFACE.] Ah, Charles, if you associated more with your brother, one might indeed hope for your reformation. He is a man of sentiment. Well, there is nothing in the world so noble as a man of sentiment.

Chas. Surf. Psha! he is too moral by half; and so apprehensive of his good name, as he calls it, that I suppose he would as soon let a priest into his house as a wench.

Sir Pet. No, no,—come, come,—you wrong him. No, no! Joseph is no rake, but he is no such saint either, in that respect.—[*Aside.*] I have a great mind to tell him—we should have such a laugh at Joseph.

Chas. Surf. Oh, hang him! he's a very anchorite, a young hermit!

Sir Pet. Hark'ee—you must not abuse him: he may chance to hear of it again, I promise you.

Chas. Surf. Why, you won't tell him?

Sir Pet. No—but—this way.—[*Aside.*] Egad, I'll tell him.—[*Aloud.*] Hark'ee —have you a mind to have a good laugh at Joseph?

Chas. Surf. I should like it of all things.

Sir Pet. Then, i'faith, we will! I'll be quit with him for discovering me. He had a girl with him when I called. [*Whispers.*

Chas. Surf. What! Joseph? you jest.

Sir Pet. Hush!—a little French milliner—and the best of the jest is—she's in the room now.

Chas. Surf. The devil she is!

Sir Pet. Hush! I tell you. [*Points to the screen.*

Chas. Surf. Behind the screen! 'Slife, let's unveil her!

Sir Pet. No, no, he's coming:—you sha'n't, indeed!

Chas. Surf. Oh, egad, we'll have a peep at the little milliner!

Sir Pet. Not for the world!—Joseph will never forgive me.

Chas. Surf. I'll stand by you——

Sir Pet. Odds, here he is! [CHARLES SURFACE *throws down the screen.*

Re-enter JOSEPH SURFACE.

Chas. Surf. Lady Teazle, by all that's wonderful!

Sir Pet. Lady Teazle, by all that's damnable!

Chas. Surf. Sir Peter, this is one of the smartest French milliners I ever saw. Egad, you seem all to have been diverting yourselves here at hide and seek, and I don't see who is out of the secret. Shall I beg your ladyship to inform me? Not a word!—Brother, will you be pleased to explain this matter? What! is Morality dumb too?—Sir Peter, though I found you in the dark, perhaps you are not so now! All mute!—Well—though I can make nothing of the affair, I suppose you perfectly understand one another; so I'll leave you to yourselves.—[*Going.*] Brother, I'm sorry to find you have given that worthy man grounds for so much uneasiness.—Sir Peter! there's nothing in the world so noble as a man of sentiment! [*Exit.*

Jos. Surf. Sir Peter—notwithstanding—I confess—that appearances are against me—if you will afford me your patience—I make no doubt—but I shall explain every thing to your satisfaction.

Sir Pet. If you please, sir.

Jos. Surf. The fact is, sir, that Lady Teazle, knowing my pretensions to your ward Maria—I say, sir, Lady Teazle, being apprehensive of the jealousy of your temper—and knowing my friendship to the family—she, sir, I say—called here—in order that—I might explain these pretensions—but on your coming—being apprehensive—as I said—of your jealousy—she withdrew—and this, you may depend on it, is the whole truth of the matter.

Sir Pet. A very clear account, upon my word; and I dare swear the lady will vouch for every article of it.

Lady Teaz. For not one word of it, Sir Peter!

Sir Pet. How! don't you think it worth while to agree in the lie?

Lady Teaz. There is not one syllable of truth in what that gentleman has told you.

Sir Pet. I believe you, upon my soul, ma'am!

Jos. Surf. [*Aside to* LADY TEAZLE.] 'Sdeath, madam, will you betray me?

Lady Teaz. Good Mr. Hypocrite, by your leave, I'll speak for myself.

Sir Pet. Ay, let her alone, sir; you'll find she'll make out a better story than you, without prompting.

Lady Teaz. Hear me, Sir Peter!—I came here on no matter relating to your ward, and even ignorant of this gentleman's pretensions to her. But I came, seduced by his insidious arguments, at least to listen to his pretended passion, if not to sacrifice your honour to his baseness.

Sir Pet. Now, I believe, the truth is coming, indeed!

Jos. Surf. The woman's mad!

Lady Teaz. No, sir; she has recovered her senses, and your own arts have furnished her with the means.—Sir Peter, I do not expect you to credit me—but the tenderness you expressed for me, when I am sure you could not think I was a witness to it, has so penetrated to my heart, that had I left the place without the shame of this discovery, my future life should have spoken the sincerity of my gratitude. As for that smooth-tongued hypocrite, who would have seduced the wife of his too credulous friend, while he affected honourable addresses to his ward—I behold him now in a light so truly despicable, that I shall never again respect myself for having listened to him.   [*Exit.*

Jos. Surf. Notwithstanding all this, Sir Peter, Heaven knows——

Sir Pet. That you are a villain! and so I leave you to your conscience.

Jos. Surf. You are too rash, Sir Peter; you shall hear me. The man who shuts out conviction by refusing to——

Sir Pet. Oh, damn your sentiments!

[*Exeunt* SIR PETER *and* JOSEPH SURFACE, *talking.*

ACT V.

SCENE I.—*The Library in* JOSEPH SURFACE'S *House.*

Enter JOSEPH SURFACE *and* SERVANT.

Jos. Surf. Mr. Stanley! and why should you think I would see him? you must know he comes to ask something.

Ser. Sir, I should not have let him in, but that Mr. Rowley came to the door with him.

Jos. Surf. Psha! blockhead! to suppose that I should now be in a temper to receive visits from poor relations!—Well, why don't you show the fellow up?

Ser. I will, sir.—Why, sir, it was not my fault that Sir Peter discovered my lady——

Jos. Surf. Go, fool!—[*Exit* SERVANT.] Sure Fortune never played a man of my policy such a trick before! My character with Sir Peter, my hopes with Maria, destroyed in a moment! I'm in a rare humour to listen to other people's distresses! I sha'n't be able to bestow even a benevolent sentiment on Stanley.—So! here he comes, and Rowley with him. I must try to recover myself, and put a little charity into my face, however.   [*Exit.*

Enter SIR OLIVER SURFACE *and* ROWLEY.

Sir Oliv. What! does he avoid us? That was he, was it not?

Row. It was, sir. But I doubt you are come a little too abruptly. His nerves are so weak, that the sight of a poor relation may be too much for him. I should have gone first to break it to him.

Sir Oliv. Oh, plague of his nerves! Yet this is he whom Sir Peter extols as a man of the most benevolent way of thinking!

Row. As to his way of thinking, I cannot pretend to decide; for, to do him justice, he appears to have as much speculative benevolence as any private gentleman in the kingdom, though he is seldom so sensual as to indulge himself in the exercise of it.

Sir Oliv. Yet he has a string of charitable sentiments at his fingers' ends.

Row. Or, rather, at his tongue's end, Sir Oliver; for I believe there is no sentiment he has such faith in as that *Charity begins at home*.

Sir Oliv. And his, I presume, is of that domestic sort which never stirs abroad at all.

Row. I doubt you'll find it so;—but he's coming. I mustn't seem to interrupt you; and you know, immediately as you leave him, I come in to announce your arrival in your real character.

Sir Oliv. True; and afterwards you'll meet me at Sir Peter's.

Row. Without losing a moment.   [*Exit.*

Sir Oliv. I don't like the complaisance of his features.

Re-enter JOSEPH SURFACE.

Jos. Surf. Sir, I beg you ten thousand pardons for keeping you a moment waiting.—Mr. Stanley, I presume.

Sir Oliv. At your service.

Jos. Surf. Sir, I beg you will do me the honour to sit down—I entreat you, sir.

Sir Oliv. Dear sir—there's no occasion.—[*Aside.*] Too civil by half!

Jos. Surf. I have not the pleasure of knowing you, Mr. Stanley; but I am extremely happy to see you look so well. You were nearly related to my mother, I think, Mr. Stanley?

Sir Oliv. I was, sir; so nearly that my present poverty, I fear, may do discredit to her wealthy children, else I should not have presumed to trouble you.

Jos. Surf. Dear sir, there needs no apology;—he that is in distress, though a stranger, has a right to claim kindred with the wealthy. I am sure I wish I was one of that class, and had it in my power to offer you even a small relief.

Sir Oliv. If your uncle, Sir Oliver, were here, I should have a friend.

Jos. Surf. I wish he was, sir, with all my heart: you should not want an advocate with him, believe me, sir.

Sir Oliv. I should not need one—my distresses would recommend me. But I imagined his bounty would enable you to become the agent of his charity.

Jos. Surf. My dear sir, you were strangely misinformed. Sir Oliver is a worthy man, a very worthy man; but avarice, Mr. Stanley, is the vice of age. I will tell you, my good sir, in confidence, what he has done for me has been a mere nothing; though people, I know, have thought otherwise, and, for my part, I never chose to contradict the report.

Sir Oliv. What! has he never transmitted you bullion—rupees—pagodas?

Jos. Surf. Oh, dear sir, nothing of the kind! No, no; a few presents now and then—china, shawls, congou tea, avadavats, and Indian crackers—little more, believe me.

Sir Oliv. Here's gratitude for twelve thousand pounds!—Avadavats and Indian crackers!   [*Aside.*

Jos. Surf. Then, my dear sir, you have heard, I doubt not, of the extravagance of my brother: there are very few would credit what I have done for that unfortunate young man.

Sir Oliv. Not I, for one!   [*Aside.*

Jos. Surf. The sums I have lent him! Indeed I have been exceedingly to blame; it was an amiable weakness; however, I don't pretend to defend it—and now I feel it doubly culpable, since it has deprived me of the pleasure of serving you, Mr. Stanley, as my heart dictates.

Sir Oliv. [*Aside.*] Dissembler!—[*Aloud.*] Then, sir, you can't assist me?

Jos. Surf. At present, it grieves me to say, I cannot; but, whenever I have the ability, you may depend upon hearing from me.

Sir Oliv. I am extremely sorry——

Jos. Surf. Not more than I, believe me; to pity, without the power to relieve, is still more painful than to ask and be denied.

Sir Oliv. Kind sir, your most obedient humble servant.

Jos. Surf. You leave me deeply affected, Mr. Stanley.—William, be ready to open the door. [*Calls to* SERVANT.

Sir Oliv. Oh, dear sir, no ceremony.

Jos. Surf. Your very obedient.

Sir Oliv. Your most obsequious.

Jos. Surf. You may depend upon hearing from me, whenever I can be of service.

Sir Oliv. Sweet sir, you are too good!

Jos. Surf. In the meantime I wish you health and spirits.

Sir Oliv. Your ever grateful and perpetual humble servant.

Jos. Surf. Sir, yours as sincerely.

Sir Oliv. [*Aside.*] Now I am satisfied. [*Exit.*

Jos. Surf. This is one bad effect of a good character; it invites application from the unfortunate, and there needs no small degree of address to gain the reputation of benevolence without incurring the expense. The silver ore of pure charity is an expensive article in the catalogue of a man's good qualities; whereas the sentimental French plate I use instead of it makes just as good a show, and pays no tax.

Re-enter ROWLEY.

Row. Mr. Surface, your servant: I was apprehensive of interrupting you, though my business demands immediate attention, as this note will inform you.

Jos. Surf. Always happy to see Mr. Rowley,—a rascal.—[*Aside. Reads the letter.*] Sir Oliver Surface!—My uncle arrived!

Row. He is, indeed: we have just parted—quite well, after a speedy voyage, and impatient to embrace his worthy nephew.

Jos. Surf. I am astonished!—William! stop Mr. Stanley, if he's not gone. [*Calls to* SERVANT.

Row. Oh! he's out of reach, I believe.

Jos. Surf. Why did you not let me know this when you came in together?

Row. I thought you had particular business. But I must be gone to inform your brother, and appoint him here to meet your uncle. He will be with you in a quarter of an hour.

Jos. Surf. So he says. Well, I am strangely overjoyed at his coming.—[*Aside.*] Never, to be sure, was any thing so damned unlucky!

Row. You will be delighted to see how well he looks.

Jos. Surf. Oh! I'm overjoyed to hear it.—[*Aside.*] Just at this time!

Row. I'll tell him how impatiently you expect him.

Jos. Surf. Do, do; pray give my best duty and affection. Indeed, I cannot express the sensations I feel at the thought of seeing him.—[*Exit* ROWLEY.] Certainly his coming just at this time is the cruellest piece of ill fortune.

[*Exit.*

SCENE II.—*A Room in* SIR PETER TEAZLE'S *House.*

Enter MRS. CANDOUR *and* MAID.

Maid. Indeed, ma'am, my lady will see nobody at present.

Mrs. Can. Did you tell her it was her friend Mrs. Candour?

Maid. Yes, ma'am; but she begs you will excuse her.

Mrs. Can. Do go again; I shall be glad to see her, if it be only for a moment, for I am sure she must be in great distress.—[*Exit* MAID.] Dear heart, how provoking! I'm not mistress of half the circumstances! We shall have the whole affair in the newspapers, with the names of the parties at length, before I have dropped the story at a dozen houses.

Enter SIR BENJAMIN BACKBITE.

Oh, dear Sir Benjamin! you have heard, I suppose——

Sir Ben. Of Lady Teazle and Mr. Surface——

Mrs. Can. And Sir Peter's discovery——

Sir Ben. Oh, the strangest piece of business, to be sure!

Mrs. Can. Well, I never was so surprised in my life. I am so sorry for all parties, indeed.

Sir Ben. Now, I don't pity Sir Peter at all: he was so extravagantly partial to Mr. Surface.

Mrs. Can. Mr. Surface! Why, 'twas with Charles Lady Teazle was detected.

Sir Ben. No, no, I tell you: Mr. Surface is the gallant.

Mrs. Can. No such thing! Charles is the man. 'Twas Mr. Surface brought Sir Peter on purpose to discover them.

Sir Ben. I tell you I had it from one——

Mrs. Can. And I have it from one——

Sir Ben. Who had it from one, who had it——

Mrs. Can. From one immediately. But here comes Lady Sneerwell; perhaps she knows the whole affair.

Enter LADY SNEERWELL.

Lady Sneer. So, my dear Mrs. Candour, here's a sad affair of our friend Lady Teazle!

Mrs. Can. Ay, my dear friend, who would have thought——

Lady Sneer. Well, there is no trusting appearances; though, indeed, she was always too lively for me.

Mrs. Can. To be sure, her manners were a little too free; but then she was so young!

Lady Sneer. And had, indeed, some good qualities.

Mrs. Can. So she had, indeed. But have you heard the particulars?

Lady Sneer. No; but every body says that Mr. Surface——

Sir Ben. Ay, there; I told you Mr. Surface was the man.

Mrs. Can. No, no: indeed the assignation was with Charles.

Lady Sneer. With Charles! You alarm me, Mrs. Candour!

Mrs. Can. Yes, yes; he was the lover. Mr. Surface, to do him justice, was only the informer.

Sir Ben. Well, I'll not dispute with you, Mrs. Candour; but, be it which it may, I hope that Sir Peter's wound will not——

Mrs. Can. Sir Peter's wound! Oh, mercy! I didn't hear a word of their fighting.

Lady Sneer. Nor I, a syllable.

Sir Ben. No! what, no mention of the duel?

Mrs. Can. Not a word.

Sir Ben. Oh, yes: they fought before they left the room.

Lady Sneer. Pray, let us hear.

Mrs. Can. Ay, do oblige us with the duel.

Sir Ben. "Sir," says Sir Peter, immediately after the discovery, "*you are a most ungrateful fellow.*"

Mrs. Can. Ay, to Charles——

Sir Ben. No, no—to Mr. Surface—*a most ungrateful fellow; and old as I am, sir,* says he, *I insist on immediate satisfaction.*

Mrs. Can. Ay, that must have been to Charles; for 'tis very unlikely Mr. Surface should fight in his own house.

Sir Ben. Gad's life, ma'am, not at all—*giving me immediate satisfaction.*—On this, ma'am, Lady Teazle, seeing Sir Peter in such danger, ran out of the room in strong hysterics, and Charles after her, calling out for hartshorn and water; then, madam, they began to fight with swords——

Enter CRABTREE.

Crab. With pistols, nephew—pistols! I have it from undoubted authority.

Mrs. Can. Oh, Mr. Crabtree, then it is all true!

Crab. Too true, indeed, madam, and Sir Peter is dangerously wounded——

Sir Ben. By a thrust in segoon quite through his left side——

Crab. By a bullet lodged in the thorax.

Mrs. Can. Mercy on me! Poor Sir Peter!

Crab. Yes, madam; though Charles would have avoided the matter, if he could.

Mrs. Can. I told you who it was; I knew Charles was the person.

Sir Ben. My uncle, I see, knows nothing of the matter.

Crab. But Sir Peter taxed him with the basest ingratitude——

Sir Ben. That I told you, you know——

Crab. Do, nephew, let me speak!—and insisted on immediate——

Sir Ben. Just as I said——

Crab. Odds life, nephew, allow others to know something too! A pair of pistols lay on the bureau (for Mr. Surface, it seems, had come home the night before late from Salthill, where he had been to see the Montem with a friend, who has a son at Eton), so, unluckily, the pistols were left charged.

Sir Ben. I heard nothing of this.

Crab. Sir Peter forced Charles to take one, and they fired, it seems, pretty nearly together. Charles's shot took effect, as I tell you, and Sir Peter's missed; but, what is very extraordinary, the ball struck against a little bronze Shakspeare that stood over the fire-place, grazed out of the window at a right angle, and wounded the postman, who was just coming to the door with a double letter from Northamptonshire.

Sir Ben. My uncle's account is more circumstantial, I confess; but I believe mine is the true one, for all that.

Lady Sneer. [*Aside.*] I am more interested in this affair than they imagine, and must have better information. [*Exit.*

Sir Ben. Ah! Lady Sneerwell's alarm is very easily accounted for.

Crab. Yes, yes, they certainly do say—but that's neither here nor there.

Mrs. Can. But, pray, where is Sir Peter at present?

Crab. Oh! they brought him home, and he is now in the house, though the servants are ordered to deny him.

Mrs. Can. I believe so, and Lady Teazle, I suppose, attending him.

Crab. Yes, yes; and I saw one of the faculty enter just before me.

Sir Ben. Hey! who comes here?

Crab. Oh, this is he: the physician, depend on 't.

Mrs. Can. Oh, certainly! it must be the physician; and now we shall know.

Enter Sir Oliver Surface.

Crab. Well, doctor, what hopes?

Mrs. Can. Ay, doctor, how's your patient?

Sir Ben. Now, doctor, isn't it a wound with a small-sword?

Crab. A bullet lodged in the thorax, for a hundred!

Sir Oliv. Doctor! a wound with a small-sword! and a bullet in the thorax! —Oons! are you mad, good people?

Sir Ben. Perhaps, sir, you are not a doctor?

Sir Oliv. Truly, I am to thank you for my degree, if I am.

Crab. Only a friend of Sir Peter's, then, I presume. But, sir, you must have heard of his accident?

Sir Oliv. Not a word!

Crab. Not of his being dangerously wounded?

Sir Oliv. The devil he is!

Sir Ben. Run through the body——

Crab. Shot in the breast——

Sir Ben. By one Mr. Surface——

Crab. Ay, the younger.

Sir Oliv. Hey! what the plague! you seem to differ strangely in your accounts: however, you agree that Sir Peter is dangerously wounded.

Sir Ben. Oh, yes, we agree in that.

Crab. Yes, yes, I believe there can be no doubt of that.

Sir Oliv. Then, upon my word, for a person in that situation, he is the most imprudent man alive; for here he comes, walking as if nothing at all was the matter.

Enter Sir Peter Teazle.

Odds heart, Sir Peter! you are come in good time, I promise you; for we had just given you over!

Sir Ben. [*Aside to* Crabtree.] Egad, uncle, this is the most sudden recovery!

Sir Oliv. Why, man! what do you out of bed with a small-sword through your body, and a bullet lodged in your thorax?

Sir Pet. A small-sword and a bullet!

Sir Oliv. Ay; these gentlemen would have killed you without law or physic, and wanted to dub me a doctor, to make me an accomplice.

Sir Pet. Why, what is all this?

Sir Ben. We rejoice, Sir Peter, that the story of the duel is not true, and are sincerely sorry for your other misfortune.

Sir Pet. So, so; all over the town already!   [*Aside.*

Crab. Though, Sir Peter, you were certainly vastly to blame to marry at your years.

Sir Pet. Sir, what business is that of yours?

Mrs. Can. Though, indeed, as Sir Peter made so good a husband, he's very much to be pitied.

Sir Pet. Plague on your pity, ma'am! I desire none of it.

Sir Ben. However, Sir Peter, you must not mind the laughing and jests you will meet with on the occasion.

Sir Pet. Sir, sir! I desire to be master in my own house.

Crab. 'Tis no uncommon case, that's one comfort.

Sir Pet. I insist on being left to myself: without ceremony, I insist on your leaving my house directly!

Mrs. Can. Well, well, we are going; and depend on 't, we'll make the best report of it we can.   [*Exit.*

Sir Pet. Leave my house!

Crab. And tell how hardly you've been treated.   [*Exit.*

Sir Pet. Leave my house!

Sir Ben. And how patiently you bear it.   [*Exit.*

Sir Pet. Fiends! vipers! furies! Oh! that their own venom would choke them!

Sir Oliv. They are very provoking indeed, Sir Peter.

Enter Rowley.

Row. I heard high words: what has ruffled you, sir?

Sir Pet. Psha! what signifies asking? Do I ever pass a day without my vexations?

Row. Well, I'm not inquisitive.

Sir Oliv. Well, Sir Peter, I have seen both my nephews in the manner we proposed.

Sir Pet. A precious couple they are!

Row. Yes, and Sir Oliver is convinced that your judgment was right, Sir Peter.

Sir Oliv. Yes, I find Joseph is indeed the man, after all.

Row. Ay, as Sir Peter says, he is a man of sentiment.

Sir Oliv. And acts up to the sentiments he professes.

Row. It certainly is edification to hear him talk.

Sir Oliv. Oh, he's a model for the young men of the age!—But how's this, Sir Peter? you don't join us in your friend Joseph's praise, as I expected.

Sir Pet. Sir Oliver, we live in a damned wicked world, and the fewer we praise the better.

Row. What! do you say so, Sir Peter, who were never mistaken in your life?

Sir Pet. Psha! plague on you both! I see by your sneering you have heard the whole affair. I shall go mad among you!

Row. Then, to fret you no longer, Sir Peter, we are indeed acquainted with it all. I met Lady Teazle coming from Mr. Surface's so humbled, that she deigned to request me to be her advocate with you.

Sir Pet. And does Sir Oliver know all this?

Sir Oliv. Every circumstance.

Sir Pet. What of the closet and the screen, hey?

Sir Oliv. Yes, yes, and the little French milliner. Oh, I have been vastly diverted with the story! ha! ha! ha!

Sir Pet. 'Twas very pleasant.

Sir Oliv. I never laughed more in my life, I assure you: ah! ah! ah!

Sir Pet. Oh, vastly diverting! ha! ha! ha!

Row. To be sure, Joseph with his sentiments! ha! ha! ha.

Sir Pet. Yes, yes, his sentiments! ha! ha! ha! Hypocritical villain!

Sir Oliv. Ay, and that rogue Charles to pull Sir Peter out of the closet: ha! ha! ha!

Sir Pet. Ha! ha! 'twas devilish entertaining, to be sure!

Sir Oliv. Ha! ha! ha! Egad, Sir Peter, I should like to have seen your face when the screen was thrown down: ha! ha!

Sir Pet. Yes, yes, my face when the screen was thrown down: ha! ha! ha! Oh, I must never show my head again!

Sir Oliv. But come, come, it isn't fair to laugh at you neither, my old friend; though, upon my soul, I can't help it.

Sir Pet. Oh, pray don't restrain your mirth on my account: it does not hurt me at all! I laugh at the whole affair myself. Yes, yes, I think being a standing jest for all one's acquaintance a very happy situation. Oh, yes, and then of a morning to read the paragraphs about Mr. S——, Lady T——, and Sir P——, will be so entertaining!

Row. Without affectation, Sir Peter, you may despise the ridicule of fools.

But I see Lady Teazle going towards the next room; I am sure you must desire a reconciliation as earnestly as she does.

Sir Oliv. Perhaps my being here prevents her coming to you. Well, I'll leave honest Rowley to mediate between you; but he must bring you all presently to Mr. Surface's, where I am now returning, if not to reclaim a libertine, at least to expose hypocrisy.

Sir Pet. Ah, I'll be present at your discovering yourself there with all my heart; though 'tis a vile unlucky place for discoveries.

Row. We'll follow. [*Exit* SIR OLIVER SURFACE.

Sir Pet. She is not coming here, you see, Rowley.

Row. No, but she has left the door of that room open, you perceive. See, she is in tears.

Sir Pet. Certainly a little mortification appears very becoming in a wife. Don't you think it will do her good to let her pine a little?

Row. Oh, this is ungenerous in you!

Sir Pet. Well, I know not what to think. You remember the letter I found of hers evidently intended for Charles?

Row. A mere forgery, Sir Peter! laid in your way on purpose. This is one of the points which I intend Snake shall give you conviction of.

Sir Pet. I wish I were once satisfied of that. She looks this way. What a remarkably elegant turn of the head she has. Rowley, I'll go to her.

Row. Certainly.

Sir Pet. Though, when it is known that we are reconciled, people will laugh at me ten times more.

Row. Let them laugh, and retort their malice only by showing them you are happy in spite of it.

Sir Pet. I'faith, so I will! and, if I'm not mistaken, we may yet be the happiest couple in the country.

Row. Nay, Sir Peter, he who once lays aside suspicion——

Sir Pet. Hold, Master Rowley! if you have any regard for me, never let me hear you utter any thing like a sentiment: I have had enough of them to serve me the rest of my life. [*Exeunt.*

SCENE III.—*The Library in* JOSEPH SURFACE'S *House.*

Enter JOSEPH SURFACE *and* LADY SNEERWELL.

Lady Sneer. Impossible! Will not Sir Peter immediately be reconciled to Charles, and of course no longer oppose his union with Maria? The thought is distraction to me.

Jos. Surf. Can passion furnish a remedy?

Lady Sneer. No, nor cunning either. Oh, I was a fool, an idiot, to league with such a blunderer!

Jos. Surf. Sure, Lady Sneerwell, I am the greatest sufferer; yet you see I bear the accident with calmness.

Lady Sneer. Because the disappointment doesn't reach your heart; your interest only attached you to Maria. Had you felt for her what I have for that ungrateful libertine, neither your temper nor hypocrisy could prevent your showing the sharpness of your vexation.

Jos. Surf. But why should your reproaches fall on me for this disappointment?

Lady Sneer. Are you not the cause of it? Had you not a sufficient field for your roguery in imposing upon Sir Peter, and supplanting your brother, but you must endeavour to seduce his wife? I hate such an avarice of crimes; 'tis an unfair monopoly, and never prospers.

Jos. Surf. Well, I admit I have been to blame. I confess I deviated from the direct road of wrong, but I don't think we're so totally defeated neither.

Lady Sneer. No!

Jos. Surf. You tell me you have made a trial of Snake since we met, and that you still believe him faithful to us?

Lady Sneer. I do believe so.

Jos. Surf. And that he has undertaken, should it be necessary, to swear and prove, that Charles is at this time contracted by vows and honour to your ladyship, which some of his former letters to you will serve to support?

Lady Sneer. This, indeed, might have assisted.

Jos. Surf. Come, come; it is not too late yet.—[*Knocking at the door.*] But hark! this is probably my uncle, Sir Oliver: retire to that room; we'll consult farther when he is gone.

Lady Sneer. Well, but if he should find you out too?

Jos. Surf. Oh, I have no fear of that. Sir Peter will hold his tongue for his own credit's sake—and you may depend on it I shall soon discover Sir Oliver's weak side!

Lady Sneer. I have no diffidence of your abilities: only be constant to one roguery at a time.

Jos. Surf. I will, I will!—[*Exit* LADY SNEERWELL.] So! 'tis confounded hard, after such bad fortune, to be baited by one's confederate in evil. Well, at all events, my character is so much better than Charles's, that I certainly—hey! —what—this is not Sir Oliver, but old Stanley again. Plague on't that he should return to tease me just now! I shall have Sir Oliver come and find him here—and——

Enter SIR OLIVER SURFACE.

Gad's life, Mr. Stanley, why have you come back to plague me at this time? You must not stay now, upon my word.

Sir Oliv. Sir, I hear your uncle Oliver is expected here, and though he has been so penurious to you, I'll try what he'll do for me.

Jos. Surf. Sir, 'tis impossible for you to stay now, so I must beg——Come any other time, and I promise you, you shall be assisted.

Sir Oliv. No: Sir Oliver and I must be acquainted.

Jos. Surf. Zounds, sir! then I insist on your quitting the room directly.

Sir Oliv. Nay, sir——

Jos. Surf. Sir, I insist on't!—Here, William! show this gentleman out. Since you compel me, sir, not one moment—this is such insolence.

[*Going to push him out.*

Enter CHARLES SURFACE.

Chas. Surf. Heyday! what's the matter now? What the devil, have you got hold of my little broker here? Zounds, brother, don't hurt little Premium. What's the matter, my little fellow?

Jos. Surf. So! he has been with you too, has he?

Chas. Surf. To be sure, he has. Why, he's as honest a little——But sure, Joseph, you have not been borrowing money too, have you?

Jos. Surf. Borrowing! no! But, brother, you know we expect Sir Oliver here every——

Chas. Surf. O Gad, that's true! Noll mustn't find the little broker here, to be sure.

Jos. Surf. Yet Mr. Stanley insists——

Chas. Surf. Stanley! why his name's Premium.

Jos. Surf. No, sir, Stanley.

Chas. Surf. No, no, Premium.

Jos. Surf. Well, no matter which—but——

Chas. Surf. Ay, ay, Stanley or Premium, 'tis the same thing, as you say; for I suppose he goes by half a hundred names, besides A. B. at the coffee-house. [*Knocking.*

Jos. Surf. 'Sdeath! here's Sir Oliver at the door.—Now I beg, Mr. Stanley——

Chas. Surf. Ay, ay, and I beg, Mr. Premium——

Sir Oliv. Gentlemen——

Jos. Surf. Sir, by Heaven you shall go!

Chas. Surf. Ay, out with him, certainly!

Sir Oliv. This violence——

Jos. Surf. Sir, 'tis your own fault.

Chas. Surf. Out with him, to be sure. [*Both forcing* SIR OLIVER *out.*

Enter SIR PETER *and* LADY TEAZLE, MARIA, *and* ROWLEY.

Sir Pet. My old friend, Sir Oliver—hey! What in the name of wonder—here are dutiful nephews—assault their uncle at first visit!

Lady Teaz. Indeed, Sir Oliver, 'twas well we came in to rescue you.

Row. Truly it was; for I perceive, Sir Oliver, the character of old Stanley was no protection to you.

Sir Oliv. Nor of Premium either: the necessities of the former could not extort a shilling from that benevolent gentleman; and with the other I stood a chance of faring worse than my ancestors, and being knocked down without being bid for.

Jos. Surf. Charles!

Chas. Surf. Joseph!

Jos. Surf. 'Tis now complete!

Chas. Surf. Very.

Sir Oliv. Sir Peter, my friend, and Rowley too—look on that elder nephew of mine. You know what he has already received from my bounty; and you also know how gladly I would have regarded half my fortune as held in trust for him: judge then my disappointment in discovering him to be destitute of truth, charity, and gratitude!

Sir Pet. Sir Oliver, I should be more surprised at this declaration, if I had not myself found him to be mean, treacherous, and hypocritical.

Lady Teaz. And if the gentleman pleads not guilty to these, pray let him call me to his character.

Sir Pet. Then, I believe, we need add no more: if he knows himself, he will consider it as the most perfect punishment, that he is known to the world.

Chas. Surf. If they talk this way to Honesty, what will they say to me, by and by?   [*Aside.*

[SIR PETER, LADY TEAZLE, *and* MARIA *retire.*

Sir Oliv. As for that prodigal, his brother, there——

Chas. Surf. Ay, now comes my turn: the damned family pictures will ruin me!   [*Aside.*

Jos. Surf. Sir Oliver—uncle, will you honour me with a hearing?

Chas. Surf. Now, if Joseph would make one of his long speeches, I might recollect myself a little.   [*Aside.*

Sir Oliv. I suppose you would undertake to justify yourself?

[*To* JOSEPH SURFACE.

Jos. Surf. I trust I could.

Sir Oliv. [*To* CHARLES SURFACE.] Well, sir!—and you could justify yourself too, I suppose?

Chas. Surf. Not that I know of, Sir Oliver.

Sir Oliv. What!—Little Premium has been let too much into the secret, I suppose?

Chas. Surf. True, sir; but they were family secrets, and should not be mentioned again, you know.

Row. Come, Sir Oliver, I know you cannot speak of Charles's follies with anger.

Sir Oliv. Odds heart, no more I can; nor with gravity either. Sir Peter, do you know the rogue bargained with me for all his ancestors; sold me judges and generals by the foot, and maiden aunts as cheap as broken china.

Chas. Surf. To be sure, Sir Oliver, I did make a little free with the family canvas, that's the truth on't. My ancestors may rise in judgment against me, there's no denying it; but believe me sincere when I tell you—and upon my soul I would not say so if I was not—that if I do not appear mortified at the exposure of my follies, it is because I feel at this moment the warmest satisfaction in seeing you, my liberal benefactor.

Sir Oliv. Charles, I believe you. Give me your hand again: the ill-looking little fellow over the settee has made your peace.

Chas. Surf. Then, sir, my gratitude to the original is still increased.

Lady Teaz. [*Advancing.*] Yet, I believe, Sir Oliver, here is one whom Charles is still more anxious to be reconciled to.   [*Pointing to* MARIA.

Sir Oliv. Oh, I have heard of his attachment there; and, with the young lady's pardon, if I construe right—that blush——

Sir Pet. Well, child, speak your sentiments!

Mar. Sir, I have little to say, but that I shall rejoice to hear that he is happy; for me, whatever claim I had to his attention, I willingly resign to one who has a better title.

Chas. Surf. How, Maria!

Sir Pet. Heyday! what's the mystery now? While he appeared an incorrigible rake, you would give your hand to no one else; and now that he is likely to reform I'll warrant you won't have him!

Mar. His own heart and Lady Sneerwell know the cause.

Chas. Surf. Lady Sneerwell!

Jos. Surf. Brother, it is with great concern I am obliged to speak on this point, but my regard to justice compels me, and Lady Sneerwell's injuries can no longer be concealed.   [*Opens the door.*

Enter LADY SNEERWELL.

Sir Pet. So! another French milliner! Egad, he has one in every room in the house, I suppose!

Lady Sneer. Ungrateful Charles! Well may you be surprised, and feel for the indelicate situation your perfidy has forced me into.

Chas. Surf. Pray, uncle, is this another plot of yours? For, as I have life, I don't understand it.

Jos. Surf. I believe, sir, there is but the evidence of one person more necessary to make it extremely clear.

Sir Pet. And that person, I imagine, is Mr. Snake.—Rowley, you were perfectly right to bring him with us, and pray let him appear.

Row. Walk in, Mr. Snake.

Enter SNAKE.

I thought his testimony might be wanted: however, it happens unluckily, that he comes to confront Lady Sneerwell, not to support her.

Lady Sneer. A villain! Treacherous to me at last! Speak, fellow, have you too conspired against me!

Snake. I beg your ladyship ten thousand pardons: you paid me extremely liberally for the lie in question; but I unfortunately have been offered double to speak the truth.

Sir Pet. Plot and counter-plot, egad! I wish your ladyship joy of your negociation.

Lady Sneer. The torments of shame and disappointment on you all!
          [*Going.*

Lady Teaz. Hold, Lady Sneerwell—before you go, let me thank you for the trouble you and that gentleman have taken, in writing letters from me to Charles, and answering them yourself; and let me also request you to make my respects to the scandalous college, of which you are president, and inform them, that Lady Teazle, licentiate, begs leave to return the diploma they granted her, as she leaves off practice, and kills characters no longer.

Lady Sneer. You too, madam!—provoking—insolent! May your husband live these fifty years! [*Exit.*

Sir Pet. Oons! what a fury!

Lady Teaz. A malicious creature, indeed!

Sir Pet. What! not for her last wish?

Lady Teaz. Oh, no!

Sir Oliv. Well, sir, and what have you to say now?

Jos. Surf. Sir, I am so confounded, to find that Lady Sneerwell could be guilty of suborning Mr. Snake in this manner, to impose on us all, that I know not what to say: however, lest her revengeful spirit should prompt her to injure my brother, I had certainly better follow her directly. For the man who attempts to—— [*Exit.*

Sir Pet. Moral to the last!

Sir Oliv. Ay, and marry her, Joseph, if you can. Oil and vinegar!—egad you'll do very well together.

Row. I believe we have no more occasion for Mr. Snake at present?

Snake. Before I go, I beg pardon once for all, for whatever uneasiness I have been the humble instrument of causing to the parties present.

Sir Pet. Well, well, you have made atonement by a good deed at last.

Snake. But I must request of the company, that it shall never be known.

Sir Pet. Hey! what the plague! are you ashamed of having done a right thing once in your life?

Snake. Ah, sir, consider—I live by the badness of my character; and, if it were once known that I had been betrayed into an honest action, I should lose every friend I have in the world.

Sir Oliv. Well, well—we'll not traduce you by saying any thing in your praise, never fear. [*Exit* SNAKE.

Sir Pet. There's a precious rogue!

Lady Teaz. See, Sir Oliver, there needs no persuasion now to reconcile your nephew and Maria.

Sir Oliv. Ay, ay, that's as it should be, and, egad, we'll have the wedding to-morrow morning.

Chas. Surf. Thank you, dear uncle.

Sir Pet. What, you rogue! don't you ask the girl's consent first?

Chas. Surf. Oh, I have done that a long time—a minute ago—and she has looked yes.

Mar. For shame, Charles!—I protest, Sir Peter, there has not been a word——

Sir Oliv. Well, then, the fewer the better; may your love for each other never know abatement.

Sir Pet. And may you live as happily together as Lady Teazle and I intend to do!

Chas. Surf. Rowley, my old friend, I am sure you congratulate me; and I suspect that I owe you much.

Sir Oliv. You do, indeed, Charles.

Sir Pet. Ay, honest Rowley always said you would reform.

Chas. Surf. Why, as to reforming, Sir Peter, I'll make no promises, and that I take to be a proof that I intend to set about it. But here shall be my monitor—my gentle guide.—Ah! can I leave the virtuous path those eyes illumine?

> Though thou, dear maid, shouldst waive thy beauty's sway,
> Thou still must rule, because I will obey:
> An humble fugitive from Folly view,
> No sanctuary near but Love and you: [*To the audience.*
> You can, indeed, each anxious fear remove,
> For even Scandal dies, if you approve.   [*Exeunt omnes.*

EPILOGUE.

BY MR. COLMAN.

SPOKEN BY LADY TEAZLE.

> I, WHO was late so volatile and gay,
> Like a trade-wind must now blow all one way,
> Bend all my cares, my studies, and my vows,
> To one dull rusty weathercock—my spouse!
> So wills our virtuous bard—the motley Bayes
> Of crying epilogues and laughing plays!
> Old bachelors, who marry smart young wives,
> Learn from our play to regulate your lives:
> Each bring his dear to town, all faults upon her—
> London will prove the very source of honour.
> Plunged fairly in, like a cold bath it serves,
> When principles relax, to brace the nerves:
> Such is my case; and yet I must deplore
> That the gay dream of dissipation's o'er.
> And say, ye fair! was ever lively wife,
> Born with a genius for the highest life,
> Like me untimely blasted in her bloom,
> Like me condemn'd to such a dismal doom?
> Save money—when I just knew how to waste it!
> Leave London—just as I began to taste it!
>   Must I then watch the early crowing cock,
> The melancholy ticking of a clock;

In a lone rustic hall for ever pounded,
With dogs, cats, rats, and squalling brats surrounded.
With humble curate can I now retire,
(While good Sir Peter boozes with the squire),
And at backgammon mortify my soul,
That pants for loo, or flutters at a vole?
Seven's the main! Dear sound that must expire,
Lost at hot cockles round a Christmas fire;
The transient hour of fashion too soon spent,
Farewell the tranquil mind, farewell content!
Farewell the plumèd head, the cushion'd tête,
That takes the cushion from its proper seat!
That spirit-stirring drum!—card drums I mean,
Spadille—odd trick—pam—basto—king and queen!
And you, ye knockers, that, with brazen throat,
The welcome visitors' approach denote;
Farewell all quality of high renown,
Pride, pomp, and circumstance of glorious town!
Farewell! your revels I partake no more,
And Lady Teazle's occupation's o'er!
All this I told our bard; he smiled, and said 'twas clear,
I ought to play deep tragedy next year.
Meanwhile he drew wise morals from his play,
And in these solemn periods stalk'd away:—
"Bless'd were the fair like you; her faults who stopp'd
And closed her follies when the curtain dropp'd!
No more in vice or error to engage,
Or play the fool at large on life's great stage."

SONGS, VERSES, PROLOGUES AND EPILOGUES

The wit which pervades Restoration and Eighteenth Century comedy is well represented by the lyrics, prologues, and epilogues of many plays which cannot be included in this small volume. A few of them are presented here as further examples of the Comic Spirit which actually ruled Britannia while Charles II, James II, William and Mary, Anne, and the Georges were the nominal rulers.

J. G.

From LOVE IN A WOOD by William Wycherley (1641–1716)

The end of marriage now is liberty.
And two are bound—to set each other free.

From POLLY: AN OPERA (sequel to *The Beggar's Opera*)

by John Gay (1685–1732)

AIR

Woman's like the flatt'ring ocean,
   Who her pathless ways can find?
Every blast directs her motion;
   Now she's angry, now she's kind.
What a fool's the vent'rous lover,
   Whirl'd and toss'd by every wind!
Can the bark the port recover
   When the silly pilot's blind?

AIR

If husbands sit unsteady,
Most wives for freaks are ready.
   Neglect the rein,
   The steed again
Grows skittish, wild, and heady.

AIR

When gold is in hand,
  It gives us command;
It makes us lov'd and respected.
  'Tis now, as of yore,
  Wit and sense, when poor,
Are scorn'd, o'erlook'd, and neglected.
  Tho' peevish and old,
  If women have gold, ˙
They have youth, good-humour, and beauty:
  Among all mankind
  Without it we find
Nor love, nor favour, nor duty.

AIR

The sportsmen keep hawks, and their quarry they gain;
Thus the woodcock, the partridge, the pheasant is slain.
What care and expence for their hounds are employ'd!
Thus the fox, and the hare, and the stag are destroy'd.
The spaniel they cherish, whose flattering way
Can as well as their masters cringe, fawn and betray.
Thus stanch politicians, look all the world round,
Love the men who can serve as hawk, spaniel, or hound.

AIR

In pimps and politicians
  The genius is the same;
Both raise their own conditions
  On others' guilt and shame:
With a tongue well-tipt with lyes
Each the want of parts supplies,
And with a heart that's all disguise,
  Keeps his schemes unknown.
Seducing as the devil,
  They play the tempter's part,
And have, when most they're civil,
  Most mischief in their heart.
Each a secret commerce drives,
First corrupts and then connives,
And by his neighbours vices thrives,
  For they are all his own.

AIR

When kings by their huffing
   Have blown up a squabble,
All the charge and cuffing
   Light upon the rabble.
Thus when man and wife
   By their mutual snubbing,
Kindle civil strife,
   Servants get the drubbing.

AIR

   Brave boys, prepare.
Ah! cease, fond wife, to cry.
   For when the danger's near,
We've time enough to fly.
How can you be disgrac'd!
For wealth secures your fame.
The rich are always plac'd
Above the sense of shame.
Let honour spur the slave,
To fight for fighting's sake:
But even the rich are brave
When money is at stake.

AIR

How faultless does the nymph appear,
When her own hand the picture draws!
   But all others only smear
Her wrinkles, cracks, and flaws.
Self-flattery is our claim and right,
   Let men say what they will;
Sure we may set our good in sight,
   When neighbours set our ill.

AIR

The manners of the great affect:
   Stint not your pleasure:
If conscience had their genius checkt,
   How got they treasure?
The more in debt, run in debt the more,
   Careless who is undone:
Morals and honesty leave to the poor,
   As they do at London.

AIR

He that weds a beauty
  Soon will find her cloy;
When pleasure grows a duty
  Farewell love and joy:
He that weds for treasure
  (Though he hath a wife)
Hath chose one lasting pleasure
  In a married life.

From LOVE FOR LOVE by William Congreve (1670–1729)

SONG BY SCANDAL'S SINGER

A nymph and a swain to Apollo once prayed,
The swain had been jilted, the nymph been betrayed:
Their intent was to try if his oracle knew
E'er a nymph that was chaste, or a swain that was true.

Apollo was mute, and had like t'have been posed,
But sagely at length he this secret disclosed:
"He alone won't betray in whom none will confide:
And the nymph may be chaste that has never been tried."

BEN'S SAILOR SONG

A soldier and a sailor,
A tinker and a tailor,
Had once a doubtful strife, sir,
To make a maid a wife, sir,
  Whose name was buxom Joan.
For now the time was ended,
When she no more intended
To lick her lips at men, sir,
And gnaw the sheets in vain, sir,
  And lie o' nights alone.

The soldier swore like thunder,
He loved her more than plunder;
And showed her many a scar, sir,
That he had brought from far, sir,
  With fighting for her sake.

The tailor thought to please her,
With offering her his measure.
The tinker too with mettle,
Said he could mend her kettle.
    And stop up every leak.

But while these three were prating,
The sailor slily waiting,
Thought if it came about, sir,
That they should all fall out, sir,
    He then might play his part.
And just e'en as he meant, sir,
To loggerheads they went, sir,
And then he let fly at her
A shot 'twixt wind and water,
    That won this fair maid's heart.

SONG FOR VALENTINE

I tell thee, Charmion, could I time retrieve,
And could again begin to love and live,
To you I should my earliest offering give;

I know, my eyes would lead my heart to you,
And I should all my vows and oaths renew;
But, to be plain, I never would be true.

For by our weak and weary truth I find,
Love hates to centre in a point assigned,
But runs with joy the circle of the mind:

Then never let us chain what should be free,
But for relief of either sex agree:
Since women love to change, and so do we.

From THE DOUBLE DEALER by William Congreve (1670–1729)

SONG BY MUSICIANS

Cynthia frowns whene'er I woo her,
Yet she's vexed if I give over;
Much she fears I should undo her,
But much more to lose her lover;
Thus in doubting she refuses:
And not winning, thus she loses.

Prithee, Cynthia, look behind you,
Age and wrinkles will o'ertake you;
Then, too late, desire will find you,
When the power must forsake you:
Think, O think, o' th' sad condition,
To be past, yet wish fruition!

LORD FROTH'S SONG

Ancient Phillis has young graces,
    'Tis a strange thing, but a true one:
        Shall I tell you how?
She herself makes her own faces,
    And each morning wears a new one;
        Where's the wonder now!

From THE RELAPSE by Sir John Vanbrugh (1664–1726)

A SONG

I

I smile at Love and all its arts,
    The charming Cynthia cried:
Take heed, for Love has piercing darts,
    A wounded swain replied.
Once free and blest as you are now,
    I trifled with his charms,
I pointed at his little bow,
    And sported with his arms:
Till urged too far, Revenge! he cries,
    A fatal shaft he drew,
It took its passage through your eyes,
    And to my heart it flew.

II

To tear it thence I tried in vain,
    To strive, I quickly found,
Was only to increase the pain,
    And to enlarge the wound.
Ah! much too well, I fear, you know
    What pain I'm to endure,
Since what your eyes alone could do,
    Your heart alone can cure.

And that (grant heaven I may mistake!)
   I doubt is doomed to bear
A burden for another's sake,
   Who ill rewards its care.

From THE BEAUX' STRATAGEM by George Farquhar
(1678–1707)

SONG

A trifling song you shall hear,
Begun with a trifle and ended:
All trifling people draw near,
And I shall be nobly attended.

Were it not for trifles, a few,
That lately have come into play;
The men would want something to do,
And the women want something to say.

What makes men trifle in dressing?
Because the ladies (they know)
Admire, by often possessing,
That eminent trifle, a beau.

When the lover his moments has trifled,
The trifle of trifles to gain:
No sooner the virgin is rifled,
But a trifle shall part 'em again.

What mortal man would be able
At White's half an hour to sit?
Or who could bear a tea-table,
Without talking of trifles for wit?

The court is from trifles secure,
Gold keys are no trifles, we see:
White rods are no trifles, I'm sure,
Whatever their bearers may be.

But if you will go to the place,
Where trifles abundantly breed,
The levee will show you His Grace
Makes promises trifles indeed.

A coach with six footmen behind,
I count neither trifle nor sin:
But, ye gods! how oft do we find
A scandalous trifle within.

A flask of champagne, people think it
A trifle, or something as bad:
But if you'll contrive how to drink it,
You'll find it no trifle, egad!

A parson's a trifle at sea,
A widow's a trifle in sorrow:
A peace is a trifle to-day,
Who knows what may happen to-morrow!

A black coat a trifle may cloak,
Or to hide it, the red may endeavor:
But if once the army is broke,
We shall have more trifles than ever.

The stage is a trifle, they say,
The reason, pray carry along,
Because at every new play,
The house they with trifles so throng.

But with people's malice to trifle,
And to set us all on a foot:
The author of this is a trifle,
And his song is a trifle to boot.

From SHE STOOPS TO CONQUER by Oliver Goldsmith
(1730–1774)

PROLOGUE

Excuse *me, Sirs, I pray—I can't yet speak—*
I'm crying now—and have been all the week!
'Tis not alone this mourning suit, *good masters;*
I've that within—for which there are no plaisters!
Pray wou'd you know the reason why I'm crying?
The Comic muse, long sick, is now a dying!
And if she goes, my tears will never stop;
For as a play'r, I can't squeeze out one drop:
I am undone, that's all—shall lose my bread—
I'd rather, but that's nothing—lose my head.

When the sweet maid is laid upon the bier,
Shuter *and* I *shall be chief mourners here.*
To her *a mawkish drab of spurious breed,*
Who deals in sentimentals *will succeed!*
Poor Ned *and* I *are dead to all intents,*
We can as soon speak Greek *as* sentiments!
Both nervous grown, to keep our spirits up,
We now and then take down a hearty cup.
What shall we do?—If Comedy forsake us!
They'll turn us out, and no one else will take us,
But why can't I be moral?—Let me try—
My heart thus pressing—fix'd my face and eye—
With a sententious look, that nothing means,
(Faces are blocks, in sentimental scenes)
Thus I begin—All is not gold that glitters,
Pleasure seems sweet, but proves a glass of bitters.
When ign'rance enters, folly is at hand;
Learning is better far than house and land.
Let not your virtue trip, who trips may stumble,
And virtue is not virtue, if she tumble.
  I give it up—morals won't do for me;
To make you laugh I must play tragedy.
One hope remains—hearing the maid was ill,
A doctor *comes this night to shew his skill.*
To cheer her heart, and give your muscles motion,
He in five draughts prepar'd, *presents a potion:*
A kind of magic charm—for be assur'd,
If you will swallow it, *the maid is cur'd:*
But desp'rate the Doctor, and her case is,
If you reject the dose, and make wry faces!
This truth he boasts, will boast it while he lives,
No pois'nous drugs *are mix'd in what he gives;*
Should he succeed, you'll give him his degree;
If not, within he will receive no fee!
The college you, *must his pretensions back,*
Pronounce him regular, *or dub him* quack.

From THE DOUBLE DEALER by William Congreve (1670–1729)

EPILOGUE

Could poets but foresee how plays would take,
Then they could tell what epilogues to make;
Whether to thank or blame their audience most:
But that late knowledge does much hazard cost:
'Till dice are thrown, there's nothing won nor lost.

So, till the thief has stolen, he cannot know
Whether he shall escape the law or no.
But poets run much greater hazards far,
Than they who stand their trials at the bar,
The law provides a curb for its own fury,
And suffers judges to direct the jury:
But in this court, what difference does appear!
For every one's both judge and jury here;
Nay, and what's worse, an executioner.
All have a right and title to some part,
Each choosing that in which he has most art.
The dreadful men of learning all confound,
Unless the fable's good, and moral sound.
The vizor-masks that are in pit and gallery,
Approve or damn the repartee and raillery.
The lady critics, who are better read,
Inquire if characters are nicely bred;
If the soft things are penned and spoke with grace:
They judge of action, too, and time, and place;
In which we do not doubt but they're discerning,
For that's a kind of assignation learning.
Beaux judge of dress; the witlings judge of songs;
The cuckoldom, of ancient right, to cits belongs.
Poor poets thus the favour are denied
Even to make exceptions, when they're tried.
'Tis hard that they must every one admit;
Methinks I see some faces in the pit
Which must of consequence be foes to wit.
You who can judge, to sentence may proceed;
But though he cannot write, let him be freed
At least from their contempt who cannot read.